Medical Law in Austria

Medical Law in Austria

Third Edition

Aline Leischner-Lenzhofer
Claudia Zeinhofer
Sibel Uranues
Christina Lindner
Christian Kopetzki

This book was originally published as a monograph in the International Encyclopaedia of Laws/Medical Law.

Founding Editor: Roger Blanpain
General Editor: Frank Hendrickx
Volume Editor: Herman Nys

Wolters Kluwer

Published by:
Kluwer Law International B.V.
PO Box 316
2400 AH Alphen aan den Rijn
The Netherlands
E-mail: international-sales@wolterskluwer.com
Website: lrus.wolterskluwer.com

Sold and distributed in North, Central and South America by:
Wolters Kluwer Legal & Regulatory U.S.
7201 McKinney Circle
Frederick, MD 21704
United States of America
Email: customer.service@wolterskluwer.com

Sold and distributed in all other countries by:
Air Business Subscriptions
Rockwood House
Haywards Heath
West Sussex
RH16 3DH
United Kingdom
Email: international-customerservice@wolterskluwer.com

Printed on acid-free paper

ISBN 978-90-411-9534-0

e-Book: ISBN 978-90-411-9535-7
web-PDF: ISBN 978-90-411-9536-4

Printed in the United Kingdom.

The Authors

Dr Aline Leischner-Lenzhofer studied Law (Dr iur. in 2006) at the University of Vienna (Austria) and the University of Oslo (Norway) and had completed a Diploma in Mediation and Alternative Dispute Resolution. After working in a medical risk management project at the Vienna General Hospital (*Allgemeines Krankenhaus der Stadt Wien*), she worked as a university assistant at the Institute of Constitutional and Administrative Law (Department of Medical Law) of the University of Vienna from 2006 until 2012. Her main research area lies in the field of Medical Law. Leischner-Lenzhofer taught Medical, Constitutional and Administrative Law at the University of Vienna, and since 2009 she has been teaching Medical Law at the Danube University of Krems.

Dr Claudia Zeinhofer studied Law (Dr iur. in 2007) at the University of Vienna (Austria). She has been working as university assistant at the Institute of Constitutional and Administrative Law (Department of Medical Law) of the University of Vienna since 2003. Her main research focus lies in the field of Medicinal Products and Medical Devices Law. Zeinhofer teaches Medical Law at the Danube University of Krems.

The Authors

Mag. Sibel Uranues studied Law (Mag. iur. in 2013) at the Karl-Franzens-University in Graz (Austria) and is currently a PhD candidate at the University of Vienna. She has been working as a university assistant at the Institute of Constitutional and Administrative Law (Department of Medical Law) of the University of Vienna since 2015. Her main research focus lies in the fields of Medical, Human Rights and Refugee Law.

Dr Christina Lindner studied Law (Dr iur. in 2010) at the University of Vienna (Austria) and the Université de Bourgogne (France). After working as a university assistant at the Institute of Constitutional and Administrative Law (Department of Medical Law) of the University of Vienna from 2004 to 2010, she is currently working as an associate in a law office.

Univ.-Prof. DDr Christian Kopetzki studied Law (Dr iur. in 1979) and Medicine (doctorate in 1984) at the University of Vienna (Austria). He was granted a postdoctoral lecturing qualification in 1995 in the fields of Constitutional law, Administrative Law and Medical Law. In 1997 he was appointed associate professor and in 2002 as University Professor for Medical Law at the Department of Constitutional and Administrative Law at the University of Vienna. Furthermore, he is deputy director of the Department of Ethics and Law in Medicine at the University of Vienna, as well as a member of the editorial boards of several national and international journals. Prof. Kopetzki is the author of numerous books and articles on Constitutional Law and Medical Law, in which he focuses on transplantation law, law of genetic engineering and biotechnology, law of reproductive medicine, European fundamental rights in the field of biomedicine, etc.

Table of Contents

General Introduction

§1. General Background of the Country

I. Geography and Climate

1. Austria is located in the centre of Europe, neighbouring Germany, the Czech Republic, Slovakia, Hungary, Slovenia, Italy, Liechtenstein and Switzerland. It covers an area of approximately 83,870 km^2. Austria's highest mountain is the Grossglockner (3798 m, on the border between East Tyrol and Carinthia), followed by other summits like Wildspitze (3768 m) or Grossvenediger (3674 m). Due to its geographical position Austria is subject to a transitional climate; the Atlantic Oceanic influence in the West (humid westerly winds) is continuously changed into the rather continental climate of the Pannonian Plain in the East (higher variation in temperature, less rainfall). As 60% of the federal territories are covered by the Alps, the corresponding Alpine climate – characterized by strong local variations, long snowy winters and short summers with high rainfall – also has a strong influence. Austria's largest rivers are the Danube *(Donau)* leading southeastwards to the Black Sea and the Rhine *(Rhein)* which flows into the North Sea. Completely surrounded by other countries, Austria does not have direct access to the sea. Due to its mountainous surface, which also forms a meteorological divide, Austria is well known for its wealth and high quality of drinking water. Its biggest freshwater lakes are Lake Neusiedl (*Neusiedlersee*) at the Hungarian and Lake Constance (*Bodensee*) at the Swiss and German border, followed by many glacial lakes, for example in the alpine uplands of the Salzkammergut region (Salzburg, Upper Austria and Styria) and in the Southern Limestone Alps in Carinthia.

II. Cultural Composition

2. The percentage of foreigners residing in Austria is about 15.3% (January 2017[1]). The total number of approximately 1,341,930 non-Austrian citizens living on Austrian territory comprises 664,729 citizens of the European Union (EU) (thereof 181,618 Germans), 118,454 Serbs and 116,838 Turks. Apart from German as the main official language (Article 8 Constitution – *Bundes-Verfassungsgesetz,* Federal Law Gazette 1930/1 as last amended by Federal Law Gazette I 2016/62)

1. Statistics Austria, Internet: www.statistik.gv.at/web_de/statistiken/bevoelkerung/bevoelkerungsstruktur/bevoelkerung_nach_staatsangehoerigkeit_geburtsland/index.html, 24 May 2017.

and sign language (*Gebärdensprache*) there are three officially spoken languages in certain municipalities with a higher proportion of constitutionally acknowledged autochthonic minorities: Hungarian, Slovenian and Burgenland-Croatian. Although constantly declining in recent years, Roman Catholicism is still by far the strongest religion in Austria (about 74%), followed by Protestantism, Islam and Eastern Orthodox Churches, Judaism, Hinduism and much more. About 12% of the population declare themselves as undenominational.

III. Political and Judicial System

3. The Republic of Austria is a democratic and federal republic consisting of nine federal states *(Bundesländer)*: Burgenland (regional capital Eisenstadt), Carinthia (Klagenfurt), Lower Austria (St. Pölten), Upper Austria (Linz), Salzburg (Salzburg), Styria (Graz), Tyrol (Innsbruck), Vorarlberg (Bregenz) and Vienna, which is a federal state and the Austrian federal capital at the same time (Articles 1 and 2 Constitution). The Austrian system of federalism is based on the allocation of powers between the federation *(Bund)* and the federal states (*see* Articles 10–15 of the Constitution; for details on the allocation of powers in the field of Medical Law *see* §3.II.B.).

4. After the Austrian State Treaty of 1955 had ended Austria's occupation by the Allied Forces following World War II, Austria was re-recognized as a sovereign and independent state. During the same year the Federal Assembly enacted a constitutional law that grants Austria's 'perpetual neutrality' and is still in force (interdiction of joining any military alliances or establishing foreign military forces on Austrian territory). Austria is a member of many international organizations including the United Nations (and the World Health Organization – WHO), the Organization for Security and Cooperation in Europe (OSCE), etc. Since 1995 Austria has been a member of the EU, which influences Austrian legislation to a significant extent.

5. The three state powers (legislation – administration – jurisdiction) are strictly separated (*see* esp. Article 94 of the Constitution). The fundamental principle of separation of powers is complemented by a system of mutual checks and balances.

The Federal Parliament is located in Vienna, the country's capital and largest city (about 1.7 million inhabitants). It consists of two chambers: the National Council and the Federal Council (Article 24 Constitution). The National Council, consisting of 183 seats, is the dominant chamber in enacting new legislation, is elected every five years by all citizens over the age of 16. Before 2007, the legislative period was four years and the minimum electoral age 18 years. Currently, there are six political parties represented in the Federal Council: Sozialdemokratische Partei Österreichs (SPÖ – Social-Democratic Party of Austria), Österreichische Volkspartei (ÖVP – Austrian People's Party), Freiheitliche Partei Österreichs (FPÖ – Freedom Party of Austria), Die Grünen (die Grüne Alternative – the Green Party), NEOS (Das Neue Österreich und Liberales Forum) and Team Stronach. In general, parties have to achieve at least 4% of all votes in general elections *(Nationalratswahlen)* in order to be represented in Parliament. Apart from that '4%-threshold' there is also the possibility of gaining direct seats *(Direktmandate)* by achieving a certain number of votes in one of the regional electoral districts. The Federal Council, that currently consists of sixty-two delegates of the nine *Landtage* (regional parliaments of the Federal Assembly), is the second chamber of the Austrian Parliament and mainly represents federal interests in the legislation process. In most cases its limited right of a suspensive veto can be overruled by the National Council. This chamber can insist on passing the respective bill by voting a second time, which is referred to as a resolution of persistence *(Beharrungsbeschluss).*

The general elections in September 2013 once more led to a relative majority of votes for the SPÖ (Social Democrats: 26.8%), who formed a Grand Coalition government with the Conservative ÖVP (Austrian People's Party: 24%), although both parties had been considerably weakened (for the benefit of the right-wing party FPÖ on the one hand and for the benefit of the two newly established parties NEOS [5%] and FRANK [5.7%] on the other hand).

The highest executive authorities in Austria are the Federal President (currently Alexander Van der Bellen), who is directly elected by the people for a period of six years (Article 60 Constitution), the Federal Cabinet and the Federal Ministers.

The legislative organs of the federal states are the State Parliaments. The highest administrative organs are the State Governments and its members. In general, the State Governor is an equal member of the State Government. Nonetheless, he plays a central role within the Indirect Federal Administration and therefore has a special position within the State Cabinet (*see* Article 102 of the Constitution).

6. The highest courts in Austria are the Supreme Court (concerning civil and criminal matters), the Administrative Court and the Constitutional Court as regards to administrative matters (including administrative criminal law). The access to the Constitutional Court is limited to alleged infringements of constitutionally guaranteed rights or substantive rights by an illegal ordinance, an unconstitutional law or an unlawful international treaty. In addition to this administrative review, the Constitutional Court decides on pecuniary claims on territorial corporate bodies, on the constitutionality of ordinances, acts and treaties, on conflicts of responsibilities, on the legitimacy of elections (of the Federal President and to popular representative bodies) and on claims against the highest authorities.[2]

The system of legal protection against administrative action or default was completely reorganized in 2014 (Federal Law Gazette I 2012/51). The former administrative levels of review were abolished in general and were replaced by administrative courts reviewing the administrative action of the authorities in the first instance. There are nine administrative courts of the federal states *(Landesverwaltungsgerichte)* and two administrative courts of the federation *(Bundesverwaltungsgericht* and *Bundesfinanzgericht*). At the same time, the access to the Administrative Court was limited to remedies regarding fundamental legal issues.

2. For details on the the Constitution of Austria *see* M. Stelzer, 'The Constitution of the Republic of Austria' (Oxford and Portland, Oregon: Hart Publishing, 2011).

IV. Population and Vital Statistics

7. In the beginning of 2017, Austria had a population of approximately 8.77 million inhabitants (census information published by Statistics Austria[3]). The continuous growth of the population since the mid-nineties is rather caused by immigration than by a high birth rate. In 2017, the average birth rate per woman was 1.49 – id est 9.8 newborn babies per 1,000 inhabitants. Although the birth rate has been rising lately and is currently higher than the death rate (9.6 per 1,000 inhabitants), this signifies that on a long-term scale the birth rate will not be able to maintain the population at its level. Life expectancy was 78.66 years for men and 83.6 for women in 2017 and is predicted to continue its steady rise – on the one hand a consequence of a high quality health care system, on the other hand one of the health and social security laws most topical challenges.

V. Social and Cultural Values Regarding Health

8. Although constantly declining, cardiovascular diseases (42.8%) followed by cancer (24.5%) are the most common causes of death in Austria. Other frequent causes of death are respiratory diseases, injuries, accidents, poisonings and gastrointestinal illnesses.[4] Many relevant risk factors have their origin in people's own health-relevant behaviour such as little health-consciousness about precautionary measures, insufficient physical activity, overweight caused by unhealthy alimentation habits, daily stress, smoking, the abuse of alcohol or illegal drugs.

§2. General Description of the Health Care System

I. General Review of the Health Care System

9. The Austrian public security system[5] is based on three pillars: social insurance, social care and social assistance. Social insurance comprises health insurance, accident insurance and pension insurance. In a broader sense, it also includes unemployment insurance, which covers insurance in case of illness of unemployed people.

10. Social insurance is compulsory in Austria. This is the major difference to private insurance systems. It does not depend on any kind of registration, but is constituted by law as soon as the legal prerequisite of gainful employment is fulfilled.

3. Statistics Austria: Internet: http://www.statistik.gv.at/web_de/statistiken/menschen_und_gesellschaft/bevoelkerung/bevoelkerungsstand_und_veraenderung/bevoelkerung_zu_jahres-_quartalsanfang/index.html, 24 May 2017.
4. Statistics Austria: Internet: http://www.statistik.at/web_de/statistiken/gesundheit/todesursachen/todesursachen_im_ueberblick/index.html, 24 May 2017.
5. For details on the following description *see,* with further references, e.g., Th. Tomandl, 'Grundriss des österreichischen Sozialrechts', 6th edn (Vienna: Manz, 2009) and W. Brodil & M. Windisch-Graetz, 'Sozialrecht in Grundzügen', 8th edn (Vienna: facultas, 2017).

Thus, it includes practically all employed people (as well as their family members on a non-contributory basis).[6] According to the principle of territoriality, social insurance generally only covers gainful occupation in Austria.

11. Social insurance is financed by the contributions of the people insured and, in case of employees, by their employers. The premiums are calculated based on the income, but only up to an annually defined top threshold. Those who seek for better insurance generally have to take out a private insurance. Non-cash benefits are, however, independent of the fees that are paid.

Thus, the social insurance system is based on the principle of social balance. The contributions depend neither on individual risks nor on the equivalence of contributions and granted benefits. Those who earn more have to pay more, even if they are prone to fewer risks.

12. Since every gainful occupation, which is subject to compulsory insurance, leads to a (separate) insurance relationship, people who have more than one employment may also be multi-insured. Regarding health insurance, the applicable regulations provide a clear order, which insurance provider is competent for granting benefits (for instance §128 of the General Social Insurance Act). There are also restrictions concerning the contributions, which generally have to be fully paid for each existing insurance relation.

13. The implementation of the insurance system is ensured by special corporate bodies ('social insurance institutions'). There are twenty-five public insurance companies, some of which cover two or more branches of social insurance. They are all united under the umbrella organization of the Main Association of Austrian Social Security Institutions. This structure, which has evolved historically, is increasingly criticized as it leads to different health services depending on where one is insured.

14. Not all social risks are covered by an insurance system though, which is why certain benefits are financed by taxes instead of compulsory contributions (social care). For example the support of war and crime victims is based on general taxes.

15. Social assistance, which comprises for example welfare, nursing and disability benefits, is also financed by general taxation. It falls within the competence of the federal states. The amount of nursing or disability benefits depends on the degree of handicap or the extent of nursing needs. Public welfare is only granted subsidiarily if the person in need cannot be helped by other social security systems.

16. The Austrian social security system has a relatively short history, as its development started only 120 years ago in the course of the Industrial Revolution.

---

6. For this reason, private insurance is primarily a voluntary additional insurance leading to the status as private patient. For details on the private insurance system in Austria *see*, with further references, W. Fischl, 'Das Recht der privaten Krankenversicherung', in *Handbuch Medizinrecht*, ed. R. Resch & F. Wallner, 2nd edn (Vienna: LexisNexis, 2015), 649 et seq.

Based on the social facilities for example of the guilds, the forerunners of the present security system emerged at the end of the nineteenth century.

In the *German Reich,* a Health and an Accident Insurance Act were passed in 1883 and 1884. Shortly afterwards, Austria followed with an Accident Insurance Act in 1887 and a Health Insurance Act in 1888. In 1906, a Pension Insurance Act for white-collar workers was passed, followed by an Unemployment Insurance Act in 1920 (the granted benefits – unlike nowadays – depended on the needs of the unemployed person), and a Pension Insurance Act for blue-collar workers in 1927 (which never entered into force). It was not until an Insurance Act was passed in the *German Reich* in 1939, that pension insurance was first introduced for blue-collar workers in Austria. The Insurance Act of the *German Reich,* which dramatically reformed the Austrian social security system, was in force until 1955. In 1956 the General Social Insurance Act, which united health, accident and pension insurance of white-collar workers and blue-collar workers, entered into force in its present form. In the subsequent decades, self-employed people, farmers and certain members of independent professions were included into the social insurance system. The amendments to the General Social Insurance Act and the Commercial Social Insurance Act in 1997 and in 1998, which also incorporated freelancers and new forms of self-employed people, were aimed at an all-embracing compulsory social insurance for everybody.

II. Regulation of the Health Care System

A. General Remarks

17. Compulsory health insurance is regulated by several different acts, depending on the source of income. Employees in all insurance branches are fully insured under the General Social Insurance Act (*Allgemeines Sozialversicherungsgesetz,* Federal Law Gazette 1955/189, as last amended by Federal Law Gazette I 2017/53).[7] The concept of employment is defined in §4(2). Independent contractors who can be compared to employees (§4[4]) are granted equality of status under the regulations of the General Social Insurance Act. Insurance for commercially self-employed people is regulated under the Commercial Social Insurance Act (*Gewerbliches Sozialversicherungsgesetz,* Federal Law Gazette 1978/560, as last amended by Federal Law Gazette I 2017/53). These insurants have compulsory health and pension insurance as long as they are members of the Commerce Chamber (§2[1] Commercial Social Insurance Act). The Commercial Social Insurance Act also covers new forms of self-employment like independent contractors (who are not similar to employees), freelancers, businessmen (and women) who lack the right to carry on a trade and so forth (§2[1] No. 4 Commercial Social Insurance Act). Farmers are subject to the Farmers' Social Security Act (*Bauern-Sozialversicherungsgesetz,* Federal Law Gazette 1978/559, as last amended by Federal Law Gazette I 2017/53), which provides compulsory insurance in all branches.

7. Sections without further specification relate to the General Social Insurance Act. Differing regulations in other acts are quoted separately.

Certain members of independent professions are insured in accordance with the Social Security Act for Independent Professions (Federal Law Gazette 1978/624, as last amended by Federal Law Gazette I 2015/162).

18. Social health insurance (§116 of the General Social Insurance Act) not only covers the insured person, but also extends to his family members (children as well as spouses or partners, who do not pay health insurance contributions themselves). As a result, about 98% of the population are covered by statutory health insurance (about two-thirds of them pay contributions and the others receive coverage for free).

19. Social insurance provides benefits in case of illness, occupational disability caused by illness and maternity, including the considerable field of preventive health care. Early diagnosis of illnesses and the preservation of public health are paid for by the insurance as well as medical measures of rehabilitation and health promotion.

20. The social insurance institutions are generally obliged to grant non-cash benefits (§135[1]). They can either provide services through their own facilities (e.g., dental ambulatories) or contract with representatives of the particular professional group in order to grant sufficient supply for the insured. In fact they mostly conclude contracts with doctors, midwives, opticians, pharmacies, hospitals and so forth. Therefore, the Austrian health care system is characterized by a contract system.

The Main Association of Austrian Social Security Institutions concludes integrated contracts with either the medical associations of the federal states or the Austrian Medical Chamber upon approval by the medical associations of the federal states (§341[1]). These integrated contracts, which can be compared to bargaining agreements, have to contain regulations about the medical job chart (listing number and local distribution), selection procedures for contracting doctors, rights and duties of the contracting doctors, especially remuneration agreements, economic aspects and provisions for termination. Generally, the insurant should have the choice between at least two (competent) contracting doctors, who can be reached within appropriate reasonable period of time. If the insurance institution provides its own facilities, there must be at least one contracting doctor in addition who can be consulted under the same conditions.

21. The individual contracting doctor concludes an own agreement with the insurance institution, which has to correspond to the integrated contract. Thus, the only function of the individual agreement is to oblige the doctor to work as contracting doctor for the insurance institution and to fix place and time of his surgery. The compensation system is a combination of charging individual performance and a basic flat rate.[8]

8. For details *see* e.g., R. Resch, 'Vertragspartnerrecht der Krankenversicherung', in *Handbuch Medizinrecht*, ed. R. Resch & F. Wallner, 2nd edn (Vienna: LexisNexis, 2015), 581 (592 et seq.).

22. If the integrated contract expires, the individual agreements end as well. In case that there is no contract, the patient's right to non-cash benefits changes into a right to cash benefits. The doctors are treated as doctors of choice, so that the patient has to pay for the treatment in cash first. The insurance institutions then have to reimburse 80% of the amount that would have been paid to a contracting doctor.

Disputes concerning integrated contracts are generally settled by arbitration (§§344 et seq.).

23. The contracting doctor is not a vicarious agent of the insurance institution, but is the patient's contracting partner and fulfils his own obligations.[9] The relationship between the contracting doctor and the patient is qualified as contract for services or contract to render services.

B. Benefits in Case of Illness

24. In case of illness, health insurance provides medical treatment (§133), which comprises medical aid (§135), medication (§136) and health aids (§137).

25. Concerning medical aid, the insured person can consult any contracting doctor of his insurance carrier (§§341 et seq.), who will be paid for by the insurance provider. The patient also has the option to consult a doctor who does not have a contract with the insurance provider ('doctor of choice'). In this case, the patient has to pay cash first, and the health insurance provider will refund 80% of the amount that would have been paid to a contracting doctor. The health insurance institutions may also reimburse 100% of the costs, if total geographical coverage with contracting doctors is not provided and this is laid down in their general terms and conditions. In contrast to general health insurance, the health insurance for civil servants, self-employed people and farmers generally requires co-payment.

Social health insurance also provides psychotherapy and clinical psychological diagnosis. The patient has to pay a contribution of approximately EUR 22 per psychotherapeutic session. Furthermore, there are various additional forms of financing in the federal states.

Services of the medical-technical professions (e.g., physiotherapeutic, logopedic and occupational therapies) are also covered by health insurance, provided that they are performed according to a doctor's prescription. If there is no contractual relationship, the health insurance reimburses 80% of the sum that would have been paid to a contract partner.

26. Medications are provided by the insurance institution, as long as they are prescribed by the doctor in observance of the Guidelines in Economic Prescribing of Medications and Medical Equipment, as well as the Code of Reimbursement, which are both edited by the Main Association of Austrian Social Security Institutions.

---

9. S. Völkl-Torggler, 'Die Rechtsnatur des ärztlichen Behandlungsvertrages in Österreich', *JBl* (1984): 77.

The Code of Reimbursement consists of three fields ('boxes'): the green box comprises medications that can be prescribed without approval by a competent head physician. The yellow box includes medications that need approval by a competent head physician. Finally new medications are temporarily listed in the red box (until they are decided upon) and also need approval by a head physician. Medications are paid for by the insurance providers, if they are prescribed by a contracting doctor or a doctor of choice with additional approval of the insurance provider. Medicinal products that are not listed in the Code of Reimbursement are generally not paid for by the health insurance provider. The Code, however, cannot restrict the legal claim for medications.[10] Thus, in case that medication which is not listed in the Code is necessary for medical treatment, the insured person can resort to litigation. Similarly to the regulations concerning medical treatment (*see* below), even unconventional and not (yet) officially approved medicinal products have to be paid for, if there is a chance of cure and conventional medications have failed.[11,12]

Medications are available in every pharmacy at the expense of the insurance institutions on the base of a contract (§§348a et seq.). The patient has to pay an excess of EUR 5 per prescription.

27. Substitutes for physiologic functions, such as glasses, shoe insoles or hernia bandages are only partly paid for by the insurance provider. Co-payments are required in addition.

28. Medical treatment must be sufficient and appropriate, but must not exceed the necessary amount (§133[2]). This legal claim cannot be restricted by contract or the general terms and conditions of insurance providers. Instead, the individual need for treatment must be considered in every single case. These rather vague requirements have been specified by jurisdiction. The insurance providers cannot simply refuse medical benefits due to high costs. Still they are not obliged to provide all treatments that are medically possible and imaginable without co-payment of the patient.[13] Nevertheless, every insured person can claim all benefits that have a fair chance of curing lege artis.[14] Furthermore, medical treatment needs to be appropriate in the sense that it must be at least promising.[15] The question, whether treatment is appropriate or not, is not only to be answered from a scientific perspective. Alternative treatment methods might be appropriate in case there are no conventional methods, that they have failed or that they lead to serious and undesirable side

10. Supreme Court 26 Mar. 1996, 10 ObS 52/96, SSV-NF 10/30.
11. Supreme Court 28 Feb. 1994 (Ukrain), SSV-NF 8/19, 10/30 = ZAS 1998, 42 *(Offenberger)*.
12. For details concerning the Code of Reimbursement *see* R. Rebhahn, '§§351c-351j ASVG' in *Der SV-Komm*, ed. R. Mosler & R. Müller & W. Pfeil (Vienna, Manz 2013 et seq.); W. Mazal (ed.), *Erstattungskodex* (Vienna: Manz, 2005); R. Rebhahn, 'Die Bereitstellung von Arzneimitteln', in *Europäisches Wirtschaftsrecht und soziale Krankenversicherung*, ed. K. Grillberger & R. Mosler (Vienna: Manz, 2003), 209 et seq.
13. Constitutional Court 18 Mar. 2000, G 24/98 ua, SozSi 2000, 738 *(Kletter)*.
14. Supreme Court of Justice 9 Nov. 1993, 10 ObS 174/93, SSV-NF 7/112.
15. Supreme Court of Justice 19 Dec. 1989, 10 ObS 211/89, SSV-NF 3/154; 23 Feb. 1993, 10 ObS 312/92, SSV-NF 7/22; 26 Apr. 1994, 10 ObS 113/94, SSV-NF 8/44.

effects, provided that the alternative treatment methods are effective or have helped the patient and lead to the same results without side effects.[16]

The reason for the restriction of medical treatments to the necessary amount is economic efficiency.[17] On the basis of a social concept of illness,[18] there is no right to benefits, unless a treatment should be paid for by the community of insured people (e.g., treatments for impotence).[19] It cannot be expected from the community to pay for the higher costs of a medically equal treatment abroad as long as a sufficient and appropriate treatment is available in Austria and the insurer provides the necessary benefits.[20] If there are several equally appropriate and straining methods of treatment, the insurance provider only has to pay for the least expensive therapy or the treatment with the best cost-benefit relation.[21] On the other hand, more expensive treatments must not be refused, if they promise a faster, more risk or painless treatment. Significantly more expensive treatments cannot be claimed for if the difference between the methods in question is only of minor relevance for the patient.[22]

Cosmetic surgeries are no medical treatments in terms of §133, since they do not influence diseases. According to §133(2), they are still seen as medical treatments in case they correct anatomical or functional diseases (like some forms of varicose veins).

29. In case medical treatment is not sufficient, every insured person has the right to hospital care (§§144–150). There are no time limitations, so that hospital stays are paid for as long as necessary. There are two categories of fees (*see* Part III, Chapter 3, §1.V. below): for the general class, the insurant has to pay a small contribution per day, which varies between EUR 8 and EUR 15, depending on the insurance provider. Patients have to pay these contributions for a maximum of twenty-eight days a year. In some cases, like childbirth, the stay in a hospital is completely financed by the insurer. Services for private patients have to be paid for by the patient or his private supplementary insurance (except for a nursing fee compensation, which is paid for by the insurance provider).

30. Unlike benefits provided by accident insurance, health insurance benefits are granted regardless of the cause of an illness. The insured person therefore receives

16. For example, Supreme Court of Justice 9 Sep. 2008, 10 ObS 68/08k. For the discussion concerning alternative methods *see* e.g., M. Binder, 'Zur Kostendeckung alternativmedizinischer Behandlungsmethoden durch die Krankenversicherung', *RdM* (1997): 39 et seq.
17. The significance of economic efficiency is discussed controversially in Austria: *See* ia Ch. Kopetzki & J. Zahrl (eds), *Behandlungsanspruch und Wirtschaftlichkeitsgebot* (Vienna: Manz, 1998); G. Luf, 'Verteilungsgerechtigkeit im Bereich der modernen Medizin – Rechtsethische Überlegungen', *RdM* (1997): 99 et seq.; W. Ettmayer & K. Posch, 'Gedanken zum Krankheitsbegriff – Erkenntnisse zur Potenz', *öRdA* (2006): 199; Supreme Court of Justice 7 Mar. 2006, 10 ObS 12/06x (erectile dysfunction).
18. For the concept of illness (§120) *see* W. Mazal, *Krankheitsbegriff und Risikobegrenzung* (Vienna: Braumüller, 1992).
19. Supreme Court of Justice 7 Mar. 2006, 10 ObS 22/06t.
20. Supreme Court of Justice 22 May 2001, 10 ObS 315/00x.
21. Supreme Court of Justice 9 Nov. 1993, 10 ObS 174/93, SSV-NF 7/112.
22. Supreme Court of Justice 26 Apr. 1994, 10 ObS 113/94, SSV-NF 8/44.

benefits even if he causes the illness himself. Cash benefits are not granted in case the insured person has caused the insured event by having intentionally committed a crime and has been sentenced to more than one year of imprisonment on that account (§88). This forfeiture of insurance coverage does not apply to non-cash benefits.

C. Occupational Disability Due to Illness

31. In case of temporary occupational disability caused by illness, employed people receive payments from the fourth day of illness up to fifty-two weeks at longest (§§139 et seq.). The individual amount of benefits depends on the most recent income and is limited by the top contribution threshold. It is 50% until the forty-third day of sick leave (afterwards it is 60%). These payments, however, are suspended as long as the sick person receives more than 50% of his salary, as long as the occupational disability is not notified (which the insured person is obliged to within one week), for example.

D. Preventive Health Care Benefits

32. Adults over 18 as well as their co-insured relatives are entitled to a free medical check-up once a year at the expense of the insurance provider (§132b). These examinations aim at an early diagnosis of widespread illnesses like cancer, diabetes and cardiovascular diseases. The same applies to insured adolescents between the age of 15 and 18 (§§132a in conjunction with 343a, 351a).

A special service for pregnant women, newborn children and infants up to the age of sixty-two months is the Mother-Child Medical Card. This standardized programme provides the following examinations for free: five general and two ultrasound examinations for pregnant women and nine general, one orthopaedic, one ENT, one ultrasonic hip examination and two eye examinations for the child. These examinations are generally voluntary, but there is a strong indirect pressure to have the check-ups done, as the entitlement to the financial Child Care Bonus depends on evidencing the Mother-Child-Medical Card check-ups after the age of twenty-one months.

Furthermore, there is a number of benefits (demonstratively listed in §§155, 156) which aim at preventing diseases and stabilizing health and the ability to work, for example health promotion programmes, (co-paid) stays in sanatoriums and convalescent homes, vaccination strategies and so forth.

E. Maternity Benefits

33. Expectant mothers are not allowed to carry on their jobs eight weeks before and eight weeks after childbirth. As a compensation for the resulting income loss during this period, women are paid maternity benefits by their health insurance, which are based on the woman's average net income during the last thirteen weeks or three months before childbirth (§§162 et seq.). In addition, the insurance providers grant the costs of doctors, nurses, midwives and medicines (§§158–161). Hospital care is provided for up to ten days.

III. Financing of the Health Care System

34. The method of calculation of the Statistics Austria (SHA – 'System of Health Accounts') indicated a total spending of EUR 35.077 million for the Austrian health care system in 2015. Health expenditure increased by 4.9% per year averagely and the proportion of the gross domestic product was 10.3%.

In 2015, the insurance institutions spent EUR 15.707 million on services for insured people. Further EUR 10.8 million were contributed by federation, federal states and *Gemeinden*. Private households paid EUR 6.287 million for health services, which is 17.9% of the current total health expenditure. Private insurances financed 4.9%, private non-commercial organizations paid 1.4% and other enterprises 0.2% of the costs.

The largest part of the expenditures for health care (EUR 13.561 million amounting to 38.7%) was paid for hospitals. Around EUR 7.67 million (21.9%) were spent on treatments by doctors and 16.8% on medicines.[23]

35. Health insurance is primarily funded by contributions, which are raised halfway through employees and halfway through employers. The contributions are calculated based on the individual income (§44) up to a certain income threshold, which is currently EUR 4,980 per month (§45). The rates of contribution to health insurance, which vary according to the type of employment, are presently 7.65% for blue-collar workers (of which 3.87% are paid by the employee and 3.78% by the employer) and white-collar workers (of which 3.87% are paid by the employee and 3.78% by the employer). For co-insured family members, the insured person has to contribute another 3.4% of the calculation basis (§51d). People with very low incomes (less than EUR 425.70 per month) do not have to contribute at all, as they are not obliged to have health insurance.

36. The contributions of self-employed people (who are subject to the Commercial Social Insurance Act) are also based on their individual income. The applicable regulations are rather complicated (§§25 et seq. Commercial Social Insurance Act). Their share is primarily calculated on a provisional basis. There are special regulations for start-up entrepreneurs (§25[4] No. 1) as well as for special cases (§26). The minimum contribution basis is EUR 425.70 and the income threshold is EUR 5,810 per month (which is 1/6 more than for employed people, as self-employed people do not receive additional payments). The contribution rate for self-employed people is 7.65%.

Farmers' contributions are calculated upon the rateable value (assessed value) ascertained by the tax office for the purpose of property tax. The rateable value must exceed EUR 1,500 though. The contribution rate to health insurance is 7.65%.

23. www.statistik.at/web_de/statistiken/gesundheit/gesundheitsausgaben/index.html, 24 May 2017.

37. People living in Austria, who are not subject to compulsory health insurance, may take advantage of self-insurance (§76). Their maximum contribution basis is 1/6 higher than it is for employed people, as they do not receive additional payments. Students can be co-insured with their parents up to the age of 28 on a non-contributory basis. Afterwards, they may also apply for self-insurance, which can be calculated on a lower basis under certain conditions.

§3. Medical Law

I. Definition and Functions of Medical Law

38. Medical law is primarily focussed on medical practice and the relationship between the patient on the one hand and health care professionals (including not only doctors, but also nurses, pharmacists, paramedical professionals and so forth) on the other hand. Additionally, it covers the organization and financing of health care as well as product-related basic conditions of medical practice (e.g., financing of health benefits, pharmaceutical drug safety, hospital law, professional representation). Thus, it comprises all regulations that directly or indirectly relate to medical science.

39. As it covers various subjects, such as criminal law, civil law, procedural law, public law, tax law, employment law, social insurance law, European law and international law, medical law is characterized by multi-disciplinarianism. Whether medical law is an independent scientific subject or rather a cross-sectional area comprising segments of other disciplines, is discussed controversially in Austria.

40. Although medical law and medical ethics (e.g., bioethics) both focus on medical practice, the two disciplines have to be distinguished from each other. Medical ethics establish moral-ethical rules, whereas medical law is exclusively about judicial regulations. These different approaches might, but do not necessarily coincide. Ethical aspects influence medical law mostly via legislation (as they are often an impulse for regulations) and indefinite legal terms, which they are sometimes able to concretize.

41. Since the 1990s, specialist literature in the field of medical law (and bioethics) has flourished; beginning from 1994, the journal ‘Recht der Medizin’ (RdM, Manz) is published six times a year, covering current topics of medical law. ‘Imago Hominis’, which focuses on ethical questions of medicine and biomedicine, has been published four times a year since 1994. In 2016, two new journals on Health Law followed: ‘Zeitschrift für Gesundheitsrecht’ (ZfG, facultas) and ‘Journal für Medizin- und Gesundheitsrecht’ (JMG, NWV). Apart from these periodicals, there are a large number of monographs and anthologies published in specialized scientific series like ‘Schriftenreihe Recht der Medizin’ (Manz), ‘Ethik und Recht in der Medizin’ (Springer), ‘Linzer Medizinrechtliche Beiträge’ (Universitätsverlag Rudolf Trauner) or ‘Schriften zum Arztrecht’ (LexisNexis).

42. Besides being published in scientific literature, medical law has been institutionalized in academic teaching for more than fifteen years. Corresponding courses are offered at the University of Vienna, where students can specialize in medical law,[24] and at the University of Graz[25] and Linz.[26] At the law faculties, there are three professorships for Medical Law (Univ. Prof. DDr Christian Kopetzki in Vienna, ao.Univ. Prof. Dr Erwin Bernat in Graz and Univ. Prof. Dr Reinhard Resch in Linz); in Vienna, the professorship is combined with its own Department of Medical Law. In addition, an interdisciplinary Department of Ethics and Medical Law was founded in Vienna in 1993 ('Institut für Ethik und Recht in der Medizin'). It incorporates members of the Catholic-Theological Faculty, the Evangelic-Theological Faculty and the Faculty of Law. Furthermore, it cooperates with the Medical University of Vienna.[27] Although neglected in earlier times, medical law has also gained importance at the Medical University of Vienna, where medical law is now an inherent part of the curriculum. The fact, that postgraduate (and other) academic medical law courses offered by private universities or other institutions boom, shows that medical law is not only of interest for jurists but also for doctors and for other health care professionals.[28]

II. Sources of Medical Law

43. In contradiction to the legal situation in the past, when medical law was only regulated by the general principles of civil and criminal law, the number of acts in specific areas has increased rapidly over the last decades. This is not only a consequence of the rising public interest in ethical (especially bioethical) topics since 1945, but also of the higher sensibility concerning individual rights (e.g., patients' rights and consumer protection). Furthermore, new medical and technological possibilities, which were not sufficiently regulated by the general rules, demanded specific regulations.

24. https://staatsrecht.univie.ac.at/team/kopetzki-christian/, 24 May 2017.
25. https://zivilrecht.uni-graz.at/de/institut/wissenschaftliche-mitarbeiterinnen/aouniv-prof-driur-erwin-bernat/, 24 May 2017.
26. www.jku.at/sdmr/content, 24 May 2017.
27. www.ierm.at, 24 May 2017.
28. For this chapter *see*, with further references, Ch. Kopetzki, 'Herausforderungen an ein integratives Medizinrecht – Rechtsvergleichung', in *Perspektiven des Medizinrechts*, ed. A. Eser, H. Just & H. G. Koch (Baden-Baden: Nomos, 2004), 277; Ch. Kopetzki, 'Rechtspolitik der Zukunft – Medizinrecht', in *Rechtspolitik der Zukunft – Zukunft der Rechtspolitik*, ed. M. Holoubek & G. Lienbacher (Vienna: Springer, 1999), 221; E. Bernat, 'Einführung in das österreichische Medizinrecht', in *Handbuch des Fachanwalts Medizinrecht*, ed. F. Wenzel (Köln: Wolters Kluwer, 2012), 1862; E. Bernat, 'Das österreichische Recht der Medizin – eine Bestandsaufnahme', in *Perspektiven des Medizinrechts*, ed. A. Eser, H. Just & H. G. Koch (Baden-Baden: Nomos, 2004), 105; E. Bernat, 'Das österreichische Recht der Medizin – eine Bestandsaufnahme', *JAP* 10 (1999/2000): 105.

A. *International and European Sources*

44. There is an enormous number of international regulations on medical law, and consequently, health law. In general, there is a trend towards legal internationalization following the internationalization in the fields of medicine and medical ethics.

45. Binding regulations of international law have to be distinguished from merely recommendatory and thus non-binding resolutions and declarations. The field of non-binding resolutions ('soft law') is much broader regarding quantity and content. Best examples therefore are the activities of the WHO concerning recommendations on current problems (like HIV, organ transplantation and in vitro fertilization) or on documentation, development and harmonization of national health legislation.

46. The regulations of the Council of Europe are also characterized by the dualism between legally binding norms and not directly binding recommendations. The number of binding regulations is higher here, though.

Non-binding recommendations on current problems are, for example, the recommendations on the use of human embryos and foetuses,[29] organ transplantation,[30] research on human beings,[31] data protection,[32] rights of the sick[33] or on the legal protection of people suffering from mental diseases.[34]

47. Besides the European Social Charta (ESC), the most important legally binding regulations are the European Convention on Human Rights (ECHR) and the Convention on Human Rights and Biomedicine.[35]

The ECHR, which is directly applicable in Austria, and the jurisdiction of the European Court of Human Rights are of major importance to medical law. Despite lacking special regulations on the specific issues of medical law, important aspects of medical practice fall within its ambit. Essential judgments concerning

29. Rec. 1046 (1986) on the use of human embryos and foetuses for diagnostic, therapeutic, scientific, industrial and commercial purposes; Rec. 1100 (1989) on the use of human embryos and foetuses in scientific research.
30. Resolution 29 (1978) on the harmonization of legislations of Member States relating to removal, grafting and transplantation of human substances.
31. Rec. R (90) 3 on medical research involving human beings.
32. Rec. R (81) 1 on regulations for automated medical data banks; Rec. R (83) 10 on the protection of personal data used for scientific research and statistics.
33. Rec. 779 (1976) on the rights of the Sick and Dying; Rec. 1418 (1999) on the protection of the human rights and dignity of the terminally ill and dying.
34. Rec. 818 (1977) on the situation of the mentally ill; Rec. R (83) 2 concerning the legal protection of persons suffering from mental disorder placed as involuntary patients; Rec. 1235 (1994) on psychiatry and human rights.
35. Convention for the Protection of Human Rights and Dignity of the Human Being with Regard to the Application of Biology and Medicine: Convention on Human Rights and Biomedicine, European Treaty Series No. 164.

compulsory medical treatment, euthanasia, data protection or transsexuality have set fundamental binding principles of medical law.

The ECHR and Biomedicine and its additional protocols are the first legally binding documents that explicitly grant human rights concerning medical law issues. Despite a clear vote of the Bioethics Committee (*see* §3)[36] and the positive declaration of intent in the recent government statements of policy, the convention has not been ratified in Austria yet.[37]

48. Apart from the domains listed in Article 168(4) of the Treaty of Lisbon, the EU has no legislative powers regarding health policy.[38] Thus, the European legislation concerning medical law has been dominated by the principles of the Community Market so far. It has especially focussed on rules and regulations dealing with health care professions (for instance concerning training, reciprocal acknowledgment and establishment) and on regulations on medicinal products, medical devices and gene technology. In contrast to the Treaty of Amsterdam, regulations on medicinal products and medical devices do not have to be based on ex-Article 95 anymore, but can be based on Article 168(4) lit c of the Treaty of Lisbon now. This adjustment allows European regulations that only refer to the safety of the products and are not in the interest of the Common Market.

Furthermore, the Charta of Fundamental Rights of the EU, especially its Article 3, grants fundamental rights (to the integrity of the person) concerning medical law issues.[39]

B. National Sources

49. There is no unitary, nationwide legislative authority for medical law. As per Article 10[1] No. 12 of the Constitution, the federation is competent for legislation and administration in the domain of 'public health', which comprises all measures for providing public medical benefits. Furthermore, the federation is competent for regulating (and administering) the matters of civil and criminal law, which play an important role for medical law (Article 10[1] No. 6).

---

36. www.bundeskanzleramt.at/DocView.axd?CobId=1111, 24 May 2017.
37. For the consequences of a ratification on national law *see* (with further references), Ch. Kopetzki, 'Landesbericht Österreich', in *The Convention on Human Rights and Biomedicine of the Council of Europe – A Suitable Model for World-Wide Regulation?*, ed. J. Taupitz (Berlin: Springer, 2002), 197.
38. For details *see* Ch. Kopetzki, 'Die EG als Normsetzer im Gesundheitsrecht vor dem Hintergrund des Art 152 EGV?', in *Standardisierung in der Medizin als Rechtsproblem*, ed. H. Lilie, E. Bernat & H. Rosenau (Baden-Baden: Nomos, 2009), 139; for regulations on tissue K. Stöger, 'Europarechtliche und verfassungsrechtliche Kompetenzfragen der Gewebesicherheit', in *Gewebesicherheitsrecht*, ed. Ch. Kopetzki (Vienna: Manz, 2009), 12.
39. For details *see* E. Dujmovits, 'Die EU-Grundrechtscharta und das Medizinrecht', *RdM* (2001): 72; E. Dujmovits, 'Grundrechtliche Aspekte des Gewebesicherheitsgesetzes', in *Gewebesicherheitsrecht*, ed. Ch. Kopetzki (Vienna: Manz, 2009), 56 (89 et seq.) with further references.

As to hospitals and nursing homes, the federation is competent for framework legislation, while the federal states are competent for the legislation and administration of implementing regulations (Article 12[1] No. 1). Thus, there are nine different hospital acts of the federal states, which implement the Frame Law on Hospitals and Sanatoria (*Krankenanstalten- und Kuranstaltengesetz,* Federal Law Gazette 1957/1, as last amended by Federal Law Gazette I 2013/81) of the federation. According to the Constitutional Court, the subject-matter of 'hospitals and nursing homes' covers all measures which were regulated by the Law on Hospitals of 1920 (Federal Law Gazette 1920/327).

According to Article 15 of the Constitution, the federal states are competent for regulating (and administering) municipal medical services, rescue services as well as corpse and funeral matters.

50. In addition to the general principles of civil and criminal law, the first specific regulations on medical practice were professional codes like the Physicians Act, the Nursing of Patients Act, the Paramedics Act, the Medical-Technical Services Act, the Perfusionist Act, the Midwives Act, the Psychotherapy Act and the Psychologists Act.

The Frame Law on Hospitals and Sanatoria and its implementing regulations focus especially on the requirements for establishing and operating hospitals. Furthermore, there are regulations that are directly addressed to doctors and other members of health care professions.

Within the last years, the number of regulations in special areas of medical law has dramatically increased, especially concerning in vitro fertilization (Artificial Procreation Act), human genetics (Gene Technology Act), organ transplantation (Organ Transplantations Act), HIV (Aids Code) and other sexually transmitted diseases (Act on Sexually Transmitted Diseases), vaccination (Vaccination Damage Act), euthanasia (Living Will Act), biomedical research on human beings (Medicinal Products Act, Medical Devices Act, Frame Law on Hospitals and Sanatoria, Act on Universities) and the safety of medicinal products and medical devices.

51. The public authorities are generally empowered to specify these acts by passing ordinances based on the general authorization of Article 18(2) of the Constitution. There is a large number of ordinances, some of which contain important concretizations and detailed practical regulations (e.g., on forms). Extensive subordinate legislation needs special statutory powers though.

52. A central role for interpreting and establishing regulations on medical law is to be assigned to the human rights, especially Articles 2, 3 and 8 ECHR and the right to liberty under Article 5 ECHR as well as the Constitutional Law on the Protection of Liberty (Federal Law Gazette 1988/684).

53. In cross-sectional areas, federation and federal states have concluded several agreements on the basis of Article 15a of the Constitution (e.g., the Patients'

Charter or agreements on financing the health care system). These agreements are, however, only binding on the participating territorial entities and are not directly applicable, and therefore not enforceable on patients and doctors.[40]

40. This chapter is based on Ch. Kopetzki, 'Herausforderungen an ein integratives Medizinrecht – Rechtsvergleichung', in *Perspektiven des Medizinrechts*, ed. A. Eser, H. Just & H. G. Koch (Baden-Baden: Nomos, 2004), 79 (87 et seq.); Ch. Kopetzki, 'Rechtspolitik der Zukunft – Medizinrecht', in *Rechtspolitik der Zukunft – Zukunft der Rechtspolitik*, ed. M. Holoubek & G. Lienbacher (Vienna: Springer, 1999), 221 (239 et seq.); E. Bernat, 'Einführung in das österreichische Medizinrecht', in *Handbuch des Fachanwalts Medizinrecht*, ed. F. Wenzel (Köln: Wolters Kluwer, 2012), 1861 (1863 et seq.). For the impact of jurisdiction on the development of medical law *see* M. Neumayr, 'Zur Rolle der Gerichte bei der Entwicklung des Medizinrechts', *RdM* (2014): 51.

Part I. The Medical Profession

Chapter 1. Access to the Medical Profession

§1. Training of Physicians

I. General Remarks

54. In Austria, medical education requires the study of human medicine at university for a minimum of six years (five years at the Paracelsus Medical Private University of Salzburg), followed by a post-gradual practical training as a doctor-in-training (*Turnusarzt*). On the one hand, the university education is regulated by the Act on Universities 2002 (*Universitätsgesetz 2002*, Federal Law Gazette I 2002/120 as last amended by Federal Law Gazette 2017/11) and by the EU Directive 2005/36/EEC of the European Parliament and the Council on the recognition of professional qualifications as last amended by EU Directive 2013/55/EU. Moreover, each university has enacted a detailed curriculum for the university studies. On the other hand, the post-gradual practical training is regulated by the Training Regulation for Physicians 2015 (*Ärztinnen-/Ärzte-Ausbildungsordnung 2015*, Federal Law Gazette II 2015/147), which also fulfils the requirements of the aforementioned EU Directives.[41]

55. Dentistry has been part of the human medicine studies as a specialist medical field since the beginning of the eighteenth century. Since Austria joined the EU in 1995, the criteria in place, in particular the EU Directives,[42] and the need to avoid any discrimination between dental specialists trained in Austria and those trained in the rest of the European community made it necessary to create an own profession of dentistry. The basis for an EU-compliant university studies of dentistry was established by the University Studies Act (*Universitäts-Studiengesetz*, Federal Law Gazette I 1997/48, ineffective since 2009). Nowadays, dentistry education requires a university study for a minimum of six years, which also includes a practical traineeship. Contrary to physicians, dentists are fully qualified to practise dentistry independently right after graduation (§§7 et seq. Dentists Act, Federal Law Gazette I 2005/126 as last amended by Federal Law Gazette I 2016/8).

41. For details on the Training Regulation for Physicians *see* Th. Holzgruber, 'ÄAO 2015', in *Gmundner Kommentar zum Gesundheitsrecht*, ed. M. Neumayr, R. Resch & F. Wallner (Vienna: Manz, 2016), 345 et seq.
42. *See* EU Directives 78/686/EEC, 78/687/EEC.

II. Medical Education at University

56. Human medicine can be studied at seven accredited universities (Federal Law Gazette II 2015/408): Karl Landsteiner Private University for health affairs, the Medical University of Graz, the Medical University of Innsbruck, the Medical University of Vienna and the Paracelsus Medical Private University of Salzburg, Sigmund Freud Private University, Faculty of Medicine at the Johannes Kepler University Linz, Medical University. Dentistry can be studied at four accredited faculties: the Medical University of Graz, the Medical University of Innsbruck, the Medical University of Vienna, and, additionally since October 2009, at the Danube Private University of Krems (Lower Austria).

57. Admission to university requires a high school diploma or an equivalent qualification. In order to reduce the increasing number of students who study human medicine and dentistry, the universities are allowed to restrict the access by an admission procedure before acceptance or by a selection procedure during the first two semesters of studies (§71d [1] University Act). Regardless of this acceptance procedure, universities have to reserve 95% of the total university places for EU citizens, but all in all 75% for students who have successfully completed their high school diploma in Austria. This restriction of admission for foreign students shall ensure that there are enough university places for Austrian students in order to secure a publicly accessible, well-balanced health care system of high standard in Austria (§71d [5] University Act).[43]

58. Due to the autonomy of the universities (Article 81c Constitution), each university enacts its own detailed curriculum for the academic medical/dental studies (§19[2] No. 4, §54 University Act). Thus, several distinctions can be found in the concepts of the medical university studies. In general, the six-year university education is divided into a basic, a pre-clinical and a clinical part and shall give the students the essential knowledge and skills of medicine that are necessary for the further post-gradual practical training. During the academic education, the students have to pass several medical and cross-sectional exams. In the clinical part the students have to complete practical training in various medical fields. Moreover, they have to undergo an obligatory medical traineeship (*Pflichtfamulatur*) which lasts between twelve and eighteen weeks.[44] During the obligatory medical traineeship students are allowed to carry out several minor medical procedures (e.g., blood taking or administration of intramuscular or subcutaneous injections), but only under guidance and supervision of a physician or at least a doctor-in-training whose necessary qualification and experience is confirmed in writing by the responsible head of the department, in which the doctor-in-training is taught (§49[4]-[5] Physicians Act, Federal Law Gazette I 1998/169 as last amended by Federal Law Gazette I

43. For further details *see* B. Perthold-Stoitzner, '§71d UG 2002', in *UG 2002*, ed. B. Perthold-Stoitzner, 3rd (Vienna: Manz, 2016), Note I.1. et seq.
44. The Paracelsus Medical Private University of Salzburg follows another concept; for details *see* http://www.pmu.ac.at/humanmedizin.html May 2017.

2017/25). Graduates of the studies of medicine are awarded the academic degree 'Doctor of Human Medicine (Dr. med. univ.)'.

59. Dentistry education requires six years of university studies, including seventy-two weeks of practical traineeship. During their practical traineeship, dental students are allowed to practise dentistry under guidance and supervision of a responsible teaching dental practitioner (§33 Dentists Act). The study is concluded with the degree 'Doctor of Dentistry (Dr. med. dent.)'.

60. After completion of the medical or dental studies the graduates are able to apply for a PhD Programme at university in order to qualify themselves for an academic career. Each PhD Programme requires a minimum of three years of studies (§54[4] University Act).

III. Postgraduate Practical Medical Training

61. After graduation the graduate has to apply for registration in the Medical Practitioner Register (*Ärzteliste*) in order to be able to start the postgraduate training. During the practical training the doctor-in-training can practise medicine under guidance and supervision of a responsible teaching practitioner (§3[3] Physicians Act). The training shall offer the possibility to enhance the medical knowledge and skills step-by-step to finally be able to practise medicine independently. Therefore the responsible teaching practitioner has to decide on a case-by-case basis which intensity of guidance and supervision is necessary. Guidance and supervision vary according to the level of qualification of the doctor-in-training and dangerousness of the medical activity.[45] Only then the physician possesses the 'ius practicandi' and may treat patients self-reliantly (*eigenverantwortlich*).[46]

62. The postgraduate training is regulated by §§6a ff Physicians Act and by the Training Regulation for Physicians 2015, an ordinance stipulated by the Federal Minister of Health after consultation of the Austrian Medical Chamber (*Österreichische Ärztekammer*). Moreover, the Austrian Medical Chamber stipulated on the basis of §24(2) Physicians Act ordinances regarding further details on the required knowledge, experience and skills for being licensed as general practitioner or medical specialist. These ordinances (KEF and RZ-Verordnung 2015; Rahmen-Spez-Verordnung 2016) are available on the homepage of the Austrian Medical Chamber.

45. For details *see* Ch. Kopetzki, *Turnusärzte und Famulanten* (Vienna: Manz, 1990), 41 et seq.; E. Wimmer, *Rechtsfragen im Turnusarztverhältnis* (Vienna: Manz, 2000), 34 et seq.; Ch. Kopetzki, 'Zum Kompetenzumfang der Turnusärzte in Lehrpraxen', *RdM* (2013): No. 141, 251.

46. For further details *see* G. Aigner, M. Kierein & Ch. Kopetzki (eds), *Ärztegesetz*, 3rd edn (Vienna: Manz, 2007), §3 Note 3 et seq.; L. Stärker, '§3 ÄrzteG', in *Ärztegesetz mit Kommentar*, ed. H. Emberger & F. Wallner. 2nd edn (Vienna: Verlagshaus der Ärzte, 2008), 26 et seq.; F. Wallner, '§ 3 ÄrzteG', in *Gmundner Kommentar zum Gesundheitsrecht*, ed. M. Neumayr, R. Resch & F. Wallner (Vienna: Manz, 2016), Note 6 et seq.; M. Grimm, *Die Weisungsbindung des Spitalsarztes* (Vienna: Manz, 1999), 59 et seq.

63. Since the enforcement of the Training Regulation 2015 all doctors-in-training receive a basic clinical training before choosing between a practical training for being licensed as a general practitioner or as a medical specialist. The basic clinical training lasts for nine month and shall give the doctors-in-training basic clinical competencies in surgical and conservative medical subjects (§6a Physicians Act).

64. After the basic clinical training the thirty-three-months practical training for general practitioners on a full-time basis includes training in general medicine, internal medicine, gynaecology, paediatrics, orthopaedics, traumatology, psychiatry or psychotherapeutic medicine as well as two other medical fields of choice (e.g., otology, dermatology or venereology). The different training parts can take place in different institutions of medical care (e.g., department of a hospital or university hospital, teaching practice, teaching group practice, outpatient teaching clinic, etc.) which are approved as teaching places by the Austrian Medical Chamber (*see* §§7, 9 Physicians Act; §12 Training Regulation). The last six months of the practical training have to take place in a teaching practice, teaching group practice or outpatient teaching clinic (§7[4] Physicians Act). If a medical institution applies for approval as teaching place, its level of equipment, provision of medical services, frequency of patients, etc. have to meet the educational goals of the Austrian Medical Chamber. The practical training is concluded by an exam that is carried out by the Austrian Medical Chamber (§7[5] Physicians Act) via the Austrian Academy for Physicians.

65. In order to be licensed as a medical specialist, following the basic clinical training a doctor-in-training has to complete a sixty-three-month practical training (on a full-time basis) in the chosen special field which is divided into a basic and a main training (in oral and maxillofacial surgery the practical training lasts at least forty-eight months; *see* for more details §17 Training Regulation 2015). §15 Training Regulation for Physicians 2015 determines thirty-two medical fields (e.g., surgical and internal special fields). The former postgraduate practical training in dentistry has been replaced by its own studies of dental medicine. A specialization in dentistry after completing the studies of human medicine is therefore no longer possible. The postgraduate training has to take place in an institution of medical care (e.g., department of a hospital or university hospital, teaching practice, teaching group practice, outpatient teaching clinic, etc.) which is approved by the Austrian Medical Chamber as a teaching place in the specific medical field (§10 Physicians Act; §18 Training Regulation 2015). After completion of the practical training, the doctor-in-training has to pass an exam that is carried out by the Austrian Medical Chamber (§8[5] Physicians Act) via the Austrian Academy for Physicians.

66. As a supervisory method for evaluating and securing the quality of the practical training, certified logbooks (*Rasterzeugnis*) have been created. In these logbooks the responsible teaching physician has to summarize and confirm the clinical work performed by the doctor-in-training (§26 Physicians Act; §§19ff Training Regulation 2015; KEF and RZ-V 2015).

IV. Further Training

67. After being registered as medical practitioner, it is mandatory to undergo further training at recognized training programmes organized by the local medical associations, the Austrian Medical Chamber or approved foreign training programmes (§49[1] Physicians Act). These training programmes shall provide the physicians with the necessary information to keep up-to-date with the national and international standard of the state-of-the-art in medical knowledge and skills, including the applicable rules and regulations and the subject-specific standards of quality. Every three years medical practitioners have to credibly show that they have undergone further training (§49[2c] Physicians Act). Similar rules apply to dentists according to §17 of the Dentists Act.

§2. Licensing of Doctors-in-Training and Medical Practitioners

68. Physicians are not automatically allowed to practise medicine merely by obtaining the degree of doctor of human medicine. In fact, the graduated physician has to apply to the Austrian Medical Chamber via the medical chamber of the respective federal state in order to be listed in the Medical Practitioner Register as doctor-in-training before he can start a postgraduate training.

69. According to §4(4) Physicians Act the license to practise medicine as a doctor-in-training has to be granted upon application, if the applicant:

(1) has full legal capacity;
(2) is trustworthy in the sense of not being guilty of a behaviour that shows his demerit or unreliability to practise the medical profession;[47]
(3) is not unable to practise the profession for health-related reasons;
(4) is competent in the German language in order to practise the profession; and
(5) is entitled to reside in Austria, including the right of establishment;
(6) has graduated from an Austrian university with the doctorate of human medicine or, if abroad, obtained an academic degree that has been accredited by an Austrian medical university as equivalent to the Doctorate of Human Medicine or possesses the formal qualifications of basic medical training referred to in Annex V, point 5.1.1. of the EU Directive 2005/36/EEC. These professional qualifications are automatically recognized under the EU Directive 2005/36/EC (§5 No. 1 Physicians Act). With regard to other professional qualifications the applicant has to successfully absolve an aptitude test in order to assess the applicant's ability to pursue the medical profession. The aptitude test is carried out by the Austrian Medical Chamber (§5a Physicians Act).

70. Since 2015 a registration as accredited medical practitioner (*approbierter Arzt*) is no longer possible (§235[2] Physicians Act). However, already registered

47. *See* Federal Administrative Court 17 Dec. 1998, 97/11/0317; 20 Jun. 2006, 2004/11/0202.

accredited medical practitioners may continue to practise general medicine, either on a freelance or employed basis (§31[1] Physicians Act).

71. After successfully completing the specific postgraduate practical training, the physician can apply for registration as general practitioner or medical specialist according to §4(1) Physicians Act. In order to be listed in the Medical Practitioner Register as general practitioner or medical specialist, the physician, in addition to all above-mentioned requirements for registration as doctor-in-training, must have obtained a diploma from the Austrian Medical Chamber that confirms the successful completion of the relevant postgraduate practical training and the conclusion of the final exam as general practitioner or medical specialist (§4[3], §15 Physicians Act), or completed a practical training that has been accredited by an Austrian medical university as equivalent and concluded a final exam that has been accredited as equivalent or is additionally concluded (§§5, 5a, 14 Physicians Act).

Registration as a medical specialist implicates that the medical specialist is only allowed to practise in the medical field in which he is specialized (§31[3] Physicians Act). Special fields partially overlap, giving reasons for liability disputes.[48]

72. The registration in the Medical Practitioner Register is an administrative act issued by the Austrian Medical Chamber (§27 Physicians Act). The Austrian Medical Chamber is obliged to register the applicant if he fulfils the above-mentioned requirements. The applicant can take legal action against a negative decision to the responsible governor. The legal authority lies with the governor of the province of the physician's principal residence in Austria, or on his last principal residence or his last domicile in Austria if he no longer lives in Austria. If the physician has not lived or worked in Austria before his application for the registration, the legal authority lies with the governor of the province that the physician is intending to move to or work in.[49]

73. Graduated dentists have to apply for registration with the Dentists Register at the Austrian Dentists Chamber via the local dentists association in order to be allowed to practise dentistry in Austria (§§6, 12 et seq. Dentists Act). The same automatic recognition of the evidence of formal qualifications according the EU Directive 2005/36/EEC applies (§31).

§3. Manpower Planning

74. There is no federal regulation that limits the number of licensed physicians, based on need in general. Pursuant to §31 of the Physicians Act, every physician who fulfils the above-mentioned requirements (*see* §2. above) has the right to be registered in the Medical Practitioner Register. After the registration the medical practitioner who holds the 'ius practicandi', may establish his own practice or carry

48. *See* e.g., Supreme Court 23 Mar. 2010, 8 Ob 115/09h, *RdM-LS* 2010/37 (Huber).
49. For details about the licensing of physicians *see* e.g., F. Wallner, *Handbuch Ärztliches Berufsrecht* (Vienna: LexisNexis, 2011), 15 et seq.

out the medical profession within an employment at a hospital or an outpatient clinic. However, if a physician wants to establish a group practice with other medical practitioners, §§52b, 52c of the Physicians Act stipulate since the amendment in 2010 (Federal Law Gazette I 2010/61) admission procedures similar to those for autonomous outpatient clinics as a consequence of the *Hartlauer*-judgment of the European Court of Justice[50] (for details *see* Part III, Chapter 1, §2.II and Chapter 3, §1.IV. below). The concessional system for establishing and operating hospitals and autonomous outpatient clinics is dealt with in Part III, Chapter 3, §1.IV. below.

75. The regulation of access to the SHI system is based on the need for health care providers in the different areas of Austria, ensuring that health care services can be offered widespread and at high quality. Approximately 98% of the Austrian population is covered by SHI. Therefore freelance physicians and group practices have a great economic interest in having a contract with a social insurance institution. The access to the SHI system is regulated by integrated contracts (*Gesamtverträgen*), concluded principally between the Main Association of Austrian Social Insurance Institutions and the Medical Chamber of the federal state or the Austrian Medical Chamber (§§341 et seq. General Social Insurance Act). On the basis of the applicable integrated contract, the respective social insurance institution in accordance with the medical chamber of the respective federal state concludes an individual contract (*Einzelvertrag*) with the physician or group practice who applied for recognition as service provider within the SHI. This system results in a de facto manpower planning, since only few freelance physicians or group practices can survive economically with private patients only. The reason for this can be found in the differing billing, as doctors of choice (who do not have a contract with a social insurance institution) have to invoice their patients for their medical treatments, instead of charging their medical services directly to the respective social insurance institution which covers for the patient (for details *see* General Introduction, §2. above).

§4. Freedom of Establishment and Providing of Services

76. The exercise of foreign physicians' freedom of establishment and freedom to provide services in Austria is regulated by the Physicians Act in response to the need to incorporate various EU Directives. §§5 and 5a of the Physicians Act therefore regulate the recognition of diplomas, certificates and other evidences of formal qualifications and licenses to practise medicine. Regarding the right of establishment of foreigners, the provisions of the Physicians Act and the Dentists Act lay down the same rules as those applying to Austrian physicians. If these physicians want to set up their own practice or work on an employment basis in Austria, they have to apply for registration at the Medical Practitioner Register or Dentists Register (§§27, 28 Physicians Act; §12 Dentists Act; for details *see* §2. above).

50. ECJ 10 Mar. 2009, C-169/07 (*Hartlauer Handelsgesellschaft*), *RdM* 2009, 126 (Stöger).

77. Pursuant to §37 of the Physicians Act, physicians from EEA-States or the Swiss Confederation who wish to provide their services in Austria on a temporary basis from their practice or working place abroad[51] are exempt from registration in the Medical Practitioner Register. However, they must inform the Austrian Medical Chamber in advance that they want to provide their service. Additionally, they have to submit evidence of their nationality, a certificate stating that they have appropriate professional qualifications and that they have not been barred temporarily or permanently from practicing medicine in the state in which they have their working place or registered practice, evidence of holding a professional liability insurance according to §52d Physicians Act as well as a statement confirming sufficient knowledge in German language to practice medicine. Temporary services are assessed on a case-by-case basis depending on their duration, frequency, recurrence and continuity of medical service. These physicians are bound to respect the professional rules in force in Austria and are subject to the respective disciplinary jurisdiction throughout their provision of services in Austria (§37[2] Physicians Act).[52]

78. In case §37 is not applicable, physicians with working places or practices abroad can provide their services in Austria without fulfilment of all requirements of §4 Physicians Act, on the basis of §36 of the Physicians Act. There are only three cases in which such provision of services in Austria is permitted: (1) the physician collaborates with a physician who is registered in Austria on a medical consultation including the whole treatment of a patient, (2) on the basis of an interstate agreement (e.g., *see* Federal Law Gazette III 1998/76 as amended by Federal Law Gazette I 2008/2) or (3) on a temporary basis for further training of registered medical practitioners in Austria or of medical studies and teaching. The physician has to inform the Austrian Medical Chamber in advance about his intention. These physicians are bound to respect the professional rules in force in Austria and are subject to the respective disciplinary jurisdiction throughout their provision of services in Austria.[53]

---

51. *See* ECJ 30 Nov. 1995, C-55/94 (*Gebhard/Consiglio Nazionale Forense*), AnwBl 1996, 18: In order to fulfil the temporary services the physician is allowed to establish the necessary infrastructure. For details *see* G. Frieders, 'Grenzziehung zwischen Dienstleistung und Niederlassung durch den EuGH: Der Fall Gebhard', *AnwBl* (1996): 9. Also *see* explanatory report to the government bill: ErläutRV 629 BlgNR 21. GP 35.
52. F. Wallner, '§37 ÄrzteG', in *Ärztegesetz mit Kommentar*, ed. H. Emberger & F. Wallner. 2nd edn (Vienna: Verlagshaus der Ärzte, 2008), 146 et seq.
53. F. Wallner, '§36 ÄrzteG', in *Ärztegesetz mit Kommentar*, ed. H. Emberger & F. Wallner. 2nd edn (Vienna: Verlagshaus der Ärzte, 2008), 138 et seq.

Chapter 2. The Practice of Medicine

§1. Definition of the Practice of Medicine

I. General Remarks

79. According to §2 of the Physicians Act, the practice of medicine is the monopoly of physicians. Therefore only physicians who obtained the 'ius practicandi' are allowed to practise medicine independently. Medical students and doctors-in-training are only allowed to practise medicine under the guidance and supervision of a responsible teaching physician (*see* Part I, Chapter 1, §1.III. below). Others are principally not allowed to carry out any activity that is qualified as a medical act (§3 Physicians Act).

80. Two criteria define the practice of medicine: first, the applied method has to be based on medical and scientific findings, meaning that the method is rationally understandable and verifiable by scientific medical methods. Second, the applied method has to be classified as scientific method according to the medical training subjects of the Training Regulation for Physicians 2015.

In his older judgments (in cases concerning criminal and competition law) the Supreme Court qualified a diagnosis or other treatments as practice of medicine by the main criterion whether the expectation of the patients was that the consultation of a physician would be unnecessary after the treatment by the non-physician or not. The Court did not take into consideration whether the diagnostic method or treatment was medically science-based, not verified or scientifically disproved.[54] In recent cases concerning competition law the court's jurisdiction has changed. The Supreme Court ruled that an activity is excluded from the monopoly of physicians if the diagnosis or treatment is not based on medical-scientific evidence. An act is classified as medical method if it entails a minimum of rationality and typically needs profound knowledge in medicine for its application that is only imparted through university education. However, the Court stated that non-physicians are obliged to inform their clients that the applied diagnosis or treatment is not based on medical-scientific evidence and does not substitute a consultation of a doctor or medical treatment, if it is verified that the applied method has no healing effect or if the method may seem scientific based to patients.[55] This Supreme Court jurisdiction has been applied to a case concerning criminal law by a Higher Regional Court of Appeal in 2006.[56]

54. Supreme Court 29 Apr. 2003, 11 Os 42/03, *RdM* 2004/21. Also *see* Supreme Court 18 Jan. 2000, 4 Ob 14/00p, *ÖBl-LS* 2000/33; Supreme Court 10 Feb. 2004, 4 Ob 19/04d.
55. Supreme Court 21 Nov. 2006, 4 Ob 151/06v, *RdM* 2007, 59; Supreme Court 4 Ob 217/04x, *SZ* 2004/171 = *ÖBl* 2005/21 (*Gamerith*) = *RdM* 2005/42 – Tuina-Massage.
56. Higher Regional Court of Appeal of Graz, 1 Mar. 2006, 9 Bs 254/05d.

However, the Supreme Court reserved methods, even if these entail no rationality, to medical practitioners in case the appliance may be dangerous for the patient's health without a prior medical consultation.[57]

II. Medical Activities

81. Any medical activity performed directly on a person or for a person is restricted to physicians (§3[4] Physicians Act). §2(2) of the Physicians Act non-exhaustively enumerates several activities as acts of medicine:

(1) the examination of the state of health and the detection of physical or mental illnesses, disabilities or pathological aberrations;
(2) the diagnosis of diseases, disabilities and pathological aberrations with the aid of medical-diagnostic facilities;
(3) the treatment of diagnosed diseases, disabilities and pathological aberrations;
(4) the performance of invasive (surgical) interventions including taking or transfusion of blood;
(5) the prevention of diseases;
(6) the supervision of pregnancy, childbirth and appliance of methods of artificial reproductive medicine;
(7) the prescription of medicine;
(8) the performance of autopsies; and
(9) the issue of a medical certificate and medical estimate.

82. The medical treatment of diagnosed diseases, disabilities and pathological aberrations includes the prescription and administration of medicine. After the diagnosis of a disease, the physician has to inform the patient about the risks of the advised treatment, other appropriate methods and the pros and cons of undergoing or denying the recommended medical treatment. Providing the patient with medical information is exclusively restricted to physicians.

83. Law reserves several medical activities explicitly to medical practitioners. For example, taking blood samples in order to determine the alcohol level or the drug addiction of a driver is reserved to medical practitioners (§5[5]–[6] of the Traffic Regulations, Federal Law Gazette 1960/159 as last amended by Federal Law Gazette I 2017/6). Additionally, only physicians may record the cerebral death and remove or transplant organs after death (§5[2] Organ Transplantations Act). In general, the termination of pregnancy has to be carried out by physicians in order to be legal (§97[1] Nos 1 and 2 Criminal Code, excluding the case of imminent danger for the pregnant woman: §97[1] No. 3 Criminal Code). Furthermore, clinical research studies involving drugs or medical devices may only be carried out under the responsibility of an appropriately qualified physician or dentist (§35 Medicinal

57. Supreme Court 5 Oct. 2010, 4 Ob 155/10p, *RdM-LS* 2011/48 = *RdM* 2011/117, 145 (Wallner) (AtlasProfilax-Methode). For more details *see* e.g., F. Wallner, 'Der Arztvorbehalt und seine Grenzen', *RdM* (2011): No 117.

Products Act and §64 Medical Devices Act). Only appropriately, qualified emergency physicians may carry out organized emergency medical service (§40 Physicians Act).[58]

III. Alternative or Complementary Medicine

84. The monopoly of physicians includes, besides conventional medicine, methods of alternative and complementary medicine, insofar as they have a medical-scientific basis (evidence-based medicine), or they are recognized as experience-based medicine. Evidence-based medicine refers to health interventions for which systematic empirical research has provided evidence of statistically significant effectiveness as treatment for a specific problem. Experience-based medicine refers to medical measures that have shown by long-term experience that they have a healing effect, although the reason for their healing effect has not been scientifically proven yet.[59]

Freelance medical practitioners are not restricted to perform only conventional medicine, but may also treat patients with their informed consent with alternative therapeutic methods as long as these are not dangerous or evidentially do not show any healing effect. Even in hospitals an individual healing attempt with alternative, complementary or new medical methods is possible, if conventional medical methods are unsuccessful and/or the physician can expect due to his medical knowledge and experience that the new or alternative method is not more risky than the conventional one (§8c Frame Law on Hospitals and Sanatoria).[60] However, if the treating clinical doctor holds the opinion that an available alternative method is not equivalent to the conventional medicine, the entity of the hospital is not obliged to treat the patient with the method in question, as long as the medical opinion is ex ante arguable.[61]

85. The Highest Medical Advisory Board (*Oberster Sanitätsrat*), a group of experts appointed to advise the Minister of Health, plays an important role in determining which alternative medical methods are recognized as performance of medicine. Its statements have a high impact on the jurisprudence regarding the question which methods are restricted to physicians, but also in the context of which methods

---

58. *See*, with further references, Ch. Kopetzki, 'Zum Kompetenzumfang der Turnusärzte in Lehrpraxen', *RdM* (2013): 251 (253 et seq.).
59. 'Komplementärmedizin in Österreich', *Der Salzburger Arzt* 5 (2008): 14–16.
60. L. Stärker, '§2 ÄrzteG', in *Ärztegesetz mit Kommentar*, ed. H. Emberger & F. Wallner. 2nd edn (Vienna: Verlagshaus der Ärzte, 2008), 13 with further references; M. Flora, 'Die Anwendung nicht-wissenschaftlicher Behandlungsmethoden durch Ärzte – ein Betrug', *RdM* (1997): No. 109; G. Aigner & Th. Holzgruber, 'Anmerkungen zu Flora, Die Anwendung nicht-wissenschaftlicher Behandlungsmethoden durch Ärzte – ein Betrug?', *RdM* (1997): 191.
61. Supreme Court 21 Feb. 2013, 9 Ob 32/12i, *RdM* 2013/101. Also *see* R. Rebhahn, 'Wann dürfen Vertragsärzte die Behandlung von Versicherten ablehnen?', *RdM* (2013): 140.

are acknowledged as state-of-the-art in cases concerning medical malpractice and social insurance benefits.[62]

86. To give some examples, in 1990 the Highest Medical Advisory Board qualified homeopathy as alternative, not scientifically verified but yet admitted therapy method and stated that only physicians shall prescribe homeopathic medication. The Supreme Court concluded that the statement of the Highest Medical Advisory Board expresses the opinion of the highest public authority in the public health care sector and serves as a rule until the contrary is stated. Therefore non-physicians are expelled from this activity.[63] The same is declared regarding (needle-)acupuncture. This alternative, scientifically proven method is considered as a medical activity since 1986. Even so, midwives are allowed to perform acupuncture independently if they have obtained the necessary knowledge and ability to treat patients according to the state-of-the-art by further training.[64] According to the Highest Medical Advisory Board in 2000, osteopathy is a complementary, not scientifically verified medical measure and shall only be performed under the instruction of a physician. Therefore physiotherapists are allowed to carry out osteopathy within the scope of their professional authorization, but sick patients may only be treated on prescription of a physician. Health-related working traders are explicitly excluded by the Supreme Court from performance of cranio-sacral osteopathy.[65]

87. Methods that are not recognized as evidence or experience-based methods are, for example, laser-acupuncture, ozone-therapy, fresh cell therapy and Bach flower therapy.[66] Therefore the Supreme Court did not qualify the irradiation with a mineral lamp and the application of flower essences carried out without a prior diagnosis as medical treatments.[67] Nevertheless, the Supreme Court considered the prescription of a Bach flower therapy as a medical treatment after the patient's description of his complaints.[68] In the end the borderline between a lawful appliance of an alternative method and the illegal practice of medicine by a non-physician is indistinct.

88. Non-physicians are only allowed to perform alternative and complementary medicine in the course of medical education or further training for a period of six month at the utmost (§42 Physicians Act). Alternative practitioners (*Heilpraktiker*) are not allowed to treat patients with alternative medicine. Furthermore, the traineeship and also the advertising and the offer of such traineeship are forbidden in

62. *See* Ch. Kopetzki, 'Behandlungen auf dem "Stand der Wissenschaft"', in *Finanzielle Grenzen des Behandlungsanspruchs*, ed. W. Pfeil (Vienna: Manz, 2010), 37 et seq.
63. Supreme Court 10 Feb. 2004, 4 Ob 19/04d, *RdM* 2004/75.
64. Order issued by the Minister of Health and Women, 16 Jun. 2004, 99200/0-I/B/6/04.
65. Supreme Court 6 Jul. 2004, 4 Ob 156/04a, *RdM* 2005, 26.
66. For details *see* S. Weiss, 'Die menschliche Gesundheit als neues berufliches Tätigkeitsgebiet', in *Jahrbuch Gesundheitsrecht 2008*, ed. M. Kierein et al. (Vienna: Neuer Wissenschaftlicher Verlag, 2008), 119 (123 et seq).
67. Supreme Court 20 Aug. 2002, 4 Ob 70/02a, *RdM* 2003/29.
68. Supreme Court 10 Feb. 2004, 4 Ob 19/04d, *RdM* 2004/75.

Austria (*see Ausbildungsvorbehaltsgesetz*, Federal Law Gazette 1996/378).[69] If an alternative practitioner wants to work in Austria, it is possible to apply for registration as an energy practitioner for humans (*Humanenergetiker*), which does not change the fact that such a free trade professional is only allowed to offer well-being treatments.[70]

§2. Exceptions of the Monopoly of Physicians

89. The Physicians Act itself explicitly regulates exceptions to the monopoly of physicians. The most important exceptions concern medical training reasons for medical students during their obligatory medical traineeship and for doctors-in-training during their practical training (§49[4]–[5]; §3[3] Physicians Act; *see* under Part I, Chapter 1, §1. and §2. above).

As far as the law does not explicitly restrict an activity to physicians, minor medical activities can be delegated to medical auxiliary staff. In these cases the personnel is only allowed to work under the physician's instruction and supervision (§49[2] Physicians Act).

I. Home Care

90. In a given case of home care, physicians can delegate single medical tasks to a relative of the patient or to a person who is in charge of the patient or who has a personal relationship to the patient as long as the patient does not reside in an institution for medical or psychosocial care, excluding institutions caring for disabled people according to §3a(3) Nursing for Patients Act (§50a Physicians Act). In this instance, the physician has to make sure that the person has the necessary skills to perform the delegated activity and has to give appropriate instructions and guidance.[71]

Since 2008, due to the increasing number of elderly people in need of a twenty-four-hour individual home care, physicians can delegate several minor medical procedures (e.g., subcutaneous injections, administration of medicine and others) under similar conditions as mentioned above to people who professionally carry out home care (§50b Physicians Act; *see also* Home Care Act, Federal Law Gazette I 2007/33).[72]

---

69. *See* for more details G. Aigner, 'Ärztliches Berufsrecht', in *Handbuch Medizinrecht*, ed. G. Aigner et al. (Vienna: Manz, 2003 et seq.), III/6 f.
70. *See* F. Bundschuh-Rieseneder, 'Berufsausübung für Heilpraktiker', *ZfG* (2017): 28; *see also* Supreme Court 17 Sep. 2014, 4 Ob 61/14w, *RdM-LS* 2015/22 (the offer of Bio-Impedanz-analysis by an energy practitioner for humans is forbidden).
71. H. Emberger, '§50a ÄrzteG', in *Ärztegesetz mit Kommentar*, ed. H. Emberger & F. Wallner. 2nd edn (Vienna: Verlagshaus der Ärzte, 2008), 236 et seq.
72. Explanatory report to the government bill: ErläutRV 435 BlgNR 23. GP.

II. Minor Medical Measures

91. Minor medical treatments, such as taking someone's temperature or treating a not too serious wound, do not require any specific medical knowledge and can therefore be carried out legally by the patient himself or by his/her friends or relatives. In this context, the Supreme Court qualified the control of the blood pressure with the aid of a fully automatic device, which for its use does not require any special medical knowledge, applied by pharmacists or by the person himself as a non-medical treatment. Thus, this activity does not violate the monopoly of physicians.[73] The same was ruled in a case in which the blood count and chemistry were controlled with the aid of a fully automatic device that did not require any special medical knowledge for its use, although a pharmacist had to prick the person's fingertip to get some blood drops in order to perform the blood check.[74] Nevertheless, diagnosis and recommended medical treatment based on automatically provided results are reserved to medical practitioners.

III. The Practice of Specific Medical Activities by Non-physicians

92. In spite of §2, §3[4] Physicians Act, some health care professions are allowed to carry out specific medical activities according to their professional regulations. §204 of the Physicians Act explicitly states that the professional regulations for dentists, nurses, midwives, medical-technical assistance professionals (e.g., perfusionists, physiotherapists, medical-technical analysts, radiographers, dieticians and medical nutritional advisers, ergotherapists, speech therapists, orthopaedists), medical assistance professionals (e.g., disinfection assistance, plaster assistance), paramedical professionals and medical masseurs do not violate the monopoly of physicians.

The exercise of medicine is not qualified as trade in terms of the Trade Regulations (*Gewerbeordnung*, Federal Law Gazette 1994/194, as last amended by Federal Law Gazette I 2016/120). Instead, such non-medical health care providers are freelance professions according to their professional regulations. Nevertheless, some medical activities can be performed legally by specific traders according to Trade Regulations without infringing the monopoly of physicians.[75]

A. Dentistry

93. With respect to the monopoly of physicians, the practice of dentistry, which is principally part of human medicine, is a legal monopoly of the holders of the academic degree of doctor of dentistry (§§3 et seq. Dentists Act). Therefore physicians

73. Supreme Court 20 Aug. 2002, 4 Ob 170/02g, *RdM* 2003/51.
74. Supreme Court 25 Mar. 2003, 4 Ob 256/02d, *RdM* 2004/71.
75. H. Emberger, '§49 ÄrzteG', in *Ärztegesetz mit Kommentar*, ed. H. Emberger & F. Wallner. 2nd edn (Vienna: Verlagshaus der Ärzte, 2008), 221 et seq.

are not allowed to practise dentistry anymore. Even so, medical specialists on stomatology, who started their studies on human medicine before January 1994 or who applied for recognition and concluded the post-gradual training in stomatology, are authorized to continue the performance of dentistry under the same conditions as doctors of dentistry (§§52 et seq. Dentists Act).

B. Psychotherapy and Psychology

94. Psychotherapy based on medical-scientific findings is an act of medicine. Even so, non-physicians are allowed to perform psychotherapy under certain conditions since 1991 (§24[2] Psychotherapy Act, Federal Law Gazette 1990/361 as amended by Federal Law Gazette I 2016/9). Non-physicians therefore have to complete a theoretical and practical education in psychotherapy that is divided in a general and specific part (§§3 et seq.) and have to be listed in the Psychotherapists Register in order to perform psychotherapy legally (§11). These psychotherapists do not need any prescription or guidance of a physician when treating patients.[76] Apart from psychotherapists, physicians who have obtained a diploma in psychotherapeutic medicine issued by the Austrian Medical Chamber may carry out psychotherapy equally to registered psychotherapists. These physicians neither have to have completed the mentioned psychotherapeutic theoretical and practical education nor have to be registered in the Psychotherapists Register according to the Psychotherapists Act in order to practise psychotherapy legally.[77]

95. Psychology does not fall within the monopoly of physicians. In fact, psychology is an independent health care profession according to the Psychologist Act (Federal Law Gazette I 2013/182, as last amended by Federal Law Gazette 2016/120).[78] Life and social coaches are authorized to help people with problems related to self-esteem, family, martial, sexual or any other social issues according to §119 of the Trade Regulations, which also includes psychological advice. Psychologists and life coaches are not allowed to perform psychotherapy if they are not registered in the Psychotherapists List pursuant to the Psychotherapy Act.

---

76. K. Kux, 'Zur Ausübung der Psychotherapie durch Ärzte, die keine Psychotherapeuten sind', *RdM* (1996): 106; S. Skiczuk, *Berufs- und Tätigkeitsschutz der österreichischen Gesundheitsberufe unter besonderer Berücksichtigung der Ärzte und Psychotherapeuten* (Vienna: NWV, 2006). For details on the Psychotherapy Act *see*, with further references, K. Firlei, 'PThG', in *Gmundner Kommentar zum Gesundheitsrecht*, ed. M. Neumayr, R. Resch & F. Wallner (Vienna: Manz, 2016), 1095 et seq.
77. Supreme Court 12 Mar. 1996, 10 ObS 241/95; Supreme Court 31 Jan. 1995, 4 Ob 125/94, *RdM* 1995/10. *See also* Administrative Court 15 Dec. 2016, Ra 2016/11/0128, *RdM* 2017/64 (*Huber/Penz*).
78. For further reading *see* e.g., K. Firlei, 'PsychG 2013', in *Gmundner Kommentar zum Gesundheitsrecht*, ed. M. Neumayr, R. Resch & F. Wallner (Vienna: Manz, 2016), 1017 et seq.; K Firlei, 'Berufsrecht der Psychotherapeuten, Psychologen und Musiktherapeuten', in *Handbuch Medizinrecht*, ed. R. Resch & F. Wallner, 2nd edn (Vienna: LexisNexis, 2015), 920 et seq.

C. Supervision of Pregnancy and Childbirth

96. According to §2(2) of the Midwives Act, midwives are authorized to independently supervise a normal pregnancy and a so-called normal delivery. In this context midwives are also allowed to administer perinatal specific pain mitigating or anticonvulsant drugs and to take blood samples from the newborn by pricking one of the baby's heels. If no medical specialist is present and it is too late to call for medical assistance in case of emergency, the midwife may legally perform all necessary medical interventions such as a manual abruption of the placenta after delivery (§2[2] No. 7). Nevertheless, midwives are obliged to call for medical assistance if complications are expected, or arise during pregnancy or childbirth. If a specialist in gynaecology is present, the midwife shall only act on instruction of and in collaboration with the medical specialist (§4).

D. Blood Taking and Analysis of Blood and Urine Samples

97. Taking blood samples out of the veins or capillaries falls within the legal monopoly of physicians. Nevertheless, nurses and medical-technical laboratory assistants or radiographers are authorized by their professional law to take blood samples on instruction but without supervision of a physician (§15[5] Nursing of Patients Act, §4[2] Medical-Technical Services Act). Since the enforcement of the Law on Medical Assistance Professions, Federal Law Gazette I 2012/89, in 2013 laboratory assistants (*Laborassistenz*) (§6) and practice assistants (*Ordinationsassistenz*) (§9) are also authorized to take blood samples on instruction and under supervision of a physician.

In the special case that a blood sample is taken to determine a driver's alcohol level, only a physician is allowed to perform the act (§5 Traffic Regulations).

98. Analysis of blood and urine samples is clearly an examination within the meaning of §2 of the Physicians Act. Even so, medical technicians may carry out analysis autonomously on instruction of a physician in accordance with §2(2) Medical-Technical Services Act.[79] Since 2013 practice assistants (*Ordinationsassistenz*) are allowed to examine blood, urine and stool by a standard stick test on instruction and supervision of the physician (§9 Law on Medical Assistance Professions).

E. Radiography

99. Radiography is principally reserved to physicians. Even so, radiography may be carried out autonomously on instruction of a physician by radiographers (§2[3] Medical-Technical Services Act) and simple standardized radiographic methods may be carried out on instruction of a medical practitioner and under supervision of

79. Supreme Court 10 Feb. 2004, 4 Ob 17/04k, *RdM* 2004/76.

a medical practitioner or radiographer by radiographic assistants (§10 Law on Medical Assistants Professions).

What is more, radiographers are authorized on instruction of and in collaboration with a physician to apply doses of radiopaque materials and radiopharmaceuticals to patients to create medical images of the human anatomy in order to aid radiologists or physicians to diagnose and treat illnesses and injuries (§2[3] Medical-Technical Services Act).[80]

F. Piercing and Tattooing

100. Invasive (surgical) interventions are principally reserved to physicians, no matter whether they are more or less invasive, or if they are necessary for medical reasons or not. Nevertheless, beauticians are authorized to carry out ear-, nose- and tongue-piercings as well as tattoos (§109[3] Trade Regulations). These traders shall only carry out ear-, nose- or tongue-piercings if the used device pierces the skin two millimetres at most and does not cause any linear or laminar injuries or cicatrizations (§109[4] Trade Regulations).[81] Beauticians (§109[6] Trade Regulations), hairdressers and wig makers (§109[1] Trade Regulations, gold- and silversmiths (§150[6] Trade Regulations) and jewellers (§154[3] Trade Regulations) may perform ear-piercing lawfully. Genital-, nipple- or navel-piercings are reserved to physicians.[82]

G. Eye Examination and the Measuring of Visual Impairment

101. Opticians are allowed to measure defective sight using a method by which the patient determines his sight defects, *inter alia* on the basis of printed scales that may be incorporated in a control instrument and which the patient himself corrects by choosing, as the optician proposes the lenses that might satisfy him. The optician may use a refractor for measuring the visual impairment, which is not classified as a medical-diagnostic facility.[83]

102. In addition, 'contact lens opticians' (*Kontaktlinsenoptiker*) are authorized to adjust contact lenses without prior medical examination of the patient. Still, they are obliged to advise the patient to consult an ophthalmologist if they detect a potential contraindication for applying contact lens during the eye examination (§2 of the Ordinance of the Ministry of Economic Affairs on the rules concerning the exercise of the profession of contact lenses opticians, Federal Law Gazette 1976/698 as last

80. Higher Regional Court of Vienna 7 Jun. 2010, 7 Ra 54/10b.
81. *See* the Ordinance of the Federal Minister of Economic Affairs and Labour on the rules for the exercise of piercing and tattooing by cosmetic traders, Federal Law Gazette II 2003/141 as amended by Federal Law Gazette II 2008/261.
82. L. Stärker, '§2 ÄrzteG', in *Ärztegesetz mit Kommentar*, ed. H. Emberger & F. Wallner. 2nd edn (Vienna: Verlagshaus der Ärzte, 2008), 16.
83. Committee Report to the government bill of the Physicians Act: AB 378 BlgNR 10. GP 1.

amended by Federal Law Gazette 1996/13). The diagnosis of visual impairment is nevertheless restricted to ophthalmologists.[84]

H. Plastering

103. Since the enforcement of the Law on Medical Assistance Professions in 2013, plastering does not fall within the monopoly of physicians anymore. The newly established profession of a plaster assistant (*Gipsassistenz*) is authorized to plaster and bandage immobilizing on instruction and under supervision of a physician (§5).[85]

84. Supreme Court 1 Oct. 1996, 4 Ob 2255/96p; *see* H. Schwamberger, 'Kontaktlinsenoptiker Änderung der Ausübungsvorschriften', *RdM* (1996): 87.
85. *See* Explanatory Report 1808 BlgNR 24. GP 4.

Chapter 3. Illegal Practice of Medicine

§1. Non-physicians

104. Due to the monopoly of physicians, alternative practitioners (*Heilpraktiker*) or other unauthorized therapists are not allowed to treat patients in any medical field. This prohibition includes the education in alternative practice.[86] If alternative practitioners or other unauthorized therapists diagnose or cure patients in spite of that, they can be prosecuted for charlatanism (*Kurpfuscherei*).

105. According to §184 of the Criminal Code (Federal Law Gazette 1974/60 as last amended by Federal Law Gazette I 2013/134), charlatanism can be committed by any person practising medicine on a commercial basis to a larger number of people without holding the necessary official qualification. 'A larger number of people' may be defined as a minimum of ten people. Therefore only an illegal treatment of at least ten patients shall give rise to a prosecution for charlatanism. The illegal acting person can be punished with imprisonment up to three months or a fine.

106. The offence can only be committed by people who do not hold an academic degree in medicine. A physician who has not passed the post-gradual training, whose medical university qualification was obtained abroad, has not been recognized yet or whose license to practise medicine is banned, can therefore not commit charlatanism.

107. For reasons of public interests, such as securing the high quality of medical services, an unauthorized person commits charlatanism regardless of whether he has provided satisfactory health care services and cured the patient's illness or not. In other words, it is sufficient to practise medicine illegally in order to render oneself liable to prosecution.

108. Charlatanism can only be committed intentionally. However, the mistaken belief that carrying out medical treatments without the appropriate medical university education is legal is culpable so that the person will nevertheless be guilty of charlatanism.[87]

109. It is discussed controversially whether one single action is sufficient to constitute charlatanism in case the unauthorized person has the intent to offer his medical services on a commercial basis to a considerable number of people, or if this intent additionally has to be objectively manifested by establishing a practice,

86. *See* ECJ 11 Jul. 2002, C-294/00 and Administrative Court 28 Oct. 2003, 2002/11/0175. Also *see* L. Stärker, '§2 ÄrzteG', in *Ärztegesetz mit Kommentar*, ed. H. Emberger & F. Wallner. 2nd edn (Vienna: Verlagshaus der Ärzte, 2008), 13 et seq.; G. Aigner, 'Ärztliches Berufsrecht', in *Handbuch Medizinrecht*, ed. G. Aigner et al. (Vienna: Manz, 2003 et seq.), III/6 et seq.

87. Supreme Court 29 Apr. 2003, 11 Os 42/03, *RdM* 2004/21.

attaching a professional sign or other signs that are publicly visible, or whether a minimum of ten illegal patients' treatments is required.[88]

110. The offence of charlatanism can concur with other offences. If harm is caused to the patient's health or life during the performance of illegal medical activities by an inadequate treatment due to lack of knowledge or skills, the person may additionally be liable for involuntary manslaughter (§§80 et seq. Criminal Code) or bodily injury caused by negligence (§88 Criminal Code). In addition, unauthorized therapists can also be liable to prosecution for fraud in exceptional cases.[89]

§2. PHYSICIANS

111. A Person who graduated from medical school but practises medicine without holding the 'ius practicandi' can be merely guilty of an administrative offence according to §199(1) Physicians Act. Physicians whose qualifications do not entitle them to perform such activities or who are temporarily banned from practising medicine may be guilty of an administrative (§199) and a disciplinary offence (§136 Physicians Act; also *see* for dentists §55 Dentists Chamber Act). The disciplinary action can range from a disciplinary warning letter to a fine up to EUR 36,340 or a temporary ban from the exercise of the profession to striking the licensed physician off the Medical Practitioner Register (§139; also *see* §58 Dentists Chamber Act).[90]

112. Although physicians are allowed to treat patients with alternative or complementary medicine, they have to inform their patients about the fact that the success of the applied method is not verified. Otherwise they can be guilty of fraud due to the pecuniary loss caused by the physician with the intent to enrich himself (§146 Criminal Code).[91]

§3. ILLEGAL MEDICAL ACTIVITIES

113. Certain medical activities such as abortion, sterilization, reproductive medicine (in vitro fertilization, insemination), prenatal or genetic diagnostics, organ transplantations and (clinical) research on human beings may only be carried out if certain legal conditions are fulfilled. Otherwise, physicians as well as all other illegally practising therapists shall be prosecuted by criminal or administrative law, depending on the medical activity in question.

88. For further details *see* V. Murschetz, '§184 StGB', in *Wiener Kommentar zum Strafgesetzbuch*, ed. F. Höpfel & E. Ratz, 2nd edn (Vienna: Manz, 2014, rdb.at), marginal number 1 et seq.
89. Supreme Court 9 Oct. 1985, 9 Os 83/85; 30 Oct. 1997, 12 Os 109/97.
90. Constitutional Court 23 Sep. 2003, B 761/03, VfSlg 16.962/2003 = *RdM* 2004/55. For more details: J. Zahrl & M. Hinterbauer, 'Entwicklungstendenzen im ärztlichen Disziplinarrecht', *RdM* (2014): 80.
91. *See* M. Flora, 'Die Anwendung nicht-wissenschaftlicher Behandlungsmethoden durch Ärzte – ein Betrug?', *RdM* (1997): 109.

It may be pointed out that only certain medical activities are prohibited by the Criminal Code, namely abortion, sterilization, genital mutilation and active euthanasia. Abortion and sterilization are only legal under the conditions stipulated in §97 and §90(2) of the Criminal Code. Genital mutilations that have a lasting negative effect on the sexual sensibility are prohibited by §90(3). If somebody intentionally carries out a forbidden genital mutilation, he is liable for the offence of intentional bodily injury with strong lasting effect (§85). Even so, genital mutilations are legal if they are performed by physicians and do not have a lasting effect on the sexual sensibility. Moreover, the opinion is held that genital mutilations may be legal medical interventions if there is a medical indication, for example in case of transsexual interventions. Active euthanasia is generally an illegal medical activity according to the Criminal Code. Thus, both the assistance in committing suicide and voluntary euthanasia are prohibited by §78 or §77 (for details *see* Part II, Chapter 3 below).

Chapter 4. Control over the Practice of Medicine

§1. Professional Liability

I. General Remarks

114. Besides disciplinary liability, the professional liability of physicians is not regulated by specific laws. Therefore, both the civil and criminal liability for damages or injuries caused by improper performance of professional duties by the physician, dentist or the supplying health care institution are determined by the general rules of the Civil and Criminal Code. Moreover, if a physician is not liable according to the Criminal Code, but has breached obligations originating from administrative law, a fine may be imposed according to the applicable administrative penal law. Additionally, the Austrian Medical Chamber or Austrian Dental Chamber may prosecute the physician or dentist disciplinarily according to the applicable professional law, if he has caused harm to the reputation of the Austrian Medical Association by his behaviour or if he has breached professional duties. In case of errors during the medical treatment, the patient or his relatives may seek damages through civil jurisdiction and may also instigate an action under criminal or administrative penal law as well as disciplinary law.

But not only can physicians be personally liable for medical errors, also the entity of the hospital, for which the physician is working for, may be liable.

II. Civil Liability

115. The civil liability of physicians and health care institutions plays a significant role in the course of the control over the practice of medicine. Many principles concerning the good practice of medicine have been determined by the civil jurisdiction of the Supreme Court.

116. Although the total number of cases of medical errors is not published, it can be stated that around twenty cases of medical errors are adjudged and published by the Supreme Court every year.[92] In many cases patients claim the lack or shortage of appropriate information necessary to consent to the medical intervention. However, this number is not representative for the question how many medical errors actually occur every year, because most cases in Austria are settled out of court.

92. A. Leischner, 'Rechtsprechungsübersicht Arzthaftung', *RdM* (2007): 180–184. A. Leischner, 'Rechtsprechungsübersicht Arzthaftung', *RdM* (2008): 181. A. Leischner, 'Rechtsprechungsübersicht Arzthaftung', *RdM* (2009): 183–187; A. Leischner, 'Rechtsprechungsübersicht Arzthaftung', *RdM* (2010): 174; A. Leischner, 'Rechtsprechungsübersicht Arzthaftung', *RdM* (2011): 223; A. Leischner-Lenzhofer, 'Rechtsprechungsübersicht Arzthaftung', *RdM* (2012): 181; A. Leischner-Lenzhofer, 'Rechtsprechungsübersicht Arzthaftung', *RdM* (2013): 290; A. Leischner-Lenzhofer, 'Rechtsprechungsübersicht Arzthaftung', *RdM* (2014): 326; A. Leischner-Lenzhofer, 'Rechtsprechungsübersicht Arzthaftung', *RdM* (2015): 292; A. Leischner-Lenzhofer, 'Rechtsprechungsübersicht Arzthaftung', *RdM* (2016): 305.

117. Civil liability may arise from breaching contractual obligations or from tort. In most cases a treatment contract is concluded between patient and physician or patient and legal entity of the health care institution, in most cases a hospital. In certain circumstances, for example, if the patient is unconscious and therefore is treated in hospital without his consent, the physician treats the patient without the previous conclusion of a treatment contract. The doctor then acts as an agent of necessity, so that a relation between the physician and the patient similar to the contractual relation is constituted (§1036 Civil Code). In case of damage to a third party or if a person other than the contracting partner (e.g., the attending clinical doctor) shall be claimed, tortious liability is relevant.[93]

A. *Treatment Contract*

118. The conclusion of the treatment contract follows the general rules on contract conclusion according to §861 of the Civil Code. The treatment contract is therefore concluded by two congruent declarations of intent. These can find their expression in form of the patient's consultation of the physician and the following start of the medical treatment. Thus, the contract does not need to be concluded in a written form.

119. The treatment contract cannot be clearly assigned to the contract for services (§§1151 et seq. Civil Code) or to the contract for work (§§1165 et seq. in conjunction with §1151). Whereas the contract for work includes the duty to offer a certain success, the contract for services does not demand the achievement of a specific result, but proper service and skill. The treatment contract can principally be characterized as a contract for services, since the physician has to provide his service personally and directly, as far as he is the contracting partner. Generally spoken, the physician cannot guarantee the success of a medical treatment due to the complexity of the human body and human functions, even if it is carried out according to the state-of-art. Therefore an operation, even if it is a cosmetic operation, is carried out on the basis of a contract for services.[94] However, the physician is not an employee of the patient, but an independent contractor in relation to the patient.

93. For details concerning the civil liability *see* e.g., Th. Juen, *Arzthaftungsrecht,* 2nd edn (Vienna: Manz, 2005); A. Leischner, *Streitbeilegung in medizinischen Haftungsfällen* (Vienna: Manz, 2007), 73 et seq.; A. Kletečka, 'Zivilrechtliche Haftung (Schadenersatz)', in *Handbuch Medizinrecht,* ed. G. Aigner et al. (Vienna: Manz, 2003 et seq.), II/1 et seq.; A. Tanczos & D. Tanczos, *Arzthaftung,* 2nd edn (Vienna: Verlag Österreich, 2016), 77 et seq.; H. Jesser-Huß, 'Zivilrechtliche Haftung und Fragen der Aufklärung', *Handbuch Medizinrecht,* eds R. Resch & F. Wallner, 2nd edn (Vienna: LexisNexis, 2015), 109 et seq.; E. Nigl, *Arzthaftung,* 3rd edn (Vienna: Orac, 2017); for developments in jurisdiction *see* E. Nigl, 'Neuere Judikatur zur Arzthaftung', *Zak* (2009): 148; E. Nigl, 'Neuere Judikatur zur Arzthaftung 2009–2013', *Zak* (2014): 43; B. Koch, 'Medical Malpractice in Austria', in Medical Malpractice and Compensation in Global Perspective, eds K. Oliphant & R. Wright (Berlin/Boston: De Gruyter, 2013), 7–34; E. Bernat, 'Entwicklungslinien des Medizinrechts. Eine Bestandsaufnahme aus Anlass von 20 Jahren "Recht der Medizin", *RdM* (2014): 36 (39 et seq.).
94. Supreme Court 4 Jul. 1991, 6 Ob 558/91, *KRES* 9/20.

Consequently, the Supreme Court defined the treatment contract as a 'freelance contract for services'.[95]

120. However, in some cases the Court has made exceptions of this rule. Besides the medical treatment as main duty, treatment contracts can also include a certain result as subsidiary duty, for example to customize a dental or other prosthesis or to supply a diagnosis by EEG-analysis. These subsidiary duties may be provided under the terms of a contract for work, which means that the patient can claim for damages if the specific result is not fulfilled. The borderline between these contracts is vague. Whereas the production and adjustment of a dental prosthesis was once characterized by the Supreme Court as a contract for work as the dentist could control the success due to his proper mechanical and technical skills,[96] the failed, but complicated adjustment of a dental prosthesis was not considered as fault of the dentist due to lack of skills.[97] Consequently the patient could not claim for damages.

121. The duration of the treatment contract is defined on a case-by-case basis. In case of doubt, the contract shall be concluded for the whole case of illness, including pre- and post-interventional supervision, and not for every single treatment.[98]

122. The patient's acceptance of the contract must not be mixed up with the patient's consent to the medical treatment. Contracting partner and patient, who consents to the treatment, can differ. In this case the treatment contract is qualified as a contract that also favours the third party (§881 Civil Code). To give an example, a 14-year old patient only has a limited capacity to contract (§170 Civil Code), but generally has the ability to consent to medical intervention (§173 Civil Code). The contract therefore only constitutes the mutual obligations and rights of the contracting partners but does not justify the medical treatment itself.

123. Medical treatments in hospitals are principally based on the medical contract between the legal entity of the hospital and the patient or his legal representative. The contract not only creates the hospital's obligation to treat the patient according to the current state of medical science and experience, but also to supply the patient with adequate in-patient care, including pre- and post-interventional supervision and appropriate accommodation and maintenance of the general safety of the patient's premises and equipment. Due to the wide scope of this treatment contract it is also called total hospital (admission) contract.[99]

---

95. For example, Supreme Court 23 May 1984, 1 Ob 550/84, *SZ* 57/98.
96. Supreme Court 12 Mar. 1991, 5 Ob 514/91; *see also* Supreme Court, 15 Jun. 2016, 4 Ob 96/16w, *RdM-LS* 2016/78, 197.
97. Supreme Court 26 Apr. 1988, 4 Ob 531/88.
98. Supreme Court 3 Apr. 2008, 8 Ob 34/08w, *RdM* 2008/126, 181.
99. For details *see* e.g., M. Kletečka-Pulker, 'Rechtsgrundlagen der Behandlung', in *Handbuch Medizinrecht*, ed. G. Aigner et al. (Vienna: Manz, 2003 et seq.), I/1 et seq.; Th. Juen, *Arzthaftungsrecht*,

B. Actionable Duties of the Physician

124. Medical malpractice[100] and violations of the physician's duty to obtain the patient's informed consent have to be considered as reasons for a breach of contract, and therefore justify a claim for damages.

1. Medical Treatment

125. The physician's main contractual duty is the patient's medical examination and treatment. Due to the nature of the medical function, the treatment contract does not oblige the physician to cure the patient, but to treat the patient according to professional standards. The Supreme Court defined this professional standard as the professional treatment according to the objective professional standard of the specific medical field.[101] In other words, the physician has to treat the patient according to the current state-of-the-art or with reasonable care and skill, which shall not be less than the ordinary care shown by a prudent and diligent standard physician in the same circumstances.[102]

126. The professional standard varies between a general practitioner and a medical specialist. The specialist therefore has to meet a higher standard of skill and knowledge in the specialized field than a general practitioner does. In a case of a failed cosmetic surgery the Supreme Court stated that the required standard of medical knowledge and skill is an objective one and shall therefore be assessed on the basis of the professional standard of cosmetic surgeons as the operating physician's respective field of expertise.[103] If the physician does not meet this professional standard, the deviation from it is considered as fault of the physician (§1299 Civil Code).

127. The medical treatment has to be carried out according to the current[104] state of medical science and experience (§8[2] Federal Frame Law on Hospitals and Sanatoria; §49[1] Physicians Act). Therefore the physician continuously has to

2nd edn (Vienna: Manz, 2005), 52 et seq.; A. Leischner, *Streitbeilegung in medizinischen Haftungsfällen* (Vienna: Manz, 2007), 8 et seq.; A. Tanczos & D. Tanczos, *Arzthaftung*, 2nd edn (Vienna: Verlag Österreich, 2016), 11 et seq.; H. Jesser-Huß, 'Zivilrechtliche Haftung und Fragen der Aufklärung', *Handbuch Medizinrecht,* ed. R. Resch & F. Wallner, 2nd edn (Vienna: LexisNexis, 2015), 91 et seq.

100. For a definition of medical malpractice *see* E. Bernat, 'Compensation For Medical Injuries: Is There a Need for a Law Reform? An Austrian Viewpoint', *European Journal of Health Law* 5 (1998): 117.

101. Supreme Court 4 Jul. 1991, 6 Ob 558/91, KRES 9/20.

102. Supreme Court 31 Jan. 1995, 4 Ob 509/95, *RdM* (1995): 91; Supreme Court 30 Mar. 2016, 4 Ob 42/16d, *RdM* 2016/111, 153 *(Leischner-Lenzhofer)*; 23 Nov. 2016, 1 Ob 138/16z, *RdM* 2017/84, 112 *(Leischner-Lenzhofer)*.

103. Supreme Court 27 Feb. 2009, 6 Ob 122/07w, *RdM-LS* 2009/33; the same is ruled in context of a medical expert witness before court: Supreme Court 30 Jul. 2015, 10 Ob 50/15y, *RdM* 2016/36, 22 *(Leischner-Lenzhofer)*.

104. *See* e.g., Supreme Court 17 Feb. 2014, 4 Ob 27/14w, *RdM-LS* 2014/21, 108.

undergo further training. These training programmes shall provide the physicians with the necessary information to keep up-to-date with the national and international standard of the state-of-the-art in medical knowledge and skills. In a case of 'wrongful birth', in which the employees of a university hospital failed to notice serious abnormities of an unborn child in the course of ultrasonic diagnostics in 1988, the Supreme Court judged that medical-technical knowledge shall not be limited to the local medical standard or the subjective opinion of the physicians who work at the hospital. Thus, it was not sufficient that the university hospital staff had the general technical-medical knowledge prevailing in Austria. It would have been necessary to adapt the standard of the ultrasonic diagnostics to the higher standard of ultrasonic diagnostics customary in Germany. The Supreme Court stated that especially a university hospital could not justify a lack of knowledge of the current international state-of-art.[105] In another case of wrongful birth, in which a small regional hospital failed to refer a pregnant woman to a counselling centre for genetic diseases although the ambulance doctor knew that some family members suffered from the genetic disease Niemann-Pick, the Supreme Court did not apply the same strict professional standard as in the above-mentioned case.[106]

128. Patients have to be treated with the currently securest medical method known to acknowledged expert groups that prevents and minimizes known operative risks.[107] A method is appropriate as long as an acknowledged medical school recommends it. However, the patient principally does not have the right to be treated with the world's best medical method existing. In this respect, a medical method can be appropriate, even if other competent physicians would have preferred to use another medical treatment. But if a significant number of medical experts deem the medical method critically, the method shall not be used anymore.[108] An alternative, complementary or new medical method can be used if the patient wants to be treated with this method after being informed appropriately about the fact that this method is an alternative, complementary or new form of treatment, its risks and alternative treatment options as long as it is not contraindicated.[109] However, if the treating clinical doctor holds the opinion that an available alternative method is not equivalent to conventional medicine, the entity of the hospital is not obliged to treat the patient with the method in question, as long as the medical opinion is ex ante arguable.[110]

---

105. Supreme Court 25 May 1999, 1 Ob 91/99k, *RdM* 1999/23.
106. Supreme Court 23 Oct. 2003, 6 Ob 303/02f, *RdM* 2004/36.
107. For example, Supreme Court 29 Jun. 1989, 6 Ob 549/89, *SZ* 62/125 and others.
108. For example, Supreme Court 16 Mar. 1989, 8 Ob 525/89 (8 Ob 526/89), *SZ 62/53*. Therefore a medical practitioner does not have the duty to inform about an obsolete method: Supreme Court 12 Feb. 2013, 4 Ob 241/12p, *RdM* 2013/102, 149 *(Leischner-Lenzhofer)*.
109. Supreme Court 29 Jan. 2001, 3 Ob 87/00s, *RdM* 2001/21. There is no duty to inform in case the alternative method is qualified with little prospect of success for the current consulted and treating medical practitioners: Supreme Court 21 Feb. 2013, 9 Ob 32/12i, *RdM* 2013/101, 145.
110. Supreme Court 21 Feb. 2013, 9 Ob 32/12i, *RdM* 2013/101 = R. Rebhahn, 'Wann dürfen Vertragsärzte die Behandlung von Versicherten ablehnen?', *RdM* (2013): 140. For details on the 'state of art' *see* Ch. Kopetzki, 'Behandlungen auf dem "Stand der Wissenschaft"', in *Finanzielle Grenzen des Behandlungsanspruches* ed. Pfeil (Verlag Manz, Vienna 2010), 9–47.

2. Information

129. Every performance of a medical act affects the physical integrity of the patient and is therefore an illegal act if it is carried out without the patient's informed consent (§110 Criminal Code, §8[3] Federal Frame Law on Hospitals and Sanatoria). Thus, every medical treatment can generally only be started after the physician has informed the patient properly and the patient has consented to the treatment. Information has to be given on the diagnosis, equal potential medical techniques (if the risks, success rate or cosmetic results vary) and about the risks and consequences of undergoing the recommended treatment or abstaining from it. The quantity and intensity of the necessary information shall be adjusted to the patient's demand and to the specific situation. The Supreme Court has developed the following two principles: The more urgent a treatment or diagnosis is, the lower the requirements on quantity of information are. The less medically indicated a medical intervention is, the higher the requirements on quantity and intensity of information are (for details *see* Part II, Chapter 1, §3. below).

130. If the patient or his legal representative has not received appropriate and sufficient information and therefore cannot understand the meaning and scope of the recommended treatment, his consent is not effective in law. Therefore, the precondition for every treatment is the patient's informed consent. If the information is insufficient in any way, the patient can claim for damages even if the medical treatment itself was carried out according to the current state of medical science and experience (*lege artis*) or if the iatrogenic damage was caused accidentally, as a result of a risk about which the patient should have been informed. Only if the physician or entity of the hospital can prove that the information was given in an appropriate way or that the patient would have gone ahead with the treatment if he had known about the relevant complications thereof, the claim will not be successful.[111]

C. *Indemnification Clause*

131. Pursuant to §6(1) No. 9 of the Consumer Protection Law (Federal Law Gazette 1979/140 as last amended by Federal Law Gazette I 2003/91), the responsibility of the physician or legal entity of the hospital for its employees regarding damages to persons cannot be limited or excluded by the treatment contract. Moreover, the contracting party cannot limit or exclude its liability for intent or gross negligence in relation to other damages of the patient.

D. *Professional Liability Insurance*

132. In 2010 (Federal Law Gazette I 2010/61 as last amended by Federal Law Gazette I 2014/82) the legislator stipulated a general duty for medical or dental

111. *See* RIS-Justiz RS0038485.

service providers to conclude professional liability insurance with a certain minimal insurance coverage. Subject to this legal obligation are all freelance physicians or dentists, group practices in the legal form of private limited companies and legal entities of a hospital which are not a political subdivision (federation, *federal state* or *Gemeinde*), public-law corporation or legal entity, which is owned by a political subdivision or public-law corporation (§52d[1]–[3] Physicians Act; §26c Dentists Act; §5c[1]–[2] Frame Law on Hospitals and Sanatoria). In case of medical malpractice both the insurer and the insurant are jointly liable and can both be claimed for damages (§52d[6] Physicians Act; §26c[3] Dentists Act; §5c[3] Frame Law on Hospitals and Sanatoria).[112]

E. The Basis of Liability and Burden of Proof

1. Fault

133. Fault is the main basis for a claim for medical error either ex contractu or ex delicto. Any deviation from the professional standard is considered as fault (§1299 Civil Code). In principle, the claiming patient has the burden to prove that the physician has neglected his duty to carry out the treatment according to the professional standard or as a prudent and diligent standard physician in the same circumstances.[113]

'If medical practitioners or doctors-in training practise beyond their medical field of expertise, the patient's burden of proof is alleviated (*Übernahmeverschulden*). The patient only has to prove that the protective law according to §1311 Civil Code has been infringed (e.g., §3[3] or §31[3] Physicians Act). As a result, the defendant has to prove his competence, that other prudent and diligent standard medical practitioners would not have acted differently and that the damage would have occurred in any way.[114]

Due to the difficulty to prove medical malpractice, the Supreme Court judges in constant jurisdiction that the burden of proof shall be alleviated in favour of the patient. If a physician fails to comply with his duty to record the treatment and thereby makes it more difficult for the patient to prove the medical malpractice, such proof is facilitated corresponding to the difficulties caused by the missing documentation in order to ensure a fair distribution of evidentiary positions between the physician and the patient.[115] If there is a lack of documentation so that proof of the medical malpractice is not possible at all, the Supreme Court goes even further and reverses the burden of proof so that the physician has to prove that the medical treatment was carried out lege artis.[116] However, in cases in which it is certain that the

112. *See* for more details e.g., Th. Holzgruber, 'Obligatorische Haftpflichtversicherung und berufsrechtliche Konsequenzen für Ärzte', *VR* (2011): 27; M.-S. Häusler, 'Haftpflichtversicherung', in *Handbuch Medizinrecht*, ed. G. Aigner et al. (Vienna: Manz, 2003 et seq.), II/83 (II/89 et seq.).
113. Supreme Court 9 Sep. 1986, 2 Ob 599/85, *JBl* 1987, 104.
114. *See* e.g., Supreme Court 30 May 2012, 8 Ob 52/12y, *RdM-LS* 2012/48, 197; 30 Jul. 2015, 10 Ob 50/15y, *RdM* 2016/36, 22 *(Leischner-Lenzhofer).*
115. Supreme Court 25 Jan. 1994, 1 Ob 532/94, *SZ* 67/9 = *RdM* 1994/25 (*Kopetzki*).
116. Supreme Court 16 Aug. 2001, 8 Ob 134/01s, *RdM* 2002, 27.

patient was informed properly and treated according to the lex-artis, the question of burden of proof is not decisive.[117,118]

134. If the patient is able to convince the judge that he has suffered damage because the contracting partner of the treatment contract did not meet his contractual duties, the defendant himself has to prove that such a breach did not occur due to his own fault or the fault of his staff (§1298 Civil Code).

The defendant may also claim that the patient has caused the suffered damage by his own fault or negligence according to §1304 Civil Code (Mitverschulden).[119] However, the defendant cannot put forward successfully that the patient has caused his need of medical service by his own fault if the physician has made a medical error in the thereby performed treatment.[120]

135. In case a certain result has to be achieved, such as an adjustment of a dental prothesis or an EEG-diagnosis, the patient only has to prove that the success or result is not obtained. After that, the physician has to prove that it was not his fault, but reasoned for example in the physiology of the patient. However, the borderline between the physician's duty to achieve a specific result and to owe proper care and skill is vague and has to be answered with respect to the individual case.

136. If the patient claims that the physician has not informed him properly and therefore has violated the patient's interest in his bodily integrity (§110 Criminal Code and §8[3] Frame Law on Hospitals and Sanatoria), the defendant has the burden to prove that the standards of informed consent were met. In other words, the burden of proof concerning the question whether the patient would have consented to the treatment in case of adequate disclosure of information or not, lies with the health care provider as this concerns the question of alternative lawful behaviour (*rechtmäßiges Alternativverhalten*). The physician can also free himself from liability by claiming and proving that the patient would have consented to the treatment even if he had received adequate information (hypothetic consent). The patient does not need to substantiate his hypothetical refusal and to present in advance whether or why he would not have consented to the recommended treatment. But if the

117. Supreme Court 17 Dec. 2014, 4 Ob 27/14w, *RdM-LS* 2014/21, 108.

118. For further details on the burden of proof in case of medical malpractice *see* e.g., A. Kletečka, 'Die zivilrechtliche Haftung (Schadenersatz)', in *Handbuch Medizinrecht*, ed. G. Aigner et al. (Vienna: Manz, 2003 et seq.), II/14 et seq.; A. Tanczos & D. Tanczos, *Arzthaftung* 2nd edn (Vienna: Verlag Österreich, 2016), 97 et seq.; W. Kolmasch & M. Neumayr, 'Rechtsprechung zur Behauptungs- und Beweislast in Arzthaftungsfällen', *Zak* (2011): 45; M. Neumayr, 'Prozessuale Fragen des Arzthaftungsprozesses', in *Handbuch Medizinrecht*, ed. R. Resch & F. Wallner, 2nd edn (Vienna: LexisNexis, 2015), 326 et seq.

119. *See* e.g., for a successful plea: Supreme Court 28 Aug. 1997, 3 Ob 2121/96z RdM 1998, 57; and for a not successful plea in a case in which the physician has not informed the patient properly about the patient's duty to comply with the requirements for the success of medical treatment: Supreme Court 27 Feb. 2002, 3 Ob 17/02z.

120. Supreme Court 25 Feb. 2016, 9 Ob 76/15i, *RdM-LS* 2016/36 = *EvBl* 2016/125 *(Rohrer/Schacherreiter)*.

defendant puts forward the plea of hypothetic consent, the patient has to give comprehensible reasons why he would have fixed the date of the operation on another date or would have rejected the medical treatment.[121]

2. Damage

137. The patient has to prove which damages were caused by the medical error. An indemnification is only possible if the claimant can prove the suffered damage.[122]

138. Concerning medical treatments, damage can occur in form of bodily injury, deformation or death of the patient. The compensation for damage is based upon the general rules of damages law. Damages for any injury of the physical or mental health or integrity is regulated by §1325 of the Civil Code. Bodily harm must not be visible, so that for example any injury of a nerve, infliction of pain or cause of a trauma can also be qualified as damage. If such damages can be proved, the aggrieved party can claim for compensation for medical expenses, loss of income[123] and immaterial loss.[124]

Medical expenses are only repaid to the patient if he paid the costs himself, as they were not covered by social or private insurance. If the medical expenses are covered by the social or private health insurance, the title to compensation for the paid medical expenses is transferred *ex lege* to the social or private insurer (§332 General Social Insurance Act; §67 Insurance Contract Act – *Versicherungsvertragsgesetz*, Federal Law Gazette 1959/2). Fictive medical expenses cannot be claimed for, but the patient can claim for advance money.[125]

139. If the bodily harm also causes a visible deformation that reduces the chances of marriage or limits the professional advancement, the claiming patient can additionally sue for compensation of deformation (§1326 Civil Code).[126]

140. If the medical error causes the patient's death, his relatives can claim compensation for caused healing costs, funeral expenses, and children as well as the

121. For example, Supreme Court 16 Sep. 2008, 1 Ob 80/08h, *RdM* 2009, 96 (*Leischner*); 14 Oct. 2008, 4 Ob 155/08k, *RdM*-LS 2009/15, 101. For an English summary of this decision *see* B.C. Steininger, 'Austria', in *European Tort Law 2008*, ed. H. Koziol & B.C. Steininger (Vienna/New York: Springer, 2009), nos 66 et seq. *See also* Supreme Court 29 Nov. 2012, 2 Ob 43/12f, *RdM* 2013/50, 71.

122. *See* e.g., Supreme Court 23 Jul. 2014, 9 Ob 45/14d *RdM-LS* 2014/62, 341.

123. *See* concerning the loss of income for housewives: RIS-Justiz RS0030922; recently Supreme Court 14 Jul. 2010, 7 Ob 14/10z, *RdM-LS* 2011/31, 99.

124. *See* for more details e.g., A. Kletečka, 'Die zivilrechtliche Haftung (Schadenersatz)', in Handbuch Medizinrecht, ed. G. Aigner et al. (Vienna: Manz, 2003 et seq.), II/16 et seq.; K.-H-Danzl, 'Aktuelle (Fort-) Entwicklungen beim Schmerzengeld', *ZVR* (2016): 456. Recently e.g., Supreme Court 7 Jun. 2016, 10 Ob 89/15h, *RdM-LS* 2016/80, 198.

125. Supreme Court 23 Oct. 1997, 2 Ob 82/97s, *SZ* 70/220; *see* recently 9 Apr. 2015, 2 Ob 173/14a, *RdM-LS* 2015/54, 156.

126. For example, Supreme Court 8 May 2001, 10 Ob 86/01x.

widow/widower can claim compensation for loss of legal maintenance costs pursuant to §1327 of the Civil Code.

141. Under certain circumstances the relatives of the dead patient including the long-term partner can claim compensation for immaterial loss according to §1325 of the Civil Code, such as suffered shock in respect to the news of the patient's death caused by negligence[127] and for sorrow if the death was caused by gross negligence.[128] In a recent judgment it was ruled that also parents of an unborn child can claim compensation for immaterial loss for suffered shock and sorrow in case the death of the unborn was caused by gross negligence.[129]

142. Due to failure of diagnosis and information about serious abnormalities of an unborn child, the Supreme Court awarded parents of disabled children compensation for their disabled children's entire maintenance costs in two wrongful birth cases,[130] provided that the parents would have been convinced to lawfully abort the disabled child if they knew about the serious malformations. In other words, the Court compared the financial situation of the parents after the birth of the disabled child with their situation after an abortion, and qualified the financial damage as compensable damage according to §1293 of the Civil Code. Even so, the disabled child cannot claim for damages. Before this jurisdiction, the Supreme Court had only awarded parents of an unwanted, disabled child the additional expenses due to the malformation of their disabled child, because the parents had only claimed for compensation of the additional maintenance costs.[131]

This new ruling has strongly been criticized as discrimination of disabled people. The most significant reason for the criticism is, that the Supreme Court has two contradictory lines of court practice, namely in the case of wrongful birth and wrongful conception. Concerning wrongful conception-cases, the deciding Court panels do not award parents of unwanted, but healthy children any compensation for their children's maintenance costs. In accordance with the uniformity-theory, the panel holds the opinion that the birth of a healthy child can never be qualified as damage

127. For example, Supreme Court 29 Aug. 2002, 8 Ob 127/02p, *JBl* 2003, 118, lately Supreme Court 11 May 2010, 4 Ob 36/10p, *RdM* 2010, 149 (*Bernat*); 8 Jun. 2010, 4 Ob 71/10k, *RdM* 2010, 154 (*Leischner*); 30 Jun. 2010, 9 Ob 83/09k, *RdM-LS* 2010/53; 25 Feb. 2016, 1 Ob 22/16s, *RdM* 2016, 306.

128. For example, Supreme Court 16 May 2001, 2 Ob 84/01v, *JBl* 2001, 660.

129. Supreme Court 30 Aug. 2016, 1 Ob 114/16w, *RdM* 2017/63, 68 (Karner).

130. Supreme Court 7 Mar. 2006, 5 Ob 165/05h, *RdM* 2006/71; Supreme Court 11 Dec. 2007, 5 Ob 148/07m, *RdM* 2008/38, 47 (*Kopetzki*) = *B.C. Steininger, ÖJZ* 2008, 436 = *K. Grüblinger, Zak* 2008/260, 143 = *D. Hinghofer-Szalkay & C. Hirsch, iFamZ* 2008, 120 = *R. Pletzer, JBl* 2008, 490 = *ecolex* 2008/109, 322 (*Wilhelm*) = *M. Leitner, ecolex* 2008, 417 = *H. Koziol & B.C. Steininger, RZ* 2008, 138. For an English summary of these decisions *see* B.C. Steininger, 'Austria', in *European Tort Law 2006*, ed. H. Koziol & B.C. Steininger (Vienna/New York: Springer, 2008), no. 5 et seq. and 61 et seq.

131. Supreme Court 25 May 1999, 1 Ob 91/99k, *RdM* 1999/23. For an English summary of this decision *see* B.C. Steininger, 'Austria', in *European Tort Law 2006*, ed. H. Koziol & B.C. Steininger (Vienna/New York: Springer, 2008), no. 13 et seq. For details *see* Ch. Hirsch, *Arzthaftung bei fehlgeschlagener Familienplanung* (Vienna: Manz, 2002). Also *see* E. Bernat, 'A Cause of Action for "Wrongful Birth" Under Austrian Tort Law: Don't Take the Civil Code too Seriously!', *Journal of International Biotechnology Law* 1 (2004): 161.

and doubts that maintenance costs are compensable at all. Only in exceptional cases, in which the maintenance obligation places an extraordinary burden on parents, they shall be granted compensation. This was stated in cases of failed sterilizations[132] and in one case in which the physician placed three embryos in the uterus of the surrogate mother instead of two as previously agreed.[133]

In the recent judgment of an unplanned birth of healthy triplets, the Supreme Court denied that the criticism of inconsistent jurisdiction is justified. Instead it holds the opinion that the cases of the birth of healthy and disabled children, and liability occurred before or after conception, are different and cannot be compared, and therefore refused to decide the case in an amplified panel. This reasoning cannot be approved, since the factual differences of the cases do not deviate from the fact that both cases prompt the fundamental question whether, and if so, to what extent maintenance costs for an unplanned child are compensable. Therefore, a contradictory Supreme Court practice is definitely not justifiable.[134] Finally, the legislator will be challenged to find a consistent solution related to the unplanned birth of a child.[135]

3. Causation

143. The claiming patient has to prove that the physician's negligence caused the suffered damage. Thus, the claimant has to prove that the medical error was *conditio-sine-qua-non* for the damage. In other words, the damage would not have been caused, if the medical error had not been made. The damage has to be typical and foreseeable, in terms of an adequate consequence of the negligence of the physician. A consequence is adequate insofar as a prudent and diligent person would have realized that this act or non-act could cause the damage. Due to the difficulty of proving the causation, the Supreme Court alleviates the burden of proof for the claiming patients.

---

132. Supreme Court 14 Sep. 2006, 6 Ob 101/06f, *ÖJZ* 2006/71; Supreme Court 30 Nov. 2006, 2 Ob 172/06t, *ecolex* 2007/69, 169 *(Wilhelm)* = D. Hinghofer-Szalkay & C. Hirsch, *EF-Z* 2007, 89. For an English summary of the Supreme Court's decision 6 Ob 101/06f *see* B.C. Steininger, 'Austria', in *European Tort Law 2006*, ed. H. Koziol & B.C. Steininger (Vienna/New York: Springer, 2008), no. 18 et seq., *see also* Supreme Court 29 Jan. 2015, 9 Ob 37/14b, *RdM* 2015/110, 149 (Bernat).
133. Supreme Court 7 Oct. 2008, 6 Ob 148/08w, *Zak* 2008/578, 336 (*Kletečka*) = *R. Fucik*, *ÖJZ* 2008/67 = *RdM-LS* 2009/5 (*Leischner*) = *ecolex* 2008/397, 1117 (*Friedl*) = *E. Karner*, *EF-Z* 2009/69, 91. For an English summary of this decision *see* B.C. Steininger, 'Austria', in *European Tort Law 2008*, ed. H. Koziol & B.C. Steininger (Vienna/New York: Springer, 2009), no. 55 et seq.
134. B.C. Steininger, 'Austria', in *European Tort Law 2008*, ed. H. Koziol & B.C. Steininger (Vienna/New York: Springer, 2009), no. 59 et seq.
135. *See* H. Koziol & B.C. Steininger, 'Schadenersatz bei ungeplanter Geburt eines Kindes', *RZ* (2008): 138. For an English summary of this article *see* B.C. Steininger, 'Austria', in *European Tort Law 2008*, ed. H. Koziol & B.C. Steininger (Vienna/New York: Springer, 2009), no. 84 et seq.; E. Bernat, 'Wrongful Birth and Wrongful Conception. Der Ersatz des Familienplanungsschadens auf dem Prüfstand des OGH', in *Körper-Codes*, ed. Ch. Kopetzki et al. (Vienna: Linde, 2010), 109; E. Bernat, 'Wrongful Birth und Wrongful Conception in der Rechtsprechung des österreichischen OGH: Kann nur die Geburt eines behinderten Kindes die Quelle eines Schadens sein?', *MedR* (2010): 169–176.

The claimants therefore merely have to prove that the damage was a typical consequence of the negligence and that it is 'highly likely' that they would not have been injured if the defendant had acted adequately considering the circumstances.[136] Prima facie evidence is only possible if experience implies a typical course of events. In turn the defendant has to rebut such proof by showing that another possible cause was more likely to have caused the damage than his negligence. In other words, the defendant (physician or hospital) has to prove that his negligence did with utmost probability not cause the patient's harm.[137]

Damages law qualifies §110 of the Criminal Code and §8(3) of the Federal Frame Law on Hospitals and Sanatoria as protective law (*Schutzgesetz*, §1311 Civil Code), so that a patient who was treated without consent only has to prove that this protective law has been infringed as well as the damages, and then the physician has the burden of proof that the damages have not been caused by himself.[138]

144. The most difficult constellations of causation concerning medical malpractice cases are cases in which negligence and coincidence are both potential causes for the patient's harm in the form of alternative causation. A coincidence is on hand if the treated patient suffers from a yet undiscovered disease, abnormality or predisposition, which is a potential cause for the patient's harm. As usual, the patient has to prove that the medical error caused the damage, although in this case the defendant can give evidence to counter this proof of causation by proving that the damage has an equal origin in the patient's bad constitution. If it cannot be clarified which of the two equally possible causes was the actual cause of the damage, the Supreme Court ruled that the damage shall be divided between the defendant and the claiming patient (in analogy to §1304 Civil Code).[139] A leading case involved a child who suffered from asphyxia at birth. In the proceedings it could not be clarified whether the cause for the damage was the negligent act of the hospital staff that diagnosed a placental insufficiency, but did not keep the mother-to-be in hospital for further medical supervision, or whether the child was strangulated by the umbilical cord wrapped around its neck in the birth canal. The Supreme Court judged that in this case the damage should be shared 50:50.[140] The advantage of this solution is that an all-or-nothing-approach can be avoided.[141]

---

136. For example, Supreme Court 13 Jun. 1989, 8 Ob 525/88, *SZ* 62/53; 5 May 1998, 4 Ob 23/98f, *RdM* 1999, 20.
137. Supreme Court 31 May 1990, 6 Ob 702/ 89; Supreme Court 5 May 1998, 4 Ob 23/98f, *RdM* 1999, 20; *see* recently Supreme Court 16 Dec. 2013, 6 Ob 212/13i, *RdM-LS* 2014/12, 72 *(Kallab)*.
138. *See* e.g., Supreme Court 25 Jan. 1994, 1 Ob 532/94, *RdM* 1994/25 (*Kopetzki*). *See* recently Supreme Court 21 Dec. 2015, 5 Ob 248/15d, *RdM-LS* 2016/35.
139. F. Bydlinski, 'Haftungsgrund und Zufall als alternative mögliche Schadensursachen', in *Aktuelle Probleme des Unternehmensrechts – Festschrift Gerhard Frotz*, ed. M. Enzinger, H.F. Hügel & W. Dillenz (Vienna: Manz, 1993), 3 et seq.; For an overview in English *see* H. Koziol, 'Problems of Alternative Causation in Tort Law', in *Developments in Austrian and Israeli Private Law*, ed. H. Hausmaninger et al. (Vienna: Springer, 1999), 177 (180 et seq.); B.A. Koch, 'Austria', in *Digests of European Tort Law*, ed. B. Winiger et al., vol. 1 (Vienna: Springer, 2006), 6a/3, 6–8.
140. Supreme Court 7 Nov. 1995, 4 Ob 554/95, *JBl* 1996, 181 = *RdM* 1996, 54.
141. Supreme Court 4 Jun. 1993, 8 Ob 608/92; 7 Nov. 1995, 4 Ob 554/95, *RdM* 1996, 54; 15 Mar. 2001, 6 Ob 36/01i; 26 Jul. 2006, 3 Ob 106/06v; 10 Jun. 2008, 4 Ob 75/08w, *ecolex* 2008, 819 = B.C. Steininger, 'Austria', in *European Tort Law 2008*, ed. H. Koziol & B.C. Steininger (Vienna/ New

145. In case of overtaking causation, the defendant can rebut the evidence of causation by proving that it was at least predictable that a similar damage would have occurred hypothetically only a short time later, due to the predisposition of the patient. In such cases the liability is split between the parties, so that the defendant is only liable for the damage endured in the time period starting from its actual occurrence to the predicted moment at which the damage would have abounded anyway (*Verfrühungsschaden* or *Verschlimmerungsschaden*). To give an example, a child had a tumour surgery that caused paraplegia as a risk occurrence. It was ruled that the operation was unlawful since his parents as consenting parties were not informed properly. However, the defendant could prove that the disease pattern of the child would have caused paraplegia only a short time later, so that the Supreme Court judged that the liability of the defendant should be restricted to the compensation for temporal acceleration.[142] However, liability is not split between the parties and the defendant is liable for the whole damage, if the medical malpractice only in conjunction with predisposition of the patient caused the severity of the damage. An unpredictable disease pattern of the patient may fall within the risk sphere of the treating physician as long as the causation is adequate.[143]

F. Aspects of Vicarious Liability

1. Liability of Entities of Hospitals for Acts of Their Medical Staff

146. As mentioned above (*see* subchapter A. above), medical treatment is principally based on a hospital admission contract, which is concluded between the legal entity of the hospital and the patient as far as the patient is treated in a private, public or private non-profit hospital. Therefore the entity is vicariously liable for any negligence of its staff (§1313a Civil Code) that constitutes a breach of the hospital's contractual duties. If there is only a contractual relationship between the entity of the hospital and the patient, the acting medical staff cannot be claimed for a breach of contractual duties. The patient's action against the individual physician can merely lie in tort liability.[144]

147. If the claim against the entity of the hospital is not directly or indirectly based on contract, §1315 Civil Code is applicable. Here the vicarious liability is limited to cases in which the contracting party uses the help of an inefficient assistant or knowingly of a dangerous assistant and in which this assistant causes damage to others in his capacity as assistant.

York: Springer, 2009), 40 et seq. In contrast, an all-or-nothing-approach was chosen in Supreme Court 10 Oct. 1993, 6 Ob 604/91, *JBl* 1992, 522; 8 Jul. 1993, 2 Ob 590/92, *JBl* 1994, 540 (*Bollenberger*). *See also* Supreme Court 17 Feb. 2014, 4 Ob 204/13y, *RdM-LS* 2014/22, 108.

142. Supreme Court 3 Sep. 1996, 10 Ob 2350/96b, *RdM* 1997, 22. *See also* Supreme Court 18 Jul. 2011, 6 Ob 168/10i, *RdM-LS* 2011/64.

143. Supreme Court 17 Feb. 2014, 4 Ob 204/13y, *RdM-LS* 2014/22, 108.

144. For example, Supreme Court 25 May 1999, 1 Ob 91/99k, *RdM* 1999/23. *See also* Supreme Court 22 Jun. 2010, 10 Ob 34/10p, RdM-LS 2010/50, 158.

2. The Physician's Liability for the Medical Activity of Other People

148. If the physician is the contracting party, he is generally only liable for his own negligent acts or breaches of contractual duties. If he employs medical auxiliary or non-medical personnel to help him to fulfil his contractual duties, he is vicariously liable for any negligence of them.[145] There are specific circumstances in which the Supreme Court judged that a physician is also vicariously liable for another physician of the same or another field of expertise.

149. First, the freelance physician is in principle obliged to treat his patients personally. Therefore, a freelance physician may only appoint a substitute in case of vacation, further training or illness (§1010 Civil Code). In these circumstances, the physician has to make the substitution visible for the patients, otherwise the substitute acts as vicarious assistant to the physician. In other words, if the patient is not informed that the medical treatment is not performed by the physician himself, he is vicariously liable for any negligence of the substitute.[146]

150. Second, vicarious liability for the negligence of non-medical assistants or other physicians can arise in the context of medical treatments by attending physicians (*Belegarzt*). These are physicians who have their own practices based elsewhere, but also have an allocated number of beds within a hospital, to which they can admit patients and treat them there themselves. In this case two contracts with the patient exist: The attending physician concludes a treatment contract and the entity of the hospital concludes a contract on the in-patient care and accommodation with the patient. The legal entity of the hospital grants to provide all necessary medical and non-medical staff as vicarious assistants for the attending physician so that he is able to fulfil his contractual duties towards the patient. If the treatment contract between the in-patient doctor and the patient does not constitute explicitly which duties are his, the affiliated doctor is vicariously liable for any negligence in the medical treatment as a whole. Whether the in-patient doctor is able to give professional instructions to his assistants or not does not change his vicarious liability. Therefore the Supreme Court decided that the in-patient doctor is liable for any negligence within the preparation of the surgery by the non-medical staff of the hospital,[147] any negligence of the performing anaesthetist during the surgery[148] and the post-interventional supervision by the medical staff of the hospital.[149] However, in certain circumstances the split of duties between the in-patient doctor and the

145. *See* for more details: e.g., O. Riss & J. Kepplinger, 'Haftungsfragen bei Delegation ärztlicher Tätigkeiten an "Nichtärzte"', *RdM* (2016): No. 134, 216.
146. Supreme Court 13 Jan. 1954, 2 Ob 805/53, *SZ* 27/6 = *JBl* 1954, 437; 22 Jan. 2008, 4 Ob 210/ 07x, RdM 2008, 88 = *JBl* 2008, 651; 10 Mar. 2008 10 Ob 119/07h, *JBl* 2008, 654 (*Dullinger*).
147. Supreme Court 27 Oct. 1999, 1 Ob 267/99t, *RdM* 2000/7 = *JBl* 2001, 56.
148. Supreme Court 23 Nov. 1999, 1 Ob 269/99m, *RdM* 2000/8 = *JBl* 2001, 58.
149. Supreme Court 11 Feb. 2009, 7 Ob 2/09h, *RdM-LS* 2009/24.

hospital can be overlapping, so that the doctor and the entity of the hospital are jointly and severally liable for negligence of the hospital staff.[150]

151. Third, in cases in which a physician consults a colleague in order to obtain a second opinion or to verify a diagnosis, there is only a contractual relationship between the patient and the first physician, so that a vicarious liability may arise for any negligence of the consulted doctor. It depends on the circumstances of the individual case whether a contract between the patient and the second doctor is also concluded or if the second doctor merely acts as vicarious assistant of the first physician. In a case in which a patient consulted a dermatologist in order to clarify an alternation of her skin, the dermatologist sent a tissue sample to a freelance pathologist for a diagnostic study. The Supreme Court judged in this case that the dermatologist acted as open sub-agent for the patient, so that a contract between the pathologist and the patient is tacitly concluded and the negligent acts of the pathologist are not covered by the contractual liability of the dermatologist.[151] In a recent judgment the Supreme Court qualified a comparable situation differently: A gynaecologist sent a pap smear to a pathologist for diagnostic study. In contrast to the older judgment, the Supreme Court qualified the gynaecologist vicariously liable for the malpractice of the pathologist, because the gynaecologist had not informed the patient about the division of labour nor about the name of the pathologist, and had not sent the findings to the patient. In these circumstances, the treatment contract shall include also the diagnostic study. The professional duty of medical specialists to only practise in the medical field in which they are specialized (§31[3] Physicians Act), is therefore not decisive in context of contractual liability.[152]

G. Aspects of Joint and Several Liability

152. Joint and several liability of a freelance physician may arise if he works together with other doctors in a group practice, insofar as it is established as a general partnership (§52a[1] No. 1 and 5 Physicians Act). In this context the treatment contract is not concluded between the patient and the physician, but with the general partnership itself. Therefore, all members of the group practice are equally liable for any negligent medical activity of any member.

Contrary to that, group practices can be also established in the legal form of a private limited company since 2010 (Federal Law Gazette I 2010/61),[153] so that in case of medical errors only the company is contractually liable. However, in case that the mandatory professional liability insurance contract does not comply with the conditions provided by law, all physicians of such a group practice, regardless of their own fault, are liable personally (§52d[3] Physicians Act).

150. Supreme Court 29 Sep. 2009, 8 Ob 103/09v, *RdM-LS* 2010/4, 27. For more details concerning the attending physician *see* e.g., P. Kunz, ' Belegarzt – Beleghebamme – Belegspital', in *Handbuch Medizinrecht*, ed. G. Aigner et al. (Vienna: Manz, 2003 et seq.), chap. IV.6.
151. Supreme Court 11 Oct. 2006, 7 Ob 136/06k, *RdM* 2007/42; also *see* Supreme Court 19 Dec. 2001, 3 Ob 237/00z, *RdM* 2002/20; 1 Sep. 2010, 7 Ob 141/10a, *RdM-LS* 2011/4, 26.
152. Supreme Court 29 Mar. 2017, 1 Ob 161/16g, *RdM* 2017/144, 187.
153. For details regarding group practices *see* Part III, Ch. 1, §2.II. below.

153. If a patient is admitted to a non-profit or university hospital as in- patient in the special fee class (*Sonderklasse*) and therefore receives a higher standard of accommodation and service, he may also agree with a specific medical specialist that he shall perform the medical intervention personally (§§16[2] and 46[1] Frame Law on Hospitals and Sanatoria).[154] If the relevant regional hospital law allows that clinical doctors of non-profit hospitals may conclude such additional agreements with patients on their personal performance, the hospital and the clinical doctor can be jointly and severally liable for any medical error (§16[2] in conjunction with §27[4] No. 1 Frame Law on Hospitals and Sanatoria).[155]

III. Public Liability

154. The legal relation between the health care provider and the patient is generally subject to civil law. The same applies to the medical treatment in public hospitals.[156] Special rules apply to university hospitals (*see* Part III, Chapter 3, §1.III. below).[157] However, if the medical act involves the enforcement of law, the legal relation is determined by public law. In such cases the physician functionally (and organizationally) acts as an organ of the federation, so that the federation is liable for any damage to any person or any property caused by unlawful acts of persons at fault when implementing the law on behalf of the federation according to the Government Liability Act (*Amtshaftungsgesetz,* Federal Law Gazette 1949/20 as last amended by Federal Law Gazette I 2013/122).

155. Public liability may arise in the context of an involuntary placement of a mentally ill patient in a psychiatric institution or department of a hospital according to the Hospitalization Act,[158] restrictions of personal freedom of mentally ill or mentally disabled residents according to the Act on the Protection of Personal Freedom of Home Residents (*see* Part II, Chapter 2, §2. below),[159] or of other medical acts performed lawfully even though the person does not want to undergo the medical intervention but has the legal obligation to tolerate the medical intervention (e.g.,

---

154. *See* Constitutional Court 17 Mar. 2007, G 119/06, VfSlg 18.116/2007 = *RdM* 2007/105; Ch. Kopetzki, 'Krankenanstaltenrecht', in *Öffentliches Wirtschaftsrecht*, ed. M. Holoubek & M. Potacs, 3rd edn, vol. 1 (Vienna: Springer, 2013), 377 (469); Ch. Kopetzki, *RdM* (2007): 148–150; K. Stöger, *Ausgewählte öffentlich-rechtliche Fragestellungen des österreichischen Krankenanstaltenrechts* (Vienna: Manz, 2008), 450 et seq., 457 et seq.; B. Raschauer, 'Zur Zulässigkeit landesgesetzlicher Regelungen auf dem Gebiet der Arzthonorare', in *Gmundner Medizinrechtskongress 2008*, ed. G. Aigner, R. Resch & F. Wallner (Vienna: Manz, 2009), 1 et seq.
155. Constitutional Court 17 Mar. 2007, G 119/06, VfSlg 18.116/2007 = *RdM* 2007/105.
156. For example, Supreme Court 17 Feb. 1966, 1 Ob 2/66, *EvBl* 1966/257. Also *see* Committee Report to the government bill: AB 515 BlgNR 5. GP. For details *see* W. Schragel, *Kommentar zum Amtshaftungsgesetz (AHG)*, 3rd edn (Vienna: Manz, 2013), online version 2.02 et seq.
157. Supreme Court 24 Nov. 1997, 6 Ob 324/97 h, *RdM* 1998, 149 = *SZ* 70/241; 25 May 1999, 1 Ob 91/99 k, *RdM* 1999, 177 = *SZ* 72/91; 3 Apr. 2008, 1 Ob 186/07w, *RdM* 2008/97, 124 (*Kopetzki*); for details *see* Ch. Kopetzki, '§29 UG', in *UG 2002*, ed. B. Perthold-Stoitzner, 3rd edn (Vienna: Manz, 2016), marginal number 16 et seq with further references.
158. For details *see* Ch. Kopetzki, *Grundriss des Unterbringungsrechts*, 3rd edn (Vienna: Springer, 2012), 278 (marginal number 767) et seq.
159. For details *see* G. Strickmann, *Heimaufenthaltsgesetz*, 2nd edn (Vienna: Linde, 2012), 224 et seq.

§5[6] Traffic Regulations, §67 Imprisonment Code, Epidemic Code, Tuberculosis Code; *see* Part II, Chapter 1, §3.VIII. below).

IV. Criminal Liability

156. Every medical treatment is qualified as an unlawful infliction of bodily harm, unless it is justified by the patient's valid (informed) consent. Concerning the legal consequences, the Criminal Code differentiates between curative treatments and treatments without medical indication.

157. A curative treatment, which the patient has not consented to, violates §110(1) Criminal Code. §110(1) states that anyone who treats another person without the person's consent, even if carried out according to the current state of medical science and knowledge, can be sentenced to prison up to six months or may be fined. Only in case of imminent severe danger to the patient's health or life, or if the physician is unaware that the situation did not demand an urgent treatment at the time he carried out the medical treatment without prior consent, the acting physician is deemed unintentional and therefore shall not be prosecuted (§110[2]). A violation of §110(1) may only be prosecuted upon request of the victim itself.[160]

If the physician or another non-medical health care provider acts with negligence in the course of the curative treatment, he may (additionally) be prosecuted for causing negligent bodily harm according to §§88 et seq. of the Criminal Code or for causing negligent death according to §§80 et seq. of the Criminal Code. However, health care providers shall not be prosecuted for causing negligent bodily harm if the physical assault or damage is not caused by gross negligence in the course of curative treatment (§88[2] No. 3 Criminal Code, as last amended by Federal Law Gazette I 2015/154).[161]

158. In cases in which the medical treatment is carried out without a medical indication, as for example a plastic surgery, sterilization or organ removal, the invasive intervention is qualified as offence of physical injury according to §§83 et seq. of the Criminal Code. However, in these cases the caused bodily harm can be justified with the informed consent of the patient and therefore can be carried out lawfully unless the act violates public policy (e.g., genital mutilations are forbidden under certain circumstances according to §90[3] of the Criminal Code; abortion and sterilization are only allowed under certain conditions according to §97 or §90[2] of the Criminal Code in conjunction with §163 of the Civil Code and others).[162] The

160. R. Soyer & S. Schuhmann, '§110 StGB', in *Wiener Kommentar zum Strafgesetzbuch*, ed. F. Höpfel & E. Ratz, 2nd edn (Vienna: Manz, 2016, rdb.at), marginal number 1 et seq. For changes in criminal liability as a consequence of the amendment of the Criminal Code of 2015 (Federal Law Gazette I 2015/112) *see* A. Birklbauer, 'Die Auswirkungen des Strafrechtsänderungsgesetzes (StRÄG) 2015 auf den medizinischen Bereich', *RdM* (2016): 4.

161. A. Tipold, 'Die strafrechtliche Verantwortung', in Handbuch Medizinrecht, ed. G. Aigner et al. (Vienna: Manz, 2003 et seq.), II/35 et seq.

162. H. Schütz, '§90 StGB', in *Wiener Kommentar zum Strafgesetzbuch*, ed. F. Höpfel & E. Ratz, 2nd edn (Vienna: Manz, 2016), marginal number 85 et seq.

specific cases of criminal liability concerning abortion, sterilization, euthanasia, aiding suicide, medical secrecy, and so on are dealt with in detail in Part II, Chapter 3 below.

159. Besides the criminal liability of individuals, legal entities can be held criminally liable in accordance with the Association Liability Act (*Verbandsverantwortlichkeitsgesetz*, Federal Law Gazette I 2005/151 as last amended by Federal Law Gazette I 2016/26) since 2006. Law defines associations as legal entities (including public corporations, as long as they are not involved in the execution of the law, and religious corporations, as long as they are not involved in pastoral care), partnerships, registered acquisition enterprises and European Economic Interest Groups. Therefore, also the legal entity of a hospital can be held criminally liable under the Association Liability Act provided that it is a legal entity. The prerequisite for criminal liability is that a criminal offence is illegally and culpably committed by a person who presides over the association as a decision-maker (in a hospital this would be the cooperative management, *Kollegiale Führung*, or the medical director, *Ärztlicher Leiter*), or illegally committed by an employee of the association, provided that the perpetration of the crime was made possible or facilitated due to a lack of technical, organizational or employment measures of the association. The criminal offence has to serve the advantage of the association or constitute a breach of an association's duty. A fine can be imposed on the liable association.[163]

§2. QUALITY ASSURANCE

160. Until the term 'quality assurance' and its specific requirements were integrated in health care laws, many professional duties had quality assurance in health care services as their objects. For example the duty to treat patients diligently and indiscriminately and to undergo further training according to §49(1) of the Physicians Act, documentation requirements in health care laws, and so on. In the meantime, specific regulations regarding quality assurance can be found in all health care professional laws (e.g., §§49[2a] and [2b], 56[1] Physicians Act) and specific medical laws (e.g., Aids Code and the corresponding ordinance on quality monitoring and quality assurance in the course of HIV-diagnosis, Blood Safety Act, Human Tissues Safety Act, and so on). Quality assurance is also taught at medical school and post-gradual practical medical trainings (*see* the Training Regulation for Physicians 2015). The further training has to include education on quality assurance. All in all, quality assurance is not only an important topic in medicine, but in all health care professions.

---

163. For an overview concerning criminal liability *see* e.g., A. Tipold, 'Die strafrechtliche Verantwortung', in *Handbuch Medizinrecht*, ed. G. Aigner et al. (Vienna: Manz, 2003 et seq.), II/34 et seq.; A. Tanczos & D. Tanczos, *Arzthaftung*, 2nd edn (Vienna: Verlag Österreich, 2016), 126 et seq.; J.W. Steiner, 'Krankenhausmanagement und Verbandsverantwortlichkeit', *RdM* (2007): 113; K. Bruckmüller & S. Schumann, 'Die Heilbehandlung im österreichischen Strafrecht', in *Handbuch des Medizinstrafrechts*, ed. C. Roxin & A. Braun, 4th edn (Stuttgart: Boorberg, 2007), 813 et seq. with further references; A. Birklbauer, 'Strafrechtliche Haftung der Gesundheitsberufe', in *Handbuch Medizinrecht*, ed. R. Resch & F. Wallner, 2nd edn (Vienna: LexisNexis, 2015), 341 et seq.

161. The Health Care Quality Act (Federal Law Gazette I 2004/179 as last amended by Federal Law Gazette I 2013/81)[164] is in force since 2005. It aims to establish a nationwide sustainable quality assurance system based on the principles of patient orientation, transparency, effectiveness and efficiency in order to continuously improve the health care services of all health care providers of the extramural and intramural sector. Structural, procedural and outcome quality standards shall be incorporated in the quality assurance system. This quality assurance system shall comply with the aims and the monitoring according to the Federal Law on 'Aim-Oriented Steering of Health' (in short: Aim Steering Health Act, *Zielsteuerung-Gesundheit Gesetz,* Federal Law Gazette I 2017/26).[165] The Aim Steering Health Act shall establish a cooperative aim regulating system in order to ensure a better coordination between the intramural and extramural sector and obliges the Minister of Health and the social insurance institutions to contribute to the aim regulation system.

According to §1(3) Health Care Quality Act, the Minister of Health is responsible for ensuring nationwide coordination among all the stakeholders involved in the quality assurance system throughout Austria and the coordination of quality actions for purposes of national and international compatibility of health care services.

The Minister of Health is entitled by law to recommend quality standards for performing health care services in form of non-binding Federal Quality Guidelines or of binding Federal Quality Policies (§4). The Federal Minister of Health has to ensure that the quality provisions on performing health care services in the sense of systematic quality work take into account structural, procedural and outcome quality, including the development of corresponding methodical work. These provisions must take established requirements of notification and documentation and international developments into consideration (§5).

A nationwide quality reporting system has been established; reports on the outcome quality have to be provided regularly since 2014 (§6). Therefore, all hospitals (*see* above §5b Frame Law on Hospitals and Sanatoria) and all extramural health care providers (*see* e.g., §49[2a] Physicians Act) shall electronically provide the necessary data (§3). With §15a Federal Law on the Health Austria limited company, Federal Law Gazette I 2008/77, this company has been awarded the task to provide quality registers for statistical purposes, as basis for planning, quality assurance and quality reporting, and for scientific purposes.

Additionally, §8 obliges the Minister of Health to establish a quality monitoring system in order to control the contribution in the quality reporting and the

164. For an English version of the Health Care Quality Act: *see* http://www.bmgf.gv.at/cms/home/attachments/2/8/0/CH1063/CMS1396521704766/health_care_quality_act.pdf, 12 May 2017.

165. The Federal Law on 'Aim-Oriented Steering of Health' has been established for reasons of transparency and conformability following the purposes and aims laid down in the Agreement according to Art. 15a of the Federal Constitution on the Organisation and the Financing of the Health Care System, Federal Law Gazette I 2008/105 as amended by Federal Law Gazette I 2013/199 and in the Agreement according to Art. 15a of the Federal Constitution on the Aim Regulation-Health, Federal Law Gazette I 2013/200.

implementation of quality standards specified by Federal Quality Policies and to evaluate the implementation and application of the Federal Quality Guidelines. The Federal Institute for Quality in the Health Care System (in short: Health Quality Institute, *Bundesinstitut für Qualität im Gesundheitswesen, see* Federal Law on the Health Quality Institute, Federal Law Gazette I 2006/132 as last amended by Federal Law Gazette I 2017/26) helps the Minister of Health in the fulfilment of his duties, most notably supporting him in developing quality standards and compiling annual quality reports (§9 Health Quality Act).

162. Regarding freelance physicians and group practices §49(2a) Physicians Act established a nationwide self-evaluating and reporting procedure to the Austrian Association for Quality Assurance and Quality Management in Medicine limited company, *Österreichischen Gesellschaft für Qualitätssicherung & Qualitätsmanagement in der Medizin GmbH* (in short: *ÖQMed,* §117b[1] No. 22, §118a Physicians Act). Outpatient clinics can also opt in (§60[4] Frame Law on Hospitals and Sanatoria). For this purpose the Austrian Medical Chamber stipulated on the basis of §117c(2) No. 8 in conjunction with §118c Physicians Act the Ordinance for Quality Assurance of the Medical Service 2012 (QS-VO 2012, Federal Law Gazette II 2011/452, which will be ineffective on the 31 December 2017 according to Federal Law Gazette I 2017/25).

In case the duty of evaluation is culpably not fulfilled by the freelance physician or group practice or if an imminent danger to health is discovered on the basis of the evaluation or in the course of control (§118e[2]–[3] Physicians Act), such incident may be deemed as gross breach of professional duties and for freelance physicians with a contract to social insurance institutions this can also form a reason for its termination according to §343(4) General Insurance Act (ASVG), as far as the quality standards of the specific field in consideration with the quality of process and structure are affected (§49[2b] Physicians Act).

163. Regarding hospitals, §5b of the Frame Law on Hospitals and Sanatoria obliges the regional legislators to ensure that the legal entities of hospitals implement structural measures to evaluate the quality of the medical activities in each hospital in order to compare the quality with other hospitals. Therefore, structural measures have to be taken in every hospital. For that reason, a quality assurance committee has to be established in every stationary hospital. It shall initiate, coordinate and support quality measures, facilitate the implementation of quality assurance and shall advise the cooperative management of the hospital. In case there is no cooperative management, the responsible manager has to take the necessary measures. In addition, the regional legislators have to ensure that the entities of hospitals participate in the nationwide quality reporting system and therefore to provide the necessary data according to §6 Health Care Quality Act. Furthermore, since the amendment in 2005 the concession for operating of hospitals is only to be granted if the requirements of quality on structure are fulfilled (§3[4] lit. c Frame

Law on Hospitals and Sanatoria). These requirements are laid down in the Austrian health structural plan 2012[166] (*Österreichischer Strukturplan Gesundheit*).[167]

§3. Review Boards

164. Ethics committees[168] are interdisciplinary review boards whose task is in particular to assess clinical trials. They are characterized by multi-disciplinarianism and the external control of research activities. They have to be distinguished from committees surveying therapy and from the Austrian Bioethics Committee, which advises the government concerning general socio-political topics such as embryo research.[169]

Ethics committees are not consistently regulated by Austrian law, but are subject to different specific acts (Frame Law on Hospitals and Sanatoria, Act on Universities, Medicinal Products Act and Medical Devices Act).

165. Organizational matters, especially the composition of ethics committees, are regulated by the Frame Law on Hospitals and Sanatoria. Pursuant to §8(4), they consist at least of one physician who is neither head of department of the hospital nor investigator (No 1); a specialist in the medical field in which the clinical trial is carried out, a dentist or another member of the respective medical profession, who is not the investigator (No 2); a member of the higher civil service for health (No 3); a jurist (No 4); a pharmacist (No 5); a patients' advocate (No 6); a person with biometric expertise (Z 7); a representative of an organization for disabled people (No 8) and a person who is competent for pastoral affairs in the hospital or who has expertise in ethical matters (Z 9). For each member an equally qualified substitute has to be nominated.

---

166. *See* Art. 4 of the Agreement according to Art. 15a of the Federal Constitution on the Organisation and the Financing of the Health Care System, Federal Law Gazette I 2008/105 as amended by Federal Law Gazette I 2013/199; *see* for the Austrian Health Structural Plan 2012 under http://www.bmg.gv.at/home/Schwerpunkte/Gesundheitssystem_Qualitaetssicherung/Planung_und_spezielle_Versorgungsbereiche/Oesterreichischer_Strukturplan_Gesundheit_OeSG_2012, 12 May 2017.

167. For details concerning quality assurance, *see* e.g., K. Stöger, 'Rechtliche Aspekte von Qualitätssicherung in der Medizin', in *Handbuch Medizinrecht*, ed. G. Aigner et al. (Vienna: Manz, 2003 et seq.), I/249 et seq.; K. Stöger & M. Szüsz, 'Rechtliche Aspekte von Qualitätssicherung in der Medizin', in *Qualitätssicherung in der Medizin*, ed. R. Fischer & K.-H. Tragl (Vienna: Österreichische Ärztekammer 2000), 127–150; P. Jabornegg, R. Resch & O. Seewald (eds), *Qualitätssicherung für Leistungen in der gesetzlichen Krankenversicherung* (Vienna: Manz, 2003).

168. For details *see* Ch. Kopetzki, '§30 UG', in *Kommentar zum Universitätsgesetz 2002*, ed. Perthold-Stoitzner, 3rd edn (Vienna: Manz, 2016); H. Eberhard, 'Forschungskontrolle durch Ethikkommissionen – von der kollegialen Beratung zur staatlichen Kontrolle?', in *Ethik und Recht in der Humanforschung*, ed. U. Körtner, Ch. Kopetzki & Ch. Druml (Vienna: Springer, 2010), 152; K. Stöger, *Ausgewählte öffentlich-rechtliche Fragestellungen des österreichischen Krankenanstaltenrechts* (Vienna: Manz, 2008), 423 et seq.

169. R. Gmeiner & U. Körtner, 'Die Bioethikkommission beim Bundeskanzleramt – Aufgaben, Arbeitsweise, Bedeutung', *RdM* (2002): 164; D. Wolfslehner, 'Bioethikkommission neu ausgerichtet', *RdM* (2007): 112.

Ethics committees have to be established by the body that is responsible for the hospital (§8[1]). The members of the committees must not be subject to any directives (§8[6] of the Frame Law on Hospitals and Sanatoria; §30[4] Act on Universities).

There are special organizational requirements for 'lead ethics committees' *(Leit-Ethikkommissionen),* which are competent to assess multi-centre clinical trials. They are regulated by the Ordinance on Lead Ethics Committees (Federal Law Gazette II 2004/214).

166. The following research projects have to be submitted to an ethics committee:

(1) Clinical trials on medicinal products (including non-interventional trials) or medical devices, which take place outside a hospital, according to §41 of the Medicinal Products Act and §57 Medical Devices Act. Pursuant to §8c of the Frame Law on Hospitals and Sanatoria, §30 Act on Universities, §§41a and 41b Medicinal Products Act and §§38 et seq. Medical Devices Act, the same applies if they are carried out in a (university) hospital. Multi-centre trials only need assessment by one 'lead ethics committee' (§41b Medicinal Products Act).
(2) 'New medical methods' in (university) hospitals (§8c of the Frame Law on Hospitals and Sanatoria, §30 Act on Universities): 'New medical methods' are procedures which anticipate progress in health care based on the findings of basic research and medical experience, but which are not in use in Austria yet and therefore need systematic examination (§8[3] of the Frame Law on Hospitals and Sanatoria).
(3) Applied medical research in (university) hospitals (§8c of the Frame Law on Hospitals and Sanatoria, §30 Act on Universities).
(4) Projects concerning nursing research and practice of new nursing and treatment concepts and methods in hospitals (§8c of the Frame Law on Hospitals and Sanatoria).

There are no further statutory duties to submit other research projects to ethics committees, but there is a large number of in-house guidelines (especially at university hospitals), which require submission to ethics committees, even for diploma or master theses.[170] De facto there are additional non-legal duties to fulfil, as international standards (especially prestigious journals) require a vote of an ethics committee as condition for publishing research studies.

170. Concerning the question of conformity with constitutional law *see* M. Pöschl, 'Von der Forschungsethik zum Forschungsrecht: Wie viel Regulierung verträgt die Forschungsfreiheit?', in *Ethik und Recht in der Humanforschung,* ed. U. Körtner, Ch. Kopetzki & Ch. Druml, *Ethik und Recht in der Humanforschung* (Vienna, New York: Springer 2010), 97 et seq.; Ch. Kopetzki, 'Braucht Österreich eine Kodifikation des biomedizinischen Forschungsrechts?', in *Ethik und Recht in der Humanforschung,* ed. U. Körtner, Ch. Kopetzki & Ch. Druml (Vienna, New York: Springer, 2010), 63 et seq.; Ch. Kopetzki, 'Muss Forschung ethisch vertretbar sein?', in *Vom praktischen Wert der Methode,* ed. C. Jabloner et al. (Vienna: Manz 2011), 253 (265).

167. Ethics committees have to assess the setting, the planning, the significance, the risk-benefit relation, the selection of test subjects, the informed consent as well as the precautionary measures in case of damage (*see* for instance §41a of the Medicinal Products Act).

168. In general the votes of the ethics committees are not strictly legally binding. Instead they prepare the decisions that other institutions have to make (e.g., concerning clinical trials on medicinal products, it is the Federal Office of Safety in Health Care that finally decides about the admissibility). Consequently their votes have not been qualified as decisions by administrative organs, but as expert opinions.[171] Nevertheless the role of Ethics Committees has been strengthened significantly in specific cases. Regarding clinical trials on medicinal products and medical devices, the positive or negative vote has direct legal consequences, as the decision of the Federal Office of Safety in Health Care strictly depends on it. Thus, there are strong arguments for qualifying them (at least partly) as decisions by administrative organs.[172]

169. The question of whether ethics committees are liable for damages in connection with their votes is discussed controversially. Some authors demand 'expert-' liability in compliance with private law for each member of the committee (§1299 of the Civil Code).[173] Others favour state liability.[174] Considering the strong position of the ethics committee concerning clinical trials on medicinal products and medical devices, the better arguments support state liability. The same applies to ethics committees in university hospitals, as they are organs 'carrying out law' in terms of §1 of the Government Liability Act with respect to their functions.[175]

§4. Disciplinary Organizations

I. Order of Physicians

170. According to the Physicians Act of 1998, doctors are represented by the medical chambers of the federal states (§§65 et seq.), which are divided into two Curia (Curia of Employed Doctors, Curia of Licensed General Practitioners). The

171. Administrative Court 23 Oct. 2012, 2009/10/0254; H. Krejci, 'Ethikkommissionen und Versicherungsfragen', *RdM* (1995): 27 (31); Ch. Kopetzki, *Unterbringungsrecht,* vol. 2 (Vienna, New York: Springer, 1995), 800 et seq.; *see* the different view of W. Schragel, *Kommentar zum Amtshaftungsgesetz (AHG),* 3rd edn (2003), marginal number 100.
172. K. Stöger, *Ausgewählte öffentlich-rechtliche Fragestellungen des österreichischen Krankenanstaltenrechts* (Vienna: Manz, 2008), 433 et seq.; Ch. Kopetzki, '§30 UG', in *Kommentar zum Universitätsgesetz 2002*, ed. Perthold-Stoitzner, 3rd edn (Vienna: Manz, 2016), I.6.
173. For example, W. Berka, 'Rechtliche Probleme im Hinblick auf die Tätigkeit der Ethikkommissionen', in *Sozialrechtliche Probleme bei der Ausübung von Heilberufen*, ed. Th. Tomandl (Vienna: Braumüller, 1996), 54 (72).
174. H. Barta & G. Kalchschmid, 'Zur Haftung der Mitglieder von Ethikkommissionen', *SozSi* (1998): 366.
175. Ch. Kopetzki, '§30 UG', in *Kommentar zum Universitätsgesetz 2002*, ed. Perthold-Stoitzner, 3rd edn (Vienna: Manz, 2016), I.7.

Austrian Medical Chamber (§§117 et seq.) represents the common interests of doctors who pursue a profession inland and who are members of the medical chambers of the federal states. It is, *inter alia*, competent for setting disciplinary action against chamber members in case of misconduct. Its members are the medical chambers of the federal states (§119).

171. The medical chambers of the federal states and the Austrian Medical Chamber are public-law corporations. They are characterized by compulsory membership, by financial and organizational autonomy (in the sense that their organs have been voted for by the members), by having sovereign powers and by being relatively independent of government bodies (in other words they are not bound to any mandatory instructions, but they are subject to supervision). Thus, they are self-governing bodies.

Beyond their autonomous sphere of powers within self-administration, the chambers also have powers which are delegated by the federation or the federal states. Within this assigned sphere of functions, they are bound by directions and there are administrative channels to government bodies (for further details *see* Part III, Chapter 1, §1. below).

II. Professional Codes

172. Doctors are subject to disciplinary law, which is executed by special bodies of the Austrian Medical Chamber. The disciplinary regulations of the Physicians Act are not applicable to employees of public-law corporations (e.g., doctors with civil service status), who are subject to the special regulations for public servants.

173. Unlike other regulations, especially those of criminal law, which have to be formulated very precisely due to the principle of mandatory prosecution, disciplinary law is characterized by a rather vague wording of the relevant professional codes (for instance, the disciplinary offence of 'diminishing the reputation of the medical profession'). As a consequence, it is up to the competent disciplinary authorities to decide, whether professional codes have been violated or not. According to the Constitutional Court, the vague wording of disciplinary codes does not violate the principle of clarity and definiteness in criminal law.[176] The court rather held that especially the contents of the 'reputation of the medical profession' could be determined by taking into consideration general social opinions and the customs of the medical profession.[177] Generally, negligent behaviour is sufficient for disciplinary responsibility.

174. Disciplinary persecution is independent of persecution under criminal law or administrative criminal law (§136[5]). As disciplinary proceedings serve different purposes from criminal proceedings, the principle 'ne bis in idem' is not violated.

176. Constitutional Court VfSlg 7907, 8349.
177. Constitutional Court VfSlg 6026.

175. The major disciplinary offence is to diminish the reputation of the medical profession (§136[1] No. 1 Physicians Act). As specified by the courts, the following examples for medical conduct violate §136[1] No. 1: The use of rude expressions getting to be known to several people; impairment by alcohol or medication leading to the inability to take a blood sample; disturbing the sense of shame of a patient in the course of an examination or the claim of a fee for services that have never been rendered. Furthermore, false testimony, mistreatment of the spouse, intentional damage to property and so forth diminish the reputation of the medical profession.[178] Because of the freedom of expression, the reputation of the medical profession is not violated, if doctors make fair comments, even if they are exaggerated.

176. Furthermore, doctors are responsible for not violating the professional duties they have committed themselves to on the occasion of their graduation or for not violating the professional regulations of the Physicians Act or of other relevant regulations (§136[1] No. 2]. Professional duties stipulated in the Physicians Act (especially §§48–57) are, for example, the duty to grant urgent and necessary medical aid, professional secrecy, the obligation to disclose and to keep records, prohibition of commission payments, requirement of conscientious care, personal and direct vocational practice, duties to report, obligations regarding surgeries (especially concerning their name, condition and medicines stock), duties in connection with issuing medical certificates and limitations for specialists. Often, the violation of professional duties is to be qualified as offence pursuant to §136(1) No. 1 (diminishing the reputation of the medical profession) too. Thus, convictions for both disciplinary offences are not rare (violations of both offences are, however, aggravating).

Further professional duties are stipulated in ordinances passed by the medical chambers on the basis of the Physicians Act, e.g., the ordinance 'Physicians and Publicity' concerning advertisement and labelling instructions for surgeries.[179]

Apart from the regulations of the Physicians Act (and the ordinances based on it), there are special professional duties in other acts such as the Medicinal Products Act, the Medical Devices Act, the Artificial Procreation Act, in the Traffic Regulations (about using the tag 'doctor on duty') and in epidemics law. Finally, violations of insurance contracts might be disciplinary offences, as they are based on resolutions passed by the medical chambers, to which doctors are bound.

177. In line with §136(2) No. 2, doctors also violate disciplinary law, if they are sentenced to prison for more than six months or to a fine of at least 360 daily rates (by a national or foreign court) for a crime they have committed intentionally.

Furthermore, it is a disciplinary offence to carry out the medical profession despite a temporary interdiction of vocational practice because of a disciplinary offence.

---

178. For further examples *see* J. Zahrl & J.W. Steiner in *Ärztegesetz*, ed. H. Emberger & F. Wallner, 2nd edn (Vienna: Verlagshaus der Ärzte, 2008), 486 et seq.

179. For details on advertising law for doctors (and other health care professions) *see* V. Blum 'Werbung im Zusammenhang mit der ärztlichen Berufsausübung' (Doctoral Thesis, University of Vienna, 2017).

178. Disciplinary punishments are (§139) letters of reprimand, fines up to EUR 36,340, temporary interdiction of vocational practice and deletion from the directory of doctors. Furthermore, the disciplinary judgment can be published by the medical chamber.

179. The disciplinary authority of first instance is the Disciplinary Board of the Austrian Medical Chamber. The Disciplinary Board consists of several disciplinary commissions, which are competent under local aspects. The second level of authority is the Disciplinary Senate of the Austrian Medical Chamber, which is established within the ministry of health.[180]

180. For further details *see* G. Aigner, 'Das ärztliche Berufsrecht', in *Handbuch Medizinrecht,* ed. G. Aigner et al. (Vienna: Manz, 2003 et seq.), III/44 et seq.; F. Wallner '§136 ÄrzteG', in *Gmundner Kommentar zum Gesundheitsrecht,* ed. M. Neumayr, R. Resch & F. Wallner (Vienna: Manz, 2016), 298 et seq.; F. Wallner, 'Berufsrecht der Ärzte', in *Handbuch Medizinrecht,* ed. R. Resch & F. Wallner, 2nd edn (Vienna: LexisNexis, 2015), 689 et seq.; G. Aigner, M. Kierein & Ch. Kopetzki (eds), *Ärztegesetz,* 3rd edn (Vienna: Manz, 2007), 304 et seq.; J. Zahrl & J.W. Steiner in *Ärztegesetz,* ed. H. Emberger & F. Wallner, 2nd edn (Vienna: Verlagshaus der Ärzte, 2008), 486 et seq.

Part II. The Physician-Patient Relationship

Chapter 1. General Description

§1. The Regulation of Rights and Duties of Physicians and Patients

180. In the Austrian legal order, patients' rights are not regulated in a separate act, but are based on several provisions of civil, criminal and administrative law as well as professional codes. The reason for this is the division of the competences between the federation and the federal states regarding health care issues (Article 10[1] No. 12, Article 12[1] No. 1 and Article 15[1] Constitution). The federation does not have the legislative power to regulate all health care matters and thus cannot enact a federal law covering all patients' rights. Since 1999, the federation has concluded agreements on patients' rights according to Article 15a of the Constitution with each of the nine federal states, the so-called Patients' Charter (*Patientencharta*).[181] The Patients' Charter declares all relevant patients' rights, but are only legally binding for the federation and the federal states. As a result, patients cannot sue for compliance with patients' rights that are only outlined in this agreement. Instead, these Patients' Charters have a more political significance than legal relevance concerning the relationship between patients and health care providers (as long as the competent legislator has not integrated these stipulated patients' rights in law). Each party of the Patients' Charter shall undertake reasonable efforts within the sphere of their responsibility for enacting and enforcing legislation to guarantee the stipulated patients' rights. In the meantime, most stipulated patients' rights of the Patients' Charta have been established by law.

181. The rights and duties of patients and physicians ruled by law vary in wording and quantity from in-patient care to treatment by a freelance physician or dentist. Regarding the extraordinary situation of in-patients, a broad range of patients' rights are stipulated by §5a of the Frame Law on Hospitals and Sanatoria. For example, every in-patient has the right to an adequate private sphere, even in shared

181. The Agreements on Guaranteeing the Rights of Patients between the federation and each federal state (*Patientencharta*): Federal Law Gazette I 1999/195 (Federation – Carinthia); Federal Law Gazette I 2001/89 (Federation – Burgenland); Federal Law Gazette I 2001/116 (Federation – Upper Austria); Federal Law Gazette I 2002/36 (Federation – Lower Austria); Federal Law Gazette I 2002/153 (Federation – Styria); Federal Law Gazette I 2003/88 (Federation – Tirol); Federal Law Gazette I 2003/127 (Federation – Vorarlberg); Federal Law Gazette I 2006/42 (Federation – Vienna); Federal Law Gazette I 2006/140 (Federation – Salzburg).

sickrooms, the right to religious care and psychological support if wished, the right to receive visits and to maintain other contacts and so on.[182]

182. In general, the treatment contract constitutes the legal basis for the medical treatment in a doctor's surgery or a hospital. This contract stipulates various duties and rights for the health care provider as well as the patient. For details concerning the characterization of the treatment contract, *see* Part I, Chapter 4, §1.II.A. above.

§2. Rights and Duties Relating to the Contractual Relationship

I. The Patient's Right to Free Choice

183. The patient has the right to choose freely of all freelance physicians, dentists and hospitals, except for some restrictions determined by law. The patient's right to freely choose between equally qualified doctors, who are working together in a group practice, is regulated explicitly in §52a(3) No. 11 of the Physicians Act.

184. On the contrary, after admission to a public or non-profit hospital or ambulatory the patient cannot choose by whom he is treated, unless there is an effective extra contractual agreement with a specific physician. Only in cases where the regional hospital laws permit clinical doctors to conclude such additional agreements with private patients, in-patients have the right to receive personal treatment by a pre-defined clinical physician.[183] However, if an in-patient only wants a surgery to be performed by a specific physician and the hospital should know so, the patient's consent to the surgery may be limited to this person of physician. This limitation of the patient's consent (although there is only a contract with the hospital) may form a reason for civil liability.[184]

II. The Physician's Right to Freely Conclude or Withdraw from a Contract

185. In general, every freelance physician or dentist has the right to freely decide whether to contract with a patient or not. In other words, the professional code does not generally oblige the physician or the dentist to contract with the patient or his legal representatives. Only if the patient's life is in imminent danger the physician

182. For a general overview concerning the rights and duties of patients and physicians *see* M. Memmer, 'Rechte und Pflichten – Patient und Behandler', in *Handbuch Medizinrecht*, ed. G. Aigner et al. (Vienna: Manz, 2003 et seq.), I /27 et seq.; K. Stellamor & J.W. Steiner, *Handbuch des österreichischen Arztrechts*, vol. 1 (Vienna: Manz, 1999), 67–199; R. Krepler, J.R. Hackl & L.-M. Marzi, *Recht im Krankenhausalltag* (Vienna: Orac, 2002), and others.
183. For further details concerning the consequences of civil liability *see* Part I, Ch. 4, §1.II.F and G. above.
184. *See* Supreme Court 26 Sep. 2003, 3 Ob 131/03s, *RdM* 2004/37; confirmed by Supreme Court 4 Oct. 2005, 4 Ob 121/05f, *RdM* 2006/29 and by 25 Nov. 2014, 8 Ob 120/14a, *RdM* 2015,153 = Ch. Huber, *RdM* (2015): 135; R. Resch, 'Freie Arztwahl in der allgemeinen Gebührenklasse im Umweg des Arzthaftungsrechts', *RdM* (2004): No. 102.

has to treat the person who needs help urgently (§48 Physicians Act). Still there are further limitations to the physicians', and dentists', right to contract freely. These are stipulated in their contracts with the respective social insurance institution regarding state-insured and co-insured patients.

186. Public and non-profit hospitals have to admit patients who are in need of in-patient care (e.g., patients who are in need of admission according to prior medical diagnosis, or healthy persons for the purpose of clinical studies: §22[2] Frame Law on Hospitals and Sanatoria) or who are going to have a surgery. Patient admission has to be adapted to the business of the hospital and to the available facilities. These hospitals are also obliged to hospitalize state-insured and co-insured patients who are entitled to health insurance benefits. Furthermore, public hospitals always have to accept patients who are in urgent need of in-patient care, in the sense that otherwise the patient's life or health would be severely endangered; especially pregnant women whose delivery is imminent. Persons, who are hospitalized by public authorities according to special legal provisions also have to be admitted to hospital (§22[2]–[4] Frame Law on Hospitals and Sanatoria).

In contrast, private hospitals are free to contract with patients of their choice. There is only one exception for cases of emergency. In this instance private hospitals (as public and non-profit hospitals) have the duty to offer at least the absolutely necessary first medical aid (§23[1] corresponding with §40[1] lit. c Frame Law on Hospitals and Sanatoria).

187. Apart from the freelance physicians' and hospitals' right to freely contract, it may be pointed out that health care providers, who are qualified as service providers for general public use, are not allowed to refuse to contract or treat a patient due to his race, colour of his skin, his national or ethnic origin, his religious denomination or any handicap. In other words, a health care provider for general public use principally needs an objective and reasonable justification when he wants to deny treating a patient (Article III[1] No. 3 Introductory Act to the administrative procedure acts, Federal Law Gazette I 2008/87 as last amended by Federal Law Gazette I 2013/33).

Exceptions exist in case of legal abortion and artificial procreation (§97[2] Criminal Code, §6 Artificial Procreation Act). In respect of these medical activities, nobody (which also includes nurses, medical-technical personnel and paramedics) is obliged to perform or help carrying out such medical activities. However, in case of emergency these professionals cannot make use of this privilege (§97[2] Criminal Code).

188. As long as there is no case of emergency, the freelance physician has the right to withdraw from the treatment contract by giving notice to the patient or the person who is in charge of him, or if necessary also to the municipality in which the ill person resides in order to safeguard the continuation of the patient's medical care (§50 Physicians Act). Dentists as well have the right to withdraw from the treatment contract by giving notice to the patient (§38 Dentists Act). Nevertheless, physicians and dentists who have a contract with a social insurance institution may only withdraw from the treatment contract for certain reasons.

189. On the contrary, the hospital's entity cannot withdraw from the hospital admission contract against the patient's wish as long as the patient is in need of in-patient care. A discharge from the hospital is therefore only possible if the patient does not depend on in-patient care, if a necessary transfer to another hospital is safeguarded or if the patient, his relatives or his legal representative are insisting on the premature discharge although the attending physician or dentist has informed about the possible dangers for the patient's health (§24[1] and [4] Frame Law on Hospitals and Sanatoria).

Nevertheless, every patient is free to drop out of the contract at his own risk at any time after being appropriately informed about the possible negative consequences of the premature discharge (unless a public authority hospitalized the patient in accordance with special provisions; *see* §24[4] Frame Law on Hospitals and Sanatoria).

III. The Physician's Right to Remuneration and Duty to Price Information

190. Every physician, dentist and other health care provider principally has the right to remuneration for his provided health care services. Since the health care provider in general merely owes proper service and skill, but not the achievement of a specific result, the patient has to pay the fee, regardless of the success of the proper treatment (for details *see* Part I, Chapter 4, §1.II.A. above).

191. State-insured patients are entitled to benefits for themselves and their co-insured relatives (§122 General Social Insurance Act). Therefore, simply spoken, the respective social insurance institution pays for the patient if the health care provider is a contracting party of the social insurance institution in question. If the patient consults a doctor of his choice or a private hospital (health care providers who are not under contract with social insurance institutions), the patient has to pay the invoiced fee in advance and can then apply for – at least partly – reimbursement of costs from the respective social insurance institution.

192. In the context of private health care services, the medical health care provider is free to determine the remuneration. If the physician and the patient have not discussed the concrete fee and also have not agreed that the medical service is free of charge, a reasonable fee shall be deemed as agreed on (§1152 Civil Code).[185]

193. Although Article 16(5) Patients' Charter stipulates the political goal that patients should be informed about the estimated doctor's remuneration in advance, the Supreme Court ruled in 2002 and in 2016 that the treatment contract (in both cases between a private hospital and a patient) shall be handled by law in relation to its remuneration for the provided services equally to other contractual relationships, which means that the private hospital is not obliged to inform or warn the patient in advance that a fee will be charged for the supplied service in case the fee

185. Supreme Court 10 Apr. 1968, 5 Ob 79/68, *EvBl* 1968, 545.

may not be covered by the (private) insurance stated by the patient. The Supreme Court stated that the price notification in advance should not be mixed up with the informed consent to the treatment itself.[186]

The Administrative Court has judged differently with regard to in-patients who are admitted in the special fee class. Regional hospital laws regulate a duty to inform the in-patient (in writing) about the patient's payment obligation before admission to the special fee class. A breach of this notification duty results in remission.[187]

194. Since the implementation of the Directive 2011/24/EU on the application of patients' rights in cross-border healthcare in 2014 (Federal Law Gazette I 2014/32), clear cost information, clear invoices, and transparent and non-discriminatory calculation is stipulated for all health care providers regarding medical or non-medical health care service which is not covered by domestic public funds or domestic social insurance.

Therefore all regional legislators of hospital law are obliged to stipulate the duty to notify all in-patients (also in the general fee class) on the estimated fee as long as the amount is foreseeable at the time of admission and in case that the fee is not covered by public funds or other domestic social insurances (§5a[4] Frame Law on Hospitals and Sanatoria). Fees of private hospitals shall be calculated according to objective and non-discriminatory criteria and private hospitals shall provide clear invoices in case that the fee is not covered by public funds or other domestic social insurances (§39[3] and §40[3] Frame Law on Hospitals and Sanatoria).[188]

Also freelance physicians are bound to this obligation with regard to patients of other Member States of the European Union as far as the costs are not covered by domestic social insurance (§51[1a] Physicians Act). Freelance working non-medical health care providers need to inform their patients about the estimated costs (*see* e.g., §36[5] Nursing of Patients Act; §9a Midwives Act; §7b[2] Medical-Technical Services Act), have to calculate according to objective and non-discriminatory criteria and to provide clear invoices (*see* e.g., §18[2] Dentists Act; §7b[2]–[3] Medical-Technical Services Act).

A special information duty on the estimated costs is regulated for dentists and cosmetic surgeons. According to §18 Dentists Act (as last amended by Federal Law Gazette I 2014/32) every dentist is obliged to disclose in advance which dental treatment is paid for by the respective social insurance institution and which one the

186. Supreme Court 19 Nov. 2002, 4 Ob 249/02z, *RdM* 2004/51; 21 Apr. 2016, 9 Ob 19/16h, *RdM* 2016, 309 *(Leischner-Lenzhofer)*, but *see also* Supreme Court 21 Jun. 2006, 7 Ob 129/06f, *RdM* 2007/115: In this case the patient had decided to undergo a surgery in a private hospital so that a specific method could be applied, but was treated with an ordinary method instead which could have been performed in every other public hospital. The Supreme Court judged that in such circumstances the surgeon is obliged to inform the patient in advance about the fact that the applied ordinary surgery can also be performed in a public hospital billed by public insurance funds.

187. Administrative Court 2003/11/0267; 16 Jun. 2014, Ro 2014/11/0032, *RdM-LS* 2015/23 (*M. Huber*); 30 Jun. 2016, Ra 2016/11/0064 *RdM-LS* 2016/96.

188. For more details *see* e.g., R. Resch, 'Wirtschaftliche Aufklärungspflicht und Behandlungsvertrag', *RdM* (2014): 321; *RdM* 2016, 309 (310 et seq.) *(Leischner-Lenzhofer)*.

patient has to pay for himself.[189] According to §4[3] Act on Aesthetic Treatments and Surgery, Federal Law Gazette I 2012/8, since 2012 cosmetic surgeons have the duty to inform their patient about the estimated costs and the follow-up costs of the planned aesthetic surgery according to §5[6–9] leg. cit. Recently an explicit price information duty has been established with regard to artificial procreation (*see* §7 Artificial Procreation Act).

§3. Rights and Duties Relating to the Patient's Self-Determination

195. In accordance with Article 8 of the ECHR, the right to respect for private or family life, which has the quality of constitutional law in Austria, everybody has the fundamental right to self-determination regarding his individual physical integrity. In fulfilment of the constitutional duty to grant patients the exercise of this right, the legislator has established the provisions of §110 of the Criminal Code and of §8(3) of the Frame Law on Hospitals and Sanatoria. Both provisions state that every medical treatment principally needs the patient's consent in advance. Thus, every medical intervention that affects the patient's physical integrity is generally an illegal act. Furthermore it is considered as an illicit infliction of a bodily injury unless it is justified, in particular by the patient's or his legal representative's valid consent.

196. It may be pointed out that the patient's acceptance of the contract must not be mixed up with the patient's informed consent to the medical treatment (*see* Part I, Chapter 4, §1.II.A. above).

197. It is generally accepted that a valid consent requires the patient's capacity to consent, appropriate information, absence of any legal obstacles to consent, and a valid declaration of will. The patient's consent should be based on a free and well-considered declaration (§869 in conjunction with §876 Civil Code) and should not be initiated by error, fraud, deception or by physical or mental pressure (§870 Civil Code).[190]

I. Capacity to Consent

198. Regarding a valid consent, not the legal capacity to contract is crucial, but the patient's capacity to consent (§173[1] [as amended by Federal Law Gazette I 2013/15, former §146c Civil Code] and §283 Civil Code [repealed and newly regulated by §252 Civil Code as amended by Federal Law Gazette I 2017/59, effective in July 2018], §8[3] Frame Law on Hospitals and Sanatoria, §36 Hospitalization Act).[191] Consequently, a minor or mentally ill patient, who possesses the ability to

189. *See* Supreme Court 24 Feb. 2010, 3 Ob 223/09d, *RdM-LS* 2010/36.

190. For details e.g., M. Ganner, *Selbstbestimmung im Alter* (Vienna: Springer, 2005), 256 et seq.

191. With the amendment Federal Law Gazette I 2017/59 the term 'ability to insight and judgement' (*Einsichts- und Urteilsfähigkeit*) used in §173, §283 Civil Code and in §36[1] Hospitalization Act

understand the information and the meaning of the planned treatment and who is able to make and express an appropriate decision, is the only one who can legitimize the medical treatment by his consent; in other words, the capacity to consent consists of a cognitive and a voluntary element. The patient has to possess the necessary insight and power of judgment as well as the reasonable willingness to determine whether to consent or to refuse the medical intervention in question. The attending physician has to judge whether the patient has the capacity to consent or not, taking into consideration the severity and medical indication of the medical treatment in question. In case of doubt, he has to consult a psychiatrist for a second opinion.[192]

199. Only if the patient himself does not have the capacity to consent, the legal representative may give his consent on behalf of the patient whom he is in charge of (for details *see* Part II, Chapter 2 below).

II. Disclosure of Information

200. In general, medical treatments can only be started if the physician or dentist has informed the patient properly and the patient has validly consented to the treatment (§49[1] Physicians Act, §18 Dentists Act, §5a Nos 2 and 3 Frame Law on Hospitals and Sanatoria). The primary purpose of giving information is to provide the competent patient with appropriate and sufficient information that enables him to meaningfully avail himself of his right to self-determination. Therefore, the given information has to enable the patient to understand the meaning and the scope of the recommended treatment in order to decide whether he ultimately wants to undergo the medical or dental intervention or not. It shall be noted that also professional health care providers need, generally spoken, to inform their patients especially about the course of the planned treatment and in case of working as a freelance physician about the costs and the professional insurance coverage (*see* §36[5] Nursing of Patients Act; §9a Midwives Act; §7b[2] Medical-Technical Services Act).

201. It is generally accepted that the duty to inform is a contractual duty resulting from the concluded treatment contract as well as a legal duty implicitly stipulated by the protective regulations such as §110 of the Criminal Code, §8(3) of the

---

is going to be changed to 'capability to make decisions' (*Entscheidungsfähigkeit*). This term is newly defined by §24(2) Civil Code, effective in July 2018. *See* for more details the explanatory report: ErlRV 1461 BlgNR 25. GP 5, 8 et seq: 'Capable to make decisions is someone, who understands the meaning and the consequences of his acting in the relevant circumstances, and is capable of forming his will and acting accordingly. In case of doubt, a person of full age is assumed to have the capacity to make decisions.'

192. For details e.g., Ch. Kopetzki, 'Einwilligung und Einwilligungsfähigkeit', in *Einwilligung und Einwilligungsfähigkeit*, ed. Ch. Kopetzki (Vienna: Manz, 2002), 1 et seq.; M. Ganner, *Selbstbestimmung im Alter* (Vienna: Springer, 2005), 237 et seq.; J. Stabentheiner, '§§146c, 146d', in *Kommentar zum Allgemeinen bürgerlichen Gesetzbuch*, ed. P. Rummel, 3rd edn (Vienna: Manz, 2003), marginal number 3 with further references.

Frame Law on Hospitals and Sanatoria and others. Nevertheless it is principally not regulated by law, which, to what extent and in which form the medical information has to be provided. In fact, the Supreme Court has developed several principles concerning the procedure of information which are applied in a flexible system, so that the courts have to decide case-by-case whether the respective physician has fulfilled his (contractual) duty to information. In certain (younger) acts, the legislator has started outlining minimum information standards, mostly regarding the scope of information (e.g., §18 Dentists Act; §4 Human Tissues Safety Act; §8 Organ Transplantations Act and others).

202. The disclosure of information is required in advance of any therapeutic or diagnostic[193] measures, prescription of medication[194] or vaccinations.[195] Regarding non-medically indicated treatments, for example plastic surgeries, the Supreme Court[196] states that in each case highly detailed information shall be given. Since 2012, this obligation is established by §5 of the Act on Aesthetic Treatments and Surgery, Federal Law Gazette I 2012/80.

203. Nowadays, faults concerning the informed consent play a major role in practice and in the Supreme Court's jurisdiction, as patients normally base their claim for damages at least partly on alleged insufficient or incorrect information. In this context only the most important principles of the Supreme Court's jurisdiction shall be pointed out.[197]

A. The Manner of Providing Information

204. The duty to medically inform is qualified as a physician's duty. Therefore, it is unlawful to delegate this duty to non-medical staff. In hospitals, the duty to inform is normally not a personal obligation of the treating physician. Any

193. *See* e.g., Supreme Court 27 Sep. 2006, 9 Ob 76/06a; 16 Sep. 2009, 1 Ob 80/08h, *RdM* 2009/62, 96 (*Leischner*).
194. Supreme Court 18 Apr. 1973, 1 Ob 66/73, *RZ* 1973, 170 and others. Regarding the information duty concerning the implantation of medical devices: with further references *see* recently Supreme Court 23 Nov. 2016, 1 Ob 138/16z, *RdM* 2017, 112 *(Leischner-Lenzhofer)*.
195. For example, Supreme Court 16 Dec. 2008, 1 Ob 84/08x, *RdM-LS* 2009/21. Also *see* recently Supreme Court 1 Mar. 2012, 1 Ob 14/12h, *RdM* 2012/84, 110 = *Zak* 2012/413, 157 = U. Edelmann, 'Schadenersatz bei Unterlassung ärztlicher Aufklärung vor Schulimpfungen', *Zak* (2012): 248. Also *see* A. Kletečka/Neumayer G., 'Die Grenzen der ärztlichen Aufklärungspflicht, insbesondere bei Schulimpfaktionen', *RdM* (2012): 44.
196. For example, recently Supreme Court 27 Feb. 2009, 6 Ob 122/07w, *RdM-LS* 2009/33.
197. For an overview and more details on the disclosure of information *see* e.g., D. Engljähringer, *Ärztliche Aufklärungspflicht vor medizinischen Eingriffen* (Vienna: Orac, 1996); F. Harrer & A.H. Graf (eds), *Ärztliche Verantwortung und Aufklärung*, (Vienna: Orac 1999); K. Prutsch, Die ärztliche Aufklärung, 2nd edn (Vienna: WUV, 2004); Th. Juen, *Arzthaftungsrecht*, 2nd edn (Vienna: Manz, 2005), 95 et seq.; A. Leischner, *Streitbeilegung in medizinischen Haftungsfällen* (Vienna: Manz, 2007), 47 et seq. and 137 et seq.; M. Memmer, 'Aufklärung', in *Handbuch Medizinrecht*, ed. G. Aigner et al. (Vienna: Manz, 2003 et seq.), I/71 et seq. and others. For an English overview *see* B.A. Koch & H. Koziol, 'Country Report – Austria', in *Cases on Medical Malpractice in a Comparative Perspective*, ed. M.G. Faure & H. Koziol, (Vienna: Springer, 2004), 57–80.

appropriately qualified physician regarding the medical measure in question can provide the information. Moreover, the communication of information is not restricted to licensed practitioners, so that the information may also be given by an appropriately qualified doctor-in-training.[198] The surgeon can usually rely on the correctness of the provided information. Nevertheless, he is obliged to control whether the patient has received appropriate information and has already consented by accessing the patient's medical records before starting the treatment.[199]

205. The information has to be given orally in a comprehensible way. Therefore, it is not sufficient to hand out a written information letter that the patient signs without having had the opportunity to ask questions to a physician.[200] Nevertheless, the oral information may be facilitated by an information letter that has to be discussed with the patient item by item.[201] The physician-patient-dialogue has to be adapted to each individual patient, particularly considering his intellectual, professional, social and cultural background as well as his language skills.[202] In case a patient does not understand German, the physician is obliged to inform the patient in a language which they both speak well enough for information purposes. Otherwise the patient has to be informed in a language he speaks with the assistance of a colleague or another staff member, a confidant of the patient or an interpreter who translates the relevant information.[203] To provide evidence, the disclosure has to be documented in the patient's medical record (§51 Physicians Act, §10 Frame Law on Hospitals and Sanatoria). Regarding specific medical activities, information has to be given orally and in writing (*see* e.g., §49[3] Medicinal Devices Act).

---

198. For example, Supreme Court 14 Apr. 1998, 10 Ob 137/98i.

199. Supreme Court 17 Nov. 2009, 1 Ob 218/09d, *RdM-LS* 2010/12 (*Leischner*); 24 Nov. 2011, 1 Ob 215/11s, *RdM-LS* 2012/6; A. Heidinger, 'Die ärztliche Aufklärung in der Rechtsprechung des Obersten Gerichtshofes', in *Ärztliche Verantwortung und Aufklärung*, ed. F. Harrer & A.-H. Graf (Vienna: Orac 1999), 26 et seq.

200. Supreme Court 31 Jan. 1995, 4 Ob 509/95, *JBl* 1995, 453 (*Steiner*) = *RdM* 1995/15 (*Kopetzki*); 30 Jan. 1996, 4 Ob 505/96, *RdM* 1996/24.

201. For example Supreme Court 4 Apr. 1998, 10 Ob 137/98i, *RdM* 1998/21; 7 Apr. 2003, 2 Ob 313/01w. The performance of certain specific medical activities requires that medical information has been given orally and in written: *see* e.g., §49(3) Medical Devices Act; §39(1) Medicinal Products Act; §8(3) Organ Transplantations Act; §6(1) Act on Aesthetic Treatments and Surgery.

202. Regarding the cultural background *see* Supreme Court 15 Mar. 2001, 6 Ob 258/00k; also *see* A. Leischner, 'Sprach- und kulturspezifische Anforderungen an die ärztliche Aufklärung', in *Interkulturell kompetent. Ein Handbuch für Ärztinnen und Ärzte*, ed. M. Peintinger (Vienna: Verlag facultas, 2011), 203 (220 et seq.). Regarding the patient's prior medical knowledge *see* e.g., Supreme Court 28 Apr. 1993, 6 Ob 542/93; 31 Mar. 2011, 1 Ob 9/11x, *RdM* 2011/138, 154 (*Leischner*).

203. *See* e.g., D. Engljähringer, *Ärztliche Aufklärungspflicht vor medizinischen Behandlungen* (Vienna: Orac, 1996), 140; A. Heidinger, 'Die ärztliche Aufklärung in der Rechtsprechung des Obersten Gerichtshofes', in *Ärztliche Verantwortung und Aufklärung*, ed. F. Harrer & A.-H. Graf (Vienna: Orac, 1999), 43; A. Leischner, 'Sprach- und kulturspezifische Anforderungen an die ärztliche Aufklärung', in *Interkulturell kompetent. Ein Handbuch für Ärztinnen und Ärzte*, ed. M. Peintinger (Vienna: Verlag facultas, 2011), 203–225; A. Leischner-Lenzhofer, 'Die ärztliche Aufklärung bei fremdsprachigen Patienten', *RdM* (2013): 12–18; M. Stadler, 'Der fremdsprachige Patient – Besonderheiten bei der ärztlichen Aufklärung', *Zak* (2013): 247; M. Kletečka-Pulker, 'Patientenrecht auf muttersprachliche Aufklärung? Videodolmetschen – neue Wege in der Kommunikation mit MigrantInnen im Gesundheitsbereich', in *Wie viel Deutsch braucht man, um gesund zu sein?*, ed. L. Kaelin et al. (Vienna: Verlag Österreich, 2013), 45–70.

B. Timeliness of Information

206. A further prerequisite for a valid consent is the timeliness of the given information. As a basic guideline the patient should have enough time to weigh the pros and cons of the planned treatment and to discuss these with a confidant or a physician of choice. The timeline has to be specified in accordance to the individual situation, taking into consideration the urgency and the severity of the treatment as well as the advance information of the patient. For instance, the Supreme Court qualified giving the information on the evening before a grave surgery as just in time, as the patient, who had already undergone the same surgery years before, had the chance to discuss the pros and cons with his wife.[204] The patient's expressed wish to combine a planned surgery with another surgery may reduce the need of time for consideration so that information given on the day of surgery or shortly before the surgery may be sufficient.[205] In any case it is too late to give the information on the way to the operating theatre.[206] However, information given to ambulatory patients or outpatients on the day of the treatment may principally be qualified as sufficient.

207. In 2009 the Supreme Court judged that information was given in time when first information was given seven months before the plastic surgery, again when the date of the surgery was fixed, and recapitulated once more on the day before the surgery. In this case, the Supreme Court followed the opinion of the German Federal Supreme Court (BGH) by stating that the disclosure of information generally has to take place on the day the date of surgery is scheduled, as far as the surgeon recommends a non-urgent surgery.[207] Since the enforcement of the Act on Aesthetic Treatments and Surgery in 2012, generally a minimum of two weeks shall lie between the information and the consent (§6). Concerning other non-medically indicated interventions a certain time for consideration between the given information and the commencement of the medical intervention is stipulated by law (*see* e.g., §7 Artificial Procreation Act).

C. Extent of Information

208. Scope and detail of the required information depend on the concrete situation regarding the planned medical treatment and the specific patient, taking into consideration his private and professional life.[208] According to the Supreme Court's

---

204. *See* Supreme Court 23 Jun. 1994, 6 Ob 555/94, *RdM* 1995/1; *see also* Supreme Court 27 Apr. 2011, 7 Ob 64/11d, *RdM-LS* 2011/53 (*Leischner*); but the information given eighteen hours before the commencement of the surgery was too late in Supreme Court 28 Jan. 2016, 1 Ob 252/15p *RdM* 2016/111, 153 *(Leischner-Lenzhofer)*.
205. Supreme Court 22 Feb. 2007, 8 Ob 140/06f, *RdM* 2007/82, 124; 18 Mar. 2015, 3 Ob 22/15d, *RdM-LS* 2015/53, 155.
206. This principle is referred to by the appellate court in Supreme Court 22 Feb. 2007, 8 Ob 140/06f, *RdM* 2007/82; 24 Nov. 2011, 1 Ob 215/11s, *RdM-LS* 2012/6.
207. Supreme Court 17 Nov. 2009, 1 Ob 218/09d, *RdM-LS* 2010/12 (*Leischner*) = *JBl* 2010, 302.
208. For example, Supreme Court 20 Feb. 2001, 10 Ob 8/01a, *RdM* 2001, 152.

jurisdiction, the following two principles have to be considered: the more urgent a treatment or diagnosis is for the patient's health, the less extensively the physician has to inform the patient. The less necessary or urgent a treatment is for a reasonable patient, the higher the requirements concerning the quantity of information are.

209. In consideration of the patient's well-being, the Supreme Court ruled in a basic judgment in 1982[209] that a physician primarily has to consider the well-being of the patient when deciding whether or not and to what extent he should inform the patient. Only secondarily the physician has to consider the patient's right to self-determination. Therefore, an extraordinarily anxious patient shall not, or merely to a minimum, be informed if he is likely to decide against the treatment with extensive information, which in turn would constitute a much higher risk to his health. In literature, this principle is called 'therapeutic privilege' of the physician.

Even if this ranking of arguments was not equally retained in subsequent judgments of the Supreme Court the principles established in the aforementioned judgments are still regarded as valid today, especially to emphasize that the duty to inform shall not be applied too strictly.[210]

210. The Supreme Court accepts that the disclosure of information regarding medically indicated treatments can be reduced to a minimum under certain circumstances, such as extraordinarily anxious, depressive or suicidal patients.[211] Although such patients shall not be excessively alarmed, the patient shall still receive at least basic information, so that he can make his decision on basis of a rough estimation of the dangers involved. In case the treatment has to be performed extremely urgently in order to save the patient's health,[212] or if only a tentative diagnosis has been made, which does not imply an action that has to be verified by the patient,[213] the disclosure of information can be limited or postponed. Nevertheless, it has to be pointed out that a patient asking for information always has to be informed truthfully.

D. Waiver of Information by the Patient

211. The physician determining the scope of necessary information in accordance with the individual situation ('therapeutic privilege') has to be distinguished from the patient's right to refuse to receive information. Every patient may legitimately refuse to receive detailed information about the medical intervention in question (also *see* Article 16[4] Patients' Charter). Nevertheless, the patient's waiver of information must be ascertained beyond any doubt within a patient-to-physician

209. Supreme Court 23 Jun. 1982, 3 Ob 545/82, *JBl* 1983, 373 (*Holzer*).
210. For example, Supreme Court 7 Apr. 2003, 2 Ob 313/01w, *RdM* 2004/53.
211. *See* recently e.g., Supreme Court 20 Dec. 2016, 4 Ob 256/26z, *EvBl-LS* 2017/58, 380.
212. For example, Supreme Court 17 Jan. 2001, 6 Ob 318/00h, *RdM* 2001/16 and others.
213. Supreme Court 7 Mar. 2006, 1 Ob 4/06d. But also *see* Supreme Court 7 Mar. 2006, 5 Ob 165/ 05h, *RdM* 2007/71.

dialogue and has to be documented for evidentiary reasons.[214] Waiver of information is explicitly not legal concerning aesthetic treatments and surgeries (§6[1] Act on Aesthetic Treatments and Surgery), artificial procreation (§7[1] Artificial Procreation Act) and organ donations (§8[3] Organ Transplantations Act).

E. Content of Information

212. Legal literature and the courts divide the disclosure of medical information in three different types of information in order to enable the patient to meaningfully avail himself of his right to self-determination: medical information concerning diagnosis, risks and therapy.

213. Information on the diagnosis is regularly necessary after the confirmation of the diagnosis. Nevertheless, information on a tentative diagnosis has to be given if the patient has to undergo further tests completed by other physicians or health care institutions on his own responsibility, after which the diagnosis is likely to be revised. In a case where a gynaecologist referred a pregnant woman to the ambulance for high-risk pregnancies, without giving her the information that he assumed that the unborn baby was going to be severely handicapped, the woman did not follow the referral and gave birth to a severely handicapped child. The woman argued that she would have had a lawful abortion according to §97 of the Criminal Code if she had known about the serious handicap of her unborn child, and sued the gynaecologist for compensation for all costs of alimentation for the disabled child. The Supreme Court judged that the gynaecologist had acted faulty; the woman would have needed information on the tentative diagnosis to decide whether she wanted to verify the tentative diagnosis or not, and in order to know why she should follow the referral.[215] In another case a gynaecologist had urgently recommended a pregnant woman to go to a hospital informing her that otherwise she would risk bleedings, spasms and possible dangers for the unborn child. The Supreme Court ruled that this given information is sufficient in the way that an average diligent woman should know that she should follow such a referral.[216]

214. The information on the therapy has to include details about the planned treatment and the consequences of undergoing the recommended treatment or abstaining from it. If several equally acceptable common medical methods[217] are in question, the physician has to discuss the pros and the cons of each possible treatment with the patient, especially the imminent risks, the intensity, success rates and cosmetic results.[218] In general, the physician does not have to inform the patient

214. *See* e.g., Supreme Court 19 Dec. 1984, 3 Ob 562/84, *JBl* 1985, 548.
215. Supreme Court 7 Mar. 2006, 5 Ob 165/05h, *RdM* 2006/71.
216. Supreme Court 4 Aug. 2009, 9 Ob 64/08i *RdM* 2009/156 = *Hubinger*, *RdM* 2010, 30.
217. *See* Supreme Court 12 Feb. 2013, 4 Ob 241/12p, *RdM* 2013/102 (*Leischner-Lenzhofer*) = S. Kallab, 'Zur Aufklärungspflicht über "Außenseitermethoden"', *RdM* (2013): 133.
218. For example, Supreme Court 7 Sep. 1993, 10 Ob 503/93, *RdM* 1994/1 (*Kopetzki*); 17 Dec. 2003, 7 Ob 299/03a, *RdM* 2004/52. This principle also applies to equally acceptable alternative methods: Supreme Court 21 Feb. 2013, 9 Ob 32/12i, *RdM* 2013/101.

about all theoretically possible treatment methods, as long as the used method can be qualified as *lege artis*. If the patient explicitly asks for information on other methods that eventually come into question if the clinical situation turns out to be different, even though they are not indicated at the moment, the physician has to inform the patient about them.[219] But if a patient consults the physician especially for a treatment with a specific method that is even medically indicated in the patient's case, the physician does not need to inform the patient about other adequate methods.[220] If a new method shall be used, the patient must be informed that the method is new and that the risks are not entirely assessable yet.[221] Similar principles apply to outsider-methods.

215. De facto, most indemnity claims are based on alleged insufficient or faulty information on the risks of the undergone treatment. There are no general criteria or a pre-defined list concerning the possible risks that have to be disclosed. Instead, there is a rather flexible set of criteria which shall be considered when determining which risks have to be disclosed. Statistical probabilities of the potential risks of the more or less urgent medical treatment[222] as well as the importance of a specific risk for the individual patient due to his private or professional life can play a more or less significant role in this process.[223] Even so, the Supreme Court has established as a general guideline pursuant to typical risks, stating that, regardless of the statistical probability, every typical risk has to be communicated which might result in a quite severe damage and is unexpected for a non-informed patient, since the patient does not connect such possible risks with the intervention in question, even though the risk is specifically associated with the intervention or method and cannot be avoided completely even if utmost care is applied.[224]

But even under this rule, it is not necessary that the patient is informed about each and every risk that could materialize. The decisive factor is solely whether the knowledge of the risk in question is likely to influence the decision of the individual patient.[225]

216. Furthermore, the Supreme Court recently had to decide whether patients have the right to be informed about the person and the qualification of the surgeon performing the upcoming surgery. The Court ruled that a patient who is admitted to hospital as an in-patient only under certain circumstances has the right to be informed on who is going to perform the surgery. In particular, the duty to disclose the person performing the surgery can only be in question, if the patient limits his consent to a specific surgeon, which is also noticeable or shall have been noticeable

219. Supreme Court 16 Apr. 2002, 10 Ob 107/02m; 8 Jul. 2003, 5 Ob 162/03i.
220. Supreme Court 29 Jan. 2001, 3 Ob 87/00s, *RdM* 2001, 21.
221. Supreme Court 26 Jul. 2006, 3 Ob 106/06v, *RdM* 2007, 181 – laser eye surgery.
222. For example, Supreme Court 12 Nov. 1992, 8 Ob 646/92; 10 Jun. 2001, 8 Ob 103/01g.
223. For example, Supreme Court 12 Jul. 1990, 7 Ob 593/90, *JBl* 1991, 316.
224. *See* recently Supreme Court 23 Nov. 2016, 1 Ob 138/16z, *RdM* 2017, 112 *(Leischner-Lenzhofer)*. Critical towards this information criterion E. Pitzl & G. W. Huber, 'Das "typische" Behandlungsrisiko als Aufklärungskriterium', *RdM* (2011): 4.
225. For example, Supreme Court 21 Sep. 1989, 8 Ob 535/89, *JBl* 1990, 459; 31 Jan. 1995, 4 Ob 509/95, *RdM* 1995/91 and many others.

with reasonable effort by the hospital staff. This was first acknowledged in 2003[226] in a case in which a physician of choice fixed a date for a surgery with his patient and as usually noted on the referral to the hospital that he would complete the surgery (namely with the comment 'ipse'). The patient consequently assumed that the physician was going to complete the surgery himself, but in the end a different surgeon performed it. The hospital had not informed the patient about the change in advance so that he did not have the opportunity to delay the surgery.

In 2009[227] the Supreme Court first had to decide whether patients have the right to be informed about the specific qualification of the surgeon regarding the method in question. The Court ruled that the physician is not obliged to inform the patient how often he has already performed the method in question. Even so, the physician has to answer truthfully, if the patient asks the physician about his range of experience with this method.

III. Legal Obstacles to Consent

217. In general, it can be pointed out that patients can freely consent to every medically indicated treatment. Legal obstacles to consent exist regarding specific medical procedures that are not medically indicated. In these cases the patient's right to consent is limited by law. Therefore, even if the patient is capable to consent and adequately informed, he can only consent to the performance of certain medical activities like sterilization, organ or blood donation or cosmetic treatments as long as a specific minimum age and the legal prerequisites are fulfilled. Regarding other special activities, for example active euthanasia, the patient can never validly consent to (*see* Part II, Chapter 3 below).

IV. The Manner of Giving Consent

218. In general, it suffices that the patient or his legal representative consents implicitly or orally. Implicit consent is also referred to as non-verbal consent, in the sense that the patient shows by his behaviour without leaving any doubt that he agrees with the proposed treatment. For evidentiary reasons the consent shall be documented in the medical records of the patient (implicitly according to §51 Physicians Act, §10 Frame Law on Hospitals and Sanatoria).

219. Regarding specific medical activities, Austrian law requires the patient's consent in written or other special forms. This is regulated particularly concerning the donation of blood (§8 Blood Safety Law), the living donation of human tissues and cells (§4[3] Human Tissue Safety Law) and of human organs (§8[4] Organ Transplantations Act), clinical trials on drugs or medical devices (§39[2] Medicinal

226. Supreme Court 26 Sep. 2003, 3 Ob 131/03s, *RdM* 2004/37; confirmed by Supreme Court 4 Oct. 2005, 4 Ob 121/05f, *RdM* 2006/29 and 25 Nov. 2014, 8 Ob 120/14a, *RdM* 2015, 153 = Ch. Huber, *RdM* (2015): 135.

227. Supreme Court 20 Jan. 2009, 4 Ob 166/08b, *RdM* 2009/128 (*Leischner*).

Products Act; §50[1] Medical Devices Act), genetic diagnostics (§69[1] Gene Technology Act), medically assisted reproduction (§§8[4], 13[1] Artificial Procreation Act), performance of cosmetic treatments and plastic surgeries according to §3 Law on the Performance of Aesthetic Treatments and Surgeries (§6) and medical interventions which have a serious or lasting impact on the person's health or personality and are necessary in the course of hospitalization in a psychiatric hospital or department in hospitals (§36 Hospitalization Act). The same applies to tattooing and piercing according to the Ordinance of the Federal Minister of Economic and Labour Affairs on the rules for the exercise of piercing and tattooing by cosmetic traders, Federal Law Gazette II 2003/141 as last amended by Federal Law Gazette II 2008/261.

V. Presumed Consent

220. The patient's consent may be presumed in case of emergency if the patient's life or health is imminently endangered. A treatment without the patient's or his legal representative's consent is only lawful if it cannot be obtained in time or if there is not enough time to figure out whether the patient has made a written statement refusing the provided services in advance, without seriously endangering the patient's life or health (§110[3] Criminal Code, §8[3] Frame Law on Hospitals and Sanatoria, §12 Living Will Act – for details *see* subchapter VII.A. below).

221. Moreover, in case a non-foreseeable enlargement or modification of a surgery is necessary, the narcotized patient's consent may be presumed. The surgeon shall decide whether to continue or stop the surgery taking into account how a 'reasonable' patient would have decided in the same circumstances. In other words, the surgeon has to consider the patient's (objective) well-being (especially the dangerousness of the termination of the surgery to the patient's health) as well as his right to self-determination when he decides whether to continue or to stop the surgery and the anaesthetics. All in all, this presumed consent can only be justified if the enlargement or modification of the surgery is urgent and the termination of the surgery is medically contraindicated, or involves a higher risk for the patient's life or health than its continuation. As a general rule, the higher the additional risks and the graver the consequences of the enlarged or modified surgery, the less justifiable is the presumption of the patient's consent. If the continuation and the termination of the surgery have almost the same impact on the patient's health, the patient's right to self-determination has priority, so that the surgery must be interrupted.[228]

VI. The Patient's Right to Withdraw or Refuse Consent

222. The patient's right to self-determination also includes the right to freely refuse the proposed medical treatment. The patient has the right to refuse or

228. Supreme Court 26 Jun. 2007, 10 Ob 50/07m, *RdM* 2007, 188; 22 Jul. 2010, 8 Ob 43/10x, *RdM-LS* 2010/58; 15 Sep. 2010, 4 Ob 145/10t, *RdM-LS* 2011/6.

withdraw his consent personally, as long as he is capable of understanding the nature and consequences of his expressed declaration of will at the time of the refusal or withdrawal. The scope of the refusal is not limited. Instead, the patient has the right to refuse any treatment, even if it is indispensable for his survival or is only one medical act out of a complete medical intervention (e.g., blood transfusion). Neither the refusal nor the withdrawal of the consent by itself terminates the legal relation between the patient and the physician or the legal entity of the health care institution. If the physician cannot render any medical services due to the refusal, the physician's duty to treatment ends. The physician has to obey the expressed will of the patient. Otherwise he may be prosecuted for treatment without consent pursuant to §110 of the Criminal Code. Correspondingly, the physician cannot be prosecuted for neglecting to start or to continue the medical treatment which caused harm to the patient (at the reverse of §2 Criminal Code).[229] Under these circumstances the treatment contract may lawfully be terminated, provided that others can appropriately supply the necessary basic care (*see* Part II, Chapter 1, §2.II. above).

VII. The Patient's Right to Medical Decisions in Advance

223. The legislator enacted two legal instruments in order to strengthen the patient's right to self-determination regarding medical treatments. Every patient shall have the opportunity to refuse medical treatment as well as to choose a person of confidence in advance, who shall give consent to medical interventions in compliance with the patient's expressed declaration of will in case that he is no longer competent himself.

A. *Living Will*

224. Every patient capable of exercising his right to self-determination in relation to medical treatments has the right to make a written statement refusing certain medical interventions in advance. Since 2006, the Living Will Act (*Patientenverfügungsgesetz,* Federal Law Gazette I 2006/55) provides two legal instruments of advanced refusal: the binding living will and the considerable living will. This right to refuse in advance can only be used personally by someone who is capable of insight and judgment regarding the medical measure that shall be denied (§3). In order that an advanced refusal to be binding, the following conditions have to be met: A binding living will concretely has to describe the refused medical treatments

229. R. Moos, 'Vor §§75–79', in *Wiener Kommentar zum Strafgesetzbuch,* ed. F. Höpfel & E. Ratz, 2nd edn (Vienna: Manz, 2003), marginal number 32 et seq. *See also* A. Mangold, J. Mascherbauer, M. Peintinger & Ch. Kopetzki, 'Behandlungsablehnung trotz vitaler Indikation', *RdM* (2010): 13; A. Polzer, G. Dinhof, A. Leischner, H. Schütz, E. Bernat, 'Verweigerung der Sectio trotz dringender medizinischer Indikation', *RdM* (2011): 123. Concerning the claim for damages in a case where a patient with belief in Jehovah's Witness refused a medical indicated blood transfusion: Supreme Court 22 Jun. 2011, 2 Ob 219/10k, *RdM* 2011, 228 *(Leischner)*; 31 Aug. 2016, 2 Ob 148/15a, *RdM-LS* 2016/89, 312.

or these at least have to emerge unambiguously from the context of the living will (§4). The written living will shall not only describe which medical measures are refused, but also the situation in which the living will shall be applied. Therefore the patient has to consult a qualified physician who has to inform him about the nature and the consequences of his advanced refusal and who evaluates the patient's capacity to insight and judgment concerning the refused medical interventions as well as for which reasons the patient appropriately evaluates the consequences of the living will. This has to be documented and confirmed by the informing physician in the living will (§5). Only hereafter the patient's living will may be executed by an attorney, notary or legally trained associate of the patient's advocacies (representatives) (§6).

225. A binding advanced refusal generally loses its binding character five years after its execution, unless a shorter expiry date is fixed. A renewal is possible under the requirements mentioned above. It may be pointed out, that the binding living will's validity may be prolonged until the patient is able to renew it, if the patient loses his ability to understand, judge or express himself during the term of validity of the binding living will (§7).

226. Besides the binding living will, the patient can also draft a merely considerable living will. This type of living will is defined as an advanced refusal that does not fulfil all prerequisites of a binding living will. A considerable living will must be taken into account for the establishment of the patient's will (§8). As a general rule the law states that the more a considerable living will meets the conditions of a binding living will, the more it shall be taken into account for the establishment of the patient's will. In particular it has to be considered to what extent the patient was able to comprehend the concrete situation the living will is relating to, as well as its consequences at the time the living will was set up, how concrete the refused medical treatments are described, how comprehensive the medical information prior to the execution was, to what extent the living will differs from the formal requirements of a binding living will, how often the living will was renewed and how long ago the most recent renewals were (§9). On the basis of this legal principle it is generally acknowledged that a considerable living will may be equally binding, as long as the physician can estimate the patient's will without any reasonable doubt.[230]

In the course of an appointment of a custodian by court, it can be subject whether the living will is binding or only considerable. In case of a binding living will, applicable for the concrete circumstances, a custodian shall not be appointed or involved (§268[2] Civil Code, repealed and newly regulated by §253[4] Civil Code, Federal Law Gazette I 2017/59). In case the living will is only considerable, the court merely appoints a custodian, who has to decide on behalf of the patient with regard to his expressed wish and his objective well-being (§281 Civil Code, repealed and newly regulated by §241 Civil Code, Federal Law Gazette I 2017/59).[231]

230. *See* U. Pesendorfer, in *Handbuch Sachwalterrecht*, ed. P. Barth & M. Ganner, 2nd edn (Vienna: Linde, 2010), 412 et seq.

231. Concerning the appointment of a custodian in despite of the patient's declared will in form of a living will: Supreme Court 8 Oct. 2012, 9 Ob 68/11g, *RdM* 2013/74 *(Kopetzki)*; 17 Sep. 2014, 6

227. A (binding or considerable) living will loses its validity, if the patient revokes it himself or shows by his behaviour that it is no longer valid. In addition, a living will is invalid if it is not based on a free and well-considered declaration of will, if it has been initiated by error, fraud, deception or by physical or mental pressure, if its content is legally unacceptable (§13) or if the standard of medical science regarding the content of the living will has essentially changed in the meantime (§10). It shall be pointed out, that a living will is legally unacceptable if the patient for example wishes the performance of active euthanasia, which is forbidden by criminal law.

228. The living will has to be documented by the informing and the attending physician in the patient's medical record (§14). Unfortunately, the Austrian legislator has not stipulated an obligatory documentation in a central register. As a result the patient has the duty to notify the attending physician of the existence and the content of the living will. If the patient is unable to do so in advance, the attending physician shall take reasonable efforts to check whether the patient has drawn up an advanced refusal or not, for example by asking his relatives or by accessing his medical records. If the time spent on searching a living will seriously endangers the patient's life or health, the attending physician is no longer obliged to search for a living will. Instead he has to provide the respective emergency medical treatment (§12).

229. Finally, a basic ruling of the Supreme Court may be pointed out. In the context of an inheritance dispute in 2008,[232] that took place before the Living Will Act entered into force, the Supreme Court stated that the termination of a total parenteral nutrition as a life-prolonging medical treatment[233] of a terminally ill, no longer competent patient may be lawful, as long as the decision on the termination was made in compliance with the patient's prior oral statements refusing this medical treatment. Therefore, the termination of medically indicated treatments can be lawful if it is performed in accordance with the presumed patient's refusal of treatment, even if the patient has not set up a written statement. Even so the Supreme Court stated that in case of uncertainty the principle 'in dubio pro vita' shall apply. Although this

Ob 147/14g, *RdM-LS* 2015/50, 120 *(Kopetzki/Leischner-Lenzhofer)*. Concerning §241 Civil Code as amended on Federal Law Gazette I 2017/59 *see* Explanatory Report to the government bill: 1461 BlgNR 25. GP 20.

232. Supreme Court 7 Jul. 2008, 6 Ob 286/07p, *RdM* 2008/119. Also *see* recently Supreme Court 8 Oct. 2012, 9 Ob 68/11g, *Zak* 2012/762, 415 (*Kletečka*) ≈ *iFamZ* 2013/14, 50 (*Ganner*) = *EvBl* 2013/60, 414 (*Pfurtscheller*) = *RdM* 2013/74, 104 (*Kopetzki*) = E. Bernat, 'Sterbehilfe und Sachwalterrecht – Zugleich eine Besprechung des Beschlusses des OGH v 8. 10. 2012, 9 Ob 68/11g', *EF-Z* (2013): 5.

233. The legislator qualified total parenteral nutrition as medical intervention, since passing a gastric tube is only performed on instruction of a physician, which implies that the act is qualified as medical act: Caucus Report to the Living Will Act 1381 BlgNR 22. GP 2. Also *see* E. Bernat, '§3 PatVG', in *ABGB Praxiskommentar*, ed. M. Schwimann, 3rd edn (Vienna: Orac, 2007), marginal number 5 et seq.

case was decided before the Living Will Act became effective, the outlined principle will have an impact on the jurisdiction to come.[234]

B. Health Care Proxy

230. Since July 2007, the Austrian civil law provides the legal institute of the health care proxy (*Vorsorgevollmacht in Gesundheitsangelegenheiten*, §§284f–284g Civil Code, Federal Law Gazette I 2006/92). With 1 July 2018 this legal institute is going to be newly, but similarly regulated by §§260 et seq. Civil Code, Federal Law Gazette I 2017/59.[235]

Every person with full legal capacity may grant a durable power of attorney regarding concretely defined affairs to a person of particular confidence. The principal can either choose to grant a health care proxy for giving consent to medical treatments, or instruct the attorney to make sure that his denial of specified medical treatments is respected. However, the validity of the latter instructions is subject to the prerequisites of the Living Will Act.[236] Since medical decisions do not require full legal capacity, but merely capacity to insight and judgment, it is generally acknowledged that also minor and mentally ill patients who are capable of understanding, judging and expressing their will, can appoint a health care proxy.[237]

231. As to legal representation concerning simple medical matters of everyday life, the health care proxy has to be set up in form of a testament. Therefore it has to be manually written and signed by the person granting the authority. If the principal only signs the document, three unbiased witnesses who have full legal capacity and are proficient in the language the document was written in have to confirm that the content of the health care proxy fully corresponds to the principal's intentions. If the principal does not sign the health care proxy, its content has to be confirmed by a notary (§284f[2]).

Concerning legal representation in serious medical matters, the health care proxy has to be drawn up before a lawyer, notary or court and shall explicitly name the respective medical matters. The lawyer, notary or judge has to inform the principal about the consequences of the health care proxy, the possibility of revocation at any time and has to confirm the provision of this instruction by indicating his name and address and personally signing the document (§284f[3]).

---

234. E. Bernat, 'Grenzen der ärztlichen Behandlungspflicht bei einwilligungsunfähigen Patienten', *JBl* (2009): 129; H. Schütz, 'Abbruch der künstlichen Ernährung bei einer einwilligungsunfähigen Patientin – vorsätzliche Tötung durch Unterlassung', *iFamZ* (2009): 32; Ch. Kopetzki, 'Abbruch der künstlichen Ernährung beim Wachkomapatienten', in *Eluana Englaro – Wachkoma und Behandlungsabbruch*, ed. W. Kröll & W. Schaupp (Vienna: Manz, 2010), 61 et seq.

235. *See* for more details explanatory report to the government bill: ErläutRV 1461 BlgNR 25. GP 36 et seq.

236. Explanatory report to the government bill: ErläutRV 1420 BlgNR 22. GP 30.

237. Explanatory report to the government bill: ErläutRV 1420 BlgNR 22. GP 28. Also *see* H. Weitzenböck, 'Vor §284f', in *ABGB Praxiskommentar*, ed. M. Schwimann, 3rd edn (Vienna: Orac, 2007), marginal number 3; M. Ganner, in *Handbuch Sachwalterrecht*, ed. P. Barth & M. Ganner, 2nd edn (Vienna: Linde, 2010), 353.

It may be pointed out that from July 2018 on all health care proxies generally have to be drawn up personally and in writing before a notary, lawyer or adults' safeguard advocacies (representatives, *Erwachsenenschutzverein*) according to §262 Civil Code, Federal Law Gazette I 2017/59.

232. The health care proxy becomes effective as soon as the patient becomes unconscious or unable to make medical decisions due to incapacity of insight and judgment or inability to express these. The health care proxy's coming into effect has to be registered by the Austrian Register of Representation (*Österreichisches Zentrales Vertretungsregister,* §284h[2], newly regulated by Federal Law Gazette I 2017/59 in §263 Civil Code, effective as of July 2018).

233. It may be pointed out, that the health care proxy is the unique case in Austrian law, in which a third party might be obliged to take care that a medical intervention is not performed or discontinued on behalf of the patient's unambiguous declaration of will, even though the decision of the third party might be against the patient's well-being from an objective point of view (§284h[1], newly regulated by Federal Law Gazette I 2017/59 in §241 Civil Code, effective as of July 2018).

VIII. The Patient's Duty to Tolerate Interventions

234. In some specially regulated cases the performance of a medical intervention does not need the patient's valid consent to be lawful. Instead, the patient is obliged by law to undergo the respective treatment. Therefore the patient is not able to restrict such an obligation by a declaration of will (§13 Living Will Act). In compliance with Article 8 of the ECHR, such a legal obligation to undergo a treatment that affects the patient's physical integrity and is performed by a physician on behalf of public authority, can only be acceptable if the medical procedure is based on laws promoting substantial public interests as stated in Article 8(2) of the ECHR (which are national security, public safety or the economic well-being of the country, the prevention of disorder or crime, the protection of health or morals, or the protection of the rights and freedom of others). In addition, the means used must be proportionate regarding the legitimate aim pursued.

235. Therefore, the obligation to tolerate such medical interventions normally does not involve compulsory physical powers, but includes other disadvantages. For example, according to §5(6) of the Traffic Regulations, under defined circumstances the driver is obliged to endure the taking of blood samples by physicians for the determination of the alcohol level or intake of drugs. In case the driver refuses the blood sampling, he is guilty of an administrative offence and is punishable with a fine of EUR 1,600–EUR 5,900 (§99[1] lit. c Traffic Regulations). Taking blood samples by physical force would not be justifiable in the light of Article 90(2) of the Constitution (the fundamental principle against self-incrimination).[238]

238. VfSlg 11.923/1988; M. Hiesel, 'Zwangsweise Blutabnahme und Anklageprinzip – Gedanken zu §5 Abs 6 StVO', in *Ein Leben für Rechtskultur, Festschrift Robert Dittrich*, ed. H. Tades (Vienna:

A further example is the legal obligation of pregnant women and their children to undergo certain examinations and treatments during pregnancy and after the delivery of the children up to early childhood. If a pregnant woman or mother does not fulfil these obligations, she risks partly losing her right to social benefits (*see* Law on Social Benefits for Childcare).[239]

236. Only under certain circumstances, ill people can be physically forced to tolerate a medically indicated treatment. If an imprisoned person does not comply with an absolutely necessary medical examination or treatment, the imprisoned person can be forced to tolerate the medical treatment as long as it does not endanger his life and can be reasonably imposed on the imprisoned person, which means that the medical treatment may not cause severe bodily harm (§84 Criminal Code). Even so, the Federal Minister of Justice has to be asked for agreement with the procedure in advance, except for cases of imminent danger. In case of hunger strike the imprisoned person shall be medically observed and when necessary force-feed on instruction and under supervision of a physician (§69 Imprisonment Code).

In case a determined epidemic plague ought to be kept at bay, ill people or people who are suspected to be ill may be forced to undergo an examination and may be isolated (Epidemic Code, Tuberculosis Code based on Article 2[1] No. 5 of the Constitutional Law on the Protection of Personal Liberty, which states that in case there is reason to presume that a person is a source of danger for the spreading of infectious diseases, he may be deprived of his personal liberty in accordance with the procedure prescribed by law).[240]

§4. Rights and Duties Relating to the Medical Treatment

I. The Physician's Duty to Help in Case of Emergency

237. Physicians are obliged to perform first medical emergency services when a person's life is imminently endangered (§48 Physicians Act). The physician himself has to check whether medical emergency services are necessary.[241] Only if an ambulance is already notified about the accident and the physician can assume on well-founded reasons that a physician will be part of the rescue team and that the

Manz, 2000), 757; Th. Öhlinger, 'Die verfassungsrechtlichen Schranken der Blutabnahme gemäß §5 Abs 6 StVO', in *Ein Leben für Rechtskultur, Festschrift Robert Dittrich*, ed. H. Tades (Vienna: Manz, 2000), 773. Also *see* §85 Alternative Dispute Resolution Act (*Außerstreitgesetz*) regarding the obligation to endure the taking of tissue samples in order to know the filiation.

239. For details regarding invasive methods of physical investigation and their legitimacy *see* Ch. Kopetzki, 'Invasive Verfahren aus rechtlicher Sicht', in *Zumutbare Maßnahmen in Diagnostik und Therapie bei der Begutachtung*, ed. Gesellschaft der Gutachterärzte Österreichs, Forschung und Praxis der Begutachtung 68 (2006/2007), 33–58.

240. *See* for more details concerning the newly regulated judicial proceedings according to Federal Law Gazette I 2016/63: C. Mokrejs-Weinhappel, 'Das neue gerichtliche Anhalteverfahren nach TuberkuloseG und EpidemieG', *ÖJZ* (2017): 345.

241. Administrative Court 2 Jun. 1965, Z 1817/64, VwSlg 6719 A/1965 = *JBl* 1966, 332.

ambulance will arrive at the place of accident before he would arrive, he does not have to make sure that his emergency services are not necessary.[242]

This duty applies to doctors-in-training as well as all other (employed or freelance) physicians registered in the Medical Practitioner Register (*see* Part I, Chapter 1, §2. above).[243] Similar rules apply to other health care providers (e.g., §4[3] Nursing of Patients Act; §6[2] Midwives Act).

238. Pursuant to §57[1] of the Physicians Act, freelance physicians are obliged to have all necessary medication for first medical emergency services in stock in their medicine chest.

239. The hospital's duty to admit and treat patients in case of emergency is broader than the physician's duty. Therefore all hospitals (public, non-profit and private) have to admit patients in case first medical emergency services are absolutely necessary (§23[1] and §40[1] lit. c in conjunction with §23[1] of the Frame Law on Hospital and Sanatoria).[244]

II. The Physician's Duty to Treat Patients State-of-the-Art

240. According to §49(1) of the Physicians Act every licensed physician is obliged to continuously undergo further training in order to safeguard the well-being of the ill and the protection of the healthy patients according to medical science and experience as well as all applicable rules and specialist standards of quality assurance, especially in accordance with the Health Quality Act. Generally speaking, every physician has to gain knowledge of the current medical state-of-the-art. Thus, it is not sufficient for a physician to have profound knowledge of the subjective opinion of the physicians working in the respective hospital and experience with this local routine.[245] This does not mean that physicians are not allowed to treat patients with medically indicated methods that are new or alternative as long as their patients have validly consented to the medical intervention in question. As a general principle may be pointed out, that every physician has to treat his patients with reasonable care and skill, which shall not be less than ordinary care shown by a prudent and diligent standard physician in the same circumstances.[246] Similar rules apply to other health care providers (e.g., §4[1] Nursing of Patients Act; §6[1] Midwives Act).

---

242. Administrative Court 12 Dec. 1967, Z 564/67, VwSlg 7244 A/1967.

243. Most recently Supreme Court 8 Jun. 2010, 4 Ob 71/10k, *RdM* 2010/154 (*Leischner*); Ch. Schneider, *Ärztliche Ordinationen und selbständige Ambulatorien* (Vienna: Verlag Österreich, 2001), 285 et seq.; E. Koschy & B. Adlassnig, '§48 ÄrzteG', in *Ärztegesetz mit Kommentar*, ed. H. Emberger & F. Wallner, 2nd edn (Vienna: Verlagshaus der Ärzte, 2008), 169 et seq.

244. *See* Administrative Court 23 Apr. 2007, 2004/110/0192 and Supreme Court 11 May 2010, 4 Ob 36/10p, *RdM* 2010/152 (*Bernat*) = *Zak* 2010/480 (*Kletečka*).

245. Supreme Court 25 Mar. 1999, 1 Ob 91/99k, *RdM* 1999/23.

246. Supreme Court 3 Dec. 1992, 12 Os 123,124/92, *RdM* 1994/13; 31 Jan. 1995, 4 Ob 509/95, *RdM* 1995, 91. Also *see* Supreme Court 16 Mar. 1989, 8 Ob 525,526/88, *SZ* 62/53. For details *see* Part I, Ch. 4, §1.II.B. above.

241. Pursuant to §8(2) of the Frame Law on Hospitals and Sanatoria, every in-patient shall only be treated in accordance with the principles and acknowledged methods of medical or dental science.[247] 'Acknowledged methods' in this sense may be defined as clinically proven and promising medical methods, which are acknowledged by the respective medical discipline at home as well as abroad. Whether a medical method may be qualified as 'acknowledged' in the meaning of an appropriate method in the concrete situation is subject to the responsibility of the attending physician.[248] Consequently the Supreme Court has judged that every in-patient has the right to be treated with the safest available method according to the common standard generally acknowledged by medical experts.[249] Nevertheless, the necessary range of medical services varies from the degree of organizational standard to the available facilities of the hospital. Therefore a regional hospital does not have to provide the same standard of medical services as a university hospital.[250] Moreover, if there are no methods acknowledged or if none of them are promising in the concrete situation, treatment with new methods is possible (§8c[3] of the Frame Law on Hospitals and Sanatoria).

In addition, every legal entity of a hospital is obliged to implement appropriate organizational measures in order to safeguard the smooth provision and the success of the supplied medical services. This especially requires sufficient staff resources and appropriate technical equipment as well as measures to safeguard the coordination between the hospital staff in the course of the treatments.[251]

242. Physicians and dentists have to treat their patients conscientiously and indiscriminately (§49[1] Physicians Act, §16 Dentists Act). This includes the duty to take care of the patient before and after the medical intervention. The physician therefore generally has to look after the patient as long as the patient needs his help. Thus, the physician or the entity of the hospital has numerous further medical duties to ensure the healing effect of the treatment and to protect the patient from other dangers and suffering (*see* e.g., §24[2] Federal Law on Hospitals and Sanatoria regarding the hospital discharge letter).[252] For example, the attending physician or the entity of the hospital is obliged to implement hygiene measures to protect patients from infections with contagious diseases while being treated.[253] Moreover,

247. *See* the corresponding wording of §35(1) Hospitalization Act.

248. Committee Report to the government bill of the Hospitalization Act: AB 164 BlgNR 8. GP 7. Also *see* recently Supreme Court 21 Feb. 2013, 9 Ob 32/12i, *RdM* 2013/101 = R. Rebhahn, 'Wann dürfen Vertragsärzte die Behandlung von Versicherten ablehnen?', *RdM* (2013): 140.

249. Supreme Court 29 Jun. 1989, 6 Ob 549/89, *SZ* 62/125. *See also* Supreme Court 17 Feb. 2014, 4 Ob 27/14w, *RdM-LS* 2014/21, 108.

250. Supreme Court 25 Mar. 1999, 1 Ob 91/99k, *RdM* 1999/23; 23 Oct. 2003, 6 Ob 303/02f, *RdM* 2004/36. Also *see* Ch. Kopetzki, 'Behandlungen auf dem "Stand der Wissenschaft"', in *Finanzielle Grenzen des Behandlungsanspruchs*, ed. W. Pfeil (Vienna: Manz, 2010), 9 et seq.

251. Higher Court of Innsbruck 16 Feb. 1992, 1a R 50/93, *ZVR* 1993/100; Supreme Court 2 Oct. 1985, 3 Ob 569/84 and 3 Dec. 1985, 5 Ob 608/84; recently Supreme Court 30 Jun. 2010, 3 Ob 77/10k, *RdM-LS* 2010/52.

252. *See* for instance recently Supreme Court 31 Jan. 2013, 1 Ob 256/12s, *RdM-LS* 2013/29 (duty to instruct the patient about necessary actions from his side after the hospital discharge); 19 Jun. 2013, 7 Ob 85/13w (duty of the anaesthetist to look after the patient during his anaesthetic recovery).

253. Supreme Court 17 Jun. 1992, 2 Ob 538/92, *JBl* 1993, 316.

appropriate measures shall be performed to prevent and ease pain (also *see* Article 15 Patients' Charter).

III. The Patient's Obligation to Cooperate

243. Even the most diligent and prudent physician can only treat his patient sufficiently on condition that the patient has given him all necessary information and cooperates with the medical treatment in question. In order to enable a state-of-the-art medical treatment, every patient is obliged to give the necessary information on, for example, previous illnesses and risks or consequences particularly significant for him. Nevertheless, every physician has to tell the patient which information is needed and which and to which extent the patient shall perform necessary measures by himself during the treatment and after-treatment-care.[254] Finally it can be summarized that the medical contract on the one hand obliges the physician to provide appropriate information and instructions, and on the other hand obliges the patient to comply with the physician's instructions. If the patient does not cooperate despite having received the necessary information, the physician either has the opportunity to drop out of the medical contract without losing his right to a reasonable fee (§50[3] Physicians Act; §38 Dentists Act) or to seek defence in the invocation of the patient's negligence if claimed by the patient because of the insufficient success of the treatment.[255]

§5. Rights Relating to the Patient's Medical Record

I. The Patient's Right to Medical Records

244. The medical contract obliges the physician, dentist or any other health care professional to document at least key aspects of the treatment provided.[256] In addition to contractual duties, §51(1) of the Physicians Act and §19(1) of the Dentists Act require documentation of the individual patient's health history concerning his past and present health status, examination findings, diagnosis, course of the disease, disclosure of information and type and degree of the provided advisory, diagnostic and therapeutic services, including medications prescribed. All other health care providers are also obliged to document according to their professional laws (e.g., §5 Nursing of Patients Act, §9 Midwives Act, etc.). According to §10 of the

254. For example, Supreme Court 23 Mar. 2000, 10 Ob 24/00b, *RdM* 2001/1; recently Supreme Court 4 Aug. 2009, 9 Ob 64/08i *RdM* 2009/156 = Hubinger, *RdM* 2010, 30; 30 Jun. 2010, 3 Ob 77/10k, *RdM-LS* 2010/52; 28 May 2013, 8 Ob 4/13s, *RdM-LS* 2013/40; 27 Aug. 2015, 9 Ob 48/15x, *RdM-LS* 2015/88.
255. For example, Supreme Court 12 Jul. 1990, 7 Ob 593/90, *JBl* 1991, 316; 28 Aug. 1997, 3 Ob 2121/96z, *RdM* 1998, 7; 23 Oct. 2003, 6 Ob 303/02f, *RdM* 2004/36; Supreme Court 27 Sep. 2005, 10 Ob 22/04i, *RdM* 2006/30; recently Supreme Court 24 Apr. 2013, 9 Ob 39/12v, *RdM-LS* 2013/37. For more details *see* e.g., S. Dullinger, 'Mitwirkungspflichten des Patienten im Rahmen der ärztlichen Behandlung', *RdM Sonderheft Gmunder Medizinrechtskongress 2012, RdM* (2012): 222.
256. Supreme Court 25 Jan. 1994, 1 Ob 532/94, *RdM* 1994/25 (*Kopetzki*).

Frame Law on Hospitals and Sanatoria, further aspects have to be recorded in the course of hospital care, especially a patient's statement refusing organ donation in the event of death as well as a patient's (binding or considerable) living will. Hospital staff (physicians, nurses, psychologists, pyschotherapeutists and medical-technical staff) has to document all services that have been rendered. The hospital staff is also obliged to document the date the patient is admitted and discharged or the reasons why a patient was not admitted at all (§10[1] No. 1). Special provisions regarding the duty to documentation are enacted in laws regulating special medical procedures (for instance §§15, 18 Artificial Procreation Act). Beginning with July 2015, EHR-health care providers will have the duty to store EHR-health data in accordance with the Health Telematics Act 2012 and the EHR-Ordinance (*see* the next chapter for details).

245. Freelance physicians and dentists have to keep patients' records for at least ten years (§51[3] Physicians Act, §19[3] Dentists Act). Special provisions apply in case the physician or dentist dies or quits during the required storage period (§51[4] and [5] Physicians Act, §19[4] and [5] Dentists Act). §10 of the Frame Law on Hospitals and Sanatoria provides that provincial legislators have to introduce laws that oblige hospitals to store patients' records for at least thirty years. A shorter period of ten years may be provided for outpatient records as well as for X-rays and other parts of the patients' records as their evidentiary value does not persist for thirty years.

246. This duty was primarily established in order to facilitate the patient's burden of proof of causation in case of damage, but also to safeguard the therapy and continuity of care and to enable the health care provider to give account. If the health care provider violates these obligations, especially if he does not document which advisory, diagnostic and therapeutic services were rendered or if he fails to submit such documentation before the court, the burden of proof is reversed. Still, these rules only apply to issues that could have been proven more easily if the documents had been brought before the court. In other words, as long as the blameworthy behaviour can be proved without the missing documentation, the failure to provide such evidence has no effect on the burden of proof.[257]

II. The Patient's Right to Access the Medical Records

247. Patients are entitled to inspect their own medical or dental records and to make photocopies at their own expenses or to be provided with copies from the documentation on request in return of an appropriate fee to cover the costs (§51

257. Supreme Court 28 Aug. 1997, 3 Ob 212/96z, *RdM* 1998, 57; 7 Nov. 1995, 4 Ob 554/95, *RdM* 1996, 54, 137 (*Gaisbauer*). For details *see* e.g., M. Kletečka-Pulker, 'Dokumentation und Datenschutz', in *Handbuch Medizinrecht*, ed. G. Aigner et al. (Vienna: Manz, 2003 et seq.), I/155 et seq.; A. Leischner, *Streitbeilegung in medizinischen Haftungsfällen* (Vienna: Manz, 2007), 63 et seq. with further references.

Physicians Act, §19 Dentists Act and §5a No. 1 Frame Law on Hospitals and Sanatoria and in accordance with the medical contract). This right to access medical records covers all documents except exclusive personal documents of the health care provider in which he reflects possible courses of therapy.[258] Only in exceptional cases, in which the knowledge about the documented course of disease would severely affect the patient's well-being, the health care provider may legitimately refuse or restrict the access to the extent unavoidable to safeguard the patient's well-being (Article 19[2] Patients' Charter; compare §39 Hospitalization Act).[259]

III. Access by Next of Kin or Heirs after the Patient's Death

248. There are no provisions regulating whether the next of kin or heirs are allowed to access the patient's medical records after his death. It is generally accepted that access shall be granted if the dead patient has consented explicitly or implicitly before his death. In any other case, the court has to decide whether the dead patient's post-mortem right to privacy and the physician's post-mortem duty of secrecy demand refusal or limited access to the records.[260]

§6. Privacy and Data Protection

249. Patients have the right to protection of their privacy and intimacy concerning any medical service, especially regarding any information provided by the patients themselves and/or acquired during the medical treatment. This right to privacy has to be distinguished from the duty to protect the intimacy of the patient while submitting personal information or receiving medical treatment. In this regard hospitals have to ensure the intimacy of patients who are accommodated in shared sickrooms (§5a[1] No. 7 Frame Law on Hospitals and Sanatoria). Moreover, Article 9 of the Patients' Charter establishes that during admission and medical treatment of several patients in one room, appropriate measures in spatial structure or organization have to be taken in order to safeguard an intimate and private sphere.

250. In this context, privacy is understood as the duty to protect health-related data while it is collected, stored, processed or lawfully transmitted. The right to data protection in the field of health care ensures the patient's right to dispose over all data regarding the personality, namely all health-related information. This right originates from the right to respect for private and family life according to

258. Elucidations to the government bill to 2nd Amendment of the Physicians Act: RV 629 BlgNR 21. GP 37.
259. *See* e.g., G. Aigner, M. Kierein & Ch. Kopetzki (eds), *Ärztegesetz*, 3rd edn (Vienna: Manz, 2007), §51 Note 5, 131; A. Leischner, *Streitbeilegung in medizinischen Haftungsfällen* (Vienna: Manz, 2007), 66 with further references.
260. Supreme Court 23 May 1984, 1 Ob 550/84, *JBl* 1985, 159; 25 May 2000, 1 Ob 341/99z, *RdM* 2001/23.

Article 8(1) of the ECHR and is explicitly guaranteed by the fundamental right to data protection in §1 of the Data Protection Act 2000.[261]

§1(1) of the Data Protection Act states that everybody shall have the right to secrecy concerning his personal data, especially with regard to his private and family life, insofar as he has an interest deserving such protection. Personal data is information related to data subjects who are identified or identifiable (§4 No. 1). Moreover, the Data Protection Act refers to 'sensitive data' or 'data deserving special protection' which encompasses data relating to natural persons concerning their racial or ethnic origin, political opinion, trade-union membership, religious or philosophical beliefs, and data concerning health or sex life. Sensitive data regarding health include information about the person's disease pattern of a past or current treatment, the person's predisposition for an illness, a physical malfunction, mental illness or information about the person's behaviour that directly influences the health state (e.g., abuse of drugs or alcohol) (§4 No. 2).[262] The interest deserving such protection under §1 is precluded when personal data cannot be subject to the right to secrecy due to its general availability or because the data cannot be traced back to the data subject.

Insofar personal data is not used in the vital interest of the data subject or with his consent (and the data subject has an interest worth being protected), restrictions to the right to secrecy are only permitted in order to safeguard overriding legitimate interests of others (§1[2]). In case of an intervention by a public authority, the restriction is only permitted based on laws serving the substantial public interests stated in Article 8(2) ECHR. Regarding the use of sensitive data deserving special protection, such laws must allow the use of such data only in order to safeguard substantial public interests and have to provide suitable safeguards for the protection of the data subjects' interest in secrecy. Even in the case of permitted restrictions the intervention with the fundamental right shall be carried out using only the least intrusive of all effective methods (§1[2]). This right is therefore not granted without reservations, but there are situations in which the individual's right must give way to the common welfare. The fundamental right to data protection (except the right to information according to §26) can be asserted before the civil courts against organizations that are established according to private law, as long as they do not act in execution of laws. In all other cases the Data Protection Authority is competent to render the decision, unless an act of Parliament or a judicial decision is concerned (§5[4]; §§30 et seq.).[263]

---

261. Federal Law Gazette I 1999/165 as last amended by Federal Law Gazette I 2015/132. For an English translation *see* www.ris.bka.gv.at last update 1 Jan. 2017.

262. D. Ennöckl, 'Datenschutzrechtliche Fragen der elektronischen Gesundheitsakte (ELGA)', in *Jahrbuch Gesundheitsrecht 2010*, ed. M. Kierein et al. (Vienna: Neuer Wissenschaftlicher Verlag, 2010), 61 with further references.

263. For a general overview on the fundamental right of data protection *see* A. Lehner, 'Recht auf Datenschutz', in *Handbuch Menschenrechte*, ed. G. Heißl (Vienna: Facultas 2009), 211 et seq.; W. Berka, *Verfassungsrecht* (Vienna: Verlag Österreich, 2014), 474.

251. The Data Protection Act is mainly based on the EU Directive 95/46/EC,[264] which was established in order to harmonize the legal frameworks in EU Member States and to establish a minimum standard in data protection. Further, it ensured that transnational data transfers within the EU were not subject to further national authorizations. However, due to the constant developments in technology and especially the advancement of the World Wide Web, the shortcomings of the framework were brought to the fore. Consequently, the European Commission initiated the revision of the directive which – after intense debates, proposals and amendments – finally resulted in an agreement on the new data protection regulation in 2015. The new so-called General Data Protection Regulation[265] entered into force on 24 May 2016, will replace the former directive and apply from 25 May 2018 on (Article 99 No. 2 of the General Data Protection Regulation). In order to ensure direct applicability in all Member States, the new framework is now a regulation which is legally binding without any implementation of the Member States (according to Article 288[2] of the Treaty on European Union and the Treaty on the Functioning of the European Union, Official Journal C 326, 26 October 2012). However, it shall be noted that the regulation leaves approximately 50 clauses open for further specification by the Member States.[266]

The Austrian Data Protection Act to date stipulates the fundamental right to data protection and determines all basic rules and principles of the Austrian system of data protection. It does not cover all cases in all fields in need of data protection. Other, more precise provisions, can be found in specific material laws and override the Data Protection Act where necessary (as long as they are in conformity with the constitutional provision of §1 of the Data Protection Act). However, if a specific legal framework does not contain any specific provisions concerning the protection of personal data, the general rules and principles apply.

The General Data Protection Regulation will in general not bring major changes to the existing framework. In general, a liberalization of the currently strict principle of purpose (personal data should be collected and processed for specified and explicit purposes only), the numerous clauses open for further specification by the Member States and the facilitation for scientific research purposes, are expected to liberalize data protection in the medical field to some extent.[267]

However, those responsible for data processing (the so-called controller) will face additional duties such as carrying out an assessment of the impact of the envisaged processing operation on the protection of personal data (Article 35), the establishment of a data protection officer (Article 37) and maintaining a record of processing

264. Directive 95/46/EC of the European Parliament and of the Council of 24 Oct. 1995 on the protection of individuals with regard to the processing of personal data and on the free movement of such data.

265. Regulation (EU) 2016/679 of the European Parliament and of the Council of 27 Apr. 2016 on the protection of natural persons with regard to the processing of personal data and on the free movement of such data, and repealing 95/46/EC (General Data Protection Regulation), Official Journal L 119/1.

266. For a detailed examination *see*: D. Ennöckl, 'Die Verarbeitung von personenbezogenen Gesundheitsdaten nach der DSGVO', *RdM* (2017): 67.

267. D. Ennöckl, 'Die Verarbeitung von personenbezogenen Gesundheitsdaten nach der DSGVO', *RdM* (2017): 67 (93).

activities. Further, non-compliance may be subject to high administrative fines up to EUR 20,000,000, or in the case of a corporation, up to 4% of the total worldwide annual turnover of the preceding financial year (Article 83 No. 6). Member States may lay down the rules on whether (and to what extent) administrative fines may be imposed on public authorities and bodies (Article 83 No. 7).[268]

I. The Use of Data

252. The use of data includes all kinds of operations involving data, meaning both the processing of data (collection, recording, storing, sorting, comparing, modification, interlinkage, reproduction, consultation, output, utilization, committing, blocking, erasure, destruction or any other kind of operation with data) as well as the transmission of data (§4 Nos 8, 9 and 12 Data Protection Act). Data application is defined as the sum of logically linked stages of data use, which are organized in order to reach a defined result and which are as a whole or partially performed automatically. In general, every controller[269] has to file a notification to the Data Protection Authority for the purpose of registration in the Data Processing Register before commencing a data application (§17[1]). Regarding the patient's administration and the corresponding invoicing, physicians and dentists as all other health care providers are freed from their duty to notify about their data use (§17[2] No. 6 in conjunction with the annex 1 of the Standard-and Model-Ordinance of the Federal Chancellor, Federal Law Gazette II 312/2004 as last amended by Federal Law Gazette II 2013/514).

253. §6 lays down the guiding principles for the use of data. First and foremost, data may only be used fairly and lawfully (§6[1] No. 1). This applies, if the use of data is compliant with all applicable provisions of the Data Protection Act and other supplementary laws. Further, the data subject must not be misinformed about the circumstances of the data use and his right to data protection and its enforcement.[270] In order to determine the fair and lawful use of data more closely in a specific field, representations of interest established by law, other professional associations and comparable bodies may draw up codes of conduct for the private sector (§6[4]). In this regard, the Austrian Medical (Dental) Chamber is authorized to draw up a code of conduct for the data use of physicians (and dentists) in good faith, but has not made use of this right yet.

---

268. For further details on the implications of the Regulation on health-data-protection, *see*: M. Kastelitz, 'Die Datenschutz-Grundverordnung im Gesundheitsbereich – ein erster Überblick', *JMG* (2016): 71; D. Ennöckl, 'Die Verarbeitung von personenbezogenen Gesundheitsdaten nach der DSGVO' *RdM* (2017): 67; B. Buchner & S. Schwichtenberg, 'Gesundheitsdatenschutz unter der Datenschutz-Grundverordnung', *GuP* (2016): 6.
269. According to §4 No. 4 of the Data Protection Act, 'controller' ('Auftraggeber') is 'a natural person or legal entity, group of persons or organ of a territorial corporate body or the offices of these organs, who decide alone or jointly with others to use data, without regard to whether they use the data by themselves (No. 8) or by a service provider (No. 5) [...]'.
270. Explanatory report to the government bill: ErläutRV 1613 BlgNR 20. GP, 39.

Primarily, data shall only be collected for specific, explicit and legitimate purposes and not further processed in ways incompatible with those purposes. According to §51 of the Physicians Act and §19 in conjunction with §21(4) of the Dentists Act, physicians and dentists are both allowed and obliged to collect data of their patients for treatment and invoicing purposes (also *see* SA024 of the Standard- and Model-Ordinance). Further use for scientific and statistical purposes is permitted by §§46 and 47 of the Data Protection Act (§6[1] No. 2 Data Protection Act; for details *see* the next subchapter II. below).

The collected data may only be used insofar as they are essential for the purpose of the data application and are not excessive in relation to the purpose (§6[1] No. 3). Data shall only be used so that the results are factually correct with regard to the purpose of the application, and the data has to be kept up-to-date when necessary (§6[1] No. 4). Factually correct is to be understood as correctness regarding the specified purpose of the data use.

Finally, the collected data shall only be kept in a form which permits identification of the data subject (here the patient), as long as this is necessary for the purpose for which the data were collected. A longer period of storage may be laid down in specific laws, particularly laws concerning archives (§6[1] No. 5).

Regarding medical records, §51(3) Physicians Act, §19(3) Dentists Act and §10 Frame Law on Hospitals and Sanatoria determine general storage periods (*see* Part II, Chapter 1, §5 above). Thus, the collected data can be stored up to thirty years after the patient's last consultation, except regulated otherwise in accordance with §6(4) Data Protection Act.

254. According to §7(1) of the Data Protection Act, the legitimate use of data requires that the collected data is processed only insofar as the purpose and content of the data application are covered by the statutory competencies or the legitimate authority of the respective controller and that the data subjects' interest in secrecy deserving protection is not infringed. The transmission of data is only legitimate if the transmitted data originate from a legal data application according to §7(1) and the recipient has satisfactorily demonstrated his statutory competence or legitimate authority with regard to the purpose of the transmission to the transmitting party, insofar as it is not beyond doubt (§7[2]). Furthermore, the interests in secrecy of the data subject deserving protection shall not be infringed by the purpose and content of the transmission. The legitimacy of a use of data requires that the intervention is carried out only to the extent required, and using the least intrusive of all effective methods and in respect of the principles laid down in §6 Data Protection Act (§7[3]).[271]

255. The provisions of §51(2) of the Physicians Act and §21(5) of the Dentists Act authorize the attending physician or dentist to electronically collect and process health data necessary for carrying out the medical or dental services, and to transmit

271. For details concerning the legitimate use of data in general *see* R. Knyrim, *Datenschutzrecht* (Vienna: Manz, 2015), 123 et seq.

the required data to the social insurance institution and to other health care providers as far as the patient consents to the transmission for further treatment purposes (also *see* §54[2] and [3] of the Physicians Act).

Moreover, §10(1) of the Frame Law on Hospitals and Sanatoria binds the entities of hospitals to collect the necessary health data of the patient. Legitimately collected data can lawfully be transmitted by hospitals in the following cases (§10[1] No. 4, 4a and 5 of the Frame Law on Hospitals and Sanatoria): to courts or public authorities in case the patient's health state is subject to a decision of public interest; to the respective social insurance institutions or to the organs or appointed expert of the health care funds of the federal state (*Landesgesundheitsfonds*) or the health care providers, as far as essential for the exercise of their functions, who had referred the patient to hospital or treats the patient after the hospital stay; to the patient; to the public authorities competent for the public health care as far as essential to fulfil their functions according to law. Furthermore, the legislators of the federal states may authorize the entities of the hospitals to engage other entities to record, process and store medical records for them, even by means of electronic data processing. This is only possible on condition that the charged entities and their staff have the legal duty to secrecy and that these entities only and exclusively transmit personal data to physicians or hospitals treating the respective patient (§10[5] Frame Law on Hospitals and Sanatoria).

256. The Health Telematics Act (*Gesundheitstelematikgesetz 2012*, Federal Law Gazette I 2012/111 as last amended by Federal Law Gazette I 2017/40) and the Health Telematics Ordinance 2013 (Federal Law Gazette II 2013/506) regulate the electronic exchange of health data and include strict provisions on data security and user authentication.[272] After the introduction of the Austrian E-Card in 2005 and the Health Care Reform in 2005,[273] the federation and the federal states agreed on an e-Health strategy. The long-term goal was the development and implementation of a decentralized electronic health record system, namely the implementation of 'ELGA' (*Elektronische Gesundheitsakte*; Electronic Health Record, in short EHR).[274] In 2012, EHR was implemented through §§13 et seq. of the Health Telematics Act 2012. EHR is an ambitious project, as patient health data shall be communicated undirected in compliance with the necessary security requirements and the system has to be easy to use, effective and search and filter functions have

---

272. An English version of the Health Telematics Act 2012 is available under www.ris.bka.gv.at, 1 May 2017.

273. Article 7 of the Agreement according to Art. 15a of the Federal Constitution on the Organisation and the Financing of the Health Care System, Federal Law Gazette I 2008/105 as amended by Federal Law Gazette I 2013/199.

274. For details on the discussion concerning the implementation of EHR *see* J. Frohner, 'Datenschutz im Gesundheitswesen', in *Handbuch Datenschutzrecht*, ed. L. Bauer & S. Reimer (Vienna: Facultas, 2009), 253 (263 et seq); J. Frohner, 'Die Elektronische Gesundheitsakte (ELGA)', in *Jahrbuch Gesundheitsrecht 2010,* ed. M. Kierein et al. (Vienna: Neuer Wissenschaftlicher Verlag, 2010), 49 et seq. D. Ennöckl, 'Datenschutzrechtliche Fragen der elektronischen Gesundheitsakte (ELGA)', in *Jahrbuch Gesundheitsrecht 2010*, ed. M. Kierein et al. (Vienna: Neuer Wissenschaftlicher Verlag, 2010), 59 et seq.

to be optimized for medical criteria. EHR shall especially help to reduce duplications and errors concerning treatment and medication (also *see* §13[1] Health Telematics Act). Federation, federal states and the Main Association of Austrian Social Security Institutions developed an electronic health record system by the end of 2013 (*see* EHR-Ordinance, Federal Law Gazette II 505/2013 last amended by Federal Law Gazette II 2015/373). Thus, the EHR-health care providers (not only freelance physicians or dentists, hospitals, health care institutions, but also pharmacists, *see* §2 No. 10 Health Telematics Act) are obliged to save EHR-patient data since July 2015 (for details on the transitional provisions *see* §20, §27 et seq. Health Telematics Act and §14[5] EHR-Ordinance in the version of Federal Law Gazette II 505/2013). EHR-patient data is defined as personal data that could be essential for further treatment, care or the assurance of health care continuity of EHR-Participants (§2 No. 9 Health Telematics Act) and which may legally be used in EHR. Such data includes *inter alia* medical records, other medical applications as for example prescriptions, discharge letters, laboratory findings and medication data, patient decree or powers of attorney. EHR-patient data is supposed to remain within the individual EHR-health care provider, but is accessible to other health care providers as well (§2 No. 2 Health Telematics Act) as far as essential for their functions (*see* §21 Health Telematics Act) and the patients themselves (§16[1] No. 1 Health Telematics Act). Access to the patient data shall be granted by the E-Card (§18[4] Health Telematics Act).

Additionally, the Main Association of Austrian Social Security Institutions had to establish (and operate) an information system on prescribed and dispensed medication ('e-Medication') as EHR-application by 31 December 2014. The information system provides an overview on the medication prescribed and dispensed to EHR-participants and EHR-health care providers (§16a Health Telematics Act).

The participation of any health-insured patient (§15[1] Health Telematics Act) in EHR may generally be objected at any time (Opt-out) in accordance with §15(2). Objecting EHR-participants have to indicate, whether this objection relates to all or just certain kinds of EHR-health data. A general objection may be given in writing to the authorities responsible for the opting-out (§2 No. 15 Health Telematics Act) or electronically via the e-Health Access Point (§23 Health Telematics Act), provided, that both the unique identity of the person not willing to participate in EHR and the authenticity of the declaration can be checked. The declaration of objection needs to be confirmed. The authorities responsible for the opting-out are located at the Main Association of Austrian Social Security Institutions (§§3 et seq. EHR-Ordinance).

The Federal Minister of Health has to operate the EHR-Ombudsman on decentralized locations. The purpose of the EHR-Ombudsman is to inform, advise and assist persons concerned in matters of EHR, especially regarding the enforcement of participants' rights (*see* §16 Health Telematics Act) and in matters of data protection (*see* §17 Health Telematics Act and §10 EHR-Ordinance). From the age of fourteen (mature minors) the responsibility for the protection of the participants' rights pursuant to §16 resides exclusively with the EHR-participants (§14[2a] Health Telematics Act).[275]

257. §§50a et seq. of the Data Protection Act (introduced by the amendment in Federal Law Gazette I 2009/133) regulate the use of data collected through video surveillance as a special use of data. Video surveillance means the systematic, most of all continuous observation of occurrences concerning a certain object (observed object) or a certain person (observed person) by technical devices designed to make or transmit images (§50a[1]). §§6 and 7 also apply to video surveillance, especially the principle of proportionality (§7[3]). Lawful purposes for video surveillance, especially analysis and transmission of the data obtained such way, under the reservation of §5, are only the protection of the object or the person observed or the fulfilment of legal duties of diligence, including securing of evidence. Personal rights according to §16 Civil Code remain unaffected. A data subject's interest for secrecy deserving protection (§7[2] No. 3) is not infringed, if the video surveillance is conducted in the vital interest of a person, or data on behaviour are processed which – without any doubt – has been intended to be publicly noticed, or the person has expressly consented to the use of this data in the context of the surveillance operation (§50a[3]). According to §50a(4) video surveillance not made in the performance of official executive tasks may be legal: (1) if certain facts justify the presumption, that the object or person surveyed could become the target or the location of a dangerous attack, or (2) directly applicable legal rules of the international or EU-Law, laws, ordinances, orders or judicial decisions oblige the controller to special duties of diligence for the protection of the object or the person surveyed, or (3) the surveillance is restricted to a mere real time reproduction of occurrences concerning the surveyed object/the surveyed person which, therefore, are neither recorded nor processed in any other way (real time surveillance) and is performed for the purpose of the protection of health, life or property of the controller. If the video surveillance is not made in the performance of official executive tasks according to §50a(4), occurrences at locations that are part of the most personal area of life of a data subject (e.g., toilets) must not be observed (§50a[5]).

Video surveillance is subject to a special duty of documentation and deletion (§50b), an obligation of notification and procedure of registration (§50c), a duty to inform by signs about the video surveillance (§50d) and a right of information (§50e). Laws regulating medical activities do not provide special rules concerning video surveillance in this context, therefore the rules according to §§50a et seq. apply.[276]

---

275. For more details regarding EHR *see* G. Aigner & Leisch, 'ELGA – Die elektronische Gesundheitsakte', *RdM* (2013): 23; Th. Riesz, *Ärztliche Verschwiegenheitspflicht* (Vienna: Manz, 2013), 307 et seq. About the consequences concerning tort law for the EHR-health care providers: S. Perner, 'Ärztliche Nachforschungspflichten und ELGA', *ÖJZ* 2013/123. For further details on the Health Telematics Act *see* L. Stärker, 'Gesundheitstelematikgesetz 2012 – GTelG 2012', in *Gmundner Kommentar zum Gesundheitsrecht*, ed. M. Neumayr, R. Resch & F. Wallner (Vienna, Manz, 2016), 2229.

276. Court decisions on the lawfulness of video surveillance in the context of the (involuntary) hospitalization of mentally ill patients (*see* Part II, Ch. 2, §2): Regional Court of St. Pölten 3 Oct. 2012,

II. Interests Justifying the Use of Sensitive Data

258. §9 of the Data Protection Act emphasizes the circumstances which exclusively legitimize the use of sensitive data without infringing interests in secrecy concerning the subjects' personal data deserving protection. In this context only the most important grounds of justification shall be pointed out.

259. The most important ground of justification for the use of data regarding medical treatments is the patient's unambiguous consent. Consent can be revoked at any time. Consequently, any further use of the data is illegal (§9 No. 6 Data Protection Act). The patient's consent (declaration of intent) is valid if it is given without constraint. It furthermore has to contain the data subject's agreement to the use of data relating to him in a given case after having been informed about the prevalent circumstances (§4 No. 14 Data Protection Act). The Supreme Court has ruled that the data subject's consent has to cover which type of data is given, to whom exactly and for what purpose.[277] Concerning the transmission of the collected and processed health data to other health care providers treating the patient, the requirement of the patient's consent is expressly stipulated in §51(2) No. 2 of the Physicians Act and §21(5) No. 2 of the Dentists Act. In case the attending physician or dentist dies or quits during the regulated storage period and the medical practice is passed on to a successor, the stored medical records may only be used further with the patient's consent (§51[4] and [5] Physicians Act, §19[4] and [5] Dentists Act).

260. In case the data use is in the vital interest of the patient and his consent cannot be obtained in time – which means that the patient is not able to consent and there is not enough time to ask the legal representative of the patient – the data may nevertheless be used lawfully (§9 No. 7 Data Protection Act). Vital interests are the imminent danger to the patient's health or life in case of medical emergency (compare §173[3] and §283[3] Civil Code, §110[2] Criminal Code, §8[3] Frame Law on Hospitals and Sanatoria). Similar rules apply in case the vital interest of a third party demands the use of data (§9 No. 8 Data Protection Act).

261. Moreover, even if there is no consent the right to data protection is not infringed, if a legal obligation or authorization to use the data is stipulated by laws, insofar as these serve important public interests (§9 No. 3 Data Protection Act). As to medical treatments, legal obligations or authorizations to disclose confidential information can for instance be found in the obligation to notification, information and disclosure according to §51(2) No. 1 and §54(2) of the Physicians Act, §21(2) and (5) No. 1 of the Dentists Act and §10(1) No. 4 and 5 and (5) of the Frame Law on Hospitals and Sanatoria. These legal obligations also justify a breach of the duty of confidentiality (for details *see* the next subchapter below).

23 R 415/12w, *iFamZ* 2013/17; Regional Court of St. Pölten 26 Jan. 2011, 23 R 11/11g, *iFamZ* 2011/164; Regional Court of St. Pölten 3 Oct. 2012, 23 R 415/12w, *iFamZ* 2013/13.

277. Supreme Court 27 Oct. 1999, 7 Ob 170/98w.

262. The use of data is lawful in case the data was collected legitimately and the use is necessary for the establishment, exercise or defence of the controller's legal claims before a public authority (§9 No. 9 Data Protection Act). This rule is also implemented in §54(2) No. 4 of the Physicians Act and §21(2) No. 3 of the Dentists Act, which stipulate that confidentiality is not infringed if higher public interests related to public health care and jurisdiction make it indispensable to reveal the confidential data (for details *see* the next subchapter below).

263. Moreover, the use of sensitive data does not infringe secrecy interests deserving protection in those cases in which the data is required for the purposes of preventive medicine, medical diagnosis, provision of health care or treatment or the management of health care services, and in which the use of data is performed by medical personnel or other persons subject to an equivalent duty of secrecy (§9 No. 12 Data Protection Act).

264. The use of health data by the controller for scientific or statistical research projects, which do not aim to obtain results in a form relating to specific data subjects, may be legitimate pursuant to §46(1) of the Data Protection Act, if the data are publicly accessible, if it was collected lawfully or if the data are only used in an indirect personal form. In the latter case, the data relate to the data subject in such a manner, that the controller, processor or recipient cannot establish the identity of the data subject by legal means (§4 No. 1). If the use of data for scientific research or statistics does not fulfil the aforementioned requirements, data may only be used pursuant to specific legal provisions, with the consent of the data subject or with a permit of the Data Protection Authority. A permit of the Data Protection Commission to use data for purposes of scientific research or statistics shall be granted upon request of the controller ordering the research project, if the consent of the data subjects is impossible to obtain because they cannot be reached or the effort would otherwise be unreasonable and there is a public interest in the use of data for which a permit is sought and the professional aptitude of the applicant has satisfactorily been demonstrated. If sensitive data are to be collected, an important public interest in the research must exist. Furthermore, it must be ensured that the data at the controller ordering the research project is only be used by persons who are subject to a statutory duty to confidentiality or whose reliability in this respect is otherwise credible. The Data Protection Authority may issue its permit subject to terms and conditions insofar as this is necessary to safeguard the data subjects' interests deserving protection, in particular, with regard to the use of sensitive data. Special rules apply to the data subject's consent concerning the use of data collected within clinical trials according to §§39 and 43a of the Medicinal Products Act and §§50 and 52a of the Medical Devices Act and within genetic diagnosis according to §§66 and 69 of the Gene Technology Act.[278]

278. A. Höhnel, N. Raschauer & W. Wessely, 'Datenschutzrechtliche Fragestellungen im Zusammenhang mit klinischen Prüfungen', *RdM* (2006): 106; R. Knyrim & V. Haidinger, 'Datenschutzrechts-Compliance in medizinischen Einrichtungen und Pharmaunternehmen', in *Jahrbuch Datenschutzrecht*, ed. D. Jahnel (Vienna: Neuer Wissenschaftlicher Verlag, 2009), 235 (243 et seq.).

Even in those cases, in which the use of data in a form permitting the identification of data subjects is legal for scientific research or statistical purposes, the data shall be encoded without delay, so that the data subjects are no longer identifiable (as long as specific phases of scientific or statistic work can be performed with only indirect personal data). Unless expressly laid down otherwise, data in a form permitting the identification of data subjects shall be rendered unidentifiable as soon as it is no longer necessary to keep them identifiable for scientific or statistic purposes (§46[5] Data Protection Act).[279]

III. Right to Information, Rectification and Erasure

265. §1(3) of the Data Protection Act establishes as a fundamental right that everybody shall have, insofar as personal data concerning him are destined for automated processing or manual processing, i.e., in filing systems without automated processing, as provided for by law, (1) the right to obtain information as to who processes which data concerning him, where the data originated from, for which purpose they are used, as well as to whom the data are transmitted; (2) the right to rectification of incorrect data and the right to erasure of illegally processed data. Restrictions of these rights are only permitted under the conditions laid out in §1(2).[280]

On that account, §51(2) of the Physicians Act and §21(4) of the Dentists Act stipulate that the patient has the right to information and rectification of incorrect data and the right to erasure of illegally processed data.

§7. Confidentiality

266. Medical confidentiality can be qualified as the counterpart to the patient's right to privacy and data protection. The constitutional basis for medical confidentiality is the fundamental right to determine the use of one's personal, especially medical data. This right originates from the right to respect for private life as stated in Article 8(1) of the ECHR and the right to data protection according to §1 of the Data Protection Act. The Austrian legislator enacted several provisions in criminal, civil, administrative and labour law in order to ensure that no health care provider or other staff members working in hospital or freelance passes on any confidential

279. V. Sorger, 'Verwendung von Gesundheitsdaten im Lichte der §§46, 47 DSG 2000', in *Jahrbuch Datenschutzrecht*, ed. D. Jahnel (Vienna: Neuer Wissenschaftlicher Verlag, 2010), 193 et seq.; R. Knyrim & V. Haidinger, 'Datenschutzrechts-Compliance in medizinischen Einrichtungen und Pharmaunternehmen', in *Jahrbuch Datenschutzrecht,* ed. D. Jahnel (Vienna: Neuer Wissenschaftlicher Verlag, 2009), 235 (244 and 248 et seq.); H. Schwamberger, 'Einige gesundheitsrechtlich relevante Aspekte des Datenschutzgesetzes 2000', *RdM* (1999): 131 (133 et seq.). For an overview *see* M. Suda, 'Datenverwendung für wissenschaftliche Forschung und Statistik', in *Handbuch Datenschutzrecht*, ed. L. Bauer & S. Reimer (Vienna: Facultas, 2009), 293 et seq.; R. Knyrim, *Datenschutzrecht* (Vienna: Manz, 2015), 408 et seq.

280. *See* for further details, A. Lehner, 'Recht auf Datenschutz', in *Handbuch Menschenrechte*, ed. G. Heißl (Vienna: Facultas, 2009), 211 (223 et seq.) R. Knyrim, *Datenschutzrecht* (Vienna: Manz, 2015), 30 et seq.

information revealed by the patient himself or emerged in another way in the course of medical treatment to anybody who should not have this information. This confidentiality is an essential accessory contractual obligation of the medical contract. However, medical confidentiality is not limited to physicians or dentists who have a contractual relationship with the patient, but also applies to persons who only assist the attending physician or dentist. Moreover, medical confidentiality encompasses any personal information revealed in preliminary talks without a subsequent conclusion of a medical contract.

I. The Physician's Duty of Confidentiality

267. According to §54(1) of the Physicians Act, physicians and their auxiliary staff are bound by professional confidentiality in all matters that have been confided to them or have otherwise become known to them in their professional capacity, as far as confidentiality is in the interest of their patients. Secrets or confidential information are defined as facts that are only known by the person himself or to a certain definable group of people, who has a reasonable interest in the non-exposure of these facts beyond that group of people. Similar rules apply to dentists according to §21 of the Dentists Act and to other health care providers (e.g., §7 Nursing to Patients Act, §6 Paramedics Act).

268. In addition to the professional duty of confidentiality, many laws regulating specific medical fields and activities lay down confidentiality obligations (*see* e.g., §18 Human Tissue Safety Act; §13 Blood Safety Act; §10[5] Act on the Protection of Personal Freedom of Home Residents; §12 Tuberculosis Act). A subsidiary legal obligation to secrecy is also established for the staff of hospitals, the members of training committees (§8[4]) and for the members of ethic committees (§8c) (§9[1] of the Frame Law on Hospitals and Sanatoria). Its aim is to impose a duty of confidentiality on all members of hospitals who are not obliged to confidentiality by other regulations. This subsidiary obligation particularly concerns medical students working as medical trainees in hospitals. Whereas the professional confidentiality pursuant to §54(1) of the Physicians Act covers all secrets, the obligation to secrecy according to the Frame Law on Hospitals and Sanatoria relates to all facts concerning the patient's health state and the patient's private, economic and other affairs that become known in their capacity as hospital staff members. In case of an organ donation, the donor and the recipient are covered by the duty of confidentiality as well.[281]

281. For details *see* e.g., M. Kletečka-Pulker, 'Schweige-, Anzeige- und Meldepflichten', in *Handbuch Medizinrecht*, ed. G. Aigner et al. (Vienna: Manz, 2003 et seq.), I/191 et seq. and, with further references, A. Leischner, *Streitbeilegung in medizinischen Haftungsfällen* (Vienna: Manz, 2007), 66 et seq.; B. Krauskopf, *Die ärztliche Anzeige- und Meldepflicht* (Vienna: Jan Sramek Verlag, 2011), 43 et seq.; F. Wallner, 'Grenzen der Verschwiegenheitspflicht der Gesundheitsberufe', *RdM* (2013): 164; Th. Riesz, *Ärztliche Verschwiegenheitspflicht* (Vienna: Manz, 2013), 29 et seq.; F. Wallner, 'Berufsgeheimnis', in *Handbuch Medizinrecht,* ed. R. Resch & F. Wallner, 2nd edn (Vienna: LexisNexis, 2015), 769 et seq.

II. Exceptions

269. §54(2) of the Physicians Act contains several exceptions to the duty of professional confidentiality in accordance with Article 8(2) ECHR. The physician does not commit a disciplinary or professional offence, if he or his staffs disclose confidential information in the following cases.

A. *Discharge of the Duty of Confidentiality*

270. According to §54(2) No. 3 of the Physicians Act, physicians can be released from their confidentiality obligation through the expressed or implicit, oral or written consent of the patient whose secrets are in question. Implicit release means that the patient shows by his behaviour without leaving any doubt that he agrees with the disclosure of confident information to a third party or with a testimony in court. A valid discharge of the duty of secrecy requires the patient's capacity to consent and a free and well-considered declaration of will that is not initiated by error, fraud, deception or physical or mental pressure (§869 et seq. Civil Code).

271. It is generally accepted that the presumable consent legitimizes the physician in exceptional cases to reveal personal information to the next of kin, provided that the patient is no longer or temporarily not able to consent to the disclosure of information and has not refused such disclosure beforehand.

272. Regarding the demonstration of patients for clinical teaching purposes at university hospitals or other teaching hospitals, §44 of the Frame Law on Hospitals and Sanatoria regulates that only patients, who consent to the disclosure of confident information for teaching purposes and whose health state is not endangered by the patient's demonstration, can be used for such purposes. Even so, patient's demonstrations are permitted in case the patients do not have the capacity to consent any more as long as it has not been refused beforehand.

273. There are no provisions regulating whether the duty to secrecy ceases after the death of the patient. The prevailing doctrine shares the opinion that the confidentiality obligation does not cease automatically. However, information may be disclosed if the dead patient has consented explicitly or implicitly prior to his death. Disclosure may also be legitimate, if the patient has not mentioned it explicitly, but acted in a way that implies that he would have consented. The physician has to evaluate faithfully the hypothetical will of the individual patient regarding the behaviour of the patient before his death.[282] In case of doubt, the confidentiality obligation overweighs the interests of the next of kin or heirs. The court has to decide whether the post-mortem right to privacy of the dead patient and the physician's post-mortem confidentiality obligation demand to refuse or to limit the

282. *See* M. Leitner, '§54 ÄrzteG', in *Ärztegesetz mit Kommentar*, ed. H. Emberger & F. Wallner, 2nd edn (Vienna: Verlagshaus der Ärzte, 2008), 261 et seq.

revelation of personal information.[283] The administrator of the inheritance is not allowed to release the physicians of their duty to confidentiality in an inheritance dispute.[284]

B. *Legal Obligation to Disclose Confidential Information*

274. In certain circumstances the law requires to disclose certain information about a patient without consent and even in view of a refusal (§54[2] No. 1 Physicians Act). The most important cases, in which a notification or report to competent authorities is compulsory, are regulated in §54(4) and (5) of the Physicians Act and in special laws on prophylaxis of epidemic diseases. Other cases, in which the duty of confidentiality is abandoned by law are for example §24a-c(1) of the Act on Addictive Drugs, §9(1) and §28(1) of the Act on the Civil Status of People 2013, §49 of the Act on the Protection of Employees, and other professional and administrative laws, cannot be dealt with here.[285]

1. Obligation to Notify and Report Criminal Acts

275. §54(4) of the Physicians Act stipulates that the physician is obliged to immediately report to the competent security authorities if he suspects that a death or a severe bodily harm of a patient may give rise for prosecution. In case a physician suspects that an adult has been ill-treated, tortured, neglected or sexually abused, the physician is allowed to notify the competent security authorities, on condition that the patient cannot exercise his interests himself. If this is the case for a child, the physician has the duty to notify the competent authorities. Special rules concerning the notification of criminal acts are stipulated for cases in which a physician suspects that a child or an adolescent has been ill-treated, tortured, neglected or sexually abused or its well-being has in other ways seriously been endangered. Under these circumstances, the physician (or the hospital) has to inform the competent security authorities and the youth welfare authorities immediately. However, if a next of kin is under suspicion, the notification can be postponed as long as it is necessary to safeguard the child's well-being and for the collaboration with the youth welfare authorities (§54[5] and [6] Physicians Act and §37 Federal Law on Child- and Youth-Welfare 2013, Federal Law Gazette I 2013/69). It shall be noted that all other health care professions regulated by law are also obliged to report their

283. Supreme Court 25 May 1984, 1 Ob 550/84, *JBl* 1985, 159.
284. Supreme Court 25 May 2000, 1 Ob 341/99z, *RdM* 2001/23.
285. For a general overview concerning all legal obligations to disclose confidential information *see* e.g., M. Kletečka-Pulker, 'Schweige-, Anzeige- und Meldepflichten', in *Handbuch Medizinrecht*, ed. G. Aigner et al. (Vienna: Manz, 2003 et seq.), I/211 et seq.; B. Krauskopf, *Die ärztliche Anzeige- und Meldepflicht* (Vienna: Jan Sramek Verlag, 2011), 99 et seq.; Th. Riesz, *Ärztliche Verschwiegenheitspflicht* (Vienna: Manz, 2013), 114 et seq.; F. Wallner, 'Ärztliche Meldepflichten', in *Handbuch Medizinrecht*, ed. R. Resch/F. Wallner (Vienna: LexisNexis, 2015), 780 et seq.; F. Wallner, 'Grenzen der Verschwiegenheitspflicht der Gesundheitsberufe' *RdM* (2013): 106.

suspicions to the youth welfare authorities according to §37 Federal Law on Child- and Youth-Welfare 2013.[286] Additionally, some professional laws regulate a notification duty to the competent security authorities (e.g., §8 Nursing of Patients Act).

276. Moreover, physicians are obliged to report imminent or committed crimes by intent that they have witnessed to the competent authorities according to the general rule of §286 of the Criminal Code. Under these circumstances, the duty of secrecy only overweighs if the caused harm of the committed or imminent crime is not severe.

2. Obligation to Report Notifiable Communicable Diseases

277. In order to prevent the increase and the circulation of certain communicable diseases among the population, several laws oblige the attending physician to report cases of notifiable diseases. This duty to report varies from law to law, particularly as to when a case shall be reported and which data shall be submitted to whom. Notifiable diseases are tuberculosis (§1 Tuberculosis Code)[287] and diseases enumerated in §1(1) of the Epidemic Code[288] and its ordinance, venereal diseases (§1 Venereal Disease Code)[289] and Aids (§2 Aids Code).[290] The most extensive duty to report is stipulated for epidemic diseases and tuberculosis. Diseases enumerated in §1(1) No. 2 of the Epidemic Code are for example diphtheria, malaria or rubella. The Minister of Health can establish further notification duties for newly arising epidemic diseases by ordinance, for instance in the case of swine influenza in 2009 (Federal Law Gazette II 2009/123). Concerning these diseases a notification of any confirmed or fatal case is compulsory (§2 Epidemic Code and §2 Tuberculosis Code). Regarding the diseases enumerated in §1(1) No. 1 of the Epidemic Code, such as cholera, yellow fever, infectious hepatitis and polio, a notification is already required when the disease is merely suspected. According to §4(1) of the Venereal Disease Code, a notification to the competent authorities is only requested in cases in which the patient does not cooperate with the treatment or a circulation of the disease is suspected. In contrast, no notification duty is established in case of HIV-infections. Only after the outbreak of the aids disease a very limited notification is compulsory for statistical purposes (§3 Aids Code).

286. Further details on confidentiality obligations in criminal proceedings regarding the Federal Law on Child- and Youth-Welfare 2013 *see* C. Burianek, 'B-KJHG 2013: Verschwiegenheitspflicht im Strafverfahren. Ausnahmen bei Auskunftsersuchen der Staatsanwaltschaften und Gerichte', *iFamZ* (2013): 128.

287. *Tuberkulosegesetz*, Federal Law Gazette I 1968/127 as last amended by Federal Law Gazette I 2016/63.

288. *Epidemiegesetz*, Federal Law Gazette 1950/186 as last amended by Federal Law Gazette I 2016/63.

289. *Geschlechtskrankheitengesetz*, State Law Gazette 1945/152 as last amended by Federal Law Gazette I 2001/98.

290. *Aids-Gesetz*, Federal Law Gazette 1993/728 (WV) as last amended by Federal Law Gazette I 2001/98.

C. *Notification to Social Insurance Institutions*

278. §54(2) No. 2 of the Physicians Act stipulates that physicians can legitimately pass on medical reports or findings to the social insurance institutions or to other end-payers for their bill of treatment or medication costs. Personal data shall be only submitted to the extent necessary for this purpose.

D. *Significant Public Interests*

279. §54(2) No. 4 of the Physicians Act stipulates that confidentiality is not infringed if higher public interests regarding public health care and jurisdiction make it indispensable to reveal the confidential information. It has to be decided case-by-case whether and to which extent a disclosure is indispensable in order to safeguard legitimate interests.

280. In case a physician is claimed for damages or is accused of a crime, professional confidentiality is not binding within very strict limits when he is defending himself.[291]

When a physician is summoned to testify in court, the physician may have the right to decline to provide evidence. In general, witnesses have to tell the truth and are not allowed to leave out any information that is known to them. This duty conflicts with the professional confidentiality. Therefore, the procedural laws provide exceptions to the duty to give evidence. In this case, it has to be distinguished between proceedings where the interests of the parties are at the fore and proceedings where the public interests of jurisdiction are at the fore.

In civil proceedings (where the interests of the parties are at the fore), a testifying physician may legitimately refuse to testify confidential information, if the patient did not release him from the professional obligation to confidentiality or has not disclosed the information himself. However, the physician has to testify in areas in which no confidential information is revealed (§321 No. 3 Civil Procedure Act, Reich Law Gazette 1895/113 as last amended by Federal Law Gazette I 2017/59). Thus, §321 of the Civil Procedure Act does not contain a general right to refuse to provide evidence. For example, when a patient claims an information deficit, the testifying physician has to give (at least general) information about the circumstances of the information disclosure as long as no confidential information is revealed against the patient's consent.[292]

In proceedings in which the public interests of jurisdiction are to the fore (e.g., proceedings concerning the custodianship or guardianship), the testifying physician

291. For example Administrative Court 13 Nov. 1981, 81/02/0252, VwSlg 10590 A/1981 = AnwBl 1985/2288, 398 = *ÖJZ* 1982/383 A (VwGH A); 16 Sep. 1986, 85/14/0007, *JBl* 1987, 336; 15 Oct. 1987, 87/02/0080, 0153, AnwBl 1988/2850; 19 Feb. 1992, 91/14/0216, AnwBl 1992/5, 405. Also *see* Supreme Court 25 Apr. 2012, 7 Ob 50/12x, *RdM-LS* 2012/50.

292. Supreme Court 23 Nov. 1999, 1 Ob 254/99f, *RdM* 2000/11.

has to disclose all information necessary to safeguard the public interests (e.g., in case the care of a child or person with mental disabilities or a mental illness is in question). Therefore, in these cases the duty to provide evidence outweighs the duty of confidentiality.[293] Similar rules apply to administrative or financial proceedings. In criminal proceedings, a physician does not have the right to refuse testimony (unless the physician is a psychiatrist), although confidential information shall only be disclosed as far as it is indispensable for procedural purposes (§157 Criminal Procedure Act).[294] A testimonial privilege applies besides psychiatrists also to psychologists, psychotherapists and certain other professionals (§157 No. 3).[295]

281. A limited disclosure of confidential information without the patient's consent is also legitimate in case it serves higher public health care interests, particularly for purposes of prophylaxis of communicable diseases (certain transmissible diseases according to special laws, *see* above) and for health statistics.

On equal terms with higher public health care interests, the Supreme Court ruled that under certain circumstances, a disclosure of secrets to public authorities by the attending physicians could be legitimate. In the case at issue, the attending physicians treated a man in hospital because of alcohol abuse. In the course of treatment they had learned that the man was working as an ambulance driver and had already committed several crimes under the influence of alcohol. The physicians informed the public authorities after they had unsuccessfully tried to convince him to undergo a treatment. Subsequently, the public authorities revoked the man's driving license. Due to the extraordinary circumstances of the case the Supreme Court decided that the physicians had not breached their confidentiality, since this had served the higher public interests to safeguard the life and health of other traffics.[296] Some legal authors argued that the same principle shall apply in the case where an HIV-positive patient refuses to inform the sex partner about the infection although repeatedly being informed about the risk of transmission to the sex partner and possible consequences in criminal law (§§178, 179 Criminal Code). In the case in which both sex partners are patients of the attending physician, it is generally accepted that the physician is, in the face of the HIV-positive patient's refusal, not only allowed to tell the other sex partner about the infection, but also has the (contractual) duty to inform the patient in order to safeguard the patient's health (in accordance with §49[1] of the Physicians Act which stipulates that the physician is also obliged to safeguard the health of his healthy patients).[297]

293. Supreme Court 28 Oct. 1997, 1 Ob 310/97p, *RdM* 1998/12.
294. Federal Law Gazette 1975/631 as last amended by Federal Law Gazette I 2016/121. *See* Supreme Court 6 Nov. 1996, 13 Os 110, 111/96, *RZ* 1997/37.
295. For details *see* M. Leitner, '§54 ÄrzteG', in *Ärztegesetz mit Kommentar*, ed. H. Emberger & F. Wallner, 2nd edn (Vienna: Verlagshaus der Ärzte, 2008), 265 et seq.; M. Kletečka-Pulker, 'Schweige-, Anzeige- und Meldepflichten', in *Handbuch Medizinrecht*, ed. G. Aigner et al. (Vienna: Manz, 2003 et seq.), I/237 et seq.
296. Supreme Court 12 Dec. 2002, 6 Ob 267/02m, *RdM* 2003/63.
297. *See* Order issued by the Federal Chancellery of the 2 Dec. 1987, 'Infektionsquellenforschung im Rahmen von HIV-Untersuchungen', GZ 61.700/90-VI/13b/87.

III. Sanctions

282. According to §121(1) of the Criminal Code, anyone shall be sentenced to prison up to six months or can be fined, who intentionally reveals or processes a secret concerning the health state of a person that was confided to him or emerged to him in another way in his function as the professional patient's health care provider or as staff member of the hospital administration or any other health care provider according to §2 No. 2 Health Telematics Act 2012 (Federal Law Gazette I 2012/111 as amended by Federal Law Gazette I 2017/40), provided that the revelation or use of the patient's private data is capable of harming his legitimate interests. This rule is also applicable for experts appointed by court or another administrative authority for specific proceedings according to §121(3) and, for auxiliary staff and persons who are trained on the job by those persons named in paragraphs 1 (§121[4]). A violation of §121 of the Criminal Code may only be prosecuted upon request of the victim himself (§121[6]).

The revelation or use of private data can be justified by legitimate private or public interests according to §121(5) of the Criminal Code. These interests justifying the intrusion of the private sphere are broader than the grounds of justification according to §54 of the Physicians Act. For that reason and due to the fact that criminal prosecution is limited to cases regarding the patient's health state, even though no criminal law sanctions may occur, a fine may be imposed on the physician as well as/or a disciplinary punishment is possible in accordance with the Physicians Act.

283. The patient whose private sphere is infringed, may also claim for material damages according to §1328a of the Civil Code. Material damages may be granted on condition that the harm is caused by negligence through the revelation or use of the patient's secret data. If the infringement of the patient's privacy amounts to a considerable invasion of the person's privacy, even immaterial damages may be awarded.

§8. Complaints

I. General Remarks

284. The patients' advocacies (patients' representations) and the arbitration boards, which are mostly located at the seat of the medical chambers of the federal state (*Landesärztekammer*), are the main institutions dealing with complaints from patients concerning their treatment and providing a first forum for resolving disputes arising from or in the course of treatment. Besides these institutions, most hospitals have established local Hospital Ombudsmen in order to help patients to enforce their rights and to resolve interpersonal disputes.[298]

298. For an English summary *see* G. Bachinger, 'The System of the Patient Advocacies in Austria', www.patientenanwalt.com, 28 Feb. 2014; B. Koch & H. Koziol, 'Compensation in the Austrian Health Care Sector', in *No-Fault Compensation in the Health care Sector*, ed. J. Dute, M.G. Faure

II. Patients' Representations

285. Since the early 1990s, each federal state has established a centrally operated patients' representation (*Patientenanwaltschaft* or *Patientenvertretung*). The legal prerequisites for the establishment of these institutions can be found in §11e of the Frame Law on Hospitals and Sanatoria, which is effectuated by the hospital laws of each federal state. As the federation only has the authority to outline basic principles, the patients' representations of the federal states differ in organization, structure and scope of functions. The patients' representations are not bound to directives in the course of their functions. Their functions are mainly restricted to complaints from hospital patients, but most patients' representations also offer help in disputes between freelance physicians or other health care providers and patients, and/or between nursing homes and their residents. All patients' representations are independent bodies established for the entire territory of a federal state and are arranged to represent the interests of the patients and to deal with complaints from patients or their relatives (also *see* Articles 29 et seq. Patients' Charta). The service of patients' advocacies is free of charge. Neither the patient nor the relative who puts the complaint forward has to cover for any costs incurred through the investigation or the representation of his interests. If a complaining patient seems to be entitled to damages on the merits, the patients' representatives also offer to negotiate directly with the respective private insurance company of the claimed physician or the entity of the respective hospital in order to settle the dispute out of court.

Additionally to the patients' representations, in some federal states ombudsmen are established which are not regulated by law and are bound to directives. To give an example, the Medical Chamber of Vienna has established a patients' ombudsman in 2013. The patients' ombudsman shall also offer help with complaints from patients or their relatives about physicians (also about freelance physicians), and shall give suggestions and recommendations on determinations of cases of maladministration especially towards the organs of the Medical Chambers. The insured patients elect the patients' ombudsman for a period of five years.

286. The patients' representations have to be distinguished from the patients' advocates (*Patientenanwaltschaft*), although they have the same name in German. These patients' advocates are exclusively representing and supporting patients who are involuntary hospitalized in psychiatric institutions or departments in order to assert their right to personal freedom (according to the Hospitalization Act, for details *see* below). To support and represent residents of homes and nursing or care facilities and hospitalized patients asserting their right to personal freedom, since 2005 residents' representatives (*Bewohnervertreter*) according to the Act on the Protection of the Personal Freedom of Residents of Homes and other Nursing and Care Facilities have been established (for details *see* below).

& H. Koziol (Vienna: Springer, 2004), 92 et seq. For details and further references *see* A. Leischner, *Streitbeilegung in medizinischen Haftungsfällen* (Vienna: Manz, 2007), 166 et seq.; B. Jahn, *Außergerichtliche Konfliktlösung im Gesundheitswesen* (Vienna: Manz, 2009), 16 et seq.; G. Bachinger, 'Außergerichtliche Streitbeilegung', in *Handbuch Medizinrecht,* ed. G. Aigner et al. (Vienna: Manz, 2003 et seq.), II/51 et seq.; M. Leitner, 'Spezielles Schlichtungsrecht', in *Handbuch Medizinrecht,* ed. R. Resch & F. Wallner, 2nd edn (Vienna: LexisNexis, 2015), 293–299.

III. Arbitration Boards of the Medical Chambers of the Federal States

287. Since the late 1980s, arbitration boards have been established by most Medical Chambers of the federal states (according to §66a[1] No. 6 Physicians Act) in order to safeguard and enhance the common professional, social and economic interests of physicians and to ensure the protection of the professional honour and the professional duties of physicians (§66[1] Physicians Act). Their main task is the extrajudicial settlement of disputes. Complaints of patients or relatives arising from or in the course of medical treatment can therefore also be addressed to the arbitration boards with a request for an extrajudicial settlement of disputes between the patient and the physician or the entity of the hospital. These arbitration boards are mostly located at the seat of the regional Medical Chamber, which also covers their costs.

288. Additionally, arbitration boards competent for disputes between dentists and patients have been established (§53 Dentists Chamber Act).

IV. Patient Compensation Funds

289. Liability arising from medical treatment is based – with rare exceptions[299] – on fault. Therefore, patient compensation funds have been established as an 'additional possibility' of extrajudicial dispute settlement for cases in which harmed patients complain, but legal proceedings are not considered advisable (although possible). After the successful establishment and operation of the Viennese compensation fund for public hospitals, the federation initiated the nationwide creation of similar patient compensation funds in 2001 (§27a[5]–[6] Frame Law on Hospitals and Sanatoria). These patient compensation funds are supposed to provide an (at least partial) compensation, first, for caused damage in those cases in which the liability of the legal entity of a hospital cannot definitely be proven according to tort (§§1293 et seq. Civil Code) and, second, in those cases in which the legal entity of a hospital is not liable, but a serious damage is caused by a rare, but fatal complication. The contributions for the compensation funds are provided by the in-patients themselves as a shared risk community. Generally spoken, every in-patient of a public or private non-profit hospital pays an amount of EUR 0.73 per day, up to a maximum of twenty-eight days per year (§27a[5] Frame Law on Hospitals and Sanatoria). In cases of poverty exceptions to this payment obligation are made. In the meantime these funds have been established in all federal states. As the federation also in this context only has the authority to outline basic principles, the

299. For example liability without fault is regulated for cases in which harm is caused in the course of certain vaccination campaigns according to the Vaccination Damage Act (*Impfschadengesetz*) or harm is caused by some defective apparatus, medication or by a unit of stored blood according to the Act on Product Liability (*Produkthaftungsgesetz*): B. Koch & H. Koziol, 'Compensation in the Austrian Health Care Sector', in *No-Fault Compensation in the Health care Sector*, ed. J. Dute, M.G. Faure & H. Koziol (Vienna: Springer, 2004), 91 et seq.

regional funds differ in their organization, structure and the rules concerning the award of compensation, which is strongly criticized by legal authors.[300]

290. In 2006, an additional shared risk fund (*Solidarfonds*) was established at the Austrian Medical Chamber. This fund shall provide (at least partial) compensation for damages culpably caused by freelance physicians including members of group practices, provided that there is no chance for the patient to receive an equivalent compensation within a reasonable time, especially from the professional liability insurance of the physician (§118[1] Physicians Act). The main difference to other compensation funds is that all freelance physicians have to pay a contribution to this shared risk community.[301]

300. E. Bernat, 'Der von der Haftung des Krankenanstaltenträgers losgelöste Ersatz des Patientenschadens nach §27a Abs 6 KAKuG', *MedR* (2004): 310; W. Kossak, 'Der Entschädigungsfonds gem §27a Abs 5 und Abs 6 Krankenanstaltengesetz', *RdM* (2002): 110; E. Pitzl & G. W. Huber, 'Verschuldensunabhängige Patientenentschädigung', *RdM* (2003): 100; A. Leischner, *Streitbeilegung in medizinischen Haftungsfällen* (Vienna: Manz, 2007), 184 et seq.; B. Jahn, *Außergerichtliche Konfliktlösung im Gesundheitswesen* (Vienna: Manz, 2009), 133 et seq.; H. Barta, M. Ganner & H. Lichtmannegger (eds), *Patientenentschädigungsfonds oder Medizinhaftung* (Innsbruck: Innsbruck University Press, 2009).
301. Constitutional Court, 10 Oct. 2007, G 187/06 10.

Chapter 2. The Physician-Patient Relationship in Specific Terms

§1. The Minor Patient

291. A person who has not reached the age of eighteen is a minor and is specially protected by law (§21 Civil Code). Minors lack legal capacity to contract so that they are generally not able to contract (§170[1] Civil Code as amended by Federal Law Gazette I 2013/15, former §151 Civil Code). Therefore the medical contract is generally concluded by the parents or another guardian on behalf of the minor patient (§881 Civil Code). In case the minor patient has reached the age of fourteen and has an own constant income and is thus state-insured, the medical contract may be validly concluded between the health care provider and the minor patient (§170[2] Civil Code as amended by Federal Law Gazette I 2013/15, former §151 Civil Code). Whether a minor patient has the capacity to contract or not depends on the amount of the doctor's fee owed by the patient (§865 Civil Code).

292. The legal capacity to contract has to be distinguished from the capacity to consent. If a minor patient possesses the necessary ability to insight and judgment as well as the reasonable willingness to determine whether to consent to or refuse the medical intervention in question, only the consent can legitimize the medical treatment. Capacity to consent is refutably presumed by law as soon as the minor reaches the age of fourteen (§173[1] Civil Code as amended by Federal Law Gazette I 2013/15, former §146c Civil Code). Before this age, minors are refutably presumed not to be able to understand and judge. The attending physician has to assess whether the minor patient has the capacity to consent. In case of doubt, the physician has to consult a psychiatrist for a second opinion or may initiate a court's decision on the minor's ability to insight and judgment (§175 Civil Code as amended by Federal Law Gazette I 2013/15, former §154b Civil Code).[302]

293. In case the minor is competent, the medical decision is generally decisive for the justification of the commencement or continuation of the medical treatment in question. Therefore, competent minors have the possibility to validly refuse a planned medical treatment in the concrete situation as well as a beforehand specified one in form of a binding or considerable living will (§3 Living Will Act; *see* Part II, Chapter 1, §3.VII. above).[303]

There is one exception to this rule: in case the medical intervention in question seriously or lastingly impacts the patient's health or personality (e.g., medication with psychotropic drugs or other more serious surgeries), the medical treatment requires the consent of the competent minor and of one of the parents (§173[2] Civil Code as amended by Federal Law Gazette I 2013/15, former §146c[2] Civil Code).

302. *See* J. Stabentheiner, '§§146c, 146d', in *Kommentar zum Allgemeinen bürgerlichen Gesetzbuch*, ed. P. Rummel, 3rd edn (Vienna: Manz, 2003), marginal number 4 with further references; P. Barth, '§146c', in *ABGB*, ed. A. Fenyves, F. Kerschner & A. Vonkilch, 3rd edn (Vienna: Verlag Österreich, 2008), marginal number 18 et seq.

303. P. Barth, '§146c', in *ABGB*, ed. A. Fenyves, F. Kerschner & A. Vonkilch, 3rd edn (Vienna: Verlag Österreich, 2008), marginal number 52 et seq.

Additionally, a competent minor patient of a minimum age of sixteen is only allowed to undergo a cosmetic treatment or plastic surgery (in the meaning of a medical treatment without any medical indication) if both, one of the parents and the competent patient, have consented in written form and all prerequisites laid down by §7 of the Act on Aesthetic Treatments and Surgery (Federal Law Gazette I 2012/80) are fulfilled. In short: the minor patient and the parent have to receive detailed information on the planned treatment, the child has to pass a psychiatric test and the appropriate waiting period between consent and commencement of the treatment of four weeks must be elapsed.

If the parent and the competent minor are not of the same opinion, the attending physician can initiate a court's decision in order to determine whether the parent entitled to custody is misusing custody by refusing to consent. If this is the case, the parent can either be divested of custody regarding the medical treatment in question, or the consent can be replaced by court (§181 Civil Code as last amended by Federal Law Gazette I 2017/59, former §176 Civil Code).[304]

294. In case the minor patient is not able to consent, generally one of the parents entitled to custody has to decide about the treatment in question (§173[1] in conjunction with §167[1] Civil Code as amended by Federal Law Gazette I 2013/15, §8[3] Frame Law on Hospitals and Sanatoria). Even a very serious medical treatment only requires one parent's consent in order to be legally valid (§167[1] Civil Code). On the contrary, in case another guardian than the parents, grandparents, foster parents or the youth welfare authority (§204 and §210[1] Civil Code as amended by Federal Law Gazette I 2013/15) is the asserting authority over the minor patient and when a serious medical treatment is in question, this guardian's consent additionally requires a medical certificate by an independent physician stating that the child is not capable of consenting and that the medical intervention is necessary for the child's (objective) well-being. In the absence of such a medical certificate or if the child's behaviour shows disapproval of the medical intervention, the legal representative has to obtain the court's approval (§213[2] Civil Code as amended by Federal Law Gazette I 2013/15).

The medical decision of the child's parent or another guardian has to serve the objective well-being of the child (§§138, 160 Civil Code as amended by Federal Law Gazette I 2013/15). As long as the well-being of the child is maintained, the will of the child shall be considered in the course of medical decisions (§160[3] Civil Code). If the parent misuses his authority by denying a necessary medical intervention, the court can divest him of his authority or may consent to the medical treatment in question instead (§181[1] Civil Code as amended by Federal Law Gazette I 2013/15).[305]

304. P. Barth, '§146c', in *ABGB,* ed. A. Fenyves, F. Kerschner & A. Vonkilch, 3rd edn (Vienna: Verlag Österreich, 2008), marginal number 26 et seq.; J. Stabentheiner, '§§146c, 146d', in *Kommentar zum Allgemeinen bürgerlichen Gesetzbuch,* ed. P. Rummel 3rd edn (Vienna: Manz, 2003), marginal number 6 et seq.; P. Barth, 'Minderjährige Patienten im Konflikt mit ihren Eltern', *ÖJZ* (2002): 596 et seq.

305. P. Barth, '§146c', in *ABGB*, ed. A. Fenyves, F. Kerschner & A. Vonkilch, 3rd edn (Vienna: Verlag Österreich, 2008), marginal number 36 et seq.; P. Barth, 'Minderjährige Patienten im Konflikt mit ihren Eltern', *ÖJZ* (2002): 596 et seq.

295. In case of emergency, the physician may treat the minor patient without asking for the consent of the competent child or approval of the guardian (§173[3] Civil Code as amended by Federal Law Gazette I 2013/15, §8[3] Frame Law on Hospitals and Sanatoria). If the legal representative refuses the treatment although the life or health of the child is seriously endangered, the youth welfare authority may be asked for approval of the treatment (§211 Civil Code as amended by Federal Law Gazette I 2013/15).

296. The same principle applies to the exercise of all other patients' rights. If a minor patient is not able to assert his rights himself, these rights are asserted by the parents or the guardian (e.g., parents may legitimately access the medical records of their incompetent child). Still minor patients shall be involved in the exercise of their rights, bearing in mind their level of maturity (§160[3] Civil Code as amended by Federal Law Gazette I 2013/15). Competent minors may exercise their patients' rights on their own behalf. The parents' right to access the medical records and to be involved in medical decisions can be limited to the extent necessary for their legal authority over the minor demanded by law. Physicians are generally bound by confidentiality even in regard to the minor's parents or other guardians concerning all matters which have been confided to them or which they have otherwise heard in their professional role.[306]

297. In general, it is accepted that the general rules of §173 of the Civil Code as amended by Federal Law Gazette I 2013/15 (former §146c Civil Code) analogously apply to tattooing and body piercing.[307] Additional rules are laid down in an ordinance of the Federal Minister of Economic and Labour Affairs[308] for cosmetic traders,[309] which instructs them how and to which extent they are allowed to perform tattoos and piercings (*see* Part I, Chapter 2, §2.III.F. above). According to that ordinance, cosmetic traders are only permitted to perform body piercings on minor persons who have reached at least the age of fourteen and tattoos to minor persons who have reached at least the age of sixteen. In general, the performance of tattooing and piercing needs the person's written consent after being informed about the risks and the after-treatment-care. In case a minor has reached the age of fourteen and wishes a body piercing which causes bodily harm for a maximum of twenty-four days, the consent of the minor is sufficient to make the intervention legal, otherwise both the

306. *See* recently E. Bernat & H. Salzer, 'Das 15-jährige Mädchen, die "Pille danach" und der Schutz des ärztlichen Berufsgeheimnisses', *RdM* (2009): 154 et seq. with further reference.

307. J. Stabentheiner, '§§146c, 146d', in *Kommentar zum Allgemeinen bürgerlichen Gesetzbuch,* ed. P. Rummel 3rd edn (Vienna: Manz, 2003), marginal number 2 with further references.

308. 'Verordnung des Bundesministers für Wirtschaft und Arbeit über Ausübungsregeln für das Piercen und Tätowieren durch Kosmetik(Schönheitspflege)-Gewerbetreibende', Federal Law Gazette II 2003/141 as last amended by Federal Law Gazette II 2008/261.

309. Beauticians may perform piercing and tattooing lawfully (§109[3] Trade Regulations). Besides beauticians (*see* §109[6] Trade Regulations), hairdressers and wig makers according to §109(1) Trade Regulations, gold- and silversmithes according to §150(6) Trade Regulations and jewellers according to §154(3) Trade Regulations may perform ear-piercing lawfully.

minor and the person entitled to custody need to give their consent. In case of tattooing, the performance always requires the consent of the minor, who has reached the age limit of sixteen, and of the person entitled to custody.[310]

298. Special rules apply to minors regarding sterilization, abortion, genetic diagnosis and organ transplants (*see* Part II, Chapter 3 below).[311]

§2. The Mentally Ill Patient

I. Medical Treatment of Mentally Ill Patients of Full Age

299. Mentally ill or disabled people (as minor patients) are specially protected by law (§21 Civil Code). Therefore, special rules have been established for mentally ill patients who are of age. According to §268 of the Civil Code, persons with mental disabilities or a mental illness who are of age, but are unable to take care of their matters without acting to their own detriment shall principally be represented by a custodian appointed by court. This representation may also cover medical decisions.[312] Even so, the appointment of a custodian by itself does not restrict the patient's capacity to consent. The custodian only has to give consent in those cases in which the patient does not have the capacity to consent to the medical treatment in question and a custodian is in charge of the medical matters, provided that the medical treatment is necessary for the mentally ill patient's (objective) well-being. Thus, even if a custodian is in charge of all medical matters of the mentally ill patient, the attending physician has the duty to assess case-by-case whether the mentally ill patient possesses the necessary ability to insight and judgment as well as the reasonable willingness to decide whether to consent or refuse the medical intervention in question. As far as the mentally ill patient has the capacity to consent, only the patient's decision is decisive and may legitimize the commencement or continuation of a medical treatment (§283[1]).

If a serious medical treatment is in question, the custodian's consent additionally requires a medical certificate by an independent physician stating the mentally ill patient's incapacity to consent and the medical intervention's necessity for the patient's well-being. In the absence of such a medical certificate or if the mentally ill and incompetent patient's behaviour shows that he refuses the medical intervention, the custodian's consent has to be approved by court. If the custodian does not give consent to a medical treatment and in that way puts the mentally ill patient's (objective) well-being at risk, the court may consent to the medical treatment in question instead of him or appoint somebody else to custodianship (§283[2]).

---

310. D. Beig, 'Tätowierungen und Piercings Minderjähriger, Zustimmungserfordernisse und gesetzliche Verbote', *EF-Z* (2009): 86.
311. For further details on the consent of minors *see*: A. Kletečka, 'Einwilligung', in *Handbuch Medizinrecht*, ed. G. Aigner et al. (Vienna: Manz, 2006 et seq.), I.4.
312. P. Barth & M. Ganner, in *Handbuch Sachwalterrecht*, ed. P. Barth & M. Ganner, 2nd edn (Vienna: Linde, 2010), 33 et seq.

In case of emergency the physician may treat the mentally ill patient without asking for the consent of the competent patient, the custodian or the court (§283[3]).[313]

300. The appointment of a custodian is ruled out, if the mentally ill patient is able to take care of his matters on his own, for example when the patient is capable to contract or to consent to the medical treatment in question in spite of the mental illness or disability. The same applies if the mentally ill patient has sufficiently provided for the case that he can no longer make medical decisions in advance or if he is sufficiently represented by next of kin.

Therefore, no custodian shall be appointed by court in those cases in which the competent patient, even if he is mentally ill or mentally disabled, has drawn up a binding or highly considerable living will or granted a person of confidence a health care proxy regarding the medical matter in question (for details *see* Part II, Chapter 1, §3.VII. above).

Moreover, no custodian shall be appointed by court if the mentally ill or mentally disabled patient, who is not competent to consent anymore, is sufficiently represented by his next of kin. However, if someone holds an appropriate health care proxy or has a custodian appointed by court, the next of kin is no longer competent to make the medical decision in question. The representation of next of kin is directly based on law and does not need any further constituting acts in order to represent the mentally ill or mentally disabled patient lawfully. Only a registration of the representation of next of kin for purposes of protection of trust is necessary according to §284e of the Civil Code. The civil law defines next of kin as parents, children of age as well as the spouse or registered partner (according to the Act on Registered Partnerships [Eingetragene Partnerschaft-Gesetz], Federal Law Gazette I 2009/135 as last amended by Federal Law Gazette I 2015/25) or life partner living in the same household. In the latter case cohabitation must have lasted for at least three years. The authority directly granted by law to next of kin shall only cover legal matters and need for care in daily life. Thus, next of kin are never entitled to consent to medical treatments that seriously or lastingly affect the person's health or personality (§§284b–284e Civil Code).

301. Special rules to the custodian's medical decision apply concerning sterilization and research (§284 Civil Code; for details *see* Part II, Chapter 3, §2 and §6 below). In the context of a cosmetic surgery or treatment a mentally ill or mentally disabled patient, who is represented by a custodian, is only allowed to undergo such a treatment or surgery, if the competent patient himself or – if he is not competent– the custodian, has consented in written form and all prerequisites laid down in §7 of the Act on Aesthetic Treatments and Surgery (Federal Law Gazette I 2012/80) are fulfilled (in short: detailed information on the planned treatment, psychiatric testing, waiting period between consent and commencement of the treatment of at least four weeks).

313. P. Barth & D. Dokalik, in *Handbuch Sachwalterrecht*, ed. P. Barth & M. Ganner, 2nd edn (Vienna: Linde, 2010), 172 et seq. (183 et seq.) with further references.

302. The concept of legal representation of mentally ill persons was widely criticized over the past years, mainly because of the extensive (and almost irreversible) infringements of the person's right to self-determination.[314] When Austria ratified the Convention on the Rights of Persons with Disabilities (CRPD) in 2008,[315] it committed to ensure the full exertion of rights and legal capacity of persons with disabilities and thus, an amendment of the law was required. Amongst others, this was certainly the most pressing argument for an amendment of the legal representation system and lead to the so-called (second) Adult-Protection Act in Federal Law Gazette I 2017/59, which will enter into force on 1 July 2018. The aim of the reform was to promote the self-determination of those persons, who – due to a mental illness or a comparable disability – are limited in their consensual ability.[316] In short, the amendment introduces four ways of legal representation (some new, some old), replaces the former title of 'Sachwalter' (custodian) with 'Erwachsenenvertreter' (representative of an adult), and specifies the consensual ability by replacing the former ability to insight and judgment.[317]

II. Involuntary Committal of Mentally Ill Patients and Medical Treatment During Hospitalization

303. The rules concerning the legal representation in medical matters of mentally ill patients of age have to be distinguished from the rules concerning the (involuntary) placement of mentally ill persons in psychiatric institutions or departments of hospitals, in which persons regardless of their age may be legitimately deprived of their personal liberty in certain cases. Since 1990, the Act on the Hospitalization of Mentally Ill Persons (*Unterbringungssgesetz*, Federal Law Gazette 1990/155, as last amended by Federal Law Gazette I 2017/131, hereinafter called Hospitalization Act)[318] exclusively regulates under which circumstances and which procedure an involuntary placement and deprivation of personal freedom in a psychiatric institution or department is allowed.

314. For a list of criticized aspects *see* R. Fritz, 'Die Sachwalterrechtsreform nimmt Gestalt an. Der Entwurf des 2. Erwachsenenschutz-Gesetzes ist in Begutachtung', *iFamZ* (2016): 293.
315. UN General Assembly, Convention on the Rights of Persons with Disabilities, A/RES/61/106 (24 Jan. 2007).
316. Vorblatt der ErläutRV 1461 BlgNR 25. GP 1.
317. For further information on the upcoming changes due to the amendment *see*: P. Barth, *Das neue Erwachsenenschutzrecht*, (Vienna: Linde, 2017); R. Hübelbauer, 'Reform des Sachwalterschaftsrechtes/2. Erwachsenenschutzgesetz', *ZfG* (2017): 4; R. Fucik, 'Novelle zum Sachwalterschaftsrecht (2. Erwachsenenschutzgesetz) in Begutachtung', *ÖJZ* 2016/98; R.- Fritz, 'Die Sachwalterrechtsreform nimmt Gestalt an. Der Entwurf des 2. Erwachsenenschutz-Gesetzes ist in Begutachtung', *iFamZ* (2016): 293.
318. Federal Law Gazette 1990/155 as last amended by Federal Law Gazette I 2017/59. For an overview on the amendment in 2010 (Federal Law Gazette I 2010/18) *see* P. Barth (ed.), 'Die Unterbringungs- und Heimaufenthaltsnovelle 2010', *iFamZ-Spezial* (2010): 4 et seq. For an overview on the Hospitalizations Act *see also* St. Koppensteiner, 'UbG', in *Gmundner Kommentar zur Gesundheitsrecht*, ed. M Neumayr, R. Resch & F. Wallner (Vienna: Manz, 2016), 2455; A. Engel, 'Unterbringungsrecht', in *Handbuch Medizinrecht*, ed. R. Resch & F. Wallner, 2nd edn (Vienna: 2015), 202 et seq

In accordance with Article 2(1) No. 5 of the Constitutional Law on the Protection of Personal Liberty (Federal Law Gazette 1988/684 as last amended by Federal Law Gazette I 2008/2), §3 of the Hospitalization Act stipulates that in the absence of any other appropriate possibility of medical treatment or care, a mentally ill patient's personal freedom may legitimately be restricted, as far as there is reason to assume that due to his psychiatric disorder the patient's life or health, or the life or health of others, is seriously and severely at risk.[319]

The admission to involuntary placement is subject to a special procedure involving prior medical inspection according to §§8 et seq. of the Hospitalization Act, which shall ensure that an involuntary placement is indispensable according to the prerequisites laid down in §3 of the Hospitalization Act.[320]

304. After admission, every involuntarily hospitalized mentally ill patient is *ex lege* represented by so-called patients' advocates (*Patientenanwalt*).[321] They represent psychiatric patients in the compulsory hospitalization procedure before court. The representation by the patients' advocacies by itself does not restrict the legal capacity of the mentally ill patient or the legal representation by others (§14).

305. Immediately after admission, a court has to be informed about the involuntary hospitalization (§17). The court is obliged to get a personal impression of the patient in the psychiatric institution or department within four days after being informed. It has to inform the patient about the reasons and purpose of the proceedings, hear the patient, the head of the psychiatric institution or department, the patient's advocate and other present representatives on these issues and inspect the medical records. The court may also consult a medical expert (§§19 et seq.). The objective of the first proceedings is to review whether the involuntary hospitalization and the restriction of freedom are provisionally admissible. If the court concludes that the measure restricting the patient's freedom is impermissible, it has to be discontinued without delay. If the court assesses the measure and finds it provisionally admissible, an oral proceeding has to take place within the next fourteen days (§§22 et seq.). If the court arrives at the same decision, it has to declare for how long the mentally ill patient shall be detained at the longest, not exceeding three months. In the case of a hospitalization for an indefinite period of time, its need must be reviewed by court in appropriate intervals (§30). The costs of the proceedings are borne by the government. As soon as the legal prerequisites are no longer met, the measures restricting the patient's freedom have to be discontinued immediately (§32).[322]

---

319. For details *see* Ch. Kopetzki, *Grundriss des Unterbringungsrechts*, 3rd edn (Vienna/New York: Springer, 2012), 31 et seq.
320. For details *see* Ch. Kopetzki, *Grundriss des Unterbringungsrechts*, 3rd edn (Vienna/New York: Springer, 2012), 59 et seq.
321. The patients' advocacies have to be distinguished from the patients' representations, which deal with complaints from patients about their medical treatments and help patients to enforce their patients' rights. *See* Part II, Ch. 1, §8.II. above.
322. For details *see* Ch. Kopetzki, *Grundriss des Unterbringungsrechts*, 3rd edn (Vienna/New York: Springer, 2012), 107 et seq.

306. A mentally ill but still competent person may even stay in a psychiatric institution or psychiatric department voluntarily, if he fears to endanger himself or others (§4). Whereas the hospitalization and the rights of these patients during their stay are the same as for involuntarily hospitalized patients, the procedure for admission and the legal protection is different. Although the patient's advocates do not, *ex lege,* represent these patients, they also provide information and advice for them.[323]

307. The Hospitalization Act stipulates special rules concerning medical treatment during the hospitalization in psychiatric institutions or departments. First, pursuant to §35, every patient shall only be treated in accordance with the principles and the acknowledged methods of medical science.[324] If acknowledged methods do not exist or are not promising, treatment with new methods is possible on condition that the provision of the proposed treatment has only therapeutic purposes (compare §284 Civil Code, §8c Frame Law on Hospitals and Sanatoria). Second, every hospitalized patient has to be informed about the reasons and the meaning of a planned medical treatment regardless of his ability to insight and judgment, as long as this does not affect his well-being. With regard to minors or mentally ill or mentally disabled patients who are represented by a custodian in medical matters, their legal representative has to be informed as well. The patients' advocate may also be informed upon request. Third, mentally ill patients shall not be treated during hospitalization if they are able to understand and assess as well as refuse the medical treatment in question. In other words, medical treatments require – as in general – the consent of the competent patient in order to be legal. If a medical intervention that seriously or lastingly affects the person's health or personality (e.g., a serious surgery) is necessary during the hospitalization in a psychiatric institution or department, the consent of the competent patient has to be given in written form. In case the hospitalized patient is not able to consent, the commencement of the medical treatment requires the consent of the appointed custodian or representative. If a serious medical treatment is in question, the appointed custodian or guardian has to consent in written form. In the absence of a legal representative, a court shall decide about the lawfulness of the treatment upon request of the patient or the patients' advocate. Nevertheless, an approval by court is indispensable concerning serious treatments, including surgeries (§36). In case of emergency (meaning that there is not enough time to ask for the consent of the patient or the legal representative without severely endangering the patient's life or health) a treatment without consent is lawful. Nevertheless, the mentally ill patient's legal representative or, in absence of a legal representative, the patients' advocate has to be notified about the medical treatment afterwards (§37).[325]

---

323. For details *see* Ch. Kopetzki, *Grundriss des Unterbringungsrechts,* 3rd edn (Vienna/New York: Springer, 2012), 90 et seq.

324. Compare the wording in §8(2) of the Frame Law on Hospitals and Sanatoria. 'Acknowledged methods' may be defined as clinically proved and promising medical methods which are acknowledged, both at home and abroad, by the respective medical discipline.

325. For details *see* Ch. Kopetzki, *Grundriss des Unterbringungsrechts,* 3rd edn (Vienna/New York: Springer, 2012), 222 et seq.

308. As in general, the attending physicians are obliged to document at least key aspects of the provided medical treatment. The legal representative may access the medical records without any restrictions. The patient, however, may only be granted access as long as this does not affect his well-being. If the attending physician refuses access, he is obliged to document the reason for the refusal (§39).[326]

III. Restrictions on Personal Freedom of Mentally Ill or Mentally Disabled Residents

309. Since 2005, the Act on the Protection of the Personal Freedom of Residents of Homes and other Nursing and Care Facilities (Act on the Protection of Personal Freedom of Home Residents)[327] regulates the protection of the personal freedom of mentally ill or disabled persons regardless of their age during their stay at old people's homes, nursing homes, homes for disabled people and other facilities. Rules concerning the medical treatment are not subject to this act.

310. A resident's freedom may only be restricted if certain criteria according to §4 are met: in the absence of any other appropriate possibility to medical treatment or care, a mentally ill or mentally disabled person's personal liberty may be legitimately restricted if there is reason to presume that due to a mental disorder or disability the resident's life or health or the life or health of others is seriously and severely at risk. A resident's freedom is restricted if he is prevented from wandering about against or without his will and if physical means are used or threatened to be used.

If the resident is able to understand and assess, and therefore agrees to being prevented from moving about, this is not qualified as a restriction of freedom (§3). Restrictions of freedom may be carried out exclusively upon the instruction of a person authorized by law. All restrictions of personal liberty must be carried out in observance of professional standards, always aiming at harming the resident as little as possible. As soon as the legal prerequisites are no longer met, the measure restricting the resident's freedom must be discontinued immediately (§5).

311. The resident may appoint a person of confidence in order to represent him asserting the right to personal freedom (§8). In addition, the residents are also represented *ex lege* by so-called residents' representatives (*Bewohnervertreter*). Every residents' representative is in particular entitled to visit the home without prior announcement to get a personal impression of the residents' state, to discuss whether the criteria requiring the restriction of freedom are fulfilled with the person authorized to order such measures and with other home personnels, and, if necessary, to inspect relevant documents (§9). Certain persons (including the resident

326. For details *see* Ch. Kopetzki, *Grundriss des Unterbringungsrechts*, 3rd edn (Vienna/New York: Springer, 2005), 251 et seq.

327. Federal Law Gazette I 2004/11 as last amended by Federal Law Gazette I 2017/59. For an overview on the amendment in 2010 *see* P. Barth (ed.), 'Die Unterbringungs- und Heimaufenthaltsnovelle 2010', *iFamZ-Spezial* (2010): 26 et seq., G. Strickmann, 'Neuerungen im Heimaufenthaltsgesetz', *iFamZ* (2010): 276.

himself and his representative) are entitled to request the court to review the measure restricting the resident's personal freedom (§11). In such a case, the court is obliged to get a personal impression of the resident in the facility within seven days after being notified. It has to inform the resident about the reasons and purpose of the proceedings, hear the resident and certain other persons on these issues and inspect the medical records. The court may also consult an expert (§12). The objective of the first hearing is to decide whether the restriction of freedom is provisionally admissible. If the court concludes that the measure restricting the resident's freedom is impermissible, it has to be discontinued without delay. If the court assesses the measure to be provisionally admissible, an oral hearing has to take place within fourteen days after the first hearing (§13). If the court in the course of the oral hearing arrives at the same decision, it has to declare for how long the restriction is lawful at the longest, not exceeding six months (§15). In case of a restriction of freedom for an indefinite period of time, its need may be reviewed by court upon the representative's request or ex officio at appropriate intervals (§19). The costs of the proceedings are borne by the federal government.[328]

IV. Controlling and Monitoring Duties of the Ombudsman Board Asserting Human Rights

312. In addition to the controlling and supporting duties of the patients' advocates and the residents' representatives, the Ombudsman Board (*Volksanwaltschaft*) was entrusted by law in 2012 with controlling and monitoring duties in order to protect and promote human rights also within the sphere of administration according to the Hospitalization Act and the Act on the Protection of Personal Freedom of the Home Residents (Article 148a of the Constitution). While the Ombudsman Board formerly only monitored the public administration, investigated complaints from citizens and assessed whether the administration was acting within the law and complied with human rights standards, it received new responsibilities in protecting and promoting compliance with human rights as the National Monitoring Body and part of a United Nations mandate. This new competence of the Ombudsman Board followed the implementation of the OPCAT (The Optional Protocol to the Convention against Torture and other Cruel, Inhuman or Degrading Treatment or Punishment) and assigned the Ombudsman Board along with its – then newly established – commissions (comprising of experts in the relevant fields) to monitor all institutions in which liberty is being (or may be) deprived or restricted. As a result, medical and care institutions are now monitored under this mandate. According to §11 of the Ombudsman Board Act 1982 (Federal Law Gazette 1982/433 as amended by Federal Law Gazette I 2012/1) the commissions set up by the Ombudsman Board shall (1) regularly visit and inspect these places of detention (broadly defined by Article 4 of the OPCAT); (2) monitor and concomitantly inspect the behaviour of executive

328. For details *see* G. Strickmann, *Heimaufenthaltsrecht,* 2nd edn (Vienna: Linde, 2012); P. Barth & A. Engel, Heimrecht (Vienna: Manz, 2004); H. P. Zierl, M. Wall & M. Zeinhofer, *Heimrecht I*, 3rd edn (Vienna: proLIBRIS, 2011); N. Herdega & C. Buerger, 'Heimaufenthaltsgesetz', in *Handbuch Medizinrecht*, ed. R. Resch & F. Wallner, 2nd edn (Vienna: LexisNexis, 2015), 232–289.

bodies authorized to issue direct orders and carry out coercive measures, and (3) regularly visit and inspect facilities and programmes designed to serve persons with disabilities and to prevent all forms of exploitation, violence and abuse. These duties correspond with the right of the commissions to be provided with information, to be allowed to inspect documents (even nursing documentation, case history, medical reports), to be granted access to the places of detentions and upon request to be provided contact with persons who are or were restricted in their personal freedom (for details *see* §11[3] leg cit). The commissions shall report to the Ombudsman Board on their visits and inspections and make suggestions on determinations of cases of maladministration and recommendations and suggestions as to measures of supervisory control, which shall be included in the report of the Ombudsman Board put forward to the Parliament (§13; Article 148d of the Constitution).[329]

§3. The Dying Patient

313. Austrian law does not provide any special rules concerning the situation of dying patients. Therefore, the general rules regarding the patient's self-determination apply (*see* Part II, Chapter 1, §3. above). A dying patient who has the necessary ability to insight and judgment as well as the willingness to decide whether to undergo or abstain from (further) medical or other treatments (§§173, 283 Civil Code), can refuse every medical treatment at any time (e.g., artificial nutrition). Additionally, every competent person can refuse the commencement or continuation of medical treatments specified by him in advance (based on the Living Will Act; for details *see* Part II, Chapter 1, §3.VII.A. above).

Even so, no patient can wish to be actively killed or to be helped to actively kill himself by others. Both voluntary euthanasia and abetment to suicide are prohibited by criminal law (for details *see* Part II, Chapter 3, §7 below).

In 2012, the Supreme Court ruled that in the absence of the (dying) patient's ability to insight and judgment (who is of full age), in general the appointed custodian and the treating physician have to decide consensual if the life-prolonging medical treatment shall be continued or terminated; in case a considerable living will exists, it shall be taken into account. In case of uncertainty or dissent the principle 'in dubio pro vita' shall apply. The court shall not play a role in this sort of decision (in contrary to the requirement of an additional consent of the court according to §283[2] or §275[2] Civil Code). This ruling has been criticized in literature.[330]

329. *See* Ch. Kopetzki, *Grundriss des Unterbringungsrechts*, 3rd edn (Vienna/New York: Springer, 2005), 280 et seq.

330. Supreme Court 8 Oct. 2012, 9 Ob 68/11g, *Zak* 2012/762, 415 (*Kletečka*) = *iFamZ* 2013/14, 50 (*Ganner*) = *EvBl* 2013/60, 414 (*Pfurtscheller*) = *RdM* 2013/74, 104 (*Kopetzki*) = Bernat, *EF-Z* 2013, 5.

Chapter 3. Specific Activities

§1. Abortion

I. Historical Development of the Law

314. Under the Austrian Criminal Code of 1945, abortion was generally indictable except in case of medical indication. The present regulation of abortion goes back to the big reform of the Austrian Criminal Code in 1975. The combination of a time-limit-regulation with an indication-model was first introduced then. Abortion goes unpunished within the first three months after nidation and in case of certain indications. Especially the time-limit-regulation was discussed controversially, also having effect on the legislative process. (Because of this question, the Criminal Code was not supported by all of the political parties in parliament). In 1974, the Austrian Constitutional Court declared the regulation to be constitutional and especially compliant with the right to life as guaranteed by Article 2 of the ECHR (VfSlg 7400). According to the Constitutional Court (as well as the Supreme Court of Justice) the unborn do not fall within the ambit of Article 2 ECHR. Its (full) protection only starts with childbirth. The Constitutional Court also accepted the gradually rising protection concept under aspects of the principle of equality. It emphasized that the unborn child did not have to be protected to the same extent in its diverse stages of development.

II. The Offence of Abortion

315. The offence of abortion (§96 Criminal Code) can be committed by physicians, the pregnant woman (by carrying out the abortion herself as well as by permitting others to do so) or any third party. The sentence depends on who actually commits the crime.

The physician, who terminates a pregnancy with the woman's consent beyond the time limit of three months or without an indication in line with §97 (*see* below), can be punished with imprisonment up to one year. If he acts on a commercial basis, he can even be sentenced to up to three years. If the abortion is performed without the woman's consent (either because she does not approve of it or because her given consent is invalid), §98 provides a punishment of up to three years of imprisonment for the physician. In case the woman dies, the sentence is between six months and five years. The termination, however, remains unpunished in case of imminent danger to the woman's life.

Under §96, non-physicians (such as back-street abortionists or charlatans) who terminate pregnancies can generally be jail sentenced up to three years. For the qualified offences of acting commercially or causing the death of the pregnant woman the punishment is imprisonment for a time period of six months to five years.

The pregnant woman, who carries out the abortion herself or who consents to termination by others can be imprisoned for not more than one year; she cannot be punished though if she merely accepts abortive measures (e.g., by not taking necessary hormone pills).

316. §96 not only protects the life of the unborn child, but also the health of the pregnant woman. In the initial stage of pregnancy (in the first three months after nidation), the woman's right to self-determination prevails over the legal interests of the unborn. The legal protection of the unborn, however, increases along with the ongoing pregnancy, so that after the time limit of three months, carrying out an abortion is not at the woman's disposal any more, but is only allowed under the strict additional requirements codified in §97.

317. The offence of abortion covers all measures aiming at terminating pregnancy, no matter if the result is achieved by mechanic action (e.g., by suction or abrasion) or by drugs (for instance by abortion pills). §96 requires intentional action in all cases, so that negligent behaviour is not punished. As to the necessary degree of intent, conditional intent is sufficient for being punishable.

318. The legal protection of the unborn starts with nidation (around the thirteenth day after conception), no matter if procreation and conception have been natural or artificial. Therefore, birth control methods which have exclusive or potential effects between conception and nidation (like the morning-after pill or intrauterine devices), do not fall within the ambit of the offence. The protection under §96 ends with childbirth. From the first stage of labour on (or the beginning of the Caesarean section), any action intended to prevent childbirth is punished under §75 Criminal Code (murder).[331]

III. Impunity of Abortion

319. Abortion remains unpunished under the premises of §97 Criminal Code. §97 combines a 'time-limit-regulation' with an 'indication-model', taking into account the woman's right to self-determination as well as the legal protection of the unborn. Naturally, the pregnant woman has to give her consent to the abortion in all cases. If the woman is able to comprehend the nature, significance and implications of the intervention and form a rational intention in the light of these facts (which is assumed from the age of fourteen on, but may also occur earlier), only the woman herself can consent to the abortion.[332] Third parties (e.g., parents as legal

331. For details *see* e.g., M. Eder-Rieder, '§96 StGB', in *Wiener Kommentar zum Strafgesetzbuch*, ed. F. Höpfel & E. Ratz, 2nd edn (Vienna: Manz, 1999 et seq.); D. Kienapfel & H.V. Schroll, *Strafrecht Besonderer Teil I*, 4th edn (Vienna: Manz, 2016), 246; A. Tipold, 'Die strafrechtliche Verantwortung', in *Handbuch Medizinrecht*, ed. G. Aigner et al. (Vienna: Manz, 2006 et seq.), II/45; E. Marek & A. Tipold, 'StGB', in *Gmundner Kommentar zum Gesundheitsrecht*, ed. M. Neumayr, R. Resch & F. Wallner (Vienna: Manz, 2016), 2423, marginal number 3 et seq.

332. §173 of the Civil Code is not applicable here: Explanatory Report 296 BlgNR 21. GP 54. For critics *see* e.g., C. Fischer-Czermak, '§173 ABGB', in *ABGB-ON1.02 (2015)* ed. A. Kletečka & M. Schauer (Vienna: Manz, 2013), marginal number 1; H. Salzer & E. Bernat, 'Das 15-jährige Mädchen, die "Pille danach" und der Schutz des ärztlichen Berufsgeheimnisses', *RdM* (2009): 154

representatives) can only give their consent, if the pregnant woman is not capable of understanding and if the abortion is for her (objective) benefit. Abortions, which are carried out without the woman's consent, are only lawful in case of imminent danger to her life (§98).

320. 1. Time-limit-regulation: pregnancies can legally be terminated within the first three months after nidation, provided that the woman has previously engaged medical consultation and the abortion is carried out by a physician. Only under these three requirements (time limit of three months, previous medical consultation and termination by physician) does abortion remain unpunished. If only one of these elements is missing, §96 is to be applied.

2. Medical indication: abortion also goes unpunished in case of serious danger to the life or (mental or physical) health of the pregnant woman. There is no time limit for this kind of abortion. Again it has to be carried out by a physician.

3. Embryopathic indication: in case of a high risk of the unborn being mentally or physically handicapped, pregnancy can lawfully be terminated by a physician without any time limit. The imminent handicap must be severe, but not necessarily permanent and incurable. For example, physical damages such as deformed extremities, paralysis, metabolic diseases and mental afflictions such as psychoses, epilepsy, amentia or schizophrenia, incurable dementia, deaf-mutism, ablepsia, Down syndrome and cleft palates or harelips can justify abortions.[333] The damage does not necessarily have to be caused by a genetic defect, but §97 also covers cases of prenatal causes such as rubella or metabolic diseases of the pregnant woman as well as intra-uterine damages caused by medication or radiation exposure.

The legitimacy of terminating pregnancy until childbirth is increasingly criticized in Austria. Opponents suggest a time limit model, for example set by viability of the foetus.

4. Minority: if the pregnant woman is under the age of fourteen at the time of impregnation, there is no time limit for abortion.[334] As in the other cases of indication, the pregnancy has to be terminated by a physician.

5. Imminent danger to the life of the pregnant woman: non-physicians carrying out an abortion are not punished in the sole case of medical indication, in which medical aid cannot be obtained in time. Unlike the regular case of medical indication, non-physicians only stay unpunished in case of danger to the life of the pregnant woman. Imminent danger of damage to health is not enough reason though.

(155 et seq.); F. Kerschner & K. Sagerer-Foriç, 'Familienrecht', in *Bürgerliches Recht,* vol. 5, ed. P. Bydlinski & F. Kerschner, 6th edn (Vienna: Springer, 2017), marginal number 3/35; C. Fischer-Czermak, 'Zur Handlungsfähigkeit Minderjähriger nach dem Kindschaftsrechts-Änderungsgesetz 2001', *ÖJZ* (2002): 293 (298).

333. Questioning M. Eder-Rieder, '§96 StGB', in *Wiener Kommentar zum Strafgesetzbuch*, ed. F. Höpfel & E. Ratz, 2nd edn (Vienna: Manz, 1999 et seq.), marginal number 17.

334. Critical K. Schmoller, '§97', in *Salzburger Kommentar zum Strafgesetzbuch,* ed. O. Triffterer, Ch. Rosbaud & H. Hinterhofer (Vienna: LexisNexis, 1992 et seq.), marginal number 35; M. Eder-Rieder, '§97 StGB', in *Wiener Kommentar zum Strafgesetzbuch*, ed. F. Höpfel & E. Ratz, 2nd edn (Vienna: Manz, 1999 et seq.), marginal number 23.

321. The legal qualification of §97 is discussed controversially in Austria: the prevailing doctrine of criminal law qualifies the three cases of indication (medical indication, embryopathic indication, minority) as legal justifications, whereas the time-limit-regulation is seen to exclude the elements of the offence.[335] Another strong position in criminal law does not differentiate between the different cases in §97 and classifies all of them as legal justifications (with the consequence that abortion is not unlawful then).[336] On the occasion of a 'wrongful-birth'-judgment, the Supreme Court qualified embryopathic indication as a legal justification.[337] Others see most[338] or all of the substantive grounds in §97 as reasons for not exacting punishment.

322. Finally §97 of the Criminal Code provides a 'moral clause': no physician (or any other member of a medical profession) can be forced to carry out or to assist in an abortion, as long as there is no case of imminent danger to the pregnant woman's life or health. It also includes a guarantee not to be discriminated against because of carrying out or assisting a lawful abortion or because of refusing to do so.

§2. Sterilization

323. §90(2) of the Criminal Code provides a special legal justification for sterilizations (within the meaning of permanent prevention of fertility) being performed on a competent adult who has given his informed consent. As medical treatments do not even fulfil the definition of the offence of physical injury (§§83 et seq. of the Criminal Code), medically indicated sterilizations do not fall within the ambit of §90(2).[339]

324. §90(2) only relates to sterilizations in terms of procedures that make someone infertile by cutting through the spermatic ducts or tubes. Other than that, interventions intending to remove the gonads (testicles and ovaries), which affect the sex drive (castration), are not covered by §90(2), but by §90(1) of the Criminal Code.

325. Pursuant to §90(2), the physician has to carry out the sterilization in accordance with the state-of-the-art. Furthermore, the person being sterilized either has to be older than twenty-five or the intervention has to be moral for other reasons. Hence sterilizations that are performed on (competent) adults over the age of

335. K. Schmoller, '§97', in *Salzburger Kommentar zum Strafgesetzbuch*, ed. O. Triffterer, Ch. Rosbaud & H. Hinterhofer (Vienna: LexisNexis, 1992 et seq.), marginal number 18 et seq.; M. Eder-Rieder, '§97 StGB', in *Wiener Kommentar zum Strafgesetzbuch*, ed. F. Höpfel & E. Ratz, 2nd edn (Vienna: Manz, 1999 et seq.), 1.
336. For example, D. Kienapfel & H.V. Schroll, *Strafrecht Besonderer Teil I*, 4th edn (Vienna: Manz, 2016), 247.
337. Supreme Court of Justice 25 May 1999, 1 Ob 91/99k.
338. P. Lewisch, *Strafrecht Besonderer Teil I*, 2nd edn (Vienna: WUV, 1999), 94.
339. With further references, H. Schütz in *Wiener Kommentar zum Strafgesetzbuch*, ed. F. Höpfel & E. Ratz, 2nd edn (Vienna: Manz, 1999 et seq.), marginal number 186.

twenty-five do not need any specific justification and are not immoral per se. For this reason the informed consent is very important and there are particularly strict requirements for the doctor's duty to inform and to verify the patient's capacity to consent.[340] In the case that an (adult) person giving his consent to a sterilization procedure is younger than twenty-five, the intervention is only justified if it is additionally not against good morals, in the sense that it must have a positive aim. A positive aim is assumed in case of a considerable health hazard to the offspring or in case of medical-social indication (meaning that the stress and strains of giving birth and raising a child would pose an extraordinary health hazard to the woman).[341] On the other hand, purely social reasons (without having any detrimental effect on the woman's health) are not sufficient.

326. Performing sterilizations on minor patients is generally forbidden in Austria. According to §163 of the Civil Code, neither the minor patient himself nor his parents as legal representatives can give their consent to medical treatments aiming at the child's permanent infertility. On the other hand, medical treatments that can cause infertility by secondary action (such as the removal of reproductive organs because of cancer) are not covered by §163 and can therefore be justified by the patient's or his parents' consent.[342]

327. The sterilization of adult, but not competent people who are under custodianship, can merely be performed under §284 of the Civil Code. According to §284, the custodian can only give his consent in case of a special medical-somatic indication. This requires that pregnancy would cause a severe threat to the disabled person's life or health because of a permanent physical deficiency like cardiac and circulatory troubles or disorders of metabolism, and that pregnancy cannot be avoided by other means of birth control.[343] Sterilizations for other reasons, for example out of fear of having disabled children or of not being capable of raising them, cannot be justified by consent. Additionally, the custodian's consent in all cases needs leave of the court.

328. If the civil law regulations concerning legal representation (§§163, 284 of the Civil Code) are disregarded, a sterilization cannot be not justified in line with §90 of the Criminal Code and is therefore punishable as dangerous physical injury

---

340. Ch. Kopetzki, 'Einwilligung und Einwilligungsfähigkeit', in *Einwilligung und Einwilligungsfähigkeit*, ed. Ch. Kopetzki (Vienna: Manz, 2002), 1 (16).
341. E. Fabrizy, *StGB Kurzkommentar,* 12th edn (Vienna: Manz, 2016), §90 marginal number 9; D. Kienapfel & H.V. Schroll, *Grundriss desStrafrechts. Besonderer Teil I*, 5th edn (Vienna: Manz, 2003), §90 marginal number 75.
342. M. Stormann, '§163 ABGB', in *ABGB Praxiskommentar,* vol. 1, ed. M. Schwimann & G. E. Kodek, 4th edn (Vienna: LexisNexis, 2016), marginal number 2; C. Fischer-Czermak, '§163 ABGB', in *ABGB-ON1.03*, ed. A. Kletečka & M. Schauer (Vienna: Manz, 2015).
343. With further references, H. Weitzenböck, '§284 ABGB', in *ABGB Praxiskommentar,* vol. 1, ed. M. Schwimann & G. E. Kodek, 4th edn (Vienna: LexisNexis, 2016), marginal number 9; J. Stabentheiner, '§284 ABGB', in *Kommentar zum Allgemeinen bürgerlichen Gesetzbuch,* ed. P. Rummel & M. Lukas, 4th edn (Vienna: Manz, 2015), marginal number 2.

(§88 of the Criminal Code). Some authors, who qualify the intervention as medical treatment, subsume this case under §110 of the Criminal Code.[344]

329. There is also a special rule concerning genital mutilation. According to §90(3) of the Criminal Code, consent cannot effectively be given to mutilation or injury to the genitals that might result in enduring damage of sexual sensation. Mutilation is understood as the removal of bodily parts in the nether regions or loss in functional efficiency (e.g., removal or chemical burn of the clitoris or the vulva). 'Other injuries resulting in enduring damage of sexual sensation' comprise interventions aimed at delaying sexual desire, for instance burning, chemical burning, abrasion of the vagina or insertion of aching herbs.[345] Although targeting at female genital mutilation, §90(3) is formulated gender-neutrally, so that mutilation of male genitals is also included. Simple circumcision or genital piercing is not covered, so that these kinds of interventions are regulated by §90(1).[346] On the other hand, injuries of other genitals like the non-therapeutic removal of testicles cannot legally be given consent to. Generally, medical treatments carried out lege artis (e.g., operations for gender reassignment) do not fall within the ambit of §90 so that the special regulation of §90(3) is not relevant to therapeutic interventions either. Regarding the question of guilt, the prevailing doctrine assumes that concerning mutilation in a narrow sense, negligent behaviour is sufficient for being punished under §90(3). Other forms of non-therapeutic interventions resulting in enduring damage of sexual sensation require that the offender has to act intentionally (as long as the intervention is carried out lege artis and the offender strives to conserve sexual sensation).[347]

§3. In Vitro Fertilization

I. Historical Background

330. The Artificial Procreation Act (*Fortpflanzungsmedizingesetz,* Federal Law Gazette 1992/275, as last amended by Federal Law Gazette I 2015/35, abbreviated 'Act' in the following) was passed in 1992 after long and detailed discussions, which had already started in the mid-1980s. The act was not intended to meet moral or religious expectations. It rather focussed on finding a compromise between the diverging interests and on disconnecting ethical arguments and reasons of legal policy. Nevertheless, the strictness of the act in most points can be rather traced back to the conservative (e.g., conservative-catholic circles, feminist movements, Consumer Protection Boards) than to the liberal interest groups in Austria.

344. J. Stabentheiner, '§146d', in *Kommentar zum Allgemeinen bürgerlichen Gesetzbuch,* ed. P. Rummel, 3rd edn (Vienna: Manz, 2003), marginal number 11.

345. D. Kienapfel & H.V. Schroll, *Strafrecht Besonderer Teil I,* 4th edn (Vienna: Manz, 2016), marginal number 85.

346. O. Maleczky, 'Das Strafrechtsänderungsgesetz 2001', *JAP* (2001/2002): 182.

347. H. Schütz, '§90 StGB', in *Wiener Kommentar zum Strafgesetzbuch,* ed. F. Höpfel & E. Ratz, 2nd edn (Vienna: Manz, 1999 et seq.), marginal number 203.

The Artificial Procreation Act was solely intended to regulate medical reproductive techniques. Methods of gene technology are excluded as well as other aspects of the utilization (and possible abuse) of biology and genetics (as far as an abuse is not enabled by artificial reproductive techniques). Thus, the Artificial Procreation Act does not include an 'Embryology Act' and does not primarily protect the embryo itself (which is especially expressed in the maximum storage period of ten years). Viable cells are rather protected as side effect, as the act aims to prohibit other undesired consequences of artificial reproductive techniques (for instance the selection of embryos or experiments). Political attempts to enforce the protection of embryos (especially by prohibiting therapeutic cloning) were not successful after a negative vote of the Bioethics Committee and other negative reactions in the legislative process.[348]

331. Until recently, Austria was amongst Europe's most conservative states in terms of access to reproductive technology.[349] However, a Constitutional Court ruling led to a comprehensive amendment of the Act in 2015.[350] The case that paved the road for this liberalization was brought before the Austrian Constitutional Court in 2013 by a lesbian couple that was denied access to reproductive technologies due to their homosexual relationship. At that time the Act only allowed different-sex couples to undertake assisted reproductive measures. The Constitutional Court declared this and several other restrictions (namely §2[1], §2[2], §3[1 and 2]) of the Artificial Procreation Act as unconstitutional.[351] The Court found the restriction to be violating Article 14 ECHR in conjunction with Article 8 ECHR and lifted the respective provision (and others) due to its discriminatory and disproportionate treatment. As a result, the legislator was urged to take legislative measures until 31 December 2014. Alongside this legislative alteration other main revisions (such as *inter alia* the permission to conduct pre-implantation diagnosis under specific circumstances and heterogeneous germ cell donation) were made in order to comply with European standards and the jurisdiction of the European Court of Human Rights.[352]

348. Ch. Kopetzki, 'Landesbericht Österreich', in *Internationale Perspektiven zu Status und Schutz des extrakorporalen Embryos*, ed. A. Eser, H.G. Koch & C. Seith (Baden-Baden: Nomos, 2007), 219 (230 et seq.) with further references. For further details on the historical background and the (political) discussions leading to the amendment of the Artificial Procreation Act *see also*: E. Bernat, 'Das Recht der Fortpflanzungsmedizin im Spiegel der sich wandelnden Sozialmoral', in *Das Recht der Fortpflanzungsmedizin 2015 – Analyse und Kritik*, ed. S. Arnold, E. Bernat & Ch. Kopetzki (Vienna: Manz, 2016), 9 (et seq).
349. M. Erlebach, 'Wo steht Österreich vor und nach der Reform des FMedG? Ein europäischer Rechtsvergleich', *iFamZ* (2015): 10.
350. Constitutional Court 10 Dec. 2013, G 16/2013 et al.
351. Constitutional Court 10 Dec. 2013, G 16/2013 et al.; Ch. Kopetzki, 'Fortpflanzungsmedizinrecht im Umbruch' *RdM* (2014): 1; C. Fischer-Czermak, 'Medizinisch unterstützte Fortpflanzung für lesbische Paare' *EF-Z* (2014): 61; *iFamZ* 2014, 5 *(Meinl)* = *RdM* 2014, 65 *(Kopetzki)* = *EF-Z* 2014, 66 = *ecolex* 2014, 478 = *ÖJZ* 2014, 376 = *ZAK* 2014, 31.
352. M. Erlebach, 'Wo steht Österreich vor und nach der Reform des FMedG? Ein europäischer Rechtsvergleich', *iFamZ* (2015): 10; S. Mauernböck, 'Das neue Fortpflanzungsmedizinrecht – Eine erste Auseinandersetzung mit den wesentlichen Änderungen', *ZTR* (2015): 107.

II. The Artificial Procreation Act

A. General Remarks

332. The Act regulates the use of medical techniques to induce child-conception through other means than copulation (§1). §1(2) lists four methods which fall within the scope of the Act, whereas the provision does not contain an exhaustive list and new techniques may also fall within the ambit of the Act. The listed methods include: the insertion of sperm into the reproductive organs of a woman, the extra-corporeal unification of ovum and sperm, the insertion of viable cells into the uterus or fallopian tube of a woman, and the insertion of ovum cells or ovum cells with sperm into the uterus or fallopian tube of a woman.

333. Until 2015, medically assisted procreation was only allowed amongst persons of a different sex living in marriage or cohabitation. Resulting from the Constitutional Court ruling in 2013 (*see* 319a),[353] the legislator was urged to take legislative measures. Consequently all provisions referring to persons of a different sex were adapted and now apply to homo- and heterosexual couples. Nevertheless, it must be noted that the amendment in fact only enables lesbian couples to benefit from assisted reproductive technology since surrogacy remains to be prohibited under Austrian law.

334. In addition to the requirement of a relationship in the sense of §2(1) medically assisted procreation may only be applied subordinately to other treatments. §2(2) specifies the cases in which medically assisted procreation can be undertaken: (i) if every other possible and reasonable treatments aimed at inducing pregnancy through sexual intercourse have failed or have no reasonable chance of success, (ii) if sexual intercourse is not reasonable to the partner due to a serious risk of transmitting a severe infectious disease, (iii) if the pregnancy shall be induced to a patient living in a lesbian relationship or (iv) for the purposes of a pre-implantation diagnosis.[354] §2(3) reiterates the principle of subsidiarity by specifying that initially only the least invasive method and the method creating the lowest number of viable cells shall be chosen.[355]

Hence, based on §2 the extraction and preservation of ovum cells for prospective artificial fertilizations without medical indication (so-called Social-Egg-Freezing) is prohibited. Such a procedure serves the purpose of taking precaution for a future family-plan under consideration of the steady reduction of ovum cell reserves and therefore does not meet any of the cases listed in §2(2). This prohibition however, is strongly criticized by scholars regarding its fundamental rights implications.[356] In

353. Constitutional Court 10 Dec. 2013, G 16/2013 et al.

354. The two last-mentioned clauses were part of the amendment in 2015.

355. For further details on the principle of subsidiarity in regards to ART *see* S. Merckens, 'FMedRÄG 2015: Zur Reform des Fortpflanzungsmedizingesetzes', *RdM* (2016): 54 (58).

356. Ch. Kopetzki, 'Das Recht der Fortpflanzungsmedizin 2015: Aktueller Stand und verfassungsrechtliche Bewertung', in *Das Recht der Fortpflanzungsmedizin 2015 – Analyse und Kritik*, ed. S. Arnold, E. Bernat & Ch. Kopetzki (Vienna: Manz, 2016), 72; P. Czech 'Zur Grundrechtskonformität des neuen Fortpflanzungsmedizinrechts', *NLMR* (2015): 297.

particular it is questionable which interest under Article 8(2) ECHR shall be protected to justify such an intervention with a woman's right to reproductive autonomy, as the preservation neither adversely affects the health of the woman (or her child) nor does it affect other rights.[357] Moreover, it seems incoherent to permit the donation of ova cells but not to ensure the use of own ova cells to induce a pregnancy at a later time.[358]

Nevertheless, §2b permits the preservation of sperm, ova cells, viable cells as well as testicle- and ovary tissue for prospective artificial fertilizations if there is a serious risk that a pregnancy can no longer be induced through sexual intercourse resulting from a disease or medical treatment.

B. Methods of Assisted Reproductive Technology (ART)

1. Use of Cells

335. In general, only ova and sperm from the respective partner are to be used for the purpose of medically assisted procreation (§3[1]).[359] However, if the partner is not capable of reproduction or the pregnancy shall be induced to a woman living in a lesbian relationship, the Act specifies exemption clauses which allow the use of the cells of a third person:[360] §3(2) permits the use of sperm from a third person and §3(3) permits the use of ova from a third person under the precaution that the woman receiving the ova is younger than 45 years.[361] Moreover, the ova donor must not be younger than 18 or older than 30 years (§2b[2]).

§3(3) caused particular attention and a viable debate over the requirements of reproductive health: According to the recommendation of the Austrian Bioethics Commission[362] the factor determining whether a woman shall receive (or donate) ova cells should be the biological-reproductive phase, yet the Commission did not define a corresponding age limit. Consequently, scholars argue that the age limit determined by the legislator (30 for the donor and 45 for the receiver) is not in accordance with the biological-reproductive phase and constitutes an attempt to formally grant the donation of ova cells but to practically hinder it by setting such a narrow age limit.[363] If there are good reasons to prohibit medically assisted

---

357. Ch. Kopetzki, 'Das Recht der Fortpflanzungsmedizin 2015: Aktueller Stand und verfassungsrechtliche Bewertung', in *Das Recht der Fortpflanzungsmedizin 2015 – Analyse und Kritik*, ed. S. Arnold, E. Bernat & Ch. Kopetzki (Vienna: Manz, 2016), 72.
358. Ch. Kopetzki, 'Das Recht der Fortpflanzungsmedizin 2015: Aktueller Stand und verfassungsrechtliche Bewertung', in *Das Recht der Fortpflanzungsmedizin 2015 – Analyse und Kritik*, ed. S. Arnold, E. Bernat & Ch. Kopetzki (Vienna: Manz, 2016), 72; P. Czech 'Zur Grundrechtskonformität des neuen Fortpflanzungsmedizinrechts', *NLMR* (2015): 303.
359. This is also referred to as the homogenous method.
360. This is also referred to as the heterogeneous method.
361. Until the amendment in 2015 ova and viable cells were only allowed to be used for the woman from whom they originated from (former §3[2]).
362. Bundeskanzleramt – Austrian Bioethics Commission, Reform of the Reproductive Medicine Act – Opinion of the Austrian Bioethics Commission (Vienna, 2012).
363. C. Wendehorst, 'Neuerungen im österreichischen Fortpflanzungsmedizinrecht durch das FMedRÄG 2015 Anpassung an europaweite Entwicklungen', *iFamZ* (2015): 4 (6); further critique

pregnancies because of an increased risk for mother and child at a certain age, then arguably this age limit would have to be applied to all IVF procedures.[364] Consequently, it seems incoherent that a woman at the age of 44 can use her own ova cells to undergo IVF-treatment but cannot use her 32-year old sisters' ova cells which may provide a higher quality.[365]

336. In this context the concept of 'egg-sharing' is also being thoroughly discussed among scholars. This method uses ova cells which were originally intended to be used for own purposes and are left over and donated for the use on other women. It was strongly discussed whether the age limit stipulated in §2b(2) of a maximum age of 30 also applies to such donations. The prevailing opinion considers §2b(2) to only refer to extractions of cells for the purpose of use on third persons. The cells gained and provided for egg-sharing however, were originally intended to be of own use which is why the passing on of cells is considered just as a 'use' of cells and not an extraction in terms of §2b(2). Consequently the age limit of ova cell donors does not apply in the context of egg-sharing.[366]

337. In order to avoid spare embryos, §10 stipulates that for the purpose of in vitro fertilization only as many ova may be fertilized as necessary for a promising and reasonable medically assisted procreation. §10 refers to the state-of-the-art in medical research, but purposely does not determine a number. Thus, the fertilization of ova 'on stock' is not allowed, and according to the travaux préparatoires, all fertilized ova should be implanted. By granting an absolute and unrestricted right to withdraw the consent before the implantation (§8[4]), the legislator nevertheless accepts the possibility of 'spare embryos'.

338. Before 2015, the use of ova cells for heterologous in vitro fertilization was prohibited. The prohibition originated from the basic principle in civil law 'mater semper certa est, pater est quem nuptiae demonstrant'[367] and thus, prevents the law to permit surrogate motherhood. Under this basic principle of civil law the mother may only be the woman who carries the child and situations of two women claiming to be the biological mother of one and the same child are to be avoided. In addition,

---

on the age limit by M. Fltascher-Thöni & C. Voithofer, 'Eizellenspende und PID: Offene Fragen des FMedRÄG 2015', *Imago hominis* (2017): 24 (45 et seq).

364. Ch. Kopetzki, 'Das Recht der Fortpflanzungsmedizin 2015: Aktueller Stand und verfassungsrechtliche Bewertung', in *Das Recht der Fortpflanzungsmedizin 2015 – Analyse und Kritik*, ed. S. Arnold, E. Bernat & Ch. Kopetzki (Vienna: Manz, 2016), 75.

365. C. Wendehorst, 'Neuerungen im österreichischen Fortpflanzungsmedizinrecht durch das FMedRÄG 2015 Anpassung an europaweite Entwicklungen', *iFamZ* (2015): 4 (6).

366. Ch. Kopetzki, 'Das Recht der Fortpflanzungsmedizin 2015: Aktueller Stand und verfassungsrechtliche Bewertung', in *Das Recht der Fortpflanzungsmedizin 2015 – Analyse und Kritik*, ed. S. Arnold, E. Bernat & Ch. Kopetzki (Vienna: Manz, 2016), 76; E. Bernat, 'Das Recht der Fortpflanzungsmedizin im Wandel – Eckpunkte des Fortpflanzungsmedizinrechts-Änderungsgesetzes 2015', *JAP* (2015/2016): 47; different view in regards to the age limit P. Barth & M. Erlebach (eds), *Handbuch des neuen Fortpflanzungsmedizinrechts* (Vienna: Linde Verlag, 2015), 223.

367. Which translates into: The mother is always certain, the father is the man whom the marriage appoints.

the legislator wanted to avoid the risk of exploitation of women.[368] Furthermore, the Act also prohibited the use of donor-sperm for IVF but allowed heterologous insemination. These prohibitions were strongly criticized under the aspects of constitutional law and legitimacy for years,[369] and thus, eventually fought before the European Court of Human Rights. Prior to that, the Austrian Constitutional Court held that these restrictions neither violated Article 8 ECHR nor the rule of equality.[370] Nevertheless, the court emphasized that the legislator's margin of appreciation might narrow in the future because of changes in the factual conditions. The European Court of Human Rights, which was then appealed in the same case, first ruled that the difference in treatment between prohibited sperm donation for in vitro fertilization (IVF) and the lawful use of sperm donation for in vivo fertilization (via insemination) was a violation of Article 14 in conjunction with Article 8 ECHR.[371] The Great Chamber however, revised the judgment of the Small Chamber and negated a violation of the ECHR by referring to the wide margin of appreciation of the Member States.[372] Even though the margin of appreciation equipped Austria with the autonomy to retain the extensive prohibitions the arguments against heterologous IVF did not seem plausible as there were no specific risks arising from heterologous IVF that could not appear through heterologous in vivo fertilization.[373] When the legislator therefore reformed this inconsistency in 2015, the inequality in regards to the prohibited use of ova cell donation was also eliminated.

2. Administrative and Organizational Remarks

339. Moreover, the following provisions are to be considered in general in the context of medically assisted procreation: the procedure may only be carried out by specialized physicians and in specifically equipped hospitals (§4[1 and 2]); homogenous insemination may also be carried out by gynaecologists in their offices (§4[2]); the spouses or partners have to provide their written consent, (§8); sperm,

---

368. To ensure full voluntary action under the amended Act, sperm and ova cell donations underlie a strict prohibition of commercialization.
369. *See*, e.g., E. Bernat (ed.), *Die Reproduktionsmedizin am Prüfstand von Recht und Ethik* (Vienna: Manz, 2000); M. Mayrhofer, *Reproduktionsmedizinrecht* (Vienna, Graz: NWV, 2003), FN 9; E. Dujmovits, 'Reproduktionsmedizin – Gesetzgebung im Wandel?', in *Biotechnologie und Recht*, ed. Ch. Kopetzki & H. Mayer (Vienna: Manz, 2002), 105; Ch. Kopetzki, 'Medizinisch unterstützte Fortpflanzung: Reformbedarf aus verfassungsrechtlicher Sicht', in *Gesundheit und Recht – Recht auf Gesundheit*, ed. Österreichische Juristenkommission (Vienna, Linde, 2013), 139.
370. Constitutional Court 14 Oct. 1999, VfSlg 15632, *RdM* 2000, 21; *JBl* 2000, 228; *MedR* 2000, 389 *(Bernat)*.
371. European Court of Human Rights 1 Apr. 2010, Application no. 57813/00 (Case of *S.H. and others v. Austria*), *RdM* 2010/88 *(Bernat)*.
372. European Court of Human Rights (Grand Chamber) 3 Nov. 2011, Application no. 57813/00 (Case of *S.H. and others v. Austria*), *RdM* 2012/53 *(Pöschl)*; *EF-Z* 2012/7 *(Bernat)*; *iFamZ* 2012/1 *(Vasek)*; also *see* for example Bernat, 'S.H. et al., gegen Österreich: Ein Schritt vorwärts, ein Schritt zurück', in *Gesundheit und Recht – Recht auf Gesundheit*, ed. Österreichische Juristenkommission (Vienna, Linde, 2013), 163.
373. Ch. Kopetzki, 'Das Recht der Fortpflanzungsmedizin 2015: Aktueller Stand und verfassungsrechtliche Bewertung', in *Das Recht der Fortpflanzungsmedizin 2015 – Analyse und Kritik*, ed. S. Arnold, E. Bernat & Ch. Kopetzki (Vienna: Manz, 2016), 73.

ova, viable cells as well as testicle and ovary tissue can be stored until the donors' death or the storage is revoked (§17[1]).

340. Further provisions to be considered in the context of heterologous methods are: the hospital carrying out the procedure needs to hold an administrative concession (§4[2] and [3]); the cells of a person may only be used in a maximum number of three marriages or comparable relationships (§14[2]) and in only one hospital (§14[1]); the mixed use of cells of more than one man and woman is prohibited (§14[3]); the spouses or partners have to provide their written consent, which requires a notarial deed in case of cohabitation or heterologous methods, and which must not be older than one year (§8[1]); the cell donor has to provide his/her written consent, which can be withdrawn at any time (§8[4]).

341. The Act also includes administrative regulations concerning *inter alia*: the approval and qualifications of the facilities carrying out the artificial procreations, the legal duty to give advice, to keep records and to report (§18), as well as the procreated child's right to demand information about its biological father from the age of fourteen on (§20).[374]

342. In 1999 the Artificial Procreation Act was supplemented by the Federal Act Establishing a Fund for Financing In-Vitro-Fertilization Treatment[375] in order to subsidize the treatment in compliance with the Artificial Procreation Act.

In addition, the Human Tissue Safety Act was passed in 2008 which also applies to germ cells and its regulations partially apply to the donation, testing, storage, etc. of these cells too. Thus, especially donation facilities need cumulative approvals.[376]

3. Extracorporeal Embryos

343. The rewriting of §3 caused a viable debate among scholars on whether a donation of extracorporeal embryos is prohibited or not; whereas the prevailing view argued that even though there is no explicit prohibition, the lack thereof can be interpreted as such.[377] Moreover the wording of §3 stipulates that ova or sperm

---

374. For details on this chapter *see* i.a. E. Bernat (ed.), *Lebensbeginn durch Menschenhand – Probleme künstlicher Befruchtungstechnologien aus medizinischer, ethischer und juristischer Sicht* (Graz: Leykam, 1985); E. Bernat, *Rechtsfragen medizinisch assistierter Zeugung* (Frankfurt, Bern, New York, Paris: Peter Lang, 1989); E. Bernat (ed.), *Fortpflanzungsmedizin, Wertung und Gesetzgebung* (Vienna: Verlag der Österreichischen Staatsdruckerei, 1991); M. Mayrhofer, *Reproduktionsmedizinrecht* (Vienna, Graz: NWV, 2003).

375. IVF-Fonds-Gesetz, Federal Law Gazette I 1999/180, as last amended by Federal Law Gazette I 2010/3.

376. For further information on the relation of the Artificial Procreation Act to the Human Tissue Safety Act *see* A. Leischner, 'Die Gewinnung von Keimzellen zur medizinisch unterstützten Fortpflanzung', *RdM* (2009): 140.

377. C. Wendehorst, 'Neuerungen im österreichischen Fortpflanzungsmedizinrecht durch das FMedRÄG 2015 Anpassung an europaweite Entwicklungen', *iFamZ* (2015): 4 (7); E. Bernat, 'Das Recht der Fortpflanzungsmedizin im Wandel – Eckpunkte des Fortpflanzungsmedizinrechts-Änderungsgesetzes 2015', *JAP* (2015/2016): 45 (48); M. Eder-Rieder, 'Medizinisch unterstütze

of a third person may exceptionally be used but does not mention embryos. In contrary however, there are convincing arguments against this opinion: The European Court of Human Rights ruled that the free disposal of the use of viable cells is covered by Article 8 ECHR and therefor any restriction must have a legal basis;[378] conversely, without a law stipulating a prohibition, there cannot be one. Moreover, it seems inconsistent to argue that the Act allows the donation of sperm and ova but not the combination in an embryo which is why it violates the general principle of equality granted by constitution.[379]

344. Extracorporeal embryos may only be stored for a maximum period of ten years (§17[1]).

345. Before 2015, any embryonic research – including Pre-Implantation Diagnosis – was prohibited under §9, as it was not considered to be a necessary measure to induce pregnancy and therefore not covered by the permission to use cells according to §9. As a result, couples were forced to undergo a 'trial-pregnancy', leaving them with no choice but to induce pregnancy first and to test the embryo through Prenatal Diagnosis. To tackle this issue, §9 was amended and now allows research on extracorporeal embryos under the specific circumstances of §2a.

The amended §9 stipulates that viable cells must not be used for purposes other than medically assisted procreation. They may only be studied and examined as far as it is necessary to induce pregnancy in light of the state-of-the-art in medical research and experience or to conduct Pre-Implantation Diagnosis in accordance with §2a(1). The same applies to sperms and ova intended to be used for medically assisted procreation. Further, any intervention in the gamete is explicitly prohibited (§9[3]) unless it is permitted under §2a.[380]

Fortpflanzung nach dem FMedRÄG 2015 – Neuerungen und Erweiterungen', *EF-Z* (2016): 127 (128); M. Mayrhofer, 'Fortpflanzungsmedizingesetz – FMedG', in *Gmundner Kommentar zum Gesundheitsrecht*, ed. M. Neumayr, R. Resch & F. Wallner (Vienna, Manz, 2016), 2198; A. Leischner-Lenzhofer 'Fortpflanzungsmedizin', in *Handbuch Medizinrecht,* ed. G. Aigner et al. (Vienna, Manz, 2016), I/BT (130 et seq); A. Zwettler, 'Durchbruch oder Zwischenschritt?', *ZfG* (2016): 49; P. Barth & M. Erlebach, *Handbuch des neuen Fortpflanzungsmedizinrechts* (Vienna: Linde, 2015), 222; for a detailed constitutional analysis *see* Ch. Kopetzki, 'Das Recht der Fortpflanzungsmedizin 2015: Aktueller Stand und verfassungsrechtliche Bewertung', in *Das Recht der Fortpflanzungsmedizin 2015 – Analyse und Kritik*, ed. S. Arnold, E. Bernat & Ch. Kopetzki (Vienna: Manz, 2016), 77 et seq.

378. European Court of Human Rights (Grand Chamber) 27 Aug. 2015, Application no 46.470/11, (Case of *Parillo v. Italy*); for further information on the judgment *see* B. Ohms & E. Handl-Petz, 'The Jurisprudence of the European Court of Human Rights in 2015: A Year of Transition', *Jahrbuch Human Rights* (2016), 275.

379. E. Bernat, 'Das Recht der Fortpflanzungsmedizin im Wandel – Eckpunkte des Fortpflanzungsmedizinrechts-Änderungsgesetzes 2015', *JAP* (2015/2016): 45 (48); Ch. Kopetzki, 'Das Recht der Fortpflanzungsmedizin 2015: Aktueller Stand und verfassungsrechtliche Bewertung', in *Das Recht der Fortpflanzungsmedizin 2015 – Analyse und Kritik*, ed. S. Arnold, E. Bernat & Ch. Kopetzki (Vienna: Manz, 2016), 77–79.

380. For further details *see* Part II, Ch. 3, §3.IV.

4. Surrogacy

346. Similar to the arguments regarding extracorporeal embryos the amendment of §3 also reopened the debate on the legitimacy of surrogate motherhood. Since the general expulsion of the use of third party ova cells was altered, one could argue, that this could pave the way for surrogacy. However, §143 of Austria's Civil Code (Allgemeines bürgerliches Gesetzbuch, National Gazette 1859/217, as last amended by Federal Law Gazette I 2016/43) stipulates, that legal motherhood may only be established by the woman who gave birth to a child. So even if assisted reproductive techniques would be applied to induce pregnancy to a surrogate mother, legally she could never transmit motherhood through other means than through adoption. Moreover, surrogate contracts would fail to meet the basic prerequisites of contractual agreements due to its violation of moral principles according to §879 of the Civil Code. Further, §2 of the Act stipulates, that assisted reproductive methods may only be applied under the strict principle of subsidiarity which would not be respected if the treatment were undergone by a surrogate of general reproductive health.[381] In addition, the strict prohibition of intermediation and remuneration (§16) consequently hinders commercial surrogacy.[382] Thus, even though there is no explicit prohibition there is no possible way that could enable legal motherhood for another woman than the one carrying the child.[383]

III. Stem Cell Research

347. The legal protection of the embryo is very heterogeneous in Austria. Full protection of a 'person' is not granted in criminal and civil law until childbirth. Although §22 of the Civil Code fictionally extends the protection to prenatal life from conception onwards, it is too vague and debated too controversially to guarantee absolute protection. In fact, the legal protection of the embryo rises gradually starting from nidation, as expressed especially in the regulations concerning abortion (*see* Part II, Chapter 3, §1. above).

Apart from criminal law, which does not provide any restrictions concerning the embryo before nidation,[384] the extracorporeal embryo is strictly protected under the provisions of administrative law: §9(1) of the Artificial Procreation Act forbids (apart from the cases allowed under §2a) any use (therapeutic, diagnostic or exploratory) of viable cells (in the sense of fertilized embryos), as long as such a use is

381. E. Bernat, 'Das Recht der Fortpflanzungsmedizin im Wandel – Eckpunkte des Fortpflanzungsmedizinrechts-Änderungsgesetzes 2015', *JAP* (2015/2016): 45 (49).

382. The institution of surrogate motherhood does, however, not violate the Austrian ordre public: Constitutional Court 14 Dec. 2012, B 13/11-10, *RdM* 2012, 104 (Bernat); *iFamZ* 2012, 63; *EF-Z* 2012, 67. For details on this chapter *see* Ch. Kopetzki, 'Das Recht der Fortpflanzungsmedizin 2015: Aktueller Stand und verfassungsrechtliche Bewertung', in *Das Recht der Fortpflanzungsmedizin 2015 – Analyse und Kritik*, ed. S. Arnold, E. Bernat & Ch. Kopetzki (Vienna: Manz, 2016), 81 et seq.

383. For details *see*, with further references: S. Arnold, 'Fortpflanzungstourismus und Leihmutterschaft im Spiegel des deutschen und österreichischen internationalen Privat- und Verfahrensrechts', in *Das Recht der Fortpflanzungsmedizin 2015 – Analyse und Kritik*, ed. S. Arnold, E. Bernat & Ch. Kopetzki (Vienna: Manz, 2016), 125 (et seq).

384. For example: E. Köck, 'Der (straf)rechtliche Schutz des Embryos', *ÖJZ* (2006): 631 (633 et seq.).

not necessary for inducing pregnancy. However, these strict prohibitions do not protect the embryo itself, but focus on forbidding certain manipulations like embryonic research and PID apart from the permitted cases under §2a. At the same time, §17(1) of the Artificial Procreation Act stipulates, that fertilized embryos are to be abolished after a maximum storage period of ten years.

348. Regarding the use of embryonic stem cells, §9(1) is only relevant to that extent, that it forbids procuring the cells from embryos. The use of legally acquired stem cells (e.g., because of being procured abroad or via somatic cell nuclear transfer) however, is not specifically regulated. It may be subject to the regulations of pharmaceutical law or the Gene Technology Act, but there are no general restrictions concerning the use of embryonic stem cells.

Unlike totipotent stem cells, legally procured pluripotent stem cells are not to be subsumed under §9(1) as this rule only refers to 'viable cells'. §1(3) of the Artificial Procreation Act defines the concept of 'viable cells' as 'fertilized ova and cells developed from them'. This definition only covers totipotent cells that can develop into a human being, but not pluripotent stem cells. They cannot be qualified as cells 'developed from fertilized ova' either, as this definition has to be interpreted restrictively. If interpreted otherwise, all human cells – those of the foetus in utero as well as every single somatic cell of an adult – would be subject to the strict regulations of the Artificial Procreation Act.

349. The intermediation of sperm, ova or viable cells between persons wishing to donate and those wishing to receive is strictly prohibited under §16(2). However, cells may still be transferred without constituting an intermediation, namely if there is no third party (acting as an agent between donor and receiver) involved.[385] §17(2) of the Artificial Procreation Act permits the transfer of sperm, ova and viable cells but only if the respective written consent of the person or couple is given. The import of embryonic stem cells is not regulated. Regarding the transfer from a foreign institution to an Austrian institution, the same restrictions apply as for national institutions.[386]

385. Ch. Kopetzki, 'Das Recht der Fortpflanzungsmedizin 2015: Aktueller Stand und verfassungsrechtliche Bewertung', in *Das Recht der Fortpflanzungsmedizin 2015 – Analyse und Kritik*, ed. S. Arnold, E. Bernat & Ch. Kopetzki (Vienna: Manz, 2016), 94; Leischner-Lenzhofer 'Fortpflanzungsmedizin', in *Handbuch Medizinrecht*, ed. G. Aigner et al. (Vienna, Manz, 2016), I/BT/168; different opinion in P. Barth & M. Erlebach (eds), *Handbuch des neuen Fortpflanzungsmedizinrechts* (Vienna: Linde, 2015), 285–286.

386. For further information *see*: Ch. Kopetzki, 'Rechtliche Aspekte des Embryonenschutzes', in *Embryonenschutz – Hemmschuh für die Biomedizin?*, ed. U. Körtner & Ch. Kopetzki (Vienna: Manz, 2003), 51; Ch. Kopetzki, 'Der Status des extrakorporalen Embryos – Landesbericht Österreich', in *Internationale Perspektiven zu Status und Schutz des extrakorporalen Embryos*, ed. A. Eser, H.G. Koch & C. Seith (Baden-Baden: Nomos, 2007), 215; Ch. Kopetzki, 'Stammzellforschung in Österreich – eine Bestandsaufnahme des geltenden Rechts', in *Stammzellforschung*, ed. U. Körtner & Ch. Kopetzki (Vienna, New York: Springer, 2008), 269. For the debate concerning constitutional rights *see* Ch. Kopetzki, 'Grundrechtliche Aspekte des therapeutischen Klonens', in *Biotechnologie und Recht*, ed. Ch. Kopetzki & H. Mayer (Vienna: Manz, 2002), 15 et seq.

350. Violations of §9(1) are penalized under administrative law. §22 stipulates a (quite mild) fine up to EUR 50,000 or alternatively a jail sentence of up to fourteen days in case of uncollectability.

IV. Cloning

351. Neither reproductive nor therapeutic cloning are explicitly regulated by Austrian law. Nevertheless, a prohibition of reproductive cloning can be derived from §9 of the Artificial Procreation Act, which forbids any intervention in the gamete.[387] Although the prohibition is not stipulated explicitly it is consequently derived from subparagraph 1 (stipulating that cells may only be used to induce pregnancy) and moreover by subparagraph 3 (reinforcing that any intervention in the gamete is prohibited). Whilst reproductive cloning is prohibited, the legitimacy of therapeutic cloning remains disputed: Therapeutic cloning is considered to be the transmission of the nucleus of a cell into an enucleated unfertilized ovum for the purpose of growing embryonic cells.[388] §9(1) prohibits interventions in viable cells for the purpose of research or therapy (unless §2a is applicable). Yet, viable cells are defined as 'fertilized ova and cells developed from them' in §1[3]. For lack of fertilization in the process of somatic cell nuclear transfer, this definition does not apply to therapeutic cloning.[389] Neither does §9(3), which extends the prohibition of manipulation on gametes in general, forbid therapeutic cloning, as it only refers to gametes used for medically assisted procreation (which is not aimed at in this case). The prohibitions of §9(1) are not applicable mutatis mutandis on viable cells gained by somatic cell nuclear transfer due to the clear wording of the law and the general prohibition of analogy in penalty law. Additionally, the legislator did not want to regulate biomedical techniques that had nothing to do with human procreation, so that there is no shortcoming that can be closed by analogy.[390] Therapeutic cloning is not restricted by §74 of the Gene Technology Act either (*see* Part II,

387. In detail: A. Miklos, 'Das Verbot des Klonens von Menschen in der österreichischen Rechtsordnung', *RdM* (2000): 35; A. Miklos, 'Rechtliche Überlegungen zum Klonen menschlicher Zellen', in *Biotechnologie und Recht,* ed. Ch. Kopetzki & H. Mayer (Vienna: Manz, 2002), 119 (147 et seq., 156 et seq.).

388. Ch. Kopetzki, 'Grundrechtliche Aspekte des therapeutischen Klonens', in *Biotechnologie und Recht,* ed. Ch. Kopetzki & H. Mayer (Vienna: Manz, 2002), 16.

389. When this method is applied, any cell may be transferred and used to implement into the cell envelope and if not implemented for the means of reproductive technology consequently does not constitute a viable cell.

390. Ch. Kopetzki, 'Stammzellforschung in Österreich – eine Bestandsaufnahme des geltenden Rechts', in *Stammzellforschung,* ed. U. Körtner & Ch. Kopetzki (Vienna, New York: Springer, 2008), 269 (282 ff); Ch. Kopetzki, 'Rechtliche Aspekte des Embryonenschutzes', in Embryonenschutz – Hemmschuh für die Biomedizin?, ed. U. Körtner & Ch. Kopetzki (Vienna: Manz, 2003), 51 (59); A. Miklos, 'Rechtliche Überlegungen zum Klonen menschlicher Zellen', in *Biotechnologie und Recht,* ed. Ch. Kopetzki & H. Mayer (Vienna: Manz, 2002), 119 (142 et seq.); E. Dujmovits, 'Reproduktionsmedizin – Gesetzgebung im Wandel?', in *Biotechnologie und Recht,* ed. Ch. Kopetzki & H. Mayer (Vienna: Manz, 2002), 98.

Chapter 3, §4. below), as it does not result in a mutation of the genetic material in the gametes. This (prevailing) doctrine however, is not undisputed in Austria.[391]

§4. GENETICS

I. Genetic Analysis

352. The Gene Technology Act (*Gentechnikgesetz,* Federal Law Gazette 1994/510, as last amended by Federal Law Gazette I 2016/112), which entered into force in January 1995, regulates the main aspects of biotechnology and genetic engineering: contained use of genetically modified organisms (GMOs), deliberate release of GMOs into the environment, placing products containing GMOs on the market and the application of biotechnology in human medicine, such as gene analysis and gene therapy.[392]

353. Genetic analysis is only partly regulated by §§65 et seq. of the Gene Technology Act, as these regulations only refer to genetic analysis for medical and scientific purposes.

Genetic analysis for medical purposes in the respective provisions cover four types: type 1 (diagnosis of an existing disease or preparation of a therapy), type 2 (diagnosis of an existing disease caused by mutation of the germline), type 3 ('predictive': diagnosis of predisposition of future disease or status of carrier, as long as prophylaxis or therapy is possible at that point), type 4 ('predictive': diagnosis of predisposition of future disease or status of carrier, as long as prophylaxis or therapy is not possible at that point). For predictive gene analyses (types 3 and 4) specific regulations exist. It is only allowed to be carried out in facilities that are approved by the minister of health (§68) and are run by a qualified laboratory head. Indication has to be stated by a medical specialist who is competent in the particular therapeutic field or by a human genetics specialist. The patient has to be thoroughly informed about nature, consequences and significance of the genetic analysis before and after the analysis (§69), which has to be confirmed in written form. If the patient is a minor, the legal representative has to provide the written consent. The patient has the right not to be informed about the results of the analysis. The all-embracing duties to inform (as defined in §69) also apply to type 2 analyses as well as the postulation of a qualified laboratory head. §71 provides special regulations about data protection. Until recently, it was prohibited for insurances and employers to demand, collect, accept or use the results of gene analyses, not even if the person

391. Different opinion argued by M. Mayrhofer, Reproduktionsmedizinrecht (Vienna, Graz: NWV, 2003), 99 et seq., who assumes a forbidden genetic manipulation of the germ line.

392. For details *see*, with further references, F. Kerschner et al., *Kommentar zum Gentechnikgesetz* (Vienna: Manz, 2007); M. Herdegen & H.-G. Dederer (eds), *Internationale Praxis Gentechnikrecht*, 33rd edn (Heidelberg: Müller, 2001), Landesbericht Österreich; M. Stelzer & K. Schmiedecker, 'Gentechnikrecht', in *Öffentliches Wirtschaftsrecht,* ed. M. Holoubek & M. Potacs, vol. 2, 3rd edn (Vienna, New York: Springer, 2013), 665; M. Stelzer, *Datenschutz im Gentechnikrecht* (Vienna: Bundesministerium für Gesundheit und Frauen, 2004); Bundesministerium für Wissenschaft und Forschung (ed.), *Gentechnologie im österreichischen Recht* (Vienna: Manz, 1991).

concerned gave consent to it (§67). However, the Austrian Constitutional Court found this prohibition for insurances to be objectively unjustified, as genetic analyses do not substantially differ from other 'conventional' examination results (in the sense of non-genetic methods).[393] Consequently, the legislator was given a time frame until 31 December 2016 to amend §67. The provision now stipulates in its subparagraph 2 that the prohibition in subparagraph 1 does not apply for insurances requesting results of a type 1 analysis as long as the findings do not provide information on type 2, 3 and 4 genetic analyses.[394]

354. Finally, gene analyses which are not used for medical, scientific or instructional purposes (e.g., for identification) do not fall within the scope of the Gene Technology Act.

II. Gene Therapy

355. Somatic gene therapy is only permitted for the purposes of therapy, prevention of severe diseases or establishing appropriate treatments in the context of clinical trials (§74 of the Gene Technology Act). It has to be carried out state-of-the-art and must not result in a mutation of the genetic material in the gametes. If the risk of a mutation cannot be completely eliminated, somatic gene therapy can only be carried out in case of infertility, given that the benefits of the therapy prevail its risks. Gametes of a treated person must not be used for procuring extracorporeal embryos.

356. Somatic gene therapy has to be carried out by a physician in a hospital. The therapy needs previous admission by the health minister, who has to consult the Gene Technology Commission and the Advisory Board for Medicinal Products (§75[3]). Gene therapies in the context of clinical trials also need previous admission by the health minister (§76). Beyond that, the special regulations of the Medicinal Products Act apply to clinical trials (*see* Part II, Chapter 3, §6.IV. below).

III. Prenatal Diagnosis (PND)

357. Prenatal genetic analysis is explicitly regulated and allowed by §69 of the Gene Technology Act, provided that the pregnant woman gives written consent and confirms that she was informed about the nature, consequences and significance of the genetic analysis comprehensively. If the woman is under the age of fourteen, her legal representatives have to provide this consent. The informed consent also has to cover the risks of the intervention. The indication and information related to the

393. Austrian Constitutional Court, 8 Oct. 2015, G 20/2015-13 and G 281/2015-8; *JBl* 2016, 311 = *ÖJZ* 2016, 329 = *ecolex* 2016, 103 = *RdW* 2015, 689.

394. For details *see* Ch. Kopetzki, 'Genetische Analysen und Versicherung – Verfassungsrechtliche Aspekte des § 67 GTG', *versicherungsrundschau* (2015/7-8): 25 et seq.; Ch. Kopetzki, 'Genetische Analysen und Versicherungsrecht', *RdM* (2015): 125.

procedure have to be explained either by a medical specialist who is competent in the particular therapeutic field or by a specialist on human genetics.

358. Other PND-methods that do not include genetic analysis (e.g., ultrasound, blood tests, microscopic analysis) are allowed under the general provisions of criminal and civil law (indication and informed consent). The patient has to be informed about the risks and significance of the analysis as well as alternative methods and the consequences of failing to carry out the analysis.[395]

359. In case of a wrong diagnosis or insufficient information about the limited significance of the analysis the physician may be liable for 'wrongful birth' (*see* Part I, Chapter 4, §1. above).[396]

IV. Pre-implantation Diagnostics (PID)

360. Until the recent amendment of the Act in 2015 the Pre-Implantation Diagnosis was unregulated but a prohibition thereof was derived from the former §9(1). Nevertheless PID was one of the most controversially debated methods over the past years.[397] Finally in 2015, among the various liberalizations that were implemented, PID was finally introduced. One of the main reasons that eventually made a regulation of PID necessary was the case of *Costa and Pavan v. Italy*[398] in which the ECtHR ruled that the identical legal situation, namely the general prohibition of PID whereas at the same time abortion is considered lawful, constitutes a violation of Article 8 ECHR.

361. It is defined in §1(4) as any method to genetically examine viable cells before implementing them into the body of a woman as well as genetic examinations of other cells resulting from the fertilization of the ova cell. The legislator made clear, that by 'other cells' only totipotent cells are covered.[399] §2a determines three scenarios as precondition for a lawful PID: First, three or more transmissions of viable cells could not induce a pregnancy and there is reason to believe, that this can be traced back to a genetic disposition of the viable cells; second, at least three spontaneous miscarriages or stillbirths were ascertained by a doctor and there is a high chance that they were linked to genetic disposition of the child; or third, the

395. Supreme Court of Justice 7 Mar. 2006, 5 Ob 165/05h, *ecolex* 2006, 564 = *EF-Z* 2006/53 *(Bernat)* = *FamZ* 2006, 63 (*Neumayr)* = *RdM* 2009, 90 = *JAP* 2006/2007, 115 *(Paparatits)* = *ZAK* 2006, 214 *(Rebhahn).*

396. For the development of the 'wrongful-birth' and 'wrongful conception'-judicature most recently E. Bernat, 'Wrongful Birth und Wrongful Conception. Der Ersatz des Familienplanungsschadens auf dem Prüfstand des OGH', in *Körper-Codes,* ed. Ch. Kopetzki, M. Pöschl, M. Reiter & M. Wittmann-Tiwald (Vienna: Linde, 2010), 109.

397. For all relevant arguments related to the prohibition of PID *see* Ch. Kopetzki, 'Altes und Neues zur Präimplantationsdiagnostik', *JRP* (2012): 317.

398. European Court of Human Rights 28 Aug. 2012, Application no. 54.270/10, *(Case of Costa and Pavan v. Italy)*; *RdM* 2013, 195 *(Kopetzki).*

399. Explanations of the governmental bill 445 BlgNR 25. GP 4.

genetic disposition of one of the parents constitutes a serious threat to the child's life or the development of a hereditary disease.[400]

Here too, the principle of subsidiarity is applicable and the least invasive method shall be chosen to examine the cells.

362. Polar body diagnosis is (and was) consistent with §9(1) in any case, as it does not affect viable cells as defined in §1(3) of the Artificial Procreation Act.[401]

363. For genetic analyses in the context of PID the above named Gene Technology Act is applicable. In the case of a conflict of laws, the Artificial Procreation Act is prioritized as *lex specialis.*

364. Finally, the institutions performing PID must be authorized according to §68 Gene Technology Act and independent (organizationally, staff-wise and financially) from the institution performing the assisted reproductive method (§4[3]). The committee for gene analysis and gene therapy has to be incorporated (§88 Gene Technology Act) in the authorization procedures of institutions.

§5. Organ Transplants

365. Organ transplantation[402] is regulated under the Organ Transplantation Act *(Organtransplantationsgesetz,* Federal Law Gazette 2012/108), which was passed

400. A detailed definition of hereditary diseases can be found in §2a(2). For a critical analysis of the definition of hereditary diseases *see* Ch. Kopetzki, 'Das Recht der Fortpflanzungsmedizin 2015: Aktueller Stand und verfassungsrechtliche Bewertung', in *Das Recht der Fortpflanzungsmedizin 2015 – Analyse und Kritik*, ed. S. Arnold, E. Bernat & Ch. Kopetzki (Vienna: Manz, 2016), 86.
401. Ch. Kopetzki, 'Das Recht der Fortpflanzungsmedizin 2015: Aktueller Stand und verfassungsrechtliche Bewertung', in *Das Recht der Fortpflanzungsmedizin 2015 – Analyse und Kritik*, ed. S. Arnold, E. Bernat & Ch. Kopetzki (Vienna: Manz, 2016), 85; P. Barth & M. Erlebach (eds), *Handbuch des neuen Fortpflanzungsmedizinrechts* (Vienna: Linde, 2015), 136. M. Mayrhofer 'Fortpflanzungsmedizingesetz – FMedG' in *Gmundner Kommentar zum Gesundheitsrecht*, ed. M. Neumayr, R. Resch & F. Wallner (Vienna, Manz, 2016), 2177; A. Leischner-Lenzhofer 'Fortpflanzungsmedizin', in *Handbuch Medizinrecht*, ed. G. Aigner et al. (Vienna, Manz, 2016), I.23.3.1.2; differing opinion C. Wendehorst, 'Neuerungen im österreichischen Fortpflanzungsmedizinrecht durch das FMedRÄG 2015 Anpassung an europaweite Entwicklungen', *iFamZ* (2015): 4 (6).
402. This chapter is based on E. Dujmovits, 'Organtransplantation', in *Handbuch Medizinrecht*, ed. G. Aigner et al. (Vienna: Manz, 2003 et seq.), I.21. For details *see also* V. Kräftner, *Organtransplantationsrecht* (Doctoral thesis, University of Vienna, 2016); E. Wagner & J. Ecker, 'OTPG', in *Gmundner Kommentar zum Gesundheitsrecht*, ed. M. Neumayr, R. Resch & F. Wallner (Vienna: Manz, 2016), 2349 et seq.; *S. Füszl*, 'Das neue Organtransplantationsgesetz', *ÖZPR* (2013): 26; W. Heissenberger, 'Das Bundesgesetz über die Transplantation menschlicher Organe und dessen wesentliche Neuerungen', *RdM* (2013): 50. For additional literature especially on the former regulation, *see* e.g., H. Barta, G. Kalchschmid & Ch. Kopetzki (eds), *Rechtspolitische Aspekte des Transplantationsrechts* (Vienna: Manz, 1999); H. Barta & K. Weber (eds), *Rechtsfragen der Transplantationsmedizin in Europa* (Vienna: WUV, 2001); W. Brandstetter & Ch. Kopetzki (eds), *Organtransplantationen. Medizinische und rechtliche Aspekte der Verwendung menschlicher Organe zu Heilzwecken* (Vienna: Facultas, 1987); Ch. Kopetzki, *Organgewinnung zu Zwecken der Transplantation. Eine systematische Analyse des geltenden Rechts* (Vienna, New York: Springer, 1988); Ch. Kopetzki, 'Krankenanstaltenrecht', in *Handbuch des öffentlichen Wirtschaftsrechts*, ed. M.

in 2012 in order to implement the Directive 2010/53/EU. Until then, only the removal of organs from cadavers was explicitly regulated by the Frame Law on Hospitals and Sanatoria (*Krankenanstalten- und Kuranstaltengesetz,* Federal Law Gazette 1957/1, as last amended by Federal Law Gazette I 2013/81). The removal of organs from living donors was subject to the general principals of civil and criminal law.

In 2008, the Human Tissue Safety Act (*Gewebesicherheitsgesetz,* Federal Law Gazette I 2008/49, as last amended by Federal Law Gazette I 2016/105) came into force. It regulates the donation of tissue and cells for application in the human body.

I. Removal of Organs from Cadavers

A. *Background and History*

366. The removal of organs from cadavers was explicitly regulated for the first time in 1982 (Federal Law Gazette 1982/273) on the occasion of a criminal trial concerning the removal of organs for tissue banks. Without the special legal justification in §62a of the Frame Law on Hospitals and Sanatoria, the removal of organs from cadavers for the purpose of storage would fall within the ambit of §190 of the Austrian Criminal Code, which protects the peace in death. The deprivation of cadavers from the people who are legally in possession of the body without their consent can only be justified in case of a lawful autopsy. Autopsy is only legally permissible for the purpose of criminal prosecution (§127 of the Criminal Code), the control of epidemics (Epidemic Code) and the protection of public or scientific interests,[403] if it is carried out in public hospitals (§25 of the Frame Law on Hospitals and Sanatoria). Before implementing the special legal justification of §62a in 1982, the removal of organs from cadavers without consent could only be justified in case of necessity as a justification, which did not include storage in tissue banks.

367. The legal principles of §62a were taken over by §5 Organ Transplantation Act, so that the removal of organs is permissible in order to save the life of another person or restore his/her health by means of transplantation, as long as the deceased person (or his legal representative) has not refused organ donation before his death.

Holoubek & M. Potacs, vol. 1, 3rd edn (Vienna, New York: Springer, 2013), 484; G. Kalchschmid, *Die Organtransplantation* (Vienna: Verlag Österreich, 1997). For further articles *see* W. Holczabek & Ch. Kopetzki, 'Rechtsgrundlagen von Organtransplantationen', *Wiener klinische Wochenschrift* 13 (1986): 417; M. Eder-Rieder, 'Strafrechtliche Aspekte der "kapselgeschützten" Organtransplantation', *ÖJZ* (1990): 627; G. Aigner, 'Organentnahmen bei Verstorbenen zu Transplantationszwecken gemäss §62a KAG; Widerspruchsregister', *RdM* (1994): 119; G. Kalchschmid, 'Die Organtransplantation', *LJZ* (1998): 1; G. Aigner, 'An Overview of Legal Aspects in Organ Transplantation – What are the Family Rights?', *Mitteilungen der Sanitätsverwaltung* 12 (2003): 8.

403. Scientific interests are, for example, the investigation of new forms of diseases, their causes and their course. They are, by nature, in the interest of the public: Supreme Court of Justice 19 Dec. 2001, 7 Ob 199/01t, *RdM* 2002/21.

This concept of donation refusal ('opting-out') naturally leads to high transplantation rates, since everybody who does not actively and explicitly refuse organ donation is a potential donor.

368. Violations of §5 are regarded as administrative offences and chargeable up to EUR 36,340. Additionally, violations are punishable under §190 of the Criminal Code.

B. Definition of Death

369. §5 (and formerly §62a) regulates the removal of organs from cadavers without specifying the concept of 'death' (neither do any other regulations in Austria). Therefore the scientific concept as defined state-of-the-art is relevant. While the traditional standard of death was seen in cardiopulmonary cessation, modern medicine states that brain death (understood as irreversible malfunction of the central nervous system) constitutes death. The advantage of this concept is that people who have been declared dead because of irreversible malfunction of the brain can be artificially ventilated in order to preserve their organs.

370. Regarding the declaration of death, §5(2) only regulates who is authorized to declare the donor dead. Only an uninvolved, independent, licensed medical practitioner, who is neither the ex- nor the implanter, is allowed to do so. He must not be involved in the process of explanation or implantation at all, which ensures that there is no collision of interests. Thus, the physician declaring the donor dead must not be a relative of the donor, be of higher or lower rank than the ex- or implanter or have other business or scientific relations to him. The Highest Medical Advisory Board (*Oberster Sanitätsrat;* hereinafter abbreviated as OSR) requires at least two experienced consultants, which is why brain death is diagnosed by mobile, local teams consisting of several consultants in practice.

371. The methods of diagnosing death are not regulated by Austrian law, for which reason the state-of-the-art in medicine is relevant. The OSR's Recommendations for Diagnosing Brain Death[404] are not legally binding. They are, however, guidelines that put the state-of-the-art in concrete terms and have the quality of general anticipated expert evidence. The OSR's recommendations define individual death as malfunction of the whole brain. According to these guidelines, methods of diagnosing death are detecting clinical symptoms (coma, lack of responses of the brain stem, apnoea) and additional examinations (EEG, Transcranial Duplex Sonography, colour-coded Duplex Sonography and CTA). The OSR suggests Cerebral Angiography only as therapeutic measure for the patients' sake. Non-therapeutic angiography without the patient's consent is qualified as bodily harm and therefore

404. ÖBIG (eds), Empfehlungen zur Durchführung der Hirntoddiagnostik bei einer geplanten Organentnahme, entsprechend dem Beschluss des OSR vom 17. Dez. 2005.

punishable under §§83 et seq. of the Austrian Criminal Code. It is only justified if the principal permission for removal of organs in §5 also covers this method.[405]

C. Coverage of §5 of the Organ Transplantation Act

372. According to the prevailing doctrine on former §§62a et seq. of the Frame Law on Hospitals and Sanatoria, the regulations on organ transplantation are qualified as part of public law, so that they apply on Austrian territory only (Article 49 of the Constitution). As a consequence, foreigners who die in Austria are also subject to the national regulations.[406]

Deceased people in terms of §5 must have necessarily been born alive, that is why the regulation does not cover stillbirths and abortions. In these cases, the removal of organs is only allowed under the general regulations of civil and criminal law, especially the power of disposal of private law and the clause of public morals as well as the regulations concerning cadaver and funeral matters.[407]

D. The Opting-Out Regulation

373. Only the potential donor himself or his legal representative can refuse organ donation before the donor's death. Third parties (for instance relatives) cannot articulate a legally binding refusal. Therefore, it is not necessary to inform or ask the bereaved about the organ harvesting.

The legal representatives who can bindingly refuse the removal of organs (during the donor's lifetime) are the guardians (mostly the parents) of minors and the custodians of mentally ill or disabled people. In this case, they do not represent the protected person, but they have an autonomous right to refuse. If the represented party is capable of understanding that special point, he also has the right to refuse organ donation.

The question of age limits for legally binding refusals of minors is not explicitly regulated by Austrian law (§173 of the Civil Code is not applicable in this case as organ donation is no curative treatment). Thus, the general regulations of the capacity to act (§16 of the Civil Code) apply. The relevant factors are the natural capacity

405. For details *see* U. Körtner & Ch. Kopetzki & S. Müller (eds), *'Hirntod und Organtransplantation'* (Vienna: Verlag Österreich, 2016); Ch. Kopetzki, 'Rechtliche Voraussetzungen der Hirntodbestimmung', in *Schädel-Hirn-Trauma/Hirntod. Beiträge zur Anästhesiologie, Intensiv- und Notfallmedizin,* ed. G. Schwarz, W. Kröll & W.F. List (Vienna, Munich, Bern: Verlag Maudrich, 1995), 45; U. Körtner, 'Ganz tot oder halbtot? Anthropologische und medizinethische Aspekte der Hirntodkontroverse', *RdM* (1995): 79; Ch. Kopetzki, 'Non-heart-beating donors aus rechtlicher Sicht', *Imago Hominis* (1998): 49; A. Haslinger, 'Hirntodfeststellung ohne Eingriffszustimmung?', *RdM* (2005): 77; T. Unger, 'Überarbeitung der Empfehlungen zur Durchführung der Hirntoddiagnostik bei einer geplanten Organentnahme', *Mitteilungen der Sanitätsverwaltung* 3 (2006): 3.

406. Ch. Kopetzki, *Organgewinnung zu Zwecken der Transplantation. Eine systematische Analyse des geltenden Rechts* (Vienna, New York: Springer, 1988), 92 et seq.

407. Tissue and cells are, however, allowed to be removed according to §4(4) of the Human Tissue Safety Act (*see* Ch. 3 §5.IV): W. Heissenberger, 'Entnahme von Zellen und Geweben einer Fehl- oder Totgeburt', *RdM* (2012): 67.

to understand and the ability to judge, but there are no fixed age limits (the age limit of fourteen, which is stated on the standard forms of the official opting-out registers kept by the Austrian Health Institute, therefore has no legal basis). The fact that a minor articulates a refusal alone can be seen as evidence of his intellectual maturity.

374. The doctors must have received a statement in which organ donation is explicitly refused, no matter how (and if) they know about it. The safest way to bail a refusal is by registering in the opting-out register, which is kept by the Austrian Health Institute (also *see* §6). Furthermore, a refusal has, e.g., also been received when registered in the clinical records or when the patient has told the doctor before his death. The explanting hospital is obliged to consult the opting-out register (§7) and the clinical records for a refusal before each removal. Beyond that, there are no special obligations to search for a refusal.

375. Organ donation must be refused explicitly. Beyond that, there are no formal requirements, so that a binding refusal can be articulated in writing or verbally. For registration in the opting-out register of the Austrian Health Institute the signature is required (§6[2]).

The potential donor can either refuse the removal of all or of single organs. However he is not allowed to refuse organ donation under special conditions or to articulate special wishes (e.g., concerning the question who should receive his organs or who should not), because public interests are stronger than the power of disposal in private law. The consequences of forbidden conditions (ineffectiveness either only of the forbidden collateral clause or of the whole refusal) have not been judicially clarified yet. Therefore, it has to be assessed in every single case (in case of doubt organ removal is, however, better refrained from).

There is no time limit for effective refusals. Once they are expressly articulated and can be received by the doctors, they are legally binding without any limits. They can be withdrawn at any time under the same conditions as the refusal itself. Refusals registered in the opting-out register have to be withdrawn in writing and, as a consequence, they have to be deleted in the register (§6[4]).

E. Limits for Organ Removal

376. Unlike in the former regulation of §62a of the Frame Law on Hospitals and Sanatoria, the concept of organ is now legally defined in the Organ Transplantation Act (§3[6]). The definition of organ is consistent with the one in Directive 2010/53. Different from the formerly relevant medical definition, which also covered tissue and cells, §3(6) only refers to solid organs. At the same time, the Human Tissue Safety Act and the Act on Medicinal Products exclude organs from their ambit. Although human skin is covered by the wording of §3(6) of the Organ Transplantation Act, it only falls within the regulations of the Human Tissue Safety Act as it is explicitly mentioned as counter-exception in its §2. For the removal of tissue and cells from cadavers, there is a parallel regulation in §4(5) of the Human Tissue Safety Act. As regards to the relation of organ and tissue removal, organ removal is to be treated preferentially (§5[4]).

Organ removal is only permissible for the purpose of transplantation for therapeutic reasons ('… in order to save the life of another person or to restore his health by means of transplantation'). Explantation for other reasons, for example for producing medicinal products,[408] is not covered by §5.

Organ removal is limited to single organs, but §5 does not name a number. Thus, multi-organ removals are permissible, but they are quantitatively limited.

Additionally, the removal of organs or parts of organs must not disfigure the corpse in any disrespectful way. §5(1) protects the integrity and outward appearance of the cadaver, which is why for example face-transplantations are forbidden. The removal of inner organs is rarely affected by this limitation though. Beyond that, even the removal of organs affecting the outward appearance of the cadaver (like the removal of the hands or feet) is permissible, as long as a dignified appearance is ensured by cosmetic or plastic reconstruction (for instance by using amputation appliance). Whether a disfiguration of the corpse is allowed with the relatives' consent, depends on who is protected by the regulation. If it does not only protect the relatives' feelings, but also has an objective component (protection of the integrity of the corpse itself), even the relatives' consent cannot avoid a violation of integrity.

F. Place of Removal

377. Only special hospitals, namely non-profit hospitals that are operated by a social insurance agency, are allowed to remove organs (§5[3]). Implantation and storage however may be carried out in other places too.

II. Removal of Organs from Living Donors

378. Unlike harvesting organs from cadavers, the removal from living donors was not explicitly regulated until 2012. Now the Organ Transplantation Act codifies the minimum requirements for organ removal from living donors (§8) and regulates aftercare (§9).

First of all, the donation has to be voluntary (§4[1]). The donor has to be legally sane in the concrete situation and there must not be any lack of willpower. Pressure from family members or due to extraordinary situations of necessity (e.g., concerning detainees) might indicate lack of willpower.

The Organ Transplantation Act introduced an explicit age limit of 18 years for organ donation in §8(1). Formerly, organ donation was only forbidden for minors who lacked the capacity to consent. This was deduced from the general principles of civil law, which are still valid for vulnerable groups of people other than minors: As organ donation usually only serves the interest of third parties and is never in the benefit of the donating party, consent to organ removal strictly has to be given

408. Supreme Court of Justice 25 Nov. 1986, 10 Os 104/86: Removal of the pituitary for producing medicinal products is not allowed under former §62a of the Frame Law on Hospitals and Sanatoria and is therefore forbidden.

personally. Consequently only legally sane people can do so. People who lack the capacity to consent (such as mentally ill or unconscious people) can therefore never donate their organs.

379. In general the same principles still apply to bone marrow donation of minor brothers and sisters, as long as they lack the capacity to consent (bone narrow donation falls within the ambit of the Human Tissue Safety Act, which does not generally prohibit donation for minors, but refers to the general principles of Civil Law). Neither their legal representatives nor (and not even) a guardian for collision of interests would be allowed to give his consent in this case. The resulting total inadmissibility of bone marrow donation is, however, seen to be intolerable in this case. So for once the concept of the 'well-being' of the child is seen with a wider perspective, so that it does not only include corporal integrity, but also the preservation of family life by the survival of the sick brother/sister. Other interventions, which are not too severe (such as taking blood or recoverable bone marrow) and might save the brother or sister's life, are therefore better for the child's 'well-being' than forbearance. As a consequence, representative consent given by the guardians is exceptionally allowed in this case.[409]

380. In consideration of the fact that the removal is not therapeutically indicated and therefore only serves the interest of third parties, §8(3) stipulates an all-embracing duty to inform: The donor has to be informed about the removal itself as well as its purpose, the consequences and risks of the operation, especially further necessary check-ups, analytical tests und the consequences of abnormal diagnostic findings, the therapeutical purpose of the removed organ and the potential benefit for the organ receiver, the chances of success of the transplantation, provisions to protect the donor and his/her data and obligations of secrecy, as well as frequent follow-ups. The donor has to be informed both orally and in written and cannot disclaim the information.

The informed consent has to be given in written form and has to be dated and signed. It can be withdrawn at any time. If the donor is not capable of signing, the informed consent has to be articulated in front of three witnesses who are neither involved in the donation nor have a personal interest in the organ transplantation and who have to confirm the consent by signature (§8[4]).

381. Organ removal must not be carried out in case of high risk for the life or health of the donor (§8[5]). The hospital that removed the organ has to offer the donator a medical check-up at least three months after the operation (§9).

382. In addition to the donor's informed consent, the removal must not be contra bones mores (§90 of the Criminal Code, §879 of the Civil Code). Relevant factors for this classification are primarily the character and severity of the operation. For this reason the donor cannot give his consent to a donation that will predictably lead to his death or mortal danger for instance. Apart from health risks in terms of §8(5), it is forbidden to donate organs that constitute the identity of the individual

409. G. Aigner, 'Einwilligung Minderjähriger in eine Knochenmarkspende', *RdM* (1998): 144.

in a relevant way such as gametes or genitals. The donation of organs for storage in an organ bank is problematic too (not so the donation of tissue and cells). As a general rule, the relation between the risks for the donor and the benefits for the recipient has to be balanced. As a result the donation of organs is limited to pairs of organs and organs that regenerate or are dispensable. It is discussed controversially in Austria whether the motivation for organ donation is a relevant factor (for instance monetary interests).

383. As long as the donation is not financially motivated (§4), there are no restrictions concerning the potential recipients of the organs. Therefore organ donation is not limited to relatives or close friends, which is why 'cross-over-donation' is permissible in Austria.

III. Financial Aspects and Allocation

384. Organ transplantation is financed by public health insurance. The costs for implantation are paid for by the organ receiver's health insurance. Organ donation from living donors as well as the necessary preliminary examinations are financed by the donor's health insurance (§120a of the General Social Insurance Act). Transplantation of organs from cadavers is financed by public funds raised by health agencies (§59d of the Frame Law on Hospitals and Sanatoria).[410]

385. There is no individual, legally enforceable right to a certain organ beyond the general right to therapeutic treatment. Health insurances are not obliged to find an organ or finance its procurement.

Organ donation from living donors is regularly dedicated to a particular person. Concerning organs from cadavers the question of allocation arises. Under Austrian law, there is no specific regulation for organ allocation (neither regarding allocation itself nor allocation agencies). Therefore, it is up to the people involved (doctors, hospitals, allocation agencies) to make these decisions. As related to international cooperation, Austria is member of the Eurotransplant International Foundation.

Since allocation is subject to contractual relationships under terms of private law and only private people are involved, fundamental rights are not applicable in this context.

The lack of special regulations is questionable in respect to constitutional and European law.[411]

410. For details *see* W. Geppert, 'Organtransplantationen als Leistung der sozialen Krankenversicherung', *SozSi* (1988): 165.

411. For further details concerning organ allocation *see* G. Aigner, 'Organersatz – Ökonomie und Allokation', *RdM* (2008): 100; F. Breyer et al., *Organmangel. Ist der Tod auf der Warteliste unvermeidbar?* (Berlin, Heidelberg, New York: Springer, 2006); W. Höfling, 'Verteilungsgerechtigkeit in der Transplantationsmedizin?', *JZ* (2007): 481; G. Luf, 'Verteilungsgerechtigkeit im Bereich der modernen Medizin', *RdM* (1997): 99; E. Bernat, 'Marketing of Human Organs?', *Med & Law* 14 (1995): 181. Also *see* K. Bruckmüller & S. Schumann, 'Organmangel und Organspende – Europarechtliche Rechtsetzung und nationaler Anpassungsbedarf', *Jahrbuch Gesundheitsrecht*, ed.

IV. The Human Tissue Safety Act

386. The Human Tissue Safety Act from 2008 implements the European Directive 2004/23/EG. It regulates the procurement of human cells and tissues for human application as well as their processing, storage and distribution, as far as they are not used for producing proprietary medicinal products, investigational medicinal products or medical devices. If human cells and tissues are not intended for human application (which especially comprises transplantations and cell therapy, but also extracorporeal applications), but are to be used for research for example, they do not fall within the ambit of the act. The Human Tissue Safety Act does not differentiate between the different types of cells. As a consequence embryonic stem cells are basically subject to the act, as long as their use is not prohibited by other regulations (especially the Artificial Procreation Act, *see* Part II, Chapter 3, §3.III. above).

The Human Tissue Safety Act does not apply to tissues and cells that are used as autologous transplants within the same medical procedure. Blood and blood components are not subject to the Act either (they are regulated by the Blood Safety Act, Federal Law Gazette I 1999/44, as last amended by Federal Law Gazette I 2009/107). Still cells including haematopoietic peripheral blood are not excluded. Furthermore, §1(3) excludes organs or parts of organs which are to be used for the same purpose as the entire organ in the human body. §2 defines organs as 'all vital parts of the human body formed by different tissues that form a functional entity as regards to structure, vascularization and capacity to develop physiological functions, except skin'.

387. The procurement of cells and tissues is only permitted in special facilities, which need to be registered at the Federal Office for Public Health Safety. The Office for Public Health Safety can forbid the procurement facilities' activities for the reasons listed in §19. The Human Tissue Safety Act provides specific regulations concerning the facilities' compulsory equipment, quality management and so forth. The procurement facilities are not allowed to advertise cell and tissue donation by announcing a profit or similar benefits (§3[9]).

388. The Human Tissue Safety Act differentiates between the removal of tissues and cells from living donors and from cadavers. Concerning the removal from living donors, all necessary medical examinations, which help exclude serious health risks for the donor, are required in advance. The donor has to give his (informed) consent in written form (either by signature or before witnesses), which can be withdrawn at any time. The preliminary information has to cover the therapeutic purpose as well as the further use of the donated material (§4[3]). These requirements also apply to tissue or cell removals for therapeutic reasons (e.g., to operation-waste or other left over substances). Finally a variety of duties to record exist.

The removal of cadavers is permissible for the purpose of saving the life of another person or restoring his health, as long as the tissues and cells are used within

M. Kierein et al. (Vienna: Neuer Wissenschaftlicher Verlag, 2010), 67; V. Kräftner, *Organtransplantationsrecht* (Doctoral thesis, University of Vienna; (2016), 217 et seq.

the ambit of the Human Tissue Safety Act or for producing medicinal products for advanced therapies (gene therapy, cell therapy medicinal products and tissue-engineered products). Furthermore, the removal of organs from cadavers is only allowed under the provisions of §5 of the Organ Transplantation Act. For this reason especially the opting-out regulation applies here.

389. Human tissues and cells have to be processed, stored and distributed in tissue banks that are approved by the Federal Office for Public Health Safety (§22). The Human Tissue Safety Act stipulates a special system for quality management, broad duties of documentation, report, governmental monitoring and inspection rights.[412]

V. Commercial Dealings

390. Prohibitions of financial profit and other restrictions on commercial dealings with bodily material exist only selectively in the Austrian legal order. The regulations are spread over the special areas of administrative law. Thus, their ambit is rather limited and they are not applicable to other matters *mutatis mutandis*.

391. The Organ Transplantation Act led to a harmonization concerning commercial dealings with donated organs. Formerly, §62a(4) of the Frame Law on Hospitals and Sanatoria only prohibited profit-oriented legal transactions on organs or parts of organs from cadavers, but there were no similar restrictions for the removal of organs from living donors. Now §4(5) does not differentiate between organs from cadavers or living donors, but forbids all profit-oriented legal transactions on organs. The prohibitions of §4(5) are not limited to organ donation, but also cover the resulting applications. They only cover profit-oriented legal transactions, so that commercial dealings are not forbidden per se. Appropriate expenses like the costs of removal, transporting and preserving the organs therefore may be paid for. Additionally, commercial exploitation, deprivation of organs or misleading is criminalized by §104a (and the §§88 et seq.) of the Criminal Code.[413]

392. §4(2) of the Organ Transplantation Act and §4(6) of the Human Tissue Safety Act forbid financial profit for donating organs, tissues and cells intended for human applications. These regulations only prohibit financial profit, but not a fee per se, so that appropriate expenses may be charged. §8(4) of the Blood Safety Act

412. For further details on the Human Tissue Safety Act *see* Ch. Kopetzki (ed.), *Gewebesicherheitsrecht* (Vienna: Manz, 2009); K. Polster, *Gewebesicherheitsrecht* (Vienna: Springer, 2011); W. Heissenberger, 'GSG', in *Gmundner Kommentar zum Gesundheitsrecht*, ed. M. Neumayr, R. Resch & F. Wallner (Vienna: Manz 2016), 1813 et seq.; F. Wallner, 'Berufs- und haftungsrechtliche Fragen iZm der Transplantation von Allografts in der Orthopädie', *RdM* (2015): 128; P. Steiner, 'Zum verpflichtenden Abschluss von Vereinbarungen nach §§6 und 8 Gewebesicherheitsgesetz', *RdM* (2012): 16; A. Joklik & T. Zivny, 'Gewebesicherheitsgesetz – das Wesentliche auf einen Blick', *RdM* (2008): 17.

413. For details *see* e.g., with further references, M. Klein, 'Organhandel und Menschenhandel zum Zwecke der Organentnahme im österreichischen Strafrecht', *RdM* (2012): 135.

forbids granting or promising financial profit for donation of blood or blood components. The donation of whole blood for direct transfusion must be completely for free. Concerning blood and tissue, the prohibition of financial profit only applies to donation, but not to the following applications.

393. On top of that, it is illegal to advertise organ, cell and tissue donation by announcing a profit or similar benefits (§4[4] of the Organ Transplantation Act and §3[9] of the Human Tissue Safety Act).

394. In accordance with §16 of the Artificial Procreation Act, the donation of sperm for artificial procreation shall not be object of non-gratuitous legal transactions; beyond that, procurement of embryos, gametes and donators is forbidden. §16 generally prohibits (even self-financing) legal transactions relating to gametes and embryos.

395. Violations of these prohibitions are qualified as administrative penalties. The maximum fines are relatively lenient (EUR 36,340).[414]

§6. Experiments on Human Beings

I. General Remarks

396. Experiments on human beings are not consistently regulated by the Austrian legal order. For lack of a general act, this topic is spread over several area specific and special regulations (clinical trials in the Medicinal Products Act and Medical Devices Act; gene analysis and gene therapy in the Gene Technology Act; embryonic research in the Artificial Procreation Act; autopsy in the Frame Law on Hospitals and Sanatoria and the necessity to consult ethics committees in the Medicinal Products Act, Medical Devices Act, Frame Law on Hospitals and Sanatoria and Act on Universities). Beyond that, the general principles of criminal and civil law determine the legitimacy of experiments on human beings.[415] Expectably, this legal situation will change as soon as Austria ratifies the Convention on Human

414. For details *see* Ch. Kopetzki, 'Ware Körper', in *Körper-Codes*, ed. Ch. Kopetzki, M. Pöschl, M. Reiter & M. Wittmann-Tiwald (Vienna: Linde, 2010), 61 et seq.; Ch. Kopetzki, 'Entnahmeeinrichtungen, Gewinnverbote, Gewinnung vom verstorbenen Spender', in *Gewebesicherheitsrecht*, ed. Ch. Kopetzki (Vienna: Manz, 2009), 142 (153 et seq.). For European regulations also *see* M. Borowski, 'Art 3', in *Charta der Grundrechte der Europäischen Union*, ed. J. Meyer, 2nd edn (Baden-Baden: Nomos, 2006), 132; E. Dujmovits, 'Die EU-Grundrechtscharta und das Medizinrecht', *RdM* (2001): 72; Ch. Schneider, 'Medizinrechtliche Werbe- und Gewinnverbote und Gemeinschaftsrecht', in *Biotechnologie und Recht*, ed. Ch. Kopetzki & H. Mayer (Vienna: Manz, 2002), 217; J. Taupitz, *Kommerzialisierung des menschlichen Körpers* (Berlin, Heidelberg: Springer, 2007).

415. For details *see* Ch. Kopetzki, 'Braucht Österreich eine Kodifikation des biomedizinischen Forschungsrechts?', in *Ethik und Recht in der Humanforschung*, ed. U. Körtner, Ch. Kopetzki & Ch. Druml (Vienna, New York: Springer, 2010), 56; M. Pöschl, 'Wie viel Regulierung verträgt die Forschungsfreiheit?', in *Ethik und Recht in der Humanforschung*, ed. U. Körtner, Ch. Kopetzki & Ch. Druml (Vienna, New York: Springer, 2010), 90. *See* the example of epidemiological studies carried

Rights and Biomedicine, especially the Additional Protocol on Biomedical Research.

397. In this context the concept of experiment has to be distinguished from individual healing attempts. Individual healing attempts are medically indicated methods that are not generally accepted yet (and are therefore not lege artis) and that anticipate an individual therapeutic success. They are subject to the same rules of civil and criminal law as curative treatments. In contrast to this, scientific experiments are often (but not necessarily; *see* especially clinical trials) related to future cases and are not medically indicated. However, the (scientific) concept of individual healing attempts partly coincides with the legal term of 'clinical trial' (*see* IV. below), which is also characterized by the novelty of the method. As long as the application of an investigated medicinal product is medically indicated and anticipates an individual therapeutic success, it can be qualified as a special form of individual healing attempt. On the other hand, not every individual healing attempt is a clinical trial, which is additionally characterized by systematic planning and analysis. In the latter case, the regulations of the Medicinal Products Act apply.

II. General Requirements

398. Generally, experiments have to keep a fair balance of benefits and risks and are to be carried out for the patient's benefit only (e.g., §49 of the Physicians Act). There are strict standards of care to be met and the experiments have to be well planned. In this respect, international 'soft law' is relevant (such as the Declaration of Helsinki). Medical action in the context of experiments is utterly reserved for medical professions (§2 of the Physicians Act). Some experiments have to be approved by ethics committees in advance (*see* Part I, Chapter 4, §3. above). According to the general principles of civil and criminal law (especially §16 of the Civil Code and §90 of the Criminal Code), the patient's informed consent to all experiments is required.

III. Experiments Beyond Special Regulations

399. Besides specific regulations, interventions in the human body always need the patient's consent in line with §90 of the Criminal Code, which certainly requires his capacity to consent. There are generally no further formal requirements for giving one's consent, but it has to be documented in any event. In case of non-therapeutic research, the informed consent strictly has to be given in person, so that it cannot be substituted by legal representatives (§173 of the Civil Code is not

out on intensive care patients: A. Valentin, G. Luf & Ch. Kopetzki, 'Der praktische Fall: Epidemiologische Studien in der Intensivmedizin – Neuland und Graubereich für Ethikkommissionen?', *RdM* (2011): 17.

applicable here, as invasive non-therapeutic research is never for the benefit of the child). As invasive experiments are mostly not medically indicated, an effective consent requires maximum information in advance (about all risks and so forth). Above all, the intended research measures must not violate bones mores (§90 of the Criminal Code).

400. Non-invasive research beyond specific regulations requires the patient's consent if it affects his personal rights (§16 of the Civil Code). Only in case that there is no personal reference at all (like anonymous data), the patient's consent is not necessary. The question, in which cases personal rights are significantly affected and thus an informed consent is necessary, is discussed controversially. In any case, research measures, which involve gaining or using personal data like photos or medical information on the patient, require the patient's informed consent. §16 always requires the balancing of interests, so that a violation of personal rights depends on the proportion of benefits and risks.[416]

401. If the patient is not capable of giving his consent, his legal representatives have to substitute the informed consent (custodians if covered by their legal purview; guardians of minors). Whether health care proxy is possible in this case, is not clear. In all cases of legal representation, the intended experiment has to be for the benefit of the protected person, which is not the case if it is non-therapeutic. §284 of the Civil Code explicitly stipulates that custodians can only give their consent to invasive bodily interventions if they are of direct benefit for the mentally ill/handicapped person. According to the regulations for custodianship, there is no exception to this principle. Neither is there basically for minor patients when it comes to invasive interventions. The sole exception refers to clinical trials on minor patients pursuant to §42(2) of the Medicinal Products Act, which implements the GCP-Guideline 2001/20/EG, and §51 of the Medical Devices Act (*see* section IV. below). The concept of the child's 'well-being' is also seen less strict in case of bone marrow donation (*see* Part II, Chapter 3, §5.II. above).

402. People, who are temporarily incapable of giving their consent and usually do not have a legal representative (for instance after an accident or an apoplectic stroke) must not be subject to (invasive) non-therapeutic research. Non-invasive experiments are only allowed as long as the patient's personal rights are not violated (§16 of the Civil Code), which requires a balancing of the involved interests. If the experiment at the same time is an individual healing attempt, it is admissible without the patient's consent in case of emergency (§110[2] of the Criminal Code).

403. In part there are specific regulations for other 'vulnerable' groups like prisoners, recruits, pregnant women and disordered people who are interned in a psychiatric institution.

Prisoners must not be involved in any medical experiment, not even if they give their consent (§67 of the Penal System Act). This prohibition, which results from

416. For details *see* e.g., J. Aicher, '§16 ABGB', in *Kommentar zum ABGB*, vol. 1, 4th edn, ed. P. Rummel & M. Lukas (Vienna: Manz, 2015), with further references.

the general situation of pressure in prisons, is restricted to experiments but does not concern individual healing attempts. It applies to all kinds of imprisonment (therefore also to pre-trial custody and arrest under administrative criminal law). Clinical trials concerning medicinal products and medical devices are forbidden in any case (§52 of the Medical Devices Act, §45[2] of the Medicinal Products Act).

Recruits and civil servants must not be subject to clinical trials on medicinal products (§45 of the Medicinal Products Act) or on medical devices (§54 of the Medical Devices Act). Beyond these specific provisions, there are no further restrictions so that research is permitted according to the general principles of civil and criminal law. Due to the recruits' extraordinary situation special attention is to be paid to the voluntariness of consent.

Apart from §44 of the Medicinal Products Act and §53 of the Medical Devices Act, which restrict clinical trails on pregnant women (*see* IV. below), there are no further specific prohibitions. Thus, experiments on pregnant women are subject to the general principles of civil and criminal law.

Regarding experiments on patients in psychiatric clinics, there are only relevant rules concerning involuntary patients. According to §45(2) of the Medicinal Products Act, clinical trials on patients who are interned in psychiatric clinics are forbidden in any case. §52 of the Medical Devices Act prohibits not only clinical investigations involving confined patients, but also concerning people under custodianship. The prohibitions of the Medicinal Products Act are applicable *mutatis mutandis* to all other kinds of experiments regarding confined patients. Beyond these regulations, other non-confined psychiatric patients can be subject to experiments under the general principles of civil and criminal law. In case of the patients' incapacity to consent, their custodians have to give their consent in favour of the well-being of the patient.

IV. Clinical Trials on Medicinal Products and Medical Devices

404. Medicinal products cannot be placed on the market, unless they are authorized by the Federal Office of Safety in Health Care (§7 of the Medicinal Products Act *[Arzneimittelgesetz]*, Federal Law Gazette 1983/185, as last amended by Federal Law Gazette I 2017/40). The marketing authorization is only granted if the product meets the requirements of safety, efficacy and quality, proven by clinical trials. The required procedure for clinical trails is strictly regulated under §§28 et seq.[417] The regulations on clinical trials (especially the authorization procedure) will partly have to be adapted to the provisions of the Regulation (EU) 536/2014, which is why an amendment is expected soon.[418]

417. For details *see* M. Haas, M.-L. Plank & B. Unterkofler, *Arzneimittelgesetz*, 2nd edn (Vienna: Verlag Österreich, 2015), 275 et seq.; E. Bernat & W. Kröll (eds), *Recht und Ethik in der Arzneimittelforschung* (Vienna: Manz, 2003).

418. For details *see* C. Zeinhofer, 'Klinische Prüfung von Arzneimitteln im Umbruch', *RdM* (2016): 8.

Medical devices[419] generally have to bear the CE marking of conformity before being placed on the market (§15 of the Medical Devices Act *[Medizinproduktegesetz]*, Federal Law Gazette 1996/657, as last amended by Federal Law Gazette I 2014/32). The CE marking of conformity is only granted if the medical device has been, *inter alia*, tested in a clinical investigation (§§38 et seq.).[420]

405. Clinical trials are defined by §2a(1) of the Medicinal Products Act as 'any systematic investigation of a medicinal product involving human subjects that is aimed at (1). investigating or verifying the pharmacological effects of the investigational product, (2). identifying its side effects, or (3). studying its absorption, distribution, metabolisation and excretion … .'

A multi-centre clinical trial is carried out at several study sites (and therefore by several investigators) according to a single study plan. The study sites may either be situated in a single or in several Member States of the EEA or in Member States and third countries (§2a[2]).

Non-interventional trials, which are defined by §2a(3) of the Medicinal Products Act as systematic studies on licensed medicinal products, are not qualified as clinical trials.

According to §8c as amended in 2009, they have to be submitted to an ethics committee as well as clinical trials.

Regarding medical devices (except in vitro diagnostics), the process of testing is called 'clinical evaluation', whereas the single study is called 'clinical investigation' (*see* the definition in §3[2] of the Medical Devices Act). In vitro diagnostics are tested in performance evaluation studies (§3[2a]).

406. Sections 28 et seq. of the Medicinal Products Act regulate the general conditions for carrying out clinical trails. These conditions are very similar to those required for clinical trials on medical devices (§§41 et seq. of the Medical Devices Act).

Most of all, the benefits and risks for the trial subjects must be balanced. While the risks for healthy humans involved in a clinical trial must be insignificant, those for ill trial subjects must be outweighed by the benefits. Clinical trials on ill people are only allowed subsidiarily to healthy test people. Additionally, the individual indication for their illness or their illness itself must be topic of the study.

The sponsor of the clinical trail has to provide a special insurance for the case of death or injury of the trial subjects, which has to cover all damages that can possibly occur in the course of the study (§32 of the Medicinal Products Act, §47 of the Medical Devices Act). The benefits of the insurance are not dependent on cases of fault or product liability. However, it does not cover genetic defects.[421]

419. For the concept of medicinal product *see*, with further references, C. Zeinhofer, *Der Begriff des Arzneimittels und seine Abgrenzung von anderen Produktkategorien* (Vienna, Graz: NWV, 2007), 275 et seq.

420. For details *see* W. Ecker et al., *Medizinprodukterecht* (Vienna: Ed. Juridica, 2004), 33 et seq.; W. Königshofer, 'Medizinprodukterecht', in *Handbuch Medizinrecht*, ed. R. Resch & F. Wallner, 2nd edn (Vienna: LexisNexis, 2015), 1137 et seq.

421. For details *see* H. Krejci, 'Ethikkommission und Versicherungsfragen', *RdM* (1995): 27; B. Windisch, *Probandenversicherung* (Vienna: Orac, 1995).

According to §§40 et seq. of the Medicinal Products Act all clinical trials are subject to a strict procedure of approval (medicinal products for gene therapy or somatic cell therapy) or prohibition (all other investigational products) by the Federal Office of Safety in Health Care, which compulsively has to consider the vote of the ethics committee (*see* Part I, Chapter 4, §3. above).

Clinical trials on medical devices and performance evaluations on in vitro diagnostics have to be notified to the Federal Office of Safety in Health Care (*see* the procedure in §40 of the Medical Devices Act) and need assessment by an ethics committee (§57).

407. Every clinical trial needs the trial subject's informed consent, which is regulated differently from the general principles by the §§38–45 of the Medicinal Products Act. There are specific formal requirements concerning the duty to inform. The information has to be granted verbally as well as in written form. Besides the generally required contents (nature, significance, consequences and risks), the information also has to cover the fact that a refusal of taking part in the trial or withdrawal will not have any negative consequences for the trial subject (§39[1]). The (informed) consent of the trial subject has to be documented in written form. It either has to be signed personally or be testified by a third person signing the document in case the trial subject is unable to write (§39[2]). In order to prevent forgery, the written consent also has to be dated. The trial subject can withdraw it at any time. In addition to the consent required by pharmaceutical law, the trial subject has to give his consent to the utilization of his data. §39(3) regulates the necessary contents of the information and refers to the Data Protection Act concerning the requirements for a valid consent. This differentiation between the two kinds of informed consent was emphasized by the amendment of 2009 (Federal Law Gazette I 2009/63).

The requirements for a valid informed consent regarding clinical investigations on medical devices are regulated identically in content in §§49 and 50 of the Medical Devices Act.

408. Regarding vulnerable groups, whose members lack the capacity to consent (esp. minors, people under custodianship, emergency patients, pregnant women), there are special regulations in §§42 et seq. of the Medicinal Products Act and §§51 et seq. of the Medical Devices Act.[422]

409. The requirements for clinical trials on minors (people under 18) were completely amended in 2004 in course of the implementation of the Guideline 2001/20/EG on Good Clinical Practice. In 2009, the regulations of the Medical Devices Act were also adapted to those in the Medicinal Products Act (*see* §51):

(1) The tested medicinal product must be intended to diagnose, treat, relieve or prevent diseases in minors.

422. For an overview on the main differences between the two acts also *see* E. Maier, 'Forschung an einwilligungsunfähigen Patienten', *RdM* (2013): 92.

(2) The usage of the investigational product must be medically indicated. It has to be of direct benefit for the test person and the benefits must outweigh the risks. Additionally, research on minors must be subsidiary to research on adults, in the sense that clinical trials on adults are not expected to show satisfactory test results.

(3) There is one exception to the requirement of a direct benefit, which is the only case in which strictly 'non-therapeutic' research involving a group of people who lack the capacity to consent is lawful. According to §42(2) clinical trials on minors are permissible without an expected individual benefit, if they significantly serve science in terms of considerably deepening scientific knowledge of the disease, if they bear a potential benefit for the group of patients suffering from the same disease as the tested person and if they only cause minimal risks and minimal burden to the tested person. Research only then bears minimal risk and minimal burden if it can be expected that it will result at the most in a very slight and temporary impairment of health and that the symptoms and the discomfort will be – at the most – temporary and very slight. In 2009 (Federal Law Gazette I 2009/143), this concept was also introduced in §51(2) of the Medical Devices Act, which had not applied to clinical investigations on medical devices until then.

(4) The clinical trial needs the legal representative's (in most cases the parents') informed written consent, which has to consider the 'well-being' of the child. In the case of a 'group-specific' benefit (as described above), there is a discussion whether the admissibility of the clinical trial despite a direct benefit modifies the general concept of the 'well-being' (which the prevailing doctrine is in favour of), or if the contrary is true and it is therefore forbidden by civil law.

(5) The minor patient always has to be informed additionally to his representative by an investigator who is experienced in dealing with minors. The test person's age has to be taken into account.

(6) If the minor is capable of understanding the nature, significance and implications of the trial and to form a rational intention in the light of these facts, he has to give his consent to the clinical trial too. Contrary to the regulation before 2004, there is no strict time limit for assuming the minor's capacity to consent, but the minor's maturity has to be assessed individually in each case (§42 is oriented on §173 of the Civil Code).

(7) If the minor lacks the capacity to consent, he at least has the right to express a veto, which has to be taken into account by the investigator. Consequently the minor's wish not to take part in the trial has to be respected.

(8) It is illegal to grant any advantages for taking part in the clinical trial, except for adequate compensation.

(9) The degree of burden and risks has to be monitored all the time and the minor should be confronted with as least pain, suffering, fear and risks as possible.

(10) The ethics committee must be specially qualified in the field of paediatrics or must have special consultants.

410. Section 43 provides a similar regulation for people under custodianship, except that there is no exception to the requirement of a direct benefit. §43 only applies if the test person has a custodian competent for medical treatments. If he lacks a custodian, he may still consent in compliance with the general provisions of §39 as long as he comprehends the nature, significance and implications of the trial and can form a rational intention in the light of these facts:

(1) As in the case of minors, the investigated medicinal product must be intended to diagnose, treat, relieve or prevent diseases.
(2) The use of the medicinal product must be medically indicated for diagnosing or treating the concerned mental illness or handicap or for preventing associated diseases.
(3) It must be of direct benefit to the person involved and the benefits must outweigh the risks. Additionally, the clinical trial must be subsidiary to studies on competent people. Contrary to §42, research on people under custodianship is not allowed for the potential benefit of the group of people suffering from the same disease as the test person. This differentiation between the situation of minor test persons and test people under custodianship has no reasonable and objective justification. The strictness in this point rather results from historical reasons (especially the Nazi crimes) and to the fact that the legislator is not forced to make any amendments due to EC-directives.
(4) The clinical trial needs the written (informed) consent of the custodian, who has to consider the 'well-being' of the protected person. If the risks are not merely insignificant, the custodian's consent needs approval of the court (except in case of emergency). When making the decision in favour or against the participation in a clinical trail, the custodian is bound to the implied will of the protected person.
(5) The test person always has to be informed additionally, taking into account his individual or extraordinary situation.
(6) If he comprehends the nature, significance and implications of the trial and is able to form a rational intention in the light of these facts, he must give his consent to the clinical trial too. Otherwise, the test person has the right to express a veto, which has to be considered by the investigator.
(7) As for minors, it is illegal to grant any advantages for taking part in the clinical trial, except for adequate compensation.
(8) The degree of burden and risks has to be monitored all the time.
(9) The ethics committee must be specially qualified in the field of the concerned mental illness or handicap and the tested group of people or must have special consultants.
(10) In addition to the custodian for medical affairs, a custodian for monetary affairs (if existent) has to be informed about the clinical trial (because of the special insurance that has to be provided for the test person).

411. Clinical trials on patients in psychiatric institutions are forbidden by §45(2) in any case, even if they have a custodian.

412. Other than under the Medicinal Products Act, clinical investigations on medical devices involving people under custodianship are forbidden in any case by

§52 of the Medical Devices Act, no matter if they are interned in a psychiatric institution or not.

413. Clinical trials on people who lack the capacity to consent due to an emergency situation (e.g., because they are unconscious after an accident or a stroke) are regulated under §43a of the Medicinal Products Act (*see* the similar regulation in §52a of the Medical Devices Act). §43a not only covers the case of a lacking legal representative, but also the case when the consent of a legal representative cannot be obtained in time:

(1) Clinical trails are permissible despite the lack of consent if there is no evidence (like a living will) that the test person would refuse to take part in a research study.
(2) Involving people in emergency situations must be subsidiary to testing people who have the capacity to consent.
(3) The use of the investigated medicinal product must be indicated and must be of individual benefit for the patient. The requirement of medical indication is regulated similarly to §43, but in this case the indication must be related to the emergency situation.
(4) The clinical trial and the test plan that it is based on must be approved by an ethics committee, which needs special qualification. The approval must be explicitly related to the emergency situation and intended to test people who lack the capacity to consent.
(5) Additionally, the public has to be informed properly about the clinical trial by the study site.
(6) As soon as the test person regains the capacity to consent, he must immediately be informed about the clinical trial and consent is to be obtained in accordance with §§38 and 39. Otherwise the study has to be stopped immediately. As soon as the consent of a legal representative can be obtained, he has to give his informed consent according to §42 or 43. Collected data may only be used further on if the patient gives his consent in compliance with the regulations of the Data Protection Act (§39[3] of the Medicinal Products Act).

414. Regarding clinical trials involving pregnant women, the use of the investigated medicinal product has to be medically indicated either for the mother or for the unborn child. The product must not bear any risks for the unborn child, and clinical research on pregnant women must be subsidiary to non-pregnant test people (§44 of the Medicinal Products Act; for medical investigations on medical devices *see* the similar regulation of §53 of the Medical Devices Act).

Clinical trials on recruits and civil servants as well as research involving prisoners are forbidden (§45 of the Medicinal Products Act; for recruits also *see* §54 of the Medical Devices Act).

§7. EUTHANASIA

415. Euthanasia is primarily regulated by criminal law, but during the last years, civil law has gained importance in this field, especially because of the legal amendments concerning living wills and legal representation in health care matters. In 2008, the Supreme Court had to decide a case of passive euthanasia in the (rather unexpected) context of litigation concerning inheritance.[423]

Direct active euthanasia in the sense of intentional killing of a terminally ill person by positive action, is punished under §§75 et seq. of the Criminal Code. Passive euthanasia within the meaning of omission of life-sustaining measures, not only remains unpunished, but may even be legally demanded, if it is the will of the patient (§110 Criminal Code).

Despite the general agreement on these basic principles (criminality of active euthanasia, impunity of passive euthanasia), the topic is discussed controversially when it comes to the details.[424]

I. Active Euthanasia

416. Direct active euthanasia is indictable according to §§75 et seq. in any case, no matter if the terminally ill person requested such measures or not and without regard to his constitution. The consent or request of the patient can never justify such action, not even in case of extreme pain and suffering.

The prohibition of direct active euthanasia does not only relate to the killing of others (§§75 et seq.), but also to assisting suicide (§78). §75 (murder) is the general statutory definition of the offence of intentional killing. Somebody who kills a person in a generally comprehensible, heavy emotion, is punishable under §76, which privileges the murderer compared to §75. In case of earnest and insistent request of the person killed, §77 applies. As per §78, everyone is punishable, who tempts or assists another person to kill himself, no matter if he acts selfishly or not. On the occasion of a case concerning the prohibition of an association acting as an accessory to suicide, the Constitutional Court declared §78 to be constitutional in line with the jurisdiction on Article 2 ECHR (especially the case *Pretty*, Appl 2346/02).[425]

417. The use of palliative medicinal substances which potentially bear the risk of shortening life (indirect active euthanasia) is not covered by §§75 et seq. though. Thus, doctors who apply such measures do not act unlawfully, if the patient explicitly or presumably desires these measures. Indirect active euthanasia, however, only includes the use of palliative medicine in a dosage that is medically indicated for relieving pain. In contrast, clear overdosage is to be qualified as punishable direct

423. Supreme Court of Justice 7 Jul. 2008, 6 Ob 286/07p, *iFamZ* 2009, 32 *(Schütz)*.

424. For the latest example *see* A. Birklbauer, 'Entscheidung zur Komforttherapie bei infauster Prognose. Ein Grenzgang zwischen zulässiger Behandlung und strafbarer Sterbehilfe', *RdM* (2017): 17.

425. Constitutional Court 8 Mar. 2016, E 1477/2015, *RdM* (2016): 108 *(Kneihs)*; *JAP* (2016/2017): 23 *(Böhm-Gratzl)*. *See also* A. Birklbauer, 'Die Kriminalisierung des assistierten Suizids (§78 StGB): Eine (un)notwendige Strafbestimmung zum Schutz des Lebens?', *RdM* (2016): 84.

active euthanasia (§§75, 77). The dogmatic foundations for the impunity of indirect active euthanasia are debated controversially in Austria.[426]

II. Passive Euthanasia

418. In contrast to active euthanasia, passive euthanasia is not characterized as hastening death by positive action, but covers all cases of omission of life-prolonging measures (no matter if such measures are not applied in the first place or if they are solely not continued).[427] Passive euthanasia also comprises withdrawal of gavage, as this measure is qualified as a medical treatment.[428] Generally, passive euthanasia fulfils the definition of §§75 et seq. as well as hastening death by positive action, if the person involved is obliged to take life-prolonging measures (§2 of the Criminal Code). Especially family members and physicians are in the position of being guarantors in terms of §2. The legal obligation to take life-prolonging measures is limited though.

Impunity of passive euthanasia first of all depends on the will of the terminally ill patient. If a doctor omits life-prolonging measures despite the expressive or presumable will of the patient to live on, he acts unlawfully, as long as he could potentially save the patient's life. Therefore, involuntary euthanasia is forbidden categorically in Austria.

On the other hand, the doctor has to obey the will of the patient if he refuses (further) treatment. The patient's right to self-determination is to be respected in all cases, no matter how irrational his decision may seem. Against a widespread misconception, the refusal of (further) treatment does not require a living will,[429] but must also be accepted if expressed by other means (e.g., orally). Otherwise, the physician is punishable in line with §110 of the Criminal Code, which also protects the patient's right to self-determination in case of mortal danger or certainty of death. §110(2) of the Criminal Code and §8(3) of the Frame Law on Hospitals and Sanatoria only allow life-saving treatments without the patient's consent if the patient lacks the capacity to consent. These regulations do not allow medical treatments that

---

426. For details and further references *see* R. Moos, 'Vorbem zu §§75–79', in *Wiener Kommentar zum Strafgesetzbuch*, ed. F. Höpfel & E. Ratz, 2nd edn (Vienna: Manz, 1999 et seq.), marginal number 26 et seq. and M. Burgstaller, 'Sterbehife und Strafrecht in Österreich', *JAP* (2009/ 2010): 200.
427. For example, with further references, R. Moos, 'Vorbem §§75–79 StGB', in *Wiener Kommentar zum Strafgesetzbuch*, ed. F. Höpfel & E. Ratz, 2nd edn (Vienna: Manz, 1999 et seq.), marginal number 45; D. Kienapfel & H.V. Schroll, *Strafrecht Besonderer Teil I*, 4th edn (Vienna: Manz, 2016), Vorbem §75 StGB marginal number 20 et seq.; R. Kert, 'Sterbehilfe. Der rechtliche Rahmen für das Ende des Lebens', *JAP* (2005/2006): 207; E. Bernat, 'Behandlungsabbruch und (mutmasslicher) Patientenwille', *RdM* (1995): 51 (59).
428. This point was clarified in the legislative process of the Living Will Act: Committee Report 1381 BlgNR 22. GP 2. Also *see inter alia*, E. Bernat, 'Planungssicherheit am Lebensende', *EF-Z* (2006): 43, 74 (76); with further references, Ch. Kopetzki, 'Patientenverfügung: Ist alles Machbare auch rechtlich geboten?', in *Recht und Risikomanagement in Anästhesie und Intensivmedizin, Festschrift Metzler*, ed. W. Kröll, W. Pateter & P. Schweppe (Vienna: Manz, 2009), 38 (44).
429. In detail Ch. Kopetzki, 'Behandlungsablehnung trotz vitaler Indikation. Juristische Stellungnahme', *RdM* (2010): 15 et seq.

the patient has already effectively refused, even if the patient lacks capacity to consent at the time of the treatment. The patient can anticipate an effective refusal of treatment by setting up a living will (*see* Part II, Chapter 1, §3.VII.A. above) or by appointing a health care proxy (§§284f et seq. of the Civil Code, *see* Part II, Chapter 1, §3.VII. above).

419. If the patient is devoid of the capacity to consent and has not anticipated a refusal as described above, it is generally up to the physicians to decide about ending treatment. The main criterion for being obliged to treat or not is the estimation, if treatment is medically indicated or promising in the individual case.

Beyond that, it is discussed controversially whether passive euthanasia is lawful on the base of a 'presumable refusal of treatment'. The Supreme Court has lately judged in favour of this concept, but only under the requirement that the assumption of the patient's will is primarily based on an oral or written demonstration of his will. According to the Court, moral concepts of the public or other people must not be considered. If the presumable will of the patient cannot be figured out, the doctors have to decide in favour of life ('in dubio pro vita').[430]

Representation by next of kin is not permissible in this case, as it only covers consent to medical treatments that 'not usually lead to a severe and enduring impairment of physical integrity'.[431]

§8. Transsexuality

420. Questions related to the legal status of transsexual people and to the medical procedure of sex transformation are not especially regulated by law.

421. Gender reassignment interventions are permitted within the general terms of criminal and civil law. Physicians who are specialized in this medical field are allowed to perform transsexual interventions in accordance with the current state of medical science and experience. Surgical transsexual interventions alter a person's physical appearance as well as the function of the existing sexual characteristics in order to resemble those of the opposite sex. In general, these surgical interventions

---

430. Supreme Court of Justice, 7 Jul. 2008, 6 Ob 286/07p, *RdM* 2008/119, *ZAK* 2008/571 *(Kletečka); JBl* 2009, 129 *(Bernat).* For further details on the problem of incapacity to consent *see, inter alia*, E. Bernat, 'Grenzen der ärztlichen Behandlungspflicht bei einwilligungsunfähigen Patienten', *JBl* (2009): 129; H. Schütz, 'Abbruch der künstlichen Ernährung bei einer einwilligungsunfähigen Patientin – vorsätzliche Tötung durch Unterlassen?', *iFamZ* (2009): 32; Ch. Kopetzki, 'Abbruch der künstlichen Ernährung beim Wachkomapatienten', in *Eluana Englaro – Wachkoma und Behandlungsabbruch,* ed. W. Kröll & W. Schaupp (Vienna: Manz, 2010), 61 et seq.; Ch. Kopetzki, 'Einleitung und Abbruch der medizinischen Behandlung beim einwilligungsunfähigen Patienten. Praktische Auswirkungen der gesetzlichen Neuerungen durch PatVG und SWRÄG', *iFamZ* (2007): 197; A. Birklbauer, 'Strafrechtliche Aspekte des Behandlungsabbruchs beim Wachkomapatienten', in *Eluana Englaro – Wachkoma und Behandlungsabbruch,* ed. W. Kröll & W. Schaupp (Vienna: Manz, 2010), 89 et seq.

431. P. Barth & M. Ganner (eds), *Handbuch des Sachwalterrechts* (Vienna: Linde, 2010), 467; Ch. Kopetzki, 'Abbruch der künstlichen Ernährung beim Wachkomapatienten', in *Eluana Englaro – Wachkoma und Behandlungsabbruch,* ed. W. Kröll & W. Schaupp (Vienna: Manz, 2010), 67.

go hand in hand with sterilization. As the sterilization is only a side effect of transsexual interventions, they are not restricted by §90(2) of the Criminal Code and §§163 and 284 of the Civil Code. In the past, these surgical procedures were qualified as aggravated assaults within the meaning of §84 of the Criminal Code and therefore needed a special justification according to §90(1) of the Criminal Code.[432] This legal opinion was revised in accordance with the Supreme Court's decision in 1996, in which it acknowledged transsexuality as an illness in terms of §120 of the General Social Insurance Act, with the result that the social insurance institutions have to pay for the costs of the necessary psychotherapeutic and surgical interventions.[433] Nowadays it is generally accepted that transsexual interventions shall principally be classified as curative treatments according to §110 of the Criminal Code. Therefore, a valid informed consent of the transsexual person as well as an absolutely certain medical indication for the transsexual intervention are necessary in every case. The medical indication and the self-determined and assured wish for a surgical intervention are intrinsically linked to each other. Consent to transsexual interventions is only valid if given personally by a person who is capable of insight and judgment regarding the medical measure in question. In general, a person is only competent after the achievement of psychosexual maturity, which is generally the case at the age of eighteen. The attending physician has to assess whether the patient seriously wishes the surgical intervention and whether he is capable of consenting. Furthermore, he has to provide the patient with detailed information to enable the patient to understand the dimension and the consequences of the transsexual intervention.[434]

422. A guideline for the medical procedure to reassign the gender is given by the official expert opinion of the Highest Medical Advisory Board (*Oberster Sanitätsrat*) of 22 October 1983, supplemented by the general suggestion concerning the medical procedure of gender reassignment interventions of the Federal Minister of Health.[435] Although these are not legally binding, they are important for the determination of the moment when a change of the gender is concluded, which for a long time was only after the person had undergone transsexual surgical interventions. Finally in 2009, both the Administrative and the Constitutional Court judged that a surgical intervention, namely the removal of the primary sexual characteristics, is not indispensable for being legally acknowledged as the opposite sex by the authorities, as long as a medical expert can determine in all probability that the person has

432. O. Edlbacher, 'Die Transsexualität im Zivil- und im Personenstandsrecht', *ÖJZ* (1981): 173 (177).
433. Supreme Court 12 Sep. 1996, 10 ObS 2303/96s, *RdM* 1997, 12.
434. M. Burgstaller & H. Schütz, '§90', in *Wiener Kommentar zum Strafgesetzbuch*, ed. F. Höpfel & E. Ratz, 2nd edn (Vienna: Manz, 2003), marginal number 155 et seq.
435. 'Gutachten des Obersten Sanitätsrats vom 22. Oktober 1983 über operative Geschlechtsumwandlungen', *Mitteilungen der Österreichischen Sanitätsverwaltung* 2 (1985): 24; 'Empfehlungen für den Behandlungsprozess bei Geschlechtsdysphorie bzw. Transsexualismus nach der Klassifikation in der derzeit gültigen DSM bzw. ICD-Fassung', available at http://www.transx.at/Pub/Behandlungsempfehlungen.php, 30 May 2017.

an irreversible need to belong to the opposite sex which is also visible in the person's physical appearance.[436]

423. There are no specific rules concerning the legal status of transsexuals. The change of the sex and the name are both administrative acts. Since 1983, the transsexual person can request a note in the birth certificate attesting the change of the sex if the birth register entry has become incorrect (§41 Act on the Civil Status of People, Federal Law Gazette I 2013/16 as last amended by Federal Law Gazette I 2016/120).[437] Correspondingly, §2(2) No. 3 of the Act on Name Changes (Federal Law Gazette 1988/195 as last amended by Federal Law Gazette I 2017/59) lays down that the person concerned can ask for a change of the first name if the original first name no longer corresponds with his civil status. These legal regulations are supplemented by consecutive orders (*Erlass*) of the Federal Minister of Interior that instruct the authorities how to proceed with such requests.[438] As the order not only provided instructions, but also limited the rights of the people applying, the Constitutional Court had to decide several times whether the line between a lawful order and a lawless ordinance was crossed. One judgment may be pointed out: the general order issued that the public authorities shall only issue a change of sex if the person is unmarried. This rule was not only an instruction for the authorities, but also limited the applicant's rights. This part of the order was qualified as a lawless ordinance and was partly suspended. As a consequence, the authorities are no longer allowed to check whether the applicant is married. Whether a marriage persists after the legal acknowledgement of a sex transformation is discussed controversially in literature.[439,440]

424. The moment the change of the sex is notified in the birth register, the person is fully acknowledged in the acquired sex and from then on, equal to other

436. Administrative Court 27 Feb. 2009, 2008/17/0054, *RdM* 2009, 159; 15 Sep. 2009, 2008/06/ 0032, *RdM-LS* 2010/15; Constitutional Court 3 Dec. 2009, B 1973/08, *RdM-LS* 2010/16.

437. At the moment, it is discussed controversially, whether the entry in the birth register can be changed to a 'third sex', which was denied by the Regional Administrative Court of Upper Austria (5 Oct. 2016, LVwG-750369/5/MZ/MR). As the regular audit was permitted, a decision of the Administrative Court is expected soon.

438. Transsexuality-Orders of the Federal Interior Minister: 'Erlass des Bundesministers für Inneres, 10582/24-IV/4/83 vom 18. 7. 1983', *ÖStA* (1983): 65; 'Order of 27 Nov. 1996, 36.250/66-IV/ 4/96', *ÖStA* (1997): 1, www.transx.at/Dokumente/Erlass96.pdf, 28 Feb. 2014; 'VA 1300/ 0013-III/ 2/2007 vom 12. 1. 2007', www.transx.at/Dokumente/TS-Erlass_BMI_2007.pdf, 28 Feb. 2014; 'BMI-VA 1300/0063-III/2/2009 vom 6. 2. 2009'.

439. J. Stabentheiner, '§44', in *Kommentar zum Allgemeinen bürgerlichen Gesetzbuch*, ed. P. Rummel, 3rd edn (Vienna: Manz, 2000), marginal number 2; P. Smutny, '§44 ABGB', in ABGB-ON1.03 (Vienna: Manz, 2016); J. Höllwerth, '§44 ABGB', in *EheG – Ehegesetz*, ed. E. Gitschthaler & J. Höllwerth (Vienna: Springer, 2008), marginal number 9 et seq.; Ch. Kopetzki, 'Transsexualität und das Wesen der Ehe', *iFamZ* (2008): 81 et seq. Other opinion e.g., W. Jaksch-Ratajczak, 'Gibt es in Österreich eine Ehe unter Gleichgeschlechtlichen?', *EF-Z* (2006): 111 et seq.; O. Edlbacher, 'Die Transsexualität im Zivil- und im Personenstandsrecht', *ÖJZ* (1981): 173 (180) and others.

440. In 2014, the Supreme Court held that concealing transsexuality is a reason for martial dissolution by fault in line with §§37 and 42(2) of the Act on Marriages (German Reichsgesetzblatt I S 807/ 1938, as last amended by Federal Law Gazette 2017/59): Supreme Court 21 May 2014, 3 Ob 84/14w, *EF-Z* (2015): 122 *(Schoditsch)*.

people of the acquired sex in the eyes of the law, but affects neither parenthood or events that occurred before the gender reassignment. For example, an unmarried person is allowed to marry a person of the opposite sex (§44 Civil Code) or to conclude a registered partnership with a person of the same sex (since 2010 according to the Act on Registered Partnerships [Eingetragene Partnerschaft-Gesetz], Federal Law Gazette I 2009/135 as last amended by Federal Law Gazette I 2017/59).[441] The person can also take advantage of medically assisted artificial procreation in order to become a parent in his acquired sex, as far as factually possible and permitted by law.[442] Principally, transsexuals are also on equal terms with people of the acquired sex regarding state pension benefits.[443,444]

§9. Aesthetic Surgery

425. In order to prevent patients from the risks of aesthetic surgery without medical indication, the Act on Aesthetic Treatments and Surgery was released in 2012 *(ÄsthOpG)*, Federal Law Gazette I 2012/80 (as last amended by Federal Law Gazette I 2012/80).

Generally, medical treatments that are no curative treatments or without indication fall within the ambit of §§83 et seq. of the Criminal Code. They are punishable unless the patient gives his informed consent in line with §90 Criminal Code. An informed consent is still not valid in case of violation of bonos mores or if it refers to treatments that are particularly dangerous to life. The Act on Aesthetic Treatments and Surgery stipulates special requirements for a valid informed consent in its §§6 and 7. If cosmetic surgery is combined with genital mutilation, §90(3) is to be applied as *lex specialis* (*see* Part II, Chapter 2 §2).

426. According to §1(2), the Act on Aesthetic Treatments and Surgery only covers medical activities in terms of §2(2) of the Physicians Act (*see* Part I, Chapter 2 §1.I).[445] It is, however, not applied to activities that fall within the ambit of the Trade Regulations *(Gewerbeordnung,* Federal Law Gazette I 1994/194, as last amended by Federal Law Gazette I 2016/120), e.g., piercing and tattooing carried

441. Administrative Court 30 Sep. 1997, 95/01/0061; EGMR U 11 Jul. 2002, *Christine Goodwin v. UK*, no. 28957/95, *ÖJZ* 2003, 766; *see* Ch. Kopetzki, 'Transsexualität und das Wesen der Ehe', *iFamZ* (2008): 81 et seq. with further references.

442. In the meanwhile probably obsolete: EGMR U 23 Apr. 1997, *X, Y, Z v. UK*, 75/1995/581/667, *ÖJZ* (1998): 271.

443. Supreme Court 21 Sep. 2009, 10 ObS 29/09a, *RdM-LS* 2009/35 (*Leischner*) and A. Leischner, 'Die Höhe der Alterspension einer postoperativen Mann-zu-Frau-Transsexuellen – Anmerkung zu OGH 21. 4. 2009, 10 ObS 29/09a', *iFamZ* (2009): 332 et seq.

444. For a general overview, even if partly superseded, *see* O. Edlbacher, 'Die Transsexualität im Zivil- und im Personenstandsrecht', *ÖJZ* (1981): 173; E. Greif, *Doing Trans/Gender* (Linz: Trauner, 2005); E. Greif, 'Körper an den Grenzen des Rechts. Transsexualität, Menschenrechte und nationales Recht', in *Recht und Medizin*, ed. E. Dujmovits et al. (Baden-Baden: Nomos, 2006), 171–190.

445. Activities that can also be carried out by traders, e.g., the application of lasers in low doses, are not covered by the Act of Aesthetic Treatment and Surgery, unless they are carried out by a doctor as medical activity.

out by cosmetic traders (§1[3]).[446] Tattooing and piercing (which also includes ear-piercing of minors) are also explicitly excluded from the ambit by §1(2), also if carried out by a physician. The Act on Aesthetic Treatments and Surgery neither applies to activities (including dental, oral and maxillofacial surgery) covered by the Dentists Act (§1[4]).

427. §3 provides the legal definitions of aesthetic surgery, aesthetic treatment and medical indication, and §4 (non-exhaustively) enumerates examples for both methods. According to §3 in conjunction with §4 the concept of aesthetic surgery includes onlay plasty, abdominoplasty, correction of the brows, breast lifting, breast enlargement and reduction, lipofilling, facelift, liposuction, bottom shaping, face implants, neck lifting, genioplasty, bodylifting, otoplasty, lip augmentation, correction of the nose (rhinoplasty), lifting of the upper arms, blepharoplasty, upper thigh and forehead lifting, penis enlargement and vaginal plasty. Medical treatments are, for example, the application of medicinal products (especially botulin toxin),[447] physical applications such as photorejuvenation (laser skin resurfacing, laserpeeling, crinkle lasering, thermage, etc.), if not carried out by traders in terms of the Trade Regulations.

428. The Act on Aesthetic Treatments and Surgery is only applicable to treatments and surgery without medical indication, which is defined in §3(4). As soon as a physician asserts that a treatment or operation is medically indicated it is excluded from its ambit (neither does the age limit in §7 apply). According to the legal definition, an aesthetic treatment or operation is medically indicated if it is caused by a reason based on medical-scientific findings. Considering the patient's living conditions, it must be objectively necessary to avoid danger to life or damage to the patient's health or to eliminate anatomic or functional disease. Furthermore, no milder means to reach these aims must be available. According to the travaux préparatoires, a treatment or operation is medically indicated if its costs are paid by the public health insurance. Furthermore, there is medical indication in case of medical-scientifically defined hereditary serious deformation or anomaly, defacing malformation, injury or scarring after accidents, tumour operation or burn injury.[448]

429. Aesthetic treatments and operations can only be carried out lawfully by specialists for plastic, aesthetic and reconstructive surgery as well as specialists in consideration of §31 of the Physicians Act, if they are allowed to do so by an act of the Physicians' Chamber[449] (e.g., specialists for surgery, ear, nose and throat surgery, skin and veneral diseases, gynaecology and urology). Furthermore, by general practitioners who are specially recognized by the Physicians' Chamber (§4[3]).

446. These are regulated by the Ordinance of the Federal Minister of Economic Affairs and Labour on the rules for the exercise of piercing and tattooing by cosmetic traders, Federal Law Gazette II 2003/141 as amended by Federal Law Gazette II 2008/261.

447. The application of botulin toxin by neurologists for the purpose of neurology without a connection to aesthetic treatment is not covered by the Act on Aesthetic Treatment and Surgery though.

448. Also *see* the examples listed in the explanatory report: ErläutRV 1807 BlgNR 24. GP 5.

449. The Physicians' Chamber may also list further treatments and operations in terms of §4(1) in such an act (§4[5]).

430. In order to prevent patients from unrealistic expectations and to make them aware of risks and possible negative consequences, §5 states an all-embracing duty to inform for physicians, which has to be given at least two weeks before giving consent to an intervention: §6[1]): The information has to comprise the method of the medical intervention, its nature, significance and consequences, applied medicinal products (and their adverse reactions) or medical devices (and their functionality and durability), alternative methods, the predicted result and possible discrepancies, the discomfort connected with the intervention, possible consequences such as scarring as well as complications such as damage to bodily functions (by possibly using pictures). The physician also has to inform the patient about the necessary after-treatment (including the expected length of inability to work and possible long-term consequences), about the fact that inability to work is not paid for by social insurance, about all known risks as well as all expected costs[450,451] (including follow-up costs) of the intervention. The information has to be given orally and in written and cannot be abstained from (§5[1]). All information also has to be given to parents of minors and procurators. The given information has to be documented and confirmed by the patient (as well as the parents and procurators).

If the physician suspects a patient to have a mental disorder, which results in the wish to have a cosmetic operation, he/she has to consult a psychologist or psychiatrist.

431. For cosmetic surgery[452] the attending physician has to make an operation pass at the first consultation (§9) including, for example, the patient's name, date of birth and Social Security Number, the physician's name and qualification, date and reason for the first consultation as well as the planned date of the operation, type of operation and if applicable designation, type and serial number of implants (including name and address of the producer or distributor).

432. According to §6(2) the patient's consent has to be documented in written form, it has to be dated and signed either by the patient or, if he/she is not capable of doing so, by an independent attestor. The medical intervention can be carried out one day after having given consent at the earliest.

433. §7 provides special regulations for viable groups of patients: It is absolutely forbidden to carry out an aesthetic treatment or operation on a person younger than sixteen (§7[1]). For minor patients over sixteen and under eighteen, §7(2) states that both the legal guardians and the minor, who is legally capable of doing so, have to give their informed consent in written form. In case of a planned cosmetic operation, possible mental disorders have to be clarified and the minor has to

450. The physician especially has to inform about the fact that the costs are not paid for by public health insurance (§5[6]). *See* §5(7).

451. For details *see* E. Pitzl & G. Huber, 'Aufklärungs-, Einwilligungs- und Informationspflichten nach dem ÄsthOpG', *RdM* (2014): 85.

452. In case of minors or patients under custodianship, such a pass also has to be made for aesthetic treatments.

consult a psychologist, psychiatrist or specialist for child and adolescent psychiatry. If the wish to be operated results from such a disease, it must not be carried out.[453]

Patients under custodianship have to give the consent themselves in case they have the capacity to consent. Otherwise, the informed consent has to be given by the custodian, who is bound by §283(2) of the Civil Code. According to §283(2), the custodian can only consent to the intervention, if there is a personal medical attendance report (given by an independent physician) confirming the incapacity to consent and that the operation or treatment is necessary for the patient's benefit. In lack of a medical attest or in case the patient expresses refusal, the custodian's consent has to be approved by court. If the custodian refuses to give his/her consent and endangers the patient's well-being, the consent can be replaced by court order or the court can appoint another person as custodian.

For both groups of patients, §7(5) stipulates a minimum period of four weeks between giving consent to an aesthetic treatment or operation and carrying it out. In case the patient withdraws his/her consent not later than one week before the planned intervention, he/she must not have any negative financial consequences or expenses.

434. §8 provides advertising restrictions and prohibits provisions. The Constitutional Court held that the advertising restrictions were within the responsibility of the federation according to Article 10(1) No. 12 of the Constitution (public health). This is why they are applicable to any kind of aesthetic treatment or surgery, no matter where it is carried out (in a clinic or not).[454,455]

435. Violations of the provisions of §§4 et seq. are punishable up to EUR 15,000, if they do not fall within the ambit of the Criminal Code (especially §§83 et seq.). In cases of serious danger to life or health as well as commercial nature, the offender has to pay a fine up to EUR 25,000.[456]

453. For details *see* I. Zerbes, 'Noch keine 14 – und schon tätowiert! Grenzen der Einwilligung zu ästhetischen Eingriffen an Kindern', in *FS Fuchs,* ed. S. Reindl-Krauskopf (Vienna: Verlag Österreich, 2014), 685.
454. Constitutional Court 29 Feb. 2016, G 384/2015, *RdM* (2016): 148 *(Stöger).*
455. A violation of §8 by a doctor was assumed in the following case: Administrative Court 20 Apr. 2016, Ra 2016/11/0049.
456. For details on this chapter *see* S. Weiss, *ÄsthOpG* (Vienna: Manz, 2014); W. Hauser & W. Stock, *ÄsthOpG* (Vienna; Graz: NWV, 2013); O. Malecky, 'ÄsthOpG', in *Gmundner Kommentar zum Gesundheitsrecht,* ed. M. Neumayr, R. Resch & F. Wallner (Vienna: Manz, 2016), 2071 et seq.

Part III. The Physician and the Health Care System

Chapter 1. Collegial Relationships

§1. ASSOCIATIONS

I. General Remarks

436. Under the Physicians Act of 1998, doctors are represented by the medical chambers of the federal states (§§65 et seq.). There is one medical chamber in each federal state, having its registered office in each capital (except The Medical Chamber of Lower Austria, which is situated in Vienna, and the Medical Chamber of Vorarlberg, which is in Dornbirn). The medical chambers of the federal states and the Austrian Medical Chamber are public-law corporations. They are characterized by compulsory membership, by financial and organizational autonomy (in the sense that their organs are elected by the members), by having sovereign powers and by being relatively independent of government bodies (they are not bound to any mandatory directions, but they are subject to supervision). Thus, they are non-territorial self-administering bodies.

The autonomous sphere of powers is limited to matters that are of exclusive or predominant interest for the members and are prone to be fulfilled by them (Article 120a of the Constitution). It can only refer to members, meaning that it must not legally bind outsiders due to the lack of democratic legitimacy. Thus, for example the former practise of registration in and deletion from the Medical Practitioner Register within the autonomous sphere of functions of the Austrian Medical Chamber was declared unconstitutional.[457] As a consequence of the judgment, the evaluation of the requirements for being registered in the Medical Practitioner Register was delegated to the assigned sphere of functions, whereas the administration of the register itself is still part of the autonomous sphere of functions (amendment 2015, Federal Law Gazette 2015/56).

Beyond their autonomous competence of self-administration, the chambers also have powers, which are delegated to them by the federation or the federal states.

457. Constitutional Court 23 Jun. 2014, G 87/2013 and G 99/2013, *RdM-LS* 2014/41; *JAP* (2014/2015): 86 *(Gratzl)*. The registration is not subject of the autonomous sphere of functions because it also binds non-members (the applicants). As to the deletion from the list, the court argued that it affected mostly common interests (of health protection).

Within the delegated sphere of powers, they are bound by directions of government bodies.

In their statutory function of representing a professional group, the chambers are subject to the control of the Austrian Court of Audit.

437. Within their autonomous sphere of self-administration, it is the duty of the chambers to represent the general interests of the medical profession. This major function is to be distinguished from the representation of individual interests of single members. This, however, does not exclude services like legal assistance or legal advice for single members. With regard to the different groups of doctors (licensed medical practitioners, employed doctors), the interests of a certain group are to be balanced with the general interests of the medical profession, which have to be defined and represented by the chambers. This may require an internal balance of interests, as long as not only specific interests of certain groups are concerned.

438. In the course of the chambers reform in 1998, the present structure of curia was established to take account of the different interests of the special groups of doctors.

II. Medical Chambers of the Federal States

A. *Functions*

439. The medical chambers of the federal states attend to and promote the general professional, social and economic interests of doctors (including the different groups of doctors and group practices) and preserve medical reputations and obligations. Their duties include, *inter alia,* reporting and passing expert opinions on health care matters, organizing advanced training for doctors, settling disputes between members of the chamber, granting benefits for members and their surviving dependants, concluding or terminating contracts between doctors and insurance institutions, visitations, providing information for members on the relevant regulations in the fields of health law and social law, assessing law drafts and participating in the control of quality management (*see* §66).

B. *Rights and Duties of the Members*

440. Every doctor who is registered in the Medical Practitioner Register listed by the Austrian Medical Chamber, who pursues his profession in the field of the medical chamber and who does not get age or disability pension from the Public Welfare Fund, is a regular member of the medical chamber (§68[1]). Doctors who receive a pension from the Public Welfare Fund are also ordinary members, as long as they pay contributions to the Public Welfare Fund and to the medical chamber due to regular medical practice. Doctors, who do not fulfil these requirements, and medical officers of health care may become extraordinary members voluntarily

(§68[5]). Medical officers of health care, who additionally pursue a medical profession, are ordinary members, but they are not bound by instructions of the chamber, which contradict their duties as medical officers of health or the instructions of their superior authority. Apart from that, the members must follow the resolutions that are passed by the chamber. Furthermore, they are obliged to pay contributions to the chamber and to the Public Welfare Fund.

441. Ordinary members have the right to elect the members of the Plenary Assembly (chamber councillors) and to stand for election. Each member of the chamber has the right to make use of the benefits of the Public Welfare Fund in conformity with the memorandum and the statutory rules. Finally, every member has the right to get an identity card for doctors (§70).

C. Structure of the Medical Chambers: Curia System

442. Taking into account the different interests of the special groups of doctors, the medical chambers are divided into a Curia of Employed Doctors and a Curia of Licensed Medical Practitioners (§71). In 2006, the dentists were excluded from the medical chamber, as a special Dentist Chamber was established.

443. Each member of the chamber can only be member of one curia. Under certain conditions, doctors, who are employed and at the same time have a private practice, have the possibility of choosing their membership in one of the curia by declaration.[458]

444. In medical chambers with more than 3,000 members, the Curia of Employed Doctors must be divided into a section of doctors who are entitled to independent practice and a section of trainee doctors. The Curia of Licensed Medical Practitioners is to be divided into a section of general practitioners and licensed physicians on the one hand and a section of specialists on the other hand. The sections may further be divided into specialized groups. Each member of the chamber can only be member of one section. In medical chambers with less than 3,000 members, the division into sections is optional (§72).

D. Organs of the Chambers

445. The medical chambers of the federal states consist of the Plenary Assembly, the Extended Plenary Assembly, the Board of the Chamber, the President and Vice-President, the Assemblies of the Curia, the Chairmen of the Curia and their deputies, the Presidium, the Management Committee and the Board of Complaint of the Public Welfare Fund (§73).

---

458. For details concerning the assignment to a certain curia *see* R. Resch, 'Die Interessenvertretung der angestellten Ärzte durch die Ärztekammer', in *Gmundner Medizinrechtskongress 2008,* ed. G. Aigner, R. Resch & F. Wallner (Vienna: Manz, 2009), 55 (60 et seq.).

The Plenary Assembly (§§74 et seq.) elects the President and the Vice-President, it passes resolutions on the annual estimate and on the statement of account as well as the resolution imposing an assessment. Furthermore, it issues the statute, the rules of procedure, rules on travel expenses and official regulations for the chamber staff.

The Extended Plenary Assembly (§§80a, 80b), which consists of the members of the Plenary Assembly and of representatives of the dentists, have functions concerning the Public Welfare Fund (such as passing the statute and rules on the contributions).

The Chamber Board (§81) comprises the President, the Vice-President, the representatives of the Curia Chairmen and other chamber councillors. It takes on all functions for which other organs are not explicitly competent.

The President (§83) represents the chamber. It is his task to preserve the unity of the medical profession and to execute the resolutions of the chamber organs (regardless of the Assemblies of the curia). Furthermore, he concludes and terminates contracts with the chamber staff, he summons the meetings of the Plenary Assembly, the Chamber Board and the Presidium and he acts as chairperson of these meetings. The duty to preserve the unity of the chamber is of major importance with regard to the curia. In case of doubt, the President has to decide if a certain matter falls within the competence of the Chamber Board or one of the Curia Assemblies. Furthermore, he can refuse to sign papers of the Curia Assemblies, if they exceed their competence. As per §83(3), he also has the right to veto, if a resolution of a Curia Assembly substantially affects the interests of the other curia. In this case, the Chamber Board makes the final decision (except for resolutions in the field of labour law or service law). The President can also submit matters in the interest of both curias to the Chamber Board, which gives a coordinating recommendation (§83[5]).

The curia councillors are elected by the members of a curia and form the Curia Assemblies (§84). They are obliged to pursue the specific professional, economic and social interests of the particular Curia. They have legal status, insofar as they have the right to fulfil their tasks in their own name. The Curia for Licensed General Practitioners, for example, represents employers' interests in terms of concluding collective contracts or integrated contracts with the insurance institutions.

The Curia Chairman (§85) executes the resolutions of the Curia Assembly and is in charge of the affairs of the curia (including summoning the Curia Assembly, fixing the agenda, acting as chairperson and signing the papers of the curia).

The Presidium (§86) consists of the President, the Vice-President and the Expert for Finances. It is summoned and led by the President. It decides urgent matters of the Chamber Board (which the Chamber Board generally has to agree on afterwards) and makes decisions in personnel matters. All decisions of the Presidium have to be brought to the Chamber Board's knowledge.

The chamber staff as well as the organs and referees of the chamber are obliged to maintain secrecy (§89).

446. The administrative and technical support of the chambers is provided for by the Chamber Department (§87), which is led by the Director of the Chamber Department. He supervises the chamber staff in his position as official and technical superior.

E. The Public Welfare Fund

447. The Public Welfare Fund (§§96 et seq.) is a fund for special purposes aimed at granting support for the members of the chamber, their children and their surviving dependants. Its benefits include age pension, disability pension, child benefit, provision for dependants (life insurance benefits to widows, widowers and orphans) and eventually compensation for funeral expenses and support for the dependants. Apart from that, the Fund may also pay for assistance during illness and other benefits (like educational costs for orphans).

The Public Welfare Fund is financed by the contributions of the members and is administered by the Administrative Board (§113). The administrative courts of the federal states are competent for appeals against decisions of the Administrative Board. The Review Board controls the management of the Public Welfare Fund at least once a year. Since the Fund provides benefits also for dentists, the representatives of the Public Welfare Fund also include members of the Dentists' Chamber.

III. The Austrian Medical Chamber

448. The Austrian Medical Chamber (§§117 et seq.) represents the common interests of doctors who pursue a profession inland and who are members of the medical chambers of the federal states. It is a public-law corporation and has its registered office in Vienna. Its members are the medical chambers of the federal states (§119).

449. The Austrian Medical Chamber is in charge of all matters that concern the common professional, social and economic interests of the members of two or more medical chambers (§118). In this regard, its functions are quite similar to those of the medical chambers of the federal states (for instance conclusion and termination of contracts with the social institutions, as long as they concern two or more chambers, periodic reporting to the Health Ministry). Furthermore, it is the Austrian Medical Chamber that sets disciplinary action against chamber members in case of misconduct. It is also responsible for passing regulations implementing the Physicians Act and for representing the medical profession abroad.

450. The Austrian Medical Chamber also has many functions in the context of governmental public authority (assigned sphere of functions). It maintains the Medical Practitioner Register (for the amendment of 2015 *see* Part III Chapter 1, §1.I., it acknowledges educational institutions and decides about their number, it issues identity cards for doctors and it issues certificates that are provided for in EC regulations.

451. The Austrian Medical Chamber has the same organs as the medical chambers of the federal states (Plenary Assembly, Chamber Board, President, Vice-President, Curia of the Federation and their Chairmen, Presidium, Administrative Board and Board of Complaint of a Common Public Welfare Fund).

The Plenary Assembly (§§121 et seq.) consists of the Presidents and the Curia Chairmen of all medical chambers of the federal states, as well as of the Chairmen of the Curia of the Federation and their representatives. It elects the President, the First Vice-President, the Expert for Finances and his representative. Furthermore, it makes decisions on the President's and the Chamber Board's statements of accounts, about the annual estimate and the closing of accounts. The Plenary Assembly also passes regulations (e.g., on travel expenses and fees and on conciliation) and makes decisions on important matters that are submitted by the Chamber Board.

The Board of the Austrian Medical Chamber (§123) consists of the Presidents of the medical chambers of the federal states and the Chairmen of the Curia of the Federation as well as their representatives. It is allowed to establish consulting committees (only the Board of Education has to be established compulsorily). The Board of the Chamber is responsible for all matters that are not assigned to other organs.

The President (§125) represents the Austrian Medical Chamber. He must preserve the unity of the medical profession and has to execute the resolutions of the organs of the Austrian Medical Chamber.

The Curia of the Federation (Curia of Licensed Medical Practitioners and Curia of Employed Doctors, §126) comprises the Chairmen of the Curia Assemblies of the medical chambers of the federal states and their representatives. They have the same functions as the Curia Assemblies of the federal states. They have legal status concerning the tasks they can fulfil in their own name. The Curia Chairmen of the Federation (§127) have the duty to execute the resolutions und to conduct the affairs of the curia (including summoning, fixing the agenda and acting as a chairperson).

The Presidium (§128) consists of the President, the Vice-President and the Referee for Finances of the Austrian Medical Chamber. It is summoned and led by the President of the Austrian Medical Chamber. It makes decisions concerning urgent matters of the Chamber Board (which generally have to be approved by the Board as soon as possible) and passes resolutions in personnel matters.

The Education Committee (§128a) consists of the chairpersons of the educational commissions of the federal states and two members of the Board of the Austrian Medical Chamber. For its duties *see* §128a(5).

452. Two or more medical chambers of the federal states can decide (by unanimous resolutions of the Plenary Assemblies) to establish a Common Public Welfare Fund within the Austrian Medical Chamber for the case of major damage (§§134 et seq.).[459]

---

459. This chapter is based on G. Aigner, 'Das ärztliche Berufsrecht', in *Handbuch Medizinrecht,* ed. G. Aigner et al. (Vienna: Manz, 2003 et seq.), III.35 et seq. For additional literature *see* F. Wallner, '§64 et seq. ÄrzteG', in *Gmundner Kommentar zum Gesundheitsrecht,* ed. M. Neumayr, R. Resch & F. Wallner (Vienna: Manz 2016), 3 (161 et seq.); F. Wallner, 'Berufsrecht der Ärzte', in Handbuch Medizinrecht, ed. R. Resch & F. Wallner, 2nd edn (Vienna: LexisNexis, 2015), 689 (785 et seq.); H. Emberger & F. Wallner (eds), *Ärztegesetz,* 2nd edn (Vienna: Verlagshaus der Ärzte, 2008), 301 et seq. and G. Aigner, M. Kierein & Ch. Kopetzki, *Ärztegesetz 1998,* 3rd edn (Vienna: Manz, 2007), 169 et seq. and K. Stellamor & W. Steiner, *Handbuch des österreichischen Arztrechts,* vol. 1 (Vienna: Manz, 1999), 485 et seq.; L. Stärker, 'ÄrzteG: Organzuständigkeit, Kompetenzübertragung und -überschreitung', *RdM* (2016): 16.

§2. HEALTH CARE CENTRES

453. Health care centres (within the meaning of outpatient facilities in which different aspects of health care are provided centrally outside the hospital system) comprise all forms of permanent cooperation of equal status between members of freelance health care professions.

454. Health care professions either can cooperate without concluding a partnership agreement or they can establish different forms of commercial law associations.[460]

455. A new type of health care centres is being established in the course of a big reform of the health care system in 2017: Primary Health Care Centers, which can be organized either as group practices, autonomous outpatient clinics or networks (*see* Chapter 3, §2).

I. Cooperation Without a Partnership Agreement

456. This form of cooperation is organized on the basis of a cooperation contract. It can either relate to patients (e.g., by recommending each other to patients) or to factors of production (by sharing surgeries, medical supplies or personnel). Cooperation beyond the rules of company law is permitted, but only under the general conditions of the particular professional codes (for instance the prohibition of commission payments for doctors, dentists, music therapists, psychologists, psychotherapists and massage therapists, the obligation of secrecy, which is inherent in most professional acts).

457. Cooperation without a partnership agreement is also subject to other general regulations like those of law on competition. The cooperation between members of the health care professions must not limit the patient's right to choosing treatment.[461] It is generally allowed to cooperate either with other members of the health care professions or with third parties.[462]

458. There are specific provisions for associations related to surgeries and medical instruments *(Ordinations- und Apparategemeinschaften,* §52 of the Physicians

460. This chapter is based on Ch. Schneider, 'Zusammenarbeit, Rechtsformgestaltung, Gruppenpraxen', in *Handbuch Medizinrecht,* ed. G. Aigner et al. (Vienna: Manz, 2003 et seq.), IV/51 et seq. For further reading: F. Wallner, '§§52-52c ÄrzteG', in *Gmundner Kommentar zum Gesundheitsrecht,* ed. M. Neumayr, R. Resch & F. Wallner (Vienna: Manz, 2016), 118 et seq.; M. Karollus, 'Vergesellschaftung von Ärzten und Zahnärzten', in *Handbuch Medizinrecht,* ed. R. Resch & F. Wallner, 2nd edn (Vienna: LexisNexis, 2015), 1037 et seq.

461. Supreme Court 21 Sep. 1976, *ÖBl* 1977, 35 (cooperation between an eye specialist and an optician).

462. Supreme Court 9 Mar. 1999, 4 Ob 21/99p (participation of a doctor in a special franchise system); Supreme Court 9 Mar. 1999, 4 Ob 16/99b, *RdM* 2000, 147 (dentist agency including consultation about dental treatments).

Act): sharing surgeries and medical instruments is only permitted between freelance doctors or freelance doctors and group practices. The association itself as well as every participating doctor can only work on a freelance basis. It is discussed controversially whether other (freelance) members of the health care professions can participate in an association related to surgeries and instruments.[463] In contrast to this, the legal situation concerning dentists is clear (§25 of the Dentists Act does not only allow associations related to surgeries and instruments between dentists, but also between dentists and freelance members of other health care professions).

II. Commercial Law Associations

459. Commercial law associations are established on the basis of partnership agreements. They are generally subject to the regulations of commercial law, except for the following restrictions.

460. Not every outpatient medical facility is a freelance surgery, but may also be qualified as hospital. Hospitals as defined in the Frame Law on Hospitals and Sanatoria do not only comprise hospitals with in-patient beds, but also autonomous outpatient clinics. Thus, an outpatient facility is qualified as hospital, if it is institutionally organized. Other than freelance surgeries, which are subject to the Physicians Act, institutionally organized outpatient clinics fall within the ambit of the Frame Law on Hospitals and Sanatoria (*see* Part III, Chapter 3, §1. below).

For this reason the distinction between freelance surgeries and outpatient clinics is of major importance. Outpatient clinics are defined as organizationally autonomous facilities for the examination and treatment of people who do not need hospital care. It does not even matter, if they have an appropriate number of in-patient beds, as long as they are indispensable for short-term stays for outpatient diagnostic or therapeutic measures (§2[1] No. 7 of the Frame Law on Hospitals and Sanatoria). According to the Constitutional Court (VfSlg 14.444), the major criterion of demarcation is the form of legal relationships. Contrary to freelance surgeries, in which treatment contracts are concluded with the doctor in charge, patients make a contract with the association (and not with the particular doctor) in case of an outpatient clinic.[464] Some authors, however, assume that a medical facility is only institutionally organized in terms of an outpatient clinic, if its personnel and technical equipment is that large and complex, that it must be run by a medical head.[465] According to this point of view, there is no institutional organization in case of medical treatments of minor intensity.

463. In favour of a participation G. Aigner, M. Kierein & Ch. Kopetzki, *Ärztegesetz 1998*, 3rd edn (Vienna: Manz, 2007), §52 marginal number 7; dissenting Ch. Schneider, *Ärztliche Ordinationen und selbständige Ambulatorien* (Vienna: Verlag Österreich, 2001), 79 et seq. with further references.

464. Constitutional Court 7 Mar. 1992, G 198/90 et al., VfSlg 13.023, Constitutional Court 1 Mar. 1996, G 1279/95, G 1280/95, VfSlg 14.444.

465. M. Windisch-Graetz, 'Selbständiges Ambulatorium und ärztliche Ordination', *RdM* (1995): 144; W. Mazal, 'Gruppenpraxis versus Anstaltsbegriff', *RdM* (2000): 129.

The major consequence of the practice of the courts for associations between doctors is that establishing a freelance association of doctors is only possible if the association is not partner to the treatment contract; otherwise, it is to be qualified as an outpatient clinic or hospital (except group practices, *see* below).

461. Commercial law associations (which are not partners of the treatment contracts and therefore no outpatient clinics) can be established in any legal form. Thus, they can be organized as partnerships (civil law partnerships, general partnerships or limited partnerships) or investment companies (public limited companies or private limited companies).

462. In case of establishing a freelance association, only the participating doctors, but not the association itself, hold the license for practising the medical profession. Thus, each of them is responsible for complying with his professional duties and rights. They especially have to consider the obligation of secrecy, the prohibition of commission payments and the patient's choice.

As the association itself does not hold the license for practising the medical profession, it cannot conclude an insurance contract. Only the participating doctors can do so.

Furthermore, it is the single participating doctor and not the association who is liable in case of medical malpractice, because the association itself is not the partner of the treatment contract.

463. Associations of freelance doctors which also share surgery and/or medical instruments, are to be qualified as associations related to surgeries and medical instruments in terms of §52 of the Physicians Act (*see* I. above). Establishment, extension and closing of surgery and instruments associations are to be notified to the Austrian Medical Chamber within one week (§29[1] No. 7 of the Physicians Act).

464. §52a of the Physicians Act provides a special form of cooperation for doctors: group practices.[466] Group practices can be established in the legal form of a general partnership and since the amendment of 2010 (Federal Law Gazette I 2010/61) also in the legal form of a private limited company (§52a[1]).

Contrary to other freelance doctors' associations, the group practice itself holds the license for practising the medical profession (§52a[1 and 3 No. 4]). It is also

466. For additional literature (related to the legal situation before the amendment of 2010) *see* i.a. G. Aigner, M. Kierein & Ch. Kopetzki, *Ärztegesetz,* 3rd edn (Vienna: Manz, 2007), 135 et seq.; H. Emberger & F. Wallner (eds), *Ärztegesetz,* 2nd edn (Vienna: Verlagshaus der Ärzte, 2008), 249 et seq.; S. Hummelbrunner, *Die ärztliche Gruppenpraxis* (Vienna: Manz, 2005); E. Dujmovits, 'Recht der freien Berufe', in *Öffentliches Wirtschaftsrecht,* ed. M. Holoubek & M. Potacs, vol. 1, 2nd edn (Vienna, New York: Springer, 2007), 396 (441 et seq.); P. Scholz, 'Gruppenpraxengesetze 2001 – eine Regelung mit verfassungsrechtlichen Problemen', *SozSi* (2001): 633. For literature on the amendment of 2010 *see* H. Aubauer & R. Thomas, 'Die Ärzte-GmbH', *taxlex* (2010): 323 L. Stärker,'Die Ärzte-GmbH (I)', *RdM* (2011): 36; J. Zahrl, 'Die Ärzte-GmbH (II)', *RdM* (2011): 77; M. Karollus, 'Vergesellschaftung von Ärzten und Zahnärzten', in *Handbuch Medizinrecht,* ed. R. Resch & F. Wallner, 2nd edn (Vienna: LexisNexis, 2015), 1037 et seq.

partner of the treatment contract, not the single doctor. Nonetheless, group practices are subject to the regulations of the Physicians Act.

465. Despite being partner of the treatment contract, group practices are not to be qualified as outpatient clinics in terms of the Frame Law on Hospitals and Sanatoria. They are an exception to the general rule the Constitutional Court has set up as described above. However, they must not reach the size and organizational complexity of a hospital which is now expressively stipulated in §52a(3). Otherwise, they have to be qualified as hospitals in terms of the Frame Law on Hospitals and Sanatoria.[467] §52a(3) enlists a number of criteria for the demarcation between group practices and autonomous outpatient clinics.

According to §52a(3) No. 1, only freelance licensed doctors are allowed to participate in a group practice (other physical or juridical persons must not be partners of the group practice). Other than the former regulation, §52a as amended in 2010 does not allow the participation of dentists any more. The partners of the group practice are bound to significant personal vocational practice. Thus, their professional practice must be focussed in the group practice.

Within a group practice, it is not permissible to employ other doctors or to have contractual relationships with other associations or doctors (especially to conclude service contracts or body shop agreements) for the purpose of performing medical services to an amount that exceeds temporary substitution (especially because of advanced training, disease or holiday). The general prohibition of employing other doctors does not, however, restrict the right to conclude additional treatment contracts with other doctors for the sake of the patient (for instance contracts on the administration of narcotics by a specialist in the field of anaesthesia).

It is legal to employ members of other health care professions to an amount that does not require regulations of a public institution *(Anstaltsordnung)*. §52a(3) No. 8 fixes a relation of 1:5 (one partner in relation to five members of another health care profession) and thirty members of another health care profession as a demarcation criterion. In case these numbers are exceeded, the institution is to be qualified as outpatient clinic. Doctors' surgery assistants are not included in this number because of their mainly administrative functions. There are also exceptions for group practices in highly technical special fields.

466. The partnership agreement must contain regulations on management and representation of the group practice. Beyond that, every partner is allowed to conclude treatment contracts (§52a[5]). Questions on the practice of a certain profession are decided by the particularly licensed partners. It is, however, not allowed to bind the freelance medical profession to any instructions or the approval of the partners.

467. The function of the association must be limited to the practice of the medical profession within the professional license including the necessary auxiliary

467. For the demarcation between group practices and outpatient clinics *see* e.g., W. Mazal, 'Gruppenpraxis versus Anstaltsbegriff', *RdM* (2000): 129; M. Stadler, 'Abgrenzung von ärztlichen Ordinationsstätten bzw Gruppenpraxen und selbständigen Ambulatorien', *RdM* (2010): 36.

activities, activities of other health care professions in direct relation to the professional license of the group practice and the administration of the partnership property (§52a[3] No. 5).

468. Generally, a group practice can only have one corporate domicile in Austria. Under the conditions of §52a(4) as amended in 2010, there are exceptions for group practices with an insurance contract. The firm name must at least consist of the name of one of the partners and the medical fields offered by the group practice. The rules on doctors of the Physicians Act apply *mutatis mutandis* for group practices. Every participating doctor has to provide for the observance of the provisions of the Physicians Act, especially by drawing up the partnership agreement correspondingly to them. Every partner is personally responsible for the observance of his personal duties, which cannot be restricted by the partnership agreement or resolutions of the partners.

Establishment, extension and closing of group practices as well as the beginning and ending of participation are to be notified to the Austrian Medical Chamber within one week (§29[1] No. 7 of the Physicians Act).

469. Group practices can be partners of insurance contracts. The regulations for insurance contracts are similar to those for doctors.

As the group practice itself is partner of the treatment contract, the general partnership itself is liable for damages resulting from it. Apart from that, the doctor carrying out the treatment is liable under general tort.

Other than conventional freelance associations, group practices are not subject to the obligation of secrecy and the prohibition of commission payments. This is also a consequence of their status as holder of the license for practising the medical profession.

470. Besides the admission of group practices in the legal form of a private limited company, §§52b, 52c stipulate admission procedures similar to those for outpatient clinics as a consequence of the *Hartlauer*-judgment of the European Court of Justice (for details *see* Part III, Chapter 3, §1.IV. below).

III. Cooperation Between Members of Other Health Care Professions

471. The rules for associations between doctors as described above apply *mutatis mutandis* for dentists (§§25 and 26 of the Dentists Act). Beyond that, §25(1) explicitly allows associations related to surgeries and instruments with any member of another freelance health care profession. In contrast to the legal situation before the amendment of 2010 (*see* above), doctors and dentists cannot cooperate in a group practice any more.

472. Cooperation between members of other health care professions is not subject to any specific restrictions of corporate law. Nonetheless, the demarcation between freelance surgeries and outpatient clinics and hospitals is as important as it is for associations between doctors. A freelance association between non-medical professions is, therefore, only permissible, if the association is not partner of the treatment contract (*see* VfSlg 14.444 concerning midwives). Thus, not the association itself, but only the treating member of the health care profession is liable for damages because of misconduct. Other than under the Physicians Act and the Dentists Act, the possibility of establishing group practices is not provided for under the professional acts of other health care professions.

Freelance associations between members of non-medical professions do not hold the license for practising the health care profession. Thus, the single participating members have to observe their professional duties.

As there is no such regulation as §52 of the Physicians Act, members of non-medical professions may not only associate with members of other health care professions but also with people who are unacquainted with the profession concerned (like family members).

Associations between members of non-medical professions cannot conclude insurance contracts since they are not holders of the license for practising the profession.

§3. Professional Duties Towards Colleagues

473. Physicians have to make all reasonable efforts to safeguard the professional reputation and to treat colleagues fairly. Therefore, §53 of the Physicians Act stipulates that physicians have to avoid proclaiming information that is not objective, untruthful or affects the professional reputation. This principle is clearly defined in the ordinance 'Physicians and Publicity' issued by the Austrian Medical Chamber.[468] Further on, physicians are not allowed to ask for or to take money for the referral to them or to other physicians. Such an unlawful transaction is void by law.[469]

474. In order to minimize legal proceedings between physicians, §94 of the Physicians Act postulates that in the case of disputes between registered physicians resulting from the exercise of the profession and their activities within the Medical Chamber, every physician has to put forward a request for a settlement to an arbitration committee of the Medical Chamber before filing a lawsuit or prosecuting privately.[470] Similar rules apply to dentists according to §54 Dentists Chamber Act.

468. http://www.aerztekammer.at/kundmachungen/-/asset_publisher/ZHk4/content/id/19117, 31 May 2017.

469. For details *see* M. Leitner, '§53 ÄrzteG', in *Ärztegesetz mit Kommentar*, ed. H. Emberger & F. Wallner, 2nd edn (Vienna: Verlagshaus der Ärzte, 2008), 254 et seq.; G. Aigner, M. Kierein & Ch. Kopetzki (eds), *Ärztegesetz*, 3rd edn (Vienna: Manz, 2007), §53 Note 1 et seq.

470. Supreme Court 23 May 2005, 6 Ob 32/05g, *RdM* (2005): no. 126. For details *see* N. Herdega, '§94 ÄrzteG', in *Ärztegesetz mit Kommentar*, ed. H. Emberger & F. Wallner, 2nd edn (Vienna: Verlagshaus der Ärzte, 2008), 383 et seq.; G. Aigner, M. Kierein & Ch. Kopetzki (eds), *Ärztegesetz*, 3rd ed. (Vienna: Manz, 2007), §94 Note 1 et seq.

Chapter 2. Relationship with Other Health Care Providers

§1. PHARMACISTS

I. General Remarks

475. There are about 1,352 public pharmacies in Austria, which are run by pharmacists as independent private enterprises. Furthermore, there are twenty-eight branches (every pharmacy is allowed to operate one branch within a radius of 4 km), 43 hospital pharmacies and 950 dispensing doctors (as of 31 December 2015). About 16,351 people, out of which 5,822 people are pharmacists, work in pharmacies (as of 31 December 2016).[471]

476. Pharmacies play a pivotal role in the distribution of medicinal products. In compliance with the Medicinal Products Act, medicinal products generally (except for physician samples, products used for clinical trials or special medicinal products) cannot be directly distributed from the manufacturer to the user, but only to pharmacies and certain other entitled institutions (§57). As per §59, they can only be distributed to the user via pharmacies (apart from some exceptions in §§57, 58 and 59). These distribution rules are partly overlapped by the provisions of the Pharmacy Act, the Regulation on the Operation of Pharmacies (2005) and the regulations on prescription requirements.[472]

II. Public Pharmacies, Distributing Doctors and the Need-Oriented System

477. The establishment of a public pharmacy needs a concession (§9), which is granted under several substantive and personal conditions listed in §§3 et seq., 10 of the Pharmacy Act (*Apothekengesetz,* Federal Law Gazette I 2004/142, as last amended by Federal Law Gazette I 2016/103). According to §10, a physician must have his permanent surgery in the community and there must be a need for a new public pharmacy. The need is defined negatively in §10(2) and §10(3): There is no need for a new pharmacy, if the distance to the next pharmacy is less than 500 m (for exceptions *see* §10[6]), or if each of the affected pharmacies has a supply of less than 5,500 people (for exceptions *see* §10[6a]). Furthermore, there is no need for a new public pharmacy, if there is a dispensing doctor in the prospective community and only (up to) two physicians with insurance contracts have their surgery there (the requirements for operating a branch are listed in §24). The same applies in case there is a dispensing doctor and a group practise with an insurance contract

471. *Source*: Österreichische Apothekerkammer, Apotheke in Zahlen (2017), www.apotheker.or.at, 24 May 2017.
472. For the question of distribution of medicinal products by (non-dispensing) physicians *see* Ch. Kopetzki, 'Arzneimittelabgabe durch und an Ärzte', in *Gmundner Medizinrechtskongress 2008*, ed. G. Aigner, R. Resch & F. Wallner (Vienna: Manz, 2009), 94.

in line with §10(3). The need-oriented distribution system has been declared constitutional by the Constitutional Court.[473]

Due to two judgments of the ECJ, the (alternative) requirement of a minimum supply of 5,500 people has been revised twice lately: The former regulation, which only referred to the rigid limit of 5,500 people remaining to be served, was first declared contrary to Article 49 TFEU in 2014, because it did not allow the competent authorities to take account of particular local geographical conditions.[474] As a consequence, the Austrian Administrative Court did not consider the former regulation to be generally inapplicable, but required an assessment on a case-by-case basis.[475] In a preliminary ruling (requested by the Regional Administrative Court of Upper Austria), the ECJ however held that the strict number of 5,500 people was not to be applied in a general manner, in every specific situation subject to an assessment.[476] The jurisdiction of the ECJ finally led to the flexible calculation, which allows the national authorities to undercut the rigid limit of §10(2) considering specific local circumstances (§10[6a]). If this is necessary, is to be assessed in each case.[477]

The Ordinance on the Operation of Pharmacies (Federal Law Gazette II 2005/65, as last amended by Federal Law Gazette II 2016/5) stipulates further details concerning equipment, required space and so forth.

478. The personal qualifications for becoming a pharmacist in a public pharmacy are (§3): Austrian citizenship or citizenship of an EEA-Member State or Switzerland, professional qualification, management permit (at least five years of

---

473. *See* the judgment of the Constitutional Court 26 Jun. 2008, G 12/08 concerning dispensing doctors. For details *see* (with further references) e.g., H. Serban & H. Heisler, *Apothekengesetz*, 2nd edn (Vienna: Verlag Österreich, 2005), 129 et seq.; M. Potacs & S. Scholz, 'Apothekenrecht', in *Handbuch Medizinrecht*, ed. R. Resch & F. Wallner, 2nd edn (Vienna: LexisNexis, 2015), 851 (858 et seq.); A. Schwabl, 'Apothekengesetz', in *Gmundner Kommentar zum Gesundheitsrecht*, ed. M. Neumayr, R. Resch & F. Wallner (Vienna: Manz, 2016), 403 (445 et seq.). The conformity of the general need-oriented system with Union Law is discussed controversially: Affirmative Ch. Schneider, 'Bedarfsprüfung für Apotheken EU-konform?', *wbl* (2007): 149; denying P. Bußjäger & G. Heißl, 'Bedarfsprüfung für Apotheken und Gemeinschaftsrecht', *ÖJZ* (2010): 209; P. Ivankovics, 'Bedarfsprüfung für Apotheken: Ein (un-)geeignetes Mittel?', *RdM* (2015): 285.
474. ECJ 13 Feb. 2014, C-367/12, *Sokoll-Seebacher*. For details *see* S. Scholz, 'EuGH: Österreichische Bedarfsprüfung für öffentliche Apotheken in einem Punkt EU-rechtswidrig', *RdM* (2014): 121.
475. Administrative Court 27 Mar. 2014, 2013/10/0209; 25 Apr. 2014, 2013/10/0022; 12 Aug. 2014, 2012/10/0181; 8 Aug. 2014, Ro 2014/10/0096 and 0098; 22 Apr. 2015, 2013/10/0077. Critical S. Scholz, 'Apothekenbedarfsprüfung, Inländerdiskriminierung und verfassungskonforme Interpretation: Überlegungen aus Anlass von VwGH 22.4.2015, Ro 2014/10/0122', in *Jahrbuch Öffentliches Recht 2016*, ed. G. Baumgartner (Vienna; Graz: NWV, 2016), 197.
476. ECJ 30 Jun. 2016, C-634/15, *Sokoll-Seebacher and Naderhirn*.
477. For details *see* M. Zirm, 'Bedarfsprüfung im Apothekenrecht endlich unionsrechtskonform?', *RdM* (2017): 56; Ch. Schneider, 'EuGH: Starre Grenze beim Mindestversorgungspotenzial für öffentliche Apotheken auch außerhalb ländlicher und abgelegener Regionen unzulässig', *RdM* (2016): 187; Ch. Schmelz & V. Wolfbauer, 'Die apothekenrechtliche Bedarfsprüfung im Lichte der EuGH-Judikatur', *ecolex* (2016): 1020. The Administrative Court did not consider the different treatment between national cases and cases linked to Community Law (within the period from the ECJ judgment to the amendment of §10 [6a]) to be a reverse discrimination: Administrative Court 29 Mar 2017, Ra 2016/10/0141.

working experience in a pharmacy), full legal capacity, reliability, good state of health and command of German necessary for running a pharmacy.

The professional qualification requires a university degree and one year of practical training (§3b in conjunction with §3a) or other evidences of education and training acknowledged by the Austrian Chamber of Pharmacists (§3c). Pharmacy can be studied in Vienna, Graz and Innsbruck. It takes at least nine semesters (the average duration is longer though) to finish the three parts of the education with the academic title 'Mag. pharm.'. The education comprises *inter alia* the pharmaceutical subjects Pharmaceutical Chemistry, Pharmacognosy, Pharmaceutical Technology, Biopharmacy, Pharmacology, Toxicology, Bromatology, Clinical Pharmacy. Students who want to specialize can write a doctor's thesis in pharmaceutical science for which they are awarded the doctorate in natural science (Dr. rer. nat.).

The fact that public pharmacies can only be run by pharmacists does not violate the freedom of establishment under Union Law.[478]

479. In line with the provisions of §§28 et seq. of the Pharmacy Act, physicians can run a pharmacy (dispensing doctors). Just like public pharmacies, dispensing doctors need a concession (§29). A concession is only granted, if the doctor has a contract with an insurance institution, if there is no local public pharmacy and if the distance from the surgery to the next public pharmacy is more than six kilometres. In case a new public pharmacy is established, the concession for being a dispensing doctor has to be withdrawn, if the distance between the surgery and the new public pharmacy is less than four kilometres and there are more than two local contracting doctors.

480. The relationship between public pharmacies and dispensing doctors has always been very tense. On the one hand, dispensing doctors play an important role as local providers in rural regions. On the other hand, dispensing doctors who are granted a concession might cause economic losses for public pharmacies. Thus, legislation in this field has been very inconsistent and has been determined by the jurisdiction of the Constitutional Court concerning the need-oriented system.[479] In 2006 (Federal Law Gazette 2006/41), the system of a general primacy of public pharmacies was changed on behalf of a dual system in rural regions (*see* §10[2] No. 1, §10[3] and §29[1]). The requirements for dispensing doctors have been further loosened by the amendment of 2016 (Federal Law Gazette 2016/30): Under certain circumstances, a concession for a dispensing doctor can now also be granted in communities with an existing public pharmacy (§28[3]; *see also* the regulation on succession in §29[1a]).

---

478. ECJ 19 May 2009, C-171/07 and 172/07, *RdM* 2009, 163 *(Potacs)*; M.-Th. Richter, 'Der Apotheker bleibt in seiner Apotheke. Der EuGH erachtet das Fremdbesitzverbot als durch den Gesundheitsschutz gerechtfertigt', *ZfRV* (2009): 100; L. Stärker, 'Beschränkungen für den Apothekenbesitz trotz Niederlassungsfreiheit zulässig', *ASok* (2009): 245.

479. For details (with further references) M. Potacs, 'Öffentliche Apotheken und ärztliche Hausapotheken – ein verfassungsrechtlicher Dauerbrenner?', *Sonderheft Gmundner Medizinrechtskongress 2009, RdM* (2009): 243. *See also* F. Wallner, 'Überlegungen zu einer verfassungs- und gemeinschaftsrechtskonformen Neuregelung der Abgrenzung zwischen öffentlichen Apotheken und ärztlichen Hausapotheken', *RdM* (2014): 116.

III. Pharmacies and Mail Order

481. According to §59(9) of the Medicinal Products Act, the distribution of medicinal products by mail order is generally prohibited. In the course of an amendment in 2013 (Federal Law Gazette 2013/48), the regulations on mail order were adapted to the provisions made by the ECJ in the *Doc Morris*-Judgment[480] by making exceptions to the general prohibition in §59(9).[481]

In line with §59(10), mail order is now allowed for medicinal products, which are authorized in Austria, are not subject to prescription and are either sold by pharmacies within the Austrian territory or by an authorized pharmacy of another Member State. §59(11) allows mail order by Austrian pharmacies to other Member States, if the medicinal product is authorized and not subject to prescription there. §59a stipulates further requirements; details are regulated under the Mail-Order-Ordinance (Federal Law Gazette II 2015/105.

IV. The Austrian Chamber of Pharmacists

482. The interests of pharmacists are represented by the Austrian Chamber of Pharmacists. It is a public-law corporation, which has an autonomous sphere of powers as well as a delegated sphere of functions. The main functions of the Austrian Chamber of Pharmacists are the assessment of bills, giving statements on health topics and expert opinions, providing advanced education and disciplinary power over the members.

§2. Nurses

483. Education and professional rules for nurses *('Diplomierte[r] Gesundheits- und Krankenpfleger[in]')* are regulated by the Nursing of Patients Act (*Gesundheits- und Krankenpflegegesetz*, Federal Law Gazette I 1997/108, as last amended by Federal Law Gazette I 2017/54), for which the federation is competent (Article 10[1] No. 12 Constitution). The act only refers to the nursing of ill people, but does not include social professions (which fall within Article 15 of the Constitution and therefore within the competence of the federal states) and commercial professions (which are subject to the Trade Regulations). Concerning social professions, federation and federal states have concluded an agreement on the basis of Article 15a of the Constitution, which regulates occupational pattern, functions and education similarly to the Nursing of Patients Act. According to the agreement, social professions include social workers in the fields of old-age relief, family support, working with disabled people and (optionally) home support. Some of these

480. ECJ 11 Dec. 2003, C-322/01. For details e.g., G. Gast & W. Reiser, 'Arzneimittel aus der Internet-Apotheke?', *RdM* (2004): 82; M. Nemetz, 'Internetapotheken – Post DocMorris', *ecolex* (2004): 991; R. Streinz, 'Das Verbot des Apothekenversandhandels mit Arzneimitteln', *EuZW* (2003): 37.
481. Before the amendment, §59(9) was not applicable to over-the-counter products in cases related to Union Law because of the primacy in application: *See* e.g., Supreme Court of Justice 13 Feb. 2007, 4 Ob 243/06y, ZfRV 2/2007, 75 = wbl 6/2007, 293 = M&R 2/2007, 96.

professions also gain the qualification in nursing in terms of the Nursing of Patients Act.

Under the strict conditions of §3b(1), certain caregivers who are not nurses are allowed to carry out single nursing functions (e.g., assistance concerning food, fluid or medication intake, concerning personal hygiene, putting on and taking off clothes) in an individual case. In case of not only temporary bodily impairment, §3c provides the possibility of delegating single nursing activities to caregivers for a limited time. Yet this is only possible if the person in need is not cared for institutionally. This form of personal assistance needs the written order of a nurse (for further conditions *see* §3c).[482]

484. The professional profile of nurses was reformed and modernized by the amendment of 2016 (Federal Law Gazette 2016/75): Especially the former differentiation between different spheres of functions (autonomous, jointly responsible and interdisciplinary functions as well as basic life support) was replaced with a new definition of competences. The scope of professional activities is more practically oriented now and meets the needs of the different settings where nursing takes place. According to the general description in §12(1), the higher service of nursing comprises the direct and indirect nursing of people of all ages, of families and population groups in mobile, outpatient and (partly) hospitalization care as well as at all levels of care. It contributes to the promotion and maintenance of health, it supports the healing process, provides relief and support in coping with health impairments and maintains the best possible quality of life by health-promoting, preventive, curative, rehabilitation and palliative measures based on scientific knowledge (§12[2]). Within the scope of medical diagnosis and therapy, nurses carry out activities that are delegated to them by physicians (§12[3]). In the field of interprofessional cooperation, nurses contribute to the continuity in treatment (§12[4]). The development, organization and implementation of nursing strategies, concepts and programmes for reinforcing health literacy, especially for chronical diseases as well as family, school and public health care are also part of the job description (§12[5]).

485. The scope of functions consists of the nursing core competence (§14), emergency competences (§14a), competences in medical diagnosis and therapy (§15), competences within the 'multiprofessional support team' (§16) and continued prescription of medical devices (§15a, which has not entered into force to date)

482. For details concerning the distinction between nurses and other commercial and social professions M. Hausreither, 'Das freie Gewerbe der Personenbetreuung im Kontrast zu den Gesundheitsberufen', *ecolex* (2007): 576; R. Thienel, 'Personenbetreuung und Gewerbekompetenz', *JRP* (2007): 150; M. Wegscheider, 'Die neuen Sozialbetreuungsberufe', *ÖJZ* (2007): 955; M. Pruckner, 'Der Betreuer pflegt (nicht)', *RdM* (2008): 4; H. Stolzlechner, 'Zur Durchführung krankenpflegerischer Hilfstätigkeiten durch Angehörige von Sozialberufen', *RdM* (2002): 35; Ch. Gepart, 'Aromapflege im Spannungsfeld zwischen Gewerberecht und Pflegerecht', *ÖZPR* (2015): 93. For the demarcation between nurses and other health care professions *see* e.g., M. Plank, 'Berufsrechtliche Abgrenzungsfragen zwischen Ärzten, Diplomkrankenpflegern und medizinisch-technischen Diensten', *UVSaktuell* (2007): 100.

The scope of functions can be extended or specialized by specific training (§§66–70a) or a special basic training (§§74–80).

Pursuant to §14, the nursing core competence comprises e.g., the overall responsibility for the nursing process, planning and carrying out nursing activities, supporting daily activities, health surveillance, guidance on nursing as well as organizing and carrying out training, health promotion and prevention of diseases. Furthermore, guidance and surveillance of support staff, instruction and chaperonage of nursing students as well as participating in nursing science, fall within their core competence. In the field of the core competence of nursing, which corresponds to the former 'autonomous' sphere of functions, nurses are free from functional directives (however regardless of orders within the hierarchic organization of the nursing service). The activities of nurses are not autonomous, if they are carried out on the basis of medical order. 'Autonomous' also means that the nurses are liable for damages they cause. The competences in emergency situations comprise identifying and assessing emergency situations and taking appropriate measures. Nurses can autonomously give basic life support, as long as a doctor is not available. Doctors are to be informed as soon as possible. Basic life support especially comprises defibrillation with semi-automatic devices and giving oxygen (*see* §14a).

The competence of medicinal diagnosis and therapy is related to diagnostic and therapeutic measures in compliance with a doctor's instruction (§15[1]; §49[3] of the Physicians Act provides a complementary legal authorization for doctors). The instruction has to be given in writing, except when there is an urgent situation or the physician is present and the instruction is clear and free of doubt (then an orally expressed instruction suffices). For these functions, doctor and nurse have shared responsibility. The instructing doctor is responsible for his instructions (responsibility for instruction) and the nurse is responsible for carrying out the action (performance responsibility). This competence area especially comprises giving medication (including cytostatics and contrast agents), preparing and giving injections and inserting infusions as well as blood withdrawal, e.g., from veins and capillary, placing, installing and washing urinary catheters. Furthermore the preparation, assistance and aftercare in the context of endoscopic interventions, assisting surgical wound care, removing drainage tubes, sutures and wound closure clips as well as applying and removing dressings, giving and removing nasogastric or transoral tubes and enemas and finally suction of the upper respiratory tract fall within this field of competence (for details *see* the demonstrative list of activities in §15[4]).

The competences within the multi-professional support team (former interdisciplinary sphere of functions) comprise all functions related to both nursing and other health care professions. Concerning these matters, nurses have the right of proposal and of co-decision. They are equal members of the team and are responsible for performance. In particular, nursing expertise with regard to measures related to the prevention of diseases and accidents and the preservation and promotion of health, admission and discharge management, health counselling, interprofessional networking, information transfer and knowledge management, coordination of the treatment process, initial assessment of patients and ethical decision making fall within the interdisciplinary scope of functions (§16[3]).

The list of functions in these spheres is demonstrative. Thus, further action might be included in the particular sphere of functions, if it is covered by the occupational pattern, if it is of comparable level of difficulty, if it is covered by the basic training or advanced education and if it does not fall within the occupational pattern of another health care profession or the extended or specialized sphere of functions.

486. The extended sphere of functions, which requires special education, comprises specialization aimed at certain target groups or settings, educational and managing functions (§17[1]). Specializations, which also require special education, are the nursing of children and adolescents, intensive care, nursing in the fields of psychiatry and anaesthesia, the nursing after renal replacement therapy and during surgery, hygiene in hospitals and – since the amendment in 2016 – wound and stoma management, palliative care and psycho-geriatric care (§17[2]). The special functions are listed exhaustively, so that other functions (like home nursing or nursing in the field of oncology) fall within the general sphere of functions. The knowledge of such functions can be deepened by making use of further education.

487. The qualifications for being entitled to work as a nurse are (§27[1]): Full legal capacity, good state of health and reliability, proof of qualification and knowledge of the German language as far as required for vocational practice. The different forms of proof of qualification are regulated by §§28 to 31: Inland diploma (§28), EEA-licenses (§§28a et seq., which were adapted to the Regulation 2013/55/EC by a further amendment in 2016 [Federal Law Gazette 2016/8], which i.a. introduced the European Professional Card in §28b and 39a and regulates partial access in §30a), proof of qualification outside the EEA (§31). The education at a nursing school generally takes three years and is regulated by §§41 et seq. It will be replaced with bachelor degree programmes by the year 2024. Further, advanced and special education is regulated by §§63 et seq.

The higher services of nursing can be practised either on a freelance base (§36) or on the base of certain employments (§35[1]).

From July 2018 on, all healthcare professionals that are subject to the Nursing of Patients Act (meaning nurses and their assistants), will have to register at the Austrian Chamber of Labour or the *Gesundheit Österreich GmbH* (depending on whether they are members of the Labour Chamber or not). The register for (non-physician) healthcare professionals was introduced by the Health Professions Registrations Act (Federal Law Gazette I 2016/87 as last amended by Federal Law Gazette I 2017/54) and comprises not only the nursing professions, but also the higher medical-technical services.

488. The general professional duties are listed in §§4–10 and §§38 and 63 of the Nursing of Patients Act. They comprise the obligation to carry out the profession conscientiously and without discriminating against anyone, to protect the benefit and health of the patient (§4[1]), to make use of further education (§4[2], §63) and the duties to render aid (§4[3]), to report (§§7[1] and 8[1]) and to disclose (§9[1]), the duty of documentation (§5[1]) and the obligation of secrecy (§6[1]). Violations of the general professional duties are administrative offences (§105). Beyond that, nurses who do not observe the professional duties might be liable under civil and criminal law (considering the higher standard of care in §6 of the Criminal Act and §1299 of the Civil Code). Further professional duties result from other acts, for instance the Law on Hospitals of the federal states, the Medical Devices Act (§70) and the Epidemic Act (§§2, 3). Other than the Physicians Act, the Nursing of Patients Act does not provide a prohibition of commission payments.

489. Nurses are assisted by carers *(Pflegeassistenz,* formerly *Pflegehilfe),* who have to attend an educational course of one year and are instructed by nurses for qualifications, sphere of functions, education and so forth *see* §§82 et seq.).[483] The amendment in 2016 introduced a second kind of higher qualified assistance, which enables nurses to delegate more functions without compulsory surveillance (for details on their sphere of functions *see* §83a).

§3. Midwives

490. The major functions of midwives are consultation, support and care for pregnant and parturient women as well as puerperas, assistance in giving birth, nursing of new born children and babies and care for mother and baby (§2[1] of the Midwives Act *[Hebammengesetz],* Federal Law Gazette 1994/310, as last amended by Federal Law Gazette I 2016/8).

491. Midwives generally work autonomously, except for irregular or dangerous situations for the woman or child. Then midwives are only allowed to perform on the orders of and in cooperation with a doctor (§4).

483. For details *see* Th. Müller, 'GuKG', in *Gmundner Kommentar zur Gesundheitsrecht,* ed. M. Neumayr, R. Resch & F. Wallner (Vienna: Manz, 2016), 577; R. Gruber, *Gesundheits- und Krankenpflegegesetz* (Graz: Leykam, 2017). For further information on the amendment of 2016 *see* M. Hausreither & A. Lust, 'Berufsbild und Kompetenzen des gehobenen Dienstes für Gesundheits- und Krankenpflege', *ÖZPR* (2016/6): I; M. Hausreither, 'GuKG-Novelle 2016 und Entwurf der Pflegeassistenzberufe-Ausbildungsverordnung', *ÖZPR* (2016): 100; M. Hausreither & A. Lust, 'GuKG-Novelle 2016: Inkrafttreten und Evaluierung der Reformmaßnahmen', *ÖZPR* (2016): 133; M. Drs, 'Neue Dreiteilung Gesundheits- und Krankenpflegeberufe. Arbeiter oder Angestellte?' *ASOK* (2016): 418; M. Hausreither & A. Lust, 'Berufsbild und Tätigkeitsbereich der Pflegeassistenzberufe', *ÖZPR* (2017): I; F. Schaup, 'Auswirkungen der GuKG-Novelle 2016 auf die Haftung', *ÖZPR* (2017): 58; C. Bretbacher, 'Auswirkungen der GuKG-Novelle 2016 auf die Pflegeorganisation im extramuralen Setting', *ÖZPR* (2017): 56; M. Stadler, 'Die GuKG-Novelle 2016 und ihre Auswirkungen für die Praxis im Spitalsbereich', *JMG* (2017): 36; W. Hauser, W. Kröll & W. Stock, *Grundzüge des Gesundheitsrechts* (Vienna, Graz: NWV, 2017), 101 et seq. For details concerning the legal situation before the amendment 2016 *see* (with further references) e.g., M. Hausreither, 'Gesundheits- und Krankenpflege', in *Handbuch Medizinrecht,* ed. G. Aigner et al. (Vienna: Manz, 2003 et seq.), III/479 et seq.; R. Wagner-Kreimer, 'Berufsrecht der Gesundheits- und Krankenpflegeberufe', in *Handbuch Medizinrecht,* ed. R. Resch & F. Wallner, 2nd edn (Vienna: LexisNexis, 2015), 879 et seq.; S. Weiss & A. Lust, *GuKG,* 7th edn (Vienna: Manz, 2014); H. Schwamberger, *Gesundheits- und Krankenpflegegesetz,* 6th edn (Vienna: Verlag Österreich, 2011); For details concerning the new Health Professions Registrations Act *see* e.g., K. Mayr, 'Änderungen im Gesundheitsberuferegister (GBRG-Novelle 2017) – gebührenfreie Registrierung!', *ÖZPR* (2017): 34; M. Hausreither & I. Hager-Ruhs, 'Das Gesundheitsberuferegister-Gesetz', *ÖZPR* (2016): 136; A. Gratzer & K. Schwaiger, 'Registrierung nichtärztlicher Gesundheitsberufe – Nutzen für alle!' *ÖZPR* (2015): 58.

Irregular and dangerous situations during pregnancy are especially a worrying anamnesis or the occurrence of diseases that need medical support, dangerous sudden occurrences and multiple pregnancies. Irregular and dangerous situations during birth are all irregular locations of the baby, prolapse of the umbilical cord, suspicion of disproportion of skull and pelvis, signs of overload, exhaustion or unusual pain, irregular heart beat of the child, suspicion of front position of the placenta, heavy bleeding from the birth canal, no afterbirth after two hours or parts of afterbirth remaining inside the body, miscarriage or premature birth, multiple birth, deformities of the baby that need immediate medical measures and all dangerous incidents, diseases and the death of the parturient woman. Irregular and dangerous situations during puerperium are premature birth, sensitive abdomen, irregular increased bleeding, absent or smelly lochia, deformities of the baby, injury of the baby during birth, threatening condition or diseases of the baby, excessive weight loss of the baby and death of puerpera or child.

492. In compliance with §5, midwives are entitled to apply medicinal products without a doctor's order in certain situations. In case of indication in the first stage of labour, midwives are allowed to administer anticonvulsant or analgesic medicinal products (that are not subject to the Act on Addictive Drugs). In case of emergency, they can intramuscularly or subcutaneously apply ecbolics or medication to stop the labour, if medical aid cannot be reached or if hospitalization is not possible in time. Midwives are also entitled to apply medication for rhesus-prophylaxis intramuscularly, if a doctor assesses it to be necessary. Directly after childbirth, they can apply prophylactic medicinal products, if recommended by midwives according to the state-of-the-art.

493. Education of midwives is regulated by the Midwives Act and the Administrative Order on the Education of Midwives (Federal Law Gazette 1995/599). The profession can be practised either on a freelance basis (§19) or on the basis of certain employments (§18).

494. The major professional duties of midwives are the duty to render aid (§6[2]), personal and direct vocational practice, the duty to report (for instance deliveries are to be reported to the competent register office within one week [§8] and the abandoning of a child must be reported to the safety authority), the duty of documentation (§9), the obligation of secrecy (§7), the duty to make use of further education (§37) and the duty to call a doctor in case of irregular and dangerous situations (§6[3]). Furthermore, there are advertising restrictions for freelance midwives (§20).[484]

484. For details *see* (with further references) M. Hausreither, 'Das Berufsrecht der Hebamme', in *Handbuch Medizinrecht*, ed. G. Aigner et al. (Vienna: Manz, 2003 et seq.), III/193 et seq.; E. Pitzl & Ch. Huber, 'HebG', in *Gmundner Kommentar zum Gesundheitsrecht*, ed. M. Neumayr, R. Resch & F. Wallner (Vienna: Manz, 2016), 743; E. Pitzl & Ch. Huber, 'Berufsrecht der Hebammen', in *Handbuch Medizinrecht*, ed. R. Resch & F. Wallner, 2nd edn (Vienna: LexisNexis, 2015), 983 et seq. W. Hauser, W. Kröll & W. Stock, *Grundzüge des Gesundheitsrechts* (Vienna, Graz: NWV, 2017), 131 et seq.; E. Sladecek, L.-M. Marzi & Th. Schmiedbauer, *Recht für Gesundheitsberufe*, 6th edn (Vienna: LexisNexis, 2012), 66 et seq.

§4. Dentists

495. Until the Dentists Act (*Zahnärztegesetz,* Federal Law Gazette I 2005/126, as last amended by Federal Law Gazette I 2016/8) was passed in 2006, dentists had been subject to the Physicians Act. The general regulations of the Physicians Act were taken over to a large extent, but they were also adapted to the professional requirements of dentists.

496. Dentistry includes all activities based on medical-scientific knowledge that are practised directly upon humans or indirectly for their benefit. It comprises especially medical examination, diagnosis and treatment of diseases. The practice of dentistry also includes surgery,[485] the prevention of diseases, the ordinance of remedies, health aids and diagnostic appliances, the fabrication of dental prosthesis, technical-mechanical work on prosthesis and the fabrication of artificial teeth (*see* §4 of the Dentists Act).[486]

497. Dentistry can be studied in Vienna, Graz and Innsbruck. Unlike doctors, dentists do not need further post-doc education after finishing their studies (by gaining their doctorate, generally after twelve semesters). They are allowed to use the professional title 'Dentist'. For becoming consultants in the field of stomatology, dentists are required to do three years of practical training and to take a specialist examination after graduation. Their professional title is either 'Consultant of stomatology' or 'Dentist'. Students of dentistry are entitled to practise under the guidance and supervision of a dentist (§33; for the practical training also *see* §§50a et seq.).

498. The personal qualifications for becoming a dentist are (§6 et seq.) Austrian citizenship or citizenship of an EEA-Member State or Switzerland, full legal capacity, reliability,[487] good state of health and a good command of German, Austrian doctorate of dentistry or an equal education of another EEA-Member State or Switzerland and registration in the directory of dentists listed by the Austrian Dentists' Chamber (§§11 et seq.).

499. Dentists can either work on a freelance basis or be employed (§23). Freelancers can also form group practices (§26) or cooperate regarding surgery and/ or medical instruments.

500. The professional duties of dentists (§§16 et seq.) correspond to those of a doctor (*see* Part II, Chapter 1 above). They are obliged to provide first aid just like everyone else (e.g., after an accident), but there is no professional duty for dentists that is comparable to the one of doctors.

485. 'Surgery' in terms of §4(3) num 4a comprises 'teeth-bleaching', which can therefore only be carried out by dentists: Supreme Court 22 Oct. 2013, 4 Ob 166/13k, *RdM* (2014): 139 *(Kopetzki)* = *ÖBl-LS* 2014/13.

486. For the demarcation between dentists and dental technicians *see* Supreme Court 18 Sep. 2012, 4 Ob 87/12s, *ÖBl* 2013/26 *(Gamerith)* = *RdM-LS* 2013/8; Supreme Court 25 Jun. 2014, 3 Ob 55/14f.

487. The requirement of reliability corresponds to the one in §4(2) num 2 Physicians Act: Administrative Court 11 Oct. 2016, Ra 2016/11/0140, *RdM-LS* 2017/7 = *ZfG* 2017, 15.

§35 prohibits professional misconduct as well as commission and provides rules for advertising.[488]

501. Dentists are represented by the Austrian Dentists' Chamber, which is competent for the representation of the common interests of all Austrian dentists, and by the dentists' chambers of the federal states. Other than doctors, who are members of the medical chambers of the federal states (*see* Part III, Chapter 1, §1.II. above), every dentist who practises in Austria and is registered in the directory of dentists is a member of the Austrian Dentists' Chamber (with a clear assignment to a chamber of the particular federal state). One of the major functions of the Dentists' Chamber is to contract with the insurance providers. It also has the disciplinary power over the dentists. Details concerning membership, rights and duties of the members, organs of Austrian Dentists' Chamber and chambers of the federal states, disciplinary law and so forth are regulated by the Professional Association of Dentists Act (Federal Law Gazette I 2005/154 as last amended by Federal Law Gazette I 2016/8).[489]

488. For details on advertising law for dentists *see* V. Blum, 'Werbung im Zusammenhang mit der ärztlichen Berufsausübung' (Doctoral Thesis, University of Vienna, 2017). *See* i.a. Supreme Court 25 Oct. 2016, 4 Ob 147/16w, *RdM-LS* 2017/34 ('Dental Hotel'); 24 May 2016, 4 Ob 58/16g (prohibition of billboard advertising), *RdM-LS* 2016/73 = *ÖBl-LS* 2016/19 *(Hinger)* = *ZfG* 2016, 84; and 30 Mar. 2016, 4 Ob 254/15d, *RdM-LS* 2016/52 = *AnwBl* 2016, 509 = *ÖBl* 2016/43 *(Graf)* = *ZfG* 2016, 54; 2 Aug. 2012, 4 Ob 79/12i (advertisement by Hungarian dentist) *ÖBl* 2013, 58 *(Gamerith)* = *RdM-LS* 2013/23.

489. For details *see* M. Hausreither, 'Zahnärzte', in *Handbuch Medizinrecht,* ed. G. Aigner et al. (Vienna: Manz, 2003 et seq.), III/235 et seq.; B. Krauskopf, 'ZÄG', in *Gmundner Kommentar zum Gesundheitsrecht,* ed. M. Neumayr, R. Resch & F. Wallner (Vienna: Manz, 2016), 1227; B. Krauskopf, 'Berufsrecht der Zahnärzte', in *Handbuch Medizinrecht,* ed. R. Resch & F. Wallner, 2nd edn (Vienna: LexisNexis, 2015), 805 et seq.; B. Krauskopf, *Das neue Zahnärzterecht* (Thesis, University of Vienna, 2008). For further reading on the Dentists' Chamber M. Fister, 'ZÄKG', in *Gmundner Kommentar zum Gesundheitsrecht,* ed. M. Neumayr, R. Resch & F. Wallner (Vienna: Manz, 2016), 1391 et seq.

Chapter 3. Relationship with Health Care Institutions

§1. Hospitals

I. General Remarks

502. Concerning hospitals, the federation is competent for framework legislation, while the federal states are competent for the legislation and administration of implementing regulations (Article 12[1] No. 1 Constitution). Thus, there are nine hospital acts of the federal states in Austria, implementing the Frame Law on Hospitals and Sanatoria (*Krankenanstalten- und Kuranstaltengesetz,* Federal Law Gazette 1957/1, as last amended by Federal Law Gazette I 2017/59) of the federation. For the executive organs, only the implementing regulations of the federal states, which are to be interpreted in conformity with the framework act, are directly applicable. According to the Constitutional Court, the subject-matter of 'hospitals and nursing homes' covers all measures that were regulated by the Hospitals Act of 1920 (Federal Law Gazette 1920/327).

503. The Frame Law on Hospitals and Sanatoria regulates the concept, establishment and operation of hospitals and also contains specific rules on public and private hospitals and sanatoria. Furthermore, it includes directly applicable regulations, for example on sanitary supervision and removal of organs from cadavers (*see* Part II, Chapter 3, §5.I. above). Beyond the ambit of the Frame Law on Hospitals and Sanatoria, there are further rules referring to hospitals spread over different acts (e.g., the General Social Insurance Act). The aims and principals of the planning of hospitals are agreed upon between federation and federal states in the Austrian Health Structural Plan *(Österreichischer Strukturplan Gesundheit)* on the basis of Article 15a of the Constitution, the concrete planning is stipulated under regional structural plans of the federal states.[490] Another agreement in line with Article 15a of the Constitution *(Zielsteuerung Gesundheit)* was implemented by the health care reform 2013 (Federal Law Gazette 2013/81, replaced by Federal Law Gazette 2017/26, Act on the Implementation of Agreements, *Vereinbarungsumsetzungsgesetz*).[491] The Act on the Implementation of Agreements i.a. contains regulations on the binding force of the Austrian Health Structural Plan and the regional structural plans of the federal states.[492]

490. For details *see* L. Stärker, 'Krankenanstaltenplanung und Krankenanstaltenfinanzierung', in *Handbuch Medizinrecht,* ed. R. Resch & F. Wallner, 2nd edn (Vienna: LexisNexis, 2015), 573 et seq., with further references.

491. For further reading *see* L. Stärker, 'Gesundheits-Zielsteuerungsgesetz', in *Gmundner Kommentar zum Gesundheitsrecht,* ed. M. Neumayr & R- Resch & F. Wallner (Vienna: Manz, 2016), 1479 et seq., with further references; N. Raschauer, 'Zielsteuerung-Gesundheit neu. Verfassungs- und verwaltungsrechtliche Fragen der "Gesundheitsreform 2013"', *RdM* (2014/5a): 204.

492. For details on the Act on the Implementation of Agreements *see* J. Souhrada, 'Verbindliche Planung, SV-Verträge und Krankenanstalten', *SozSi* (2017): 104; B. Schrattbauer, 'Ergänzung zum Beitrag "Zur Bedarfsprüfung bei der geplanten Änderung einer Krankenanstalt" – Auswirkungen des neuen Vereinbarungsumsetzungsgesetzes 2017 (VUG 2017)', *DRdA* (2017): 186.

II. The Definition of Hospital

504. §1 of the Frame Law on Hospitals and Sanatoria defines hospitals as institutions for checking and monitoring the state of health by examination, surgery, the prevention and healing of diseases by treatment, delivery or medically assisted reproduction. Furthermore, the concept of hospital comprises institutions for the medical support and special care for chronically sick people (but not nursing homes where nursing prevails). §2(2) excludes certain institutions despite their similar purpose: institutions for interning mentally ill criminals, medical wards in prisons, institutions in companies for first aid, industrial clinics and the Austrian Agency for Health and Food Safety *(Österreichische Agentur für Gesundheit und Ernährungssicherheit GmbH)*.

505. Thus, one of the characteristics of a hospital is the purpose of the institution, which is to be assessed on the basis of objective criteria (equipment and management) and not on the basis of the expression of will of the responsible body.[493] Nonetheless, the major criterion is the organization of the institution. For being qualified as hospital, it must be organized appropriately to a hospital.[494] According to the Constitutional Court, the decisive elements of an appropriate organization are regulations of a public institution *(Anstaltsordnung)* and a contractual relationship between the patient and the holder of the institution that is subject to sanitary supervision. Furthermore, the Court found that other than a hospital, a freelance surgery was characterized by the direct responsibility of the doctor carrying out the treatment.[495] For the demarcation between outpatient clinics and hospitals by the size of organization *see* Part III, Chapter 1, §2.II. above.

506. Every natural or juridical person can be the holder of a hospital. Public hospitals, however, can only be run by a juridical person (§15). The main holders of hospitals are the federation, the federal states, the *Gemeinden,* district boards, public-law entities established by specific regulations, social insurance carriers, clerical legal entities, associations, commercial law associations (especially outsourced entities) and individuals.

III. Types of Hospitals

507. There are different types of hospitals, which can be distinguished according to the type of operation, according to the level of care, and according to the duty of medical treatment and funding.

---

493. For example Administrative Court 10 Sep. 1986, 85/09/125, ZfVB 1987/3/1217.

494. For instance Administrative Court 19 Jan. 1990, 89/18/0138, VwSlg 13.102 A/1990; Administrative Court 15 Dec. 1989, 89/18/0105, VwSlg 13090 A/1989; Administrative Court 8 Oct. 1986, 85/09/0144, ZfVB 1987/3/1218.

495. Constitutional Court 7 Mar. 1992, G 198/90 et al., VfSlg 13023/1992. The practice of the court has been criticized: M. Windisch-Graetz, 'Selbstständiges Ambulatorium und ärztliche Ordination', *RdM* (1995): 144; Ch. Schneider, *Ärztliche Ordinationen und selbständige Ambulatorien* (Vienna: Verlag Österreich, 2001).

508. According to the type of operation, there are general hospitals (§2[1] No. 1, for everyone without distinction of person, sex or type of treatment); hospitals for special needs *(Sonderkrankenanstalten,* (§2[1] No. 2 for treating people suffering from certain diseases, of a certain age or for a certain purpose); homes for convalescents (§2[1] No. 3) or chronically ill people (§2[1] No. 4), who need medical treatment and special care; maternity hospitals (§2[1] No. 5); sanatoria (§2[1] No. 7), which have a higher standard in care because of their special equipment, and autonomous outpatient clinics (§2[1] No. 7, *see* Part III, Chapter 1, §2.II. above).

509. From the aspect of the level of care, general hospitals (not other types of hospitals) can be divided into standard hospitals, hospitals focussing on a special field *(Schwerpunktkrankenanstalten)* and central hospitals (§2a[1]). This differentiation is especially important in conjunction with §18(2), which stipulates the establishment of these types of hospitals depending on the population. Standard hospitals have departments with in-patient beds at least in the fields of surgery and internal medicine. Furthermore, they must have facilities for anaesthesiology, diagnostic radiology and for autopsy, which are supervised by specialists. In other fields of medicine that might be relevant because of the purpose and range of services of the hospital, medical attendance by medical consultants must be guaranteed. Hospitals focussed on a special field must have departments with in-patient beds at least in the fields of ophthalmology, surgery, gynaecology and obstetrics (including perinatology), otorhinolaryngology, skin and venereal diseases, internal medicine, paediatrics including neonatology, neurology and psychiatry, orthopaedics, accident surgery and urology. Furthermore, it must have facilities for anaesthesiology, haemodialysis, radiation diagnostics and therapy as well as nuclear medicine, for physical medicine, intensive care and dentistry, which are supervised by specialists.[496] Concerning other fields of medicine that must be considered because of the purpose and range of services, medical attendance by consultants must be guaranteed. Finally, there must be a hospital pharmacy, a department for pathologics and a department for medical and chemical laboratory diagnostics. Central hospitals generally must have all departments and facilities that are state-of-the-art.

Medical attendance by consultants in standard or hospitals focussing on a special field is only permissible, if a patient who is treated because of a 'major disease' also needs treatment because of an 'additional disease' that falls within a special field of medicine not covered by the range of services offered by the hospital. It is, however, not possible to extend the range of services by offering the attendance of a consultant in the first place. Medical treatment by consultants does not have to be guaranteed unrestrictedly, but only insofar as the range of services and the purpose of the hospital require it.

---

496. According to §2a(3-5) the *Länder* may modify or 'reduce' these standards and can provide more flexible forms of organization, especially since the amendment of 2011 (2011/147). For details *see* e.g., T. Worel & U. Schermann & P. Richter, 'Änderungen im Bereich der Krankenanstalten durch die Novelle zum Krankenanstalten- und Kuranstaltengesetz 2011, BGBl I 2011/147', in: *Gesundheitsrecht. Jahrbuch 2012*, ed. S. Wenda & M. Kierein & P. Lanske (Vienna: NWV, 2012), 75; L. Stärker, 'Das reduzierte Krankenhaus nach der KAKuG-Novelle 2012', *RdM* (2013): 268.

Within their implementing legislation, the federal states are competent to stipulate certain restrictions and modifications of the range of services.

510. Concerning the duty of medical treatment and funding, hospitals can be divided into non-profit making hospitals (§16), public hospitals (§14) and private hospitals (§39). Since the introduction of the performance-oriented payment scheme ('LKF-system') in 1997, there have been 'fund hospitals' *(Fondskrankenanstalten),* which are defined as hospitals that are integrated into the performance-oriented system funded by funds of the federal states. Fund hospitals include public general hospitals, special hospitals (except nursing departments in public hospitals for psychiatry) and non-profit making private hospitals.

511. Public hospitals (§14) have more rights than private hospitals (especially concerning financing within the performance-oriented system) on the one hand, but on the other hand, they have more duties, too. Typical characteristics of public hospitals are the general obligation to admit all people in need of hospital care, the duty to have at least 75% of the beds in the general class and financing by the performance-oriented system as described above. Furthermore, only juridical persons can be holders of public hospitals.

The requirements for becoming a public hospital are permanent continuance and practical operation of the hospital, non-profit making character, admission of every person in need of hospitalization (for admission and demission *see* §§22–24), treatment as long as the state of health requires it, nursing and treatment according to the state-of-the-art, equal fees for all patients of the same class, no payment of hospital employees by patients, beds for private patients may not exceed the amount of a fourth of all beds. For the different fee classes *see* below.

512. University hospitals are organizational units of Medical Universities, which do not only have scientific and educational tasks, but render medical services directly to humans (§31[2] of the Act on Universities). They are to be distinguished from clinical departments, which render medical services only indirectly to humans. Together with clinical departments, university hospitals form the 'clinical area' of a medical university and are part of a public hospital (§29[5] of the Act on Universities) at the same time. They have a (historically grown) dual function including scientific and educational tasks on the one hand and medical treatment on the other hand. The major consequence of this model is varying responsibility corresponding to the area of activity. While the university is charged with scientific and educational tasks as well as university administration, the holder of the hospital is responsible for patient care. Thus, there are different relationships of control, a differing answerability as the proper party and many conflicts at the interface of competencies. There is a large number of specific provisions for university hospitals both under the Frame Law on Hospitals and Sanatoria and under the Act on Universities.[497]

497. For details *see*, Ch. Kopetzki, '§§29 et seq. UG', in *Kommentar zum Universitätsgesetz 2002*, ed. B. Perthold-Stoitzner, 3rd edn (Vienna: Manz, 2016).

IV. Concession for Establishing and Operating a Hospital

513. All hospitals are subject to a concessional system. Both establishment and operation of hospitals need a regulatory license (§3[1]) regardless of other required concessions (such as planning permissions).

514. All hospitals need a concession of the federal state government for being established, except those that are run by social institutions (they only need to be notified). Social institutions merely need a license for establishing autonomous outpatient clinics (for the protection of licensed freelance practitioners), which is to be granted in case of mutual consent of the insurance provider and the Medical Chamber and Dentists' Chamber (§3[5]).

515. The concession is to be granted, if there is a need for a new hospital, if ownership or other rights to use the plant are proven, if the project complies with the building, fire and safety regulations and if there are no objections against the applicant (§3[2]). In case of fund hospitals, the establishment additionally needs to comply with the 'plan of *Land* hospitals' *(Landeskrankenanstaltenplan)*.

The major criterion for granting a concession is the question of need for the hospital. The need is to be evaluated with regard to the range of existing services of public, private non-profitmaking and other hospitals with insurance contracts. If an autonomous outpatient clinic is being planned, the need also has to be evaluated with regard to the existing services offered by ambulances of public, private non-profitmaking and other hospitals with insurance contracts as well as by licensed medical practitioners with insurance contracts. Within this evaluation, the hospital being planned may only be compared with hospitals or other institutions that serve an equal or similar purpose. According to the unanimous jurisdiction of the Constitutional Court and the Administrative Court, there is a need for a hospital, if the medical supply of the population is substantially facilitated, accelerated, intensified or helped another way.[498] It is not sufficient that new equipment is desirable for an improvement of the supply or that a new institution might result in some kind of time saving for the patient though. Thus, not only size and number of other providers are relevant factors, but also the range of services offered as a whole – also considering the situation on the roads and the potential users.

516. The concession for operating a hospital has to be granted, if there is a concession for establishment, if there is sufficient medical equipment and technical supply for direct operation complying with the safety and health safety rules, if the conditions of the plan of *Land* hospitals and the requirements of quality of structure are fulfilled, if there are no objections against the regulations of the institution and if a head of the medical service, the heads of the departments and the necessary personnel have been named (§3[4]).

498. For example, Administrative Court VwSlg 5823 A/1962; ZfVB 1999/4/1414, 1415, ZfVB 2000/1113; ZfVB 2004/453; Constitutional Court VfSlg 14.840/1997; 15.449/1999, 15456/1999.

517. The ECJ held that the present need-oriented system for autonomous outpatient clinics violated the freedom of establishment and therefore Union Law.[499] It did not object to the possibility of a need-oriented system concerning ambulatory supply itself. It rather objected to the differentiation between outpatient clinics which need a concession based on the question of need, and group practices, which did not (until the amendment in 2010, *see* below), although being comparable. On the other hand, the ECJ questioned the regulation of the need-oriented system, which is not based on objective, non-discriminating criteria that are known in advance, but which is handled differently by each federal state.[500]

As a consequence of the *Hartlauer*-judgment, there was a big reform of the regulations on group practices in 2010 (Federal Law Gazette 2010/63, also *see* Part III, Chapter 1, §2.II. above). Different from the former rules, the establishment of a group practice generally needs a regulatory license (of the governor) now (§52b in conjunction with §52c of the Physicians Act). In accordance with §52c(2), a license is to be granted with regard to the regional health structural plan *(Regionaler Strukturplan Gesundheit)*, if a substantial improvement of the range of services can be achieved. Within this evaluation, the local conditions (population structure and rural population) and the relevant transport situation, the use of existing providers and the development trends in medicine have to be considered. Exceptions from the admission procedures are provided basically for group practices that offer only non-refundable services like beauty surgery (§52b[1] No. 2 lit b). Under the conditions of §52b(1) No. 2 lit a in conjunction with §52b(2), the establishment conditions are easier for certain group practices: if each partner of the group practice already has an insurance contract, the establishment of a group practice only has to be notified to the governor, provided that it complies with the regional health structural plan and there is a written commitment between the association and the competent insurance provider about an insurance contract with the group practice. For the admission procedures *see* §§52b and 52c.

V. Fee Categories

518. In public and non-profit making hospitals, there are two different fee categories. Public and non-profit making hospitals primarily have to offer medical services in the general class, which embodies the standard of health care paid by public funds.

---

499. ECJ 10 Mar. 2009, C-169/07 *(Hartlauer Handelsgesellschaft), RdM* 2009, 126 *(Stöger).*

500. For details K. Stöger, 'Anm zu EuGH 10. 3. 2009, C-169/07', *RdM* (2009): 130; M. Karollus & J. Villotti, 'Zur EU-Konformität der Bedarfsprüfung bei der Errichtung von Krankenanstalten', *ZESAR* 5–6 (2010): 225; A. Joklik, 'Das "Hartlauer-Urteil" des EuGH und seine Folgen für die Bedarfsprüfung. Sind Gruppenpraxen und selbständige Ambulatorien tatsächlich vergleichbare Leistungserbringer?', *RdM* (2009): 147; Th. Zivny & H. Kristoferitsch, 'EuGH erzwingt Neuregelung der Bedarfsprüfung', *Die Presse – Rechtspanorama,* 16 Mar. 2009; already Th. Eilmansberger, 'Die Bedarfsprüfung im österreichischen Krankenanstaltenwesen', in *Aktuelle Entwicklungen in der Krankenversicherung,* ed. P. Jabornegg, R. Resch & O. Seewald (Essen: Haarfeld, 2008), 91; Th. Kröll, 'Scheitert die Bedarfsprüfung für Ambulatorien an der Niederlassungsfreiheit nach Art 43 EG-Vertrag?', *ZfV* (2008): 316.

Medical services in the general class are financed and completely covered by LKF-fees or nursing fees (§27[1]). Other payments are not lawful (§27[5]). The services in the general fee class are qualified as overall performance, so that there is no direct professional charge of the hospital that can be claimed against the patient. The LKF-fees are to be evaluated in a cost-covering way by the holder of the hospital. They consist of LKF-points for each patient and the amount of Euros fixed by the federal state government for each LKF-point (for details *see* §28). In-patient services for insured patients are to be cashed up by the Funds of the federal states in the name of the social institution and according to the principles of the performance-oriented system (§27b). In practice, not the LKF-fees, but an LKF-charging rate calculated according to the criteria in §27b(2) (i.e., generally lower than the LKF-fees) is billed.

519. Whether and under which conditions hospitals may establish a special fee class additionally to the general class, is regulated by the federal states (§16[2]). The number of beds for the special fee class must not exceed a fourth of all beds (§16[1]). The special fee class is characterized by a higher standard concerning board and lodging as well as accommodation (component of comfort). Nonetheless, there must not be a difference to the general class concerning medical treatment (which is not always the case in practice). Special fee classes have been established in each federal state.

The fees of the special fee class are regulated by the federal states (§27[4]). They must be evaluated according to statutory criteria and are fixed by ministerial order of the federal state government. There are different implementing regulations concerning classification and amount, especially diverging regulations on doctor's fees.[501]

VI. Organization and Patients' Rights

520. The organization of a hospital and its organs are regulated by §§6a et seq. of the Frame Law on Hospitals and Sanatoria. Concerning patients' rights and specific regulations concerning treatment contracts, *see* Part II, Chapter 1 above.[502]

501. For an overview over the regulations of the *Länder see* N. Herdega, 'Aufteilung der Sondergebühren in der Bundesländerübersicht', in *Gmundner Medizinrechtskongress 2008,* ed. G. Aigner, R. Resch & F. Wallner (Vienna: Manz, 2009), 26. For the (constitutional) problems concerning doctors' fees *see* the judgment of the Constitutional Court, G 119/06, *RdM* 2007, 149 *(Kopetzki);* with further references, D. Ennöckl & K. Stöger, 'Ärztliche Honorare in der Sonderklasse: Viel Neues vom VfGH', *ZfV* (2007): 770; B. Raschauer, 'Zur Zulässigkeit landesgesetzlicher Regelungen auf dem Gebiet der Arzthonorare', in *Gmundner Medizinrechtskongress 2008*, ed. G. Aigner, R. Resch & F. Wallner (Vienna: Manz, 2009), 1.

502. For details on hospitals *see* (with further references), K. Stöger, *Ausgewählte öffentlich-rechtliche Fragestellungen des österreichischen Krankenanstaltenrechts* (Vienna: Manz, 2008); E. Berglez, *Kooperationen zwischen Krankenanstalten* (Vienna, Manz, 2017); Ch. Kopetzki, 'Krankenanstaltenrecht', in *Handbuch des öffentlichen Wirtschaftsrechts,* ed. M. Holoubek & M. Potacs, vol. 1, 3rd edn (Vienna, New York: Springer, 2013), 377; K. Stöger, 'KAKuG', in *Gmundner Kommentar zum Gesundheitsrecht,* ed. M. Neumayr, R. Resch & F. Wallner (Vienna: Manz, 2016), 1523; L. Stärker, 'Krankenanstaltenrecht', in *Handbuch Medizinrecht,* ed. R. Resch & F. Wallner, 2nd edn (Vienna:

§2. Primary Health Care

521. In the course of a big health care reform in 2017 (Federal Law Gazette 2017/131, *Gesundheitsreformumsetzungsgesetz),* primary health care is being reorganized in Austria at the moment: The act establishes interdisciplinary Primary Health Care Centers characterized by good access conditions, longer opening hours and a broad range of services (for details *see* §4 and §5). Around 75 of these centres are planned by the end of 2021. One of the main legislative objectives is to reduce the excessive use of hospital ambulances. Apart from that, the reorganization is seen to be in the interest of a continuous and holistic treatment for patients and to enhance the status of the general practitioner.

522. Health Care Centers at least consist of general practitioners and nurses (§2[2]) and, if required, paediatricians and other members of health or social care professions (such as midwives, psychologists, *see* §2[3]).

523. In line with §3(5), Health Care Centers can be organized as group practices (in line with §52a of the Physicians Act, for details *see* §9), autonomous outpatient clinics (pursuant to the Frame Law on Hospitals and Sanatoria, for details *see* §10) or networks (in case of several locations). A network (e.g., in the legal form of an association) can only be established with doctors on a freelance base, with group practices or other members of health and social care professions (or their sponsoring organizations). Health Care Centers have legal personality and must be part of the regional health structural plan (§3[4]).

524. They will have individual contracts on Primary Health Care *(Primärversorgungsvertrag)* with (at least) the local competent health insurance company (for details *see* §8) on the legal basis of a new integrated contract on Primary Health Care between the Main Association of Austrian Social Security Institutions and the Austrian Medical Chamber (in line with §342b of the General Social Insurance Act). The integrated contract must contain regulations on the minimal range of services, the basic principles of compensation and remuneration agreements. It does, however, not apply to Primary Health Care Centers in the form of autonomous outpatient clinics (as they are members of the Chamber of Commerce).

LexisNexis, 2015), 403; S. Füszl, 'Krankenanstaltenrecht', in *Handbuch Medizinrecht*, ed. G. Aigner et al. (Vienna: Manz, 2003 et seq.), IV/1 et seq.; W. Hauser, W. Kröll & W. Stock, *Grundzüge des Gesundheitsrechts* (Vienna, Graz: NWV, 2017), 25 et seq.; Ch. Schneider & M. Szüsz, *Grundzüge des österreichischen Krankenanstaltenrechts* (Vienna: Verlag Österreich, 2003); K. Stellamor & W. Steiner (eds), *Handbuch des österreichischen Arztrechts*, vol. 1 (Vienna: Manz, 1999), 574 et seq.

Selected Bibliography

Aigner, G., et al. (eds). *Handbuch Medizinrecht für die Praxis*. Vienna: Manz, 2003 et seq.

Aigner, G., Kierein, M & Kopetzki, Ch. (eds). *Ärztegesetz,* 3rd edn. Vienna: Manz, 2007.

Aigner, G., Resch, R. & Wallner, F. (eds). *Gmundner Medizinrechtskongress 2008*. Vienna: Manz, 2009.

Apathy, P. (ed.). *Bürgerliches Recht,* vol. 5, 3rd edn. Vienna: Springer, 2008.

Arnold, S., Bernat, E. & Kopetzki, Ch. *Das Recht der Fortpflanzungsmedizin 2015 – Analyse und Kritik*, Vienna: Manz, 2016.

Barta, H. & Weber, K. (eds). *Rechtsfragen der Transplantationsmedizin in Europa*. Vienna: WUV, 2001.

Barta, H., Ganner, M. & Lichtmannegger, H. (eds). *Patientenentschädigungsfonds oder Medizinhaftung*. Innsbruck: innsbruck university press, 2009.

Barta, H., Kalchschmid, G. & Kopetzki, Ch. (eds). *Rechtspolitische Aspekte des Transplantationsrechts*. Vienna: Manz, 1999.

Barth, P. & Erlebach, M. (eds). *Handbuch des neuen Fortpflanzungsmedizinrechts,* Vienna: Linde Verlag, 2015.

Barth, P. & Ganner, M. (eds). *Handbuch Sachwalterrecht.* 2nd edn. Vienna: Linde, 2010.

Bauer, L. & Reimer, S. (eds). *Handbuch Datenschutzrecht*. Vienna: Facultas, 2009.

Berka, W. 'Rechtliche Probleme im Hinblick auf die Tätigkeit der Ethikkommissionen'. In *Sozialrechtliche Probleme bei der Ausübung von Heilberufen,* edited by Th. Tomandl. Vienna: Braumüller, 1996.

Berglez, E. *Kooperationen zwischen Krankenanstalten*, Vienna: Manz, 2017.

Bernat, E. & Kröll, W. (eds). *Recht und Ethik in der Arzneimittelforschung*. Vienna: Manz, 2003.

Bernat, E. (ed.). Die Reproduktionsmedizin am Prüfstand von Recht und Ethik. Vienna: Manz, 2000.

Bernat, E. (ed.). *Fortpflanzungsmedizin, Wertung und Gesetzgebung*. Vienna: Verlag der Österreichischen Staatsdruckerei, 1991.

Bernat, E. (ed.). *Lebensbeginn durch Menschenhand – Probleme künstlicher Befruchtungstechnologien aus medizinischer, ethischer und juristischer Sicht.* Graz: Leykam, 1985.

Bernat, E. 'Das österreichische Recht der Medizin – eine Bestandsaufnahme'. In *Perspektiven des Medizinrechts,* edited by Eser, A, Just, H. & Koch, H.G. Baden-Baden: Nomos, 2004.

Bernat, E. 'Einführung in das österreichische Medizinrecht'. In *Handbuch des Fachanwalts Medizinrecht,* edited by Wenzel, F. Köln: Wolters Kluwer, 2012.

Selected Bibliography

Bernat, E. 'Recht und Humangenetik – ein österreichischer Diskussionsbeitrag'. In *Festschrift Steffen*, edited by Deutsch, E., Klingmüller, E. & Kullmann, H. J. Berlin: de Gruyter, 1995.

Bernat, E. *Rechtsfragen medizinisch assistierter Zeugung*. Frankfurt, Bern, New York, Paris: Peter Lang, 1989.

Brandstetter, W. & Kopetzki, Ch. *Organtransplantationen. Medizinische und rechtliche Aspekte der Verwendung menschlicher Organe zu Heilzwecken*. Vienna: Facultas, 1987.

Breyer, F., et al. *Organmangel. Ist der Tod auf der Warteliste unvermeidbar?*. Berlin, Heidelberg, New York: Springer, 2006.

Brodil, W. & Windisch-Graetz, M. *Sozialrecht in Grundzügen*, Vienna: facultas, 2017.

Bruckmüller, K. & Schuhmann, S. 'Die Heilbehandlung im österreichischen Strafrecht'. In *Handbuch des Medizinstrafrechts,* edited by Roxin, C. & Braun, A. 4th edn. Stuttgart et al.: Boorberg, 2007.

Bundesministerium für Wissenschaft und Forschung (ed.). *Gentechnologie im österreichischen Recht*. Vienna: Manz, 1991.

Bydlinski, F. 'Haftungsgrund und Zufall als alternative mögliche Schadensursachen'. In *Aktuelle Probleme des Unternehmensrechts – Festschrift Gerhard Frotz,* edited by Enzinger, M., Hügel, H.F. & Dillenz, W. Vienna: Manz, 1993.

Ecker, W., et al. *Medizinprodukterecht*. Vienna: Ed. Juridica, 2004.

Eilmansberger, Th. 'Die Bedarfsprüfung im österreichischen Krankenanstaltenwesen'. In *Aktuelle Entwicklungen in der Krankenversicherung,* edited by Jabornegg, P., Resch, R. & Seewald, O. Essen: Haarfeld, 2008.

Emberger, H. & Wallner, F. (eds). *Ärztegesetz mit Kommentar*, 2nd edn. Vienna: Verlagshaus der Ärzte, 2008.

Engljähringer, D. *Ärztliche Aufklärungspflicht vor medizinischen Eingriffen*. Vienna: Orac, 1996.

Fabrizy, E. *StGB Kurzkommentar.* 12th edn. Vienna: Manz, 2016.

Fenyves, A., Kerschner, F. & Vonklich, A. (eds). *ABGB,* 3rd edn. Vienna: Verlag Österreich, 2008.

Flemmich, G. & Nöstlinger, W. *Gesundheits- und Krankenpflegegesetz*. Vienna: ÖGB-Verlag, 2004.

Ganner, M. *Selbstbestimmung im Alter.* Vienna: Springer, 2005.

Greif, E. 'Körper an den Grenzen des Rechts. Transsexualität, Menschenrechte und nationales Recht'. In *Recht und Medizin*, edited by Dujmovits, E., et al. Baden-Baden: Nomos, 2006.

Greif, E. *Doing Trans/Gender.* Linz: Trauner, 2005.

Grimm, M. *Die Weisungsbindung des Spitalsarztes*. Vienna: Manz, 1999.

Haas, M., Plank, M.-L & Unterkofler, B. *Arzneimittelgesetz*. 2nd edn. Vienna: Verlag Österreich, 2015.

Harrer, F. & Graf, A.-H. (eds). *Ärztliche Verantwortung und Aufklärung*. Vienna: Orac 1999.

Hauser, W., Kröll, W. & Stock, W. *Grundzüge des Gesundheitsrechts*. Vienna, Graz: NWV, 2017.

Herdegen, M. & Dederer, H.-G. (eds). 'Landesbericht Österreich'. In *Internationale Praxis Gentechnikrecht*, 33rd edn. Heidelberg: Müller, 2001.

Hirsch, Ch. *Arzthaftung bei fehlgeschlagener Familienplanung*. Vienna: Manz, 2002.

Höpfel, F. & Ratz, E. (eds). *Wiener Kommentar zum Strafgesetzbuch*. 2nd edn. Vienna: Manz, 2000 et seq.

Hummelbrunner, S. *Die ärztliche Gruppenpraxis*. Vienna: Manz, 2005.

Jabornegg, P., Resch, R. & Seewald, O. (eds). *Qualitätssicherung für Leistungen in der gesetzlichen Krankenversicherung*. Vienna: Manz, 2003.

Jahn, B. *Außergerichtliche Konfliktlösung im Gesundheitswesen*. Vienna: Manz, 2009.

Jahnel, D. (ed.). *Jahrbuch Datenschutzrecht*. Vienna: Neuer Wissenschaftlicher Verlag, 2010.

Juen, Th. *Arzthaftungsrecht*, 2nd edn. Vienna: Manz, 2005.

Kalchschmid, G. *Die Organtransplantation*. Vienna: Verlag Österreich, 1997.

Kerschner, F., et al. *Kommentar zum Gentechnikgesetz*. Vienna: Manz, 2007.

Kienapfel, D. & Schroll, H.V. *Grundriß des Strafrechts. Besonderer Teil I*, 5th edn. Vienna: Manz, 2003.

Kienapfel, D. & Schroll, H.V. *Strafrecht Besonderer Teil I*, 4th edn. Vienna: Manz, 2016.

Kierein, M. et al. (eds). *Jahrbuch Gesundheitsrecht 2010*. Vienna: Neuer Wissenschaftlicher Verlag, 2010.

Kletečka, A. & Schauer, M. (eds). *Kommentar zum Allgemeinen bürgerlichen Gesetzbuch*. Vienna: Manz, 2010.

Knyrim, R. *Datenschutzrecht*, Vienna: Manz, 2015.

Kopetzki, Ch. & Mayer, H. (eds). *Biotechnologie und Recht*. Vienna: Manz, 2002.

Kopetzki, Ch. & Zahrl, J. (eds). *Behandlungsanspruch und Wirtschaftlichkeitsgebot*. Vienna: Manz, 1998.

Kopetzki, Ch. (ed.). *Einwilligung und Einwilligungsfähigkeit*. Vienna: Manz, 2002.

Kopetzki, Ch. (ed.). *Gewebesicherheitsrecht*. Vienna: Manz, 2009.

Kopetzki, Ch. 'Behandlungen auf dem "Stand der Wissenschaft"'. In *Finanzielle Grenzen des Behandlungsanspruchs*, edited by Pfeil, W. Vienna: Manz, 2010.

Kopetzki, Ch. 'Die EG als Normsetzer im Gesundheitsrecht vor dem Hintergrund des Art 152 EGV?'. In *Standardisierung in der Medizin als Rechtsproblem*, edited by Lilie, H., Bernat, E. & Rosenau, H. Baden-Baden: Nomos, 2009.

Kopetzki, Ch. 'Herausforderungen an ein integratives Medizinrecht – Rechtsvergleichung'. In *Perspektiven des Medizinrechts*, edited by Eser, A., Just, H. & Koch, H.G. Baden-Baden: Nomos, 2004.

Kopetzki, Ch. 'Invasive Verfahren aus rechtlicher Sicht'. In *Zumutbare Maßnahmen in Diagnostik und Therapie bei der Begutachtung*, edited by Gesellschaft der Gutachterärzte Österreichs. Forschung und Praxis der Begutachtung 68 (2006/2007): 33-58.

Kopetzki, Ch. 'Krankenanstaltenrecht'. In *Öffentliches Wirtschaftsrecht*, edited by Holoubek, M. & Potacs, M., 3rd edn, vol. 1. Vienna: Springer, 2013.

Kopetzki, Ch. 'Landesbericht Österreich'. In *Internationale Perspektiven zu Status und Schutz des extrakorporalen Embryos*, edited by Eser, A., Koch, H.G. & Seith, C. Baden-Baden: Nomos, 2007.

Kopetzki, Ch. 'Landesbericht Österreich'. In *The Convention on Human Rights and Biomedicine of the Council of Europe – a Suitable Model for World-Wide Regulation?*, edited by Taupitz, J. Berlin: Springer, 2002.

Kopetzki, Ch. 'Patientenverfügung: Ist alles Machbare auch rechtlich geboten?'. In *Recht und Risikomanagement in Anästhesie und Intensivmedizin*, Festschrift Metzler, edited by Kröll, W., Pateter, W. & Schweppe, P. Vienna: Manz, 2009.

Kopetzki, Ch. 'Rechtliche Voraussetzungen der Hirntodbestimmung'. In *Schädel-Hirn-Trauma/Hirntod. Beiträge zur Anästhesiologie, Intensivund Notfallmedizin*, edited by Schwarz, G., Kröll, W. & List, W. F. Vienna, Munich, Bern: Verlag Maudrich, 1995.

Kopetzki, Ch. 'Rechtspolitik der Zukunft – Medizinrecht'. In *Rechtspolitik der Zukunft – Zukunft der Rechtspolitik*, edited by Holoubek, M. & Lienbacher, G. Vienna: Springer, 1999.

Kopetzki, Ch. 'Medizinisch unterstützte Fortpflanzung: Reformbedarf aus verfassungsrechtlicher Sicht', in *Gesundheit und Recht – Recht auf Gesundheit*, ed. Österreichische Juristenkommission (Vienna, Linde, 2013).

Kopetzki, Ch. *Grundriss des Unterbringungsrechts*, 3rd edn. Vienna/New York: Springer, 2012.

Kopetzki, Ch. *Organgewinnung zu Zwecken der Transplantation. Eine systematische Analyse des geltenden Rechts*. Vienna, New York: Springer, 1988.

Kopetzki, Ch. *Turnusärzte und Famulanten*. Vienna: Manz, 1990.

Kopetzki, Ch. *Unterbringungsrecht*. Vienna, New York: Springer, 1995.

Kopetzki, Ch.& Druml, Ch. (eds). *Ethik und Recht in der Humanforschung*. Vienna: Springer, 2010.

Kopetzki, Ch., et al. (eds). *Körper-Codes*. Vienna: Linde, 2010.

Körtner, U. & Kopetzki, Ch. (eds). *Embryonenschutz – Hemmschuh für die Biomedizin?* Vienna: Manz, 2003.

Körtner, U. & Kopetzki, Ch. (eds). *Stammzellforschung*. Vienna, New York: Springer, 2008. Körtner, U., Ch.

Krauskopf, B. *Die ärztliche Anzeige- und Meldepflicht*,. Vienna: Jan Sramek Verlag, 2011.

Krepler, R., Hackl, J.R. & Marzi, L.-M. *Recht im Krankenhausalltag*. Vienna: Orac, 2002.

Kröll, W. & Schaupp, W. (eds). *Eluana Englaro – Wachkoma und Behandlungsabbruch*. Vienna: Manz, 2010.

Lehner, A. 'Recht auf Datenschutz'. In *Handbuch Menschenrechte*, edited by Heißl, G. Vienna: Facultas 2009.

Leischner, A. 'Sprach- und kulturspezifische Anforderungen an die ärztliche Aufklärung'. In *Interkulturell kompetent. Ein Handbuch für Ärztinnen und Ärzte*, edited by Peintinger, M. Vienna: Verlag facultas, 2011, 203–225.

Leischner, A. *Streitbeilegung in medizinischen Haftungsfällen*. Vienna: Manz, 2007.

Lewisch, P. *Strafrecht Besonderer Teil I*. 2nd edn. Vienna: WUV, 1999.

Mayrhofer, M. *Reproduktionsmedizinrecht*. Vienna, Graz: NWV, 2003.

Mazal, W. (ed.). *Erstattungskodex*. Vienna: Manz, 2005.

Mazal, W. *Krankheitsbegriff und Risikobegrenzung*. Vienna: Braumüller, 1992.

Neumayr, M., Resch R. & Wallner F., *Gmundner Kommentar zum Gesundheitsrecht*, Vienna: Manz, 2016.

Perthold-Stoitzner, B. UG[3], Vienna: Manz, 2016.
Prutsch, K. *Die ärztliche Aufklärung*. 2nd edn. Vienna: WUV, 2004.
Rebhahn, R. 'Die Bereitstellung von Arzneimitteln'. In *Europäisches Wirtschaftsrecht und soziale Krankenversicherung,* edited by Grillberger, K. & Mosler, R. Vienna: Manz, 2003.
Resch, R. & Wallner, F. (eds.). *Handbuch Medizinrecht.* 2nd edn. Vienna: LexisNexis, 2015.
Riesz, Th. *Ärztliche Verschwiegenheitspflicht.* Vienna: Manz, 2013.
Rummel, P. & Lukas, M. (ed.). *Kommentar zum Allgemeinen bürgerlichen Gesetzbuch.* 4th edn. Vienna: Manz, 2016.
Schneider, Ch. & Szüsz, M. *Grundzüge des österreichischen Krankenanstaltenrechts.* Vienna: Verlag Österreich, 2003.
Schneider, Ch. *Ärztliche Ordinationen und selbständige Ambulatorien im Verwaltungs-, Sozial- und Steuerrecht.* Vienna: Verlag Österreich, 2001.
Schragel, W. *Kommentar zum Amtshaftungsgesetz (AHG).* 3rd edn. Vienna: Manz, 2003.
Schwamberger, H. 'Berufsrecht für Ärzte, Pflegepersonal und medizinisch-technische Dienste'. In *Medizinrecht für Gesundheitsberufe,* edited by Barta, H., Schwamberger, H. & Staudinger, R. Hall in Tirol: Berenkamp, 1999.
Schwamberger, H. *Gesundheits- und Krankenpflegegesetz.* 5th edn. Vienna: Verlag Österreich, 2008.
Schwimann, M. & Kodek, G. E. (ed.). *ABGB Praxiskommentar.* 4th edn. Vienna: LexisNexis, 2016.
Serban, H., & Heisler, H. *Apothekengesetz.* 2nd edn. Vienna: Verlag Österreich, 2005.
Skiczuk, S. *Berufs- und Tätigkeitsschutz der österreichischen Gesundheitsberufe unter besonderer Berücksichtigung der Ärzte und Psychotherapeuten.* Vienna: NWV, 2006.
Sladecek, E., Marzi, L.-M. & Schmiedbauer, Th. *Recht für Gesundheitsberufe.* 6th edn. Vienna: LexisNexis, 2012.
Stellamor, K. & Steiner, J. W. *Handbuch des österreichischen Arztrechts.* vol. 1. Vienna: Manz, 1999.
Stelzer, M. & Schmiedecker, K. 'Gentechnikrecht'. In *Öffentliches Wirtschaftsrecht,* edited by Holoubek, M. & Potacs, M. vol. 2, 3rd edn. Vienna, New York: Springer, 2013.
Stelzer, M. *Datenschutz im Gentechnikrecht.* Vienna: Bundesministerium für Gesundheit und Frauen, 2004.
Stöger, K. & Szüsz, M. 'Rechtliche Aspekte von Qualitätssicherung in der Medizin'. In *Qualitätssicherung in der Medizin*, edited by Fischer, R. & Tragl, K.-H. Vienna: Österreichische Ärztekammer 2000.
Stöger, K. *Ausgewählte öffentlich-rechtliche Fragestellungen des österreichischen Krankenanstaltenrechts.* Vienna: Manz, 2008.
Strickmann, G. *Heimaufenthaltsgesetz.* 2nd edn. Vienna: Linde, 2012.
Tades, H. (ed.). *Ein Leben für Rechtskultur, Festschrift Robert Dittrich.* Vienna: Manz, 2000.
Tanczos, A. & Tanczos, D. *Arzthaftung.* Vienna: Orac, 2010.

Selected Bibliography

Taupitz, J. *Kommerzialisierung des menschlichen Körpers*. Berlin, Heidelberg: Springer, 2007.

Tomandl, Th. *Grundriss des österreichischen Sozialrechts*. Vienna: Manz, 2009.

Triffterer, O., Rosbaud, Ch. & Hinterhofer, H.(eds). *Salzburger Kommentar zum Strafgesetzbuch*. Vienna: LexisNexis, 1992 et seq.

Wallner, F. *Handbuch Ärztliches Berufsrecht*. Vienna: LexisNexis, 2011.

Weiss, S. 'Die menschliche Gesundheit als neues berufliches Tätigkeitsgebiet'. In *Jahrbuch Gesundheitsrecht 2008*, edited by Kierein, M., et al. Vienna: Neuer Wissenschaftlicher Verlag, 2008.

Weiß-Faßbinder, S. & Lust, A. *GuKG*, 6th edn. Vienna: Manz, 2010.

Wimmer, E. *Rechtsfragen im Turnusarztverhältnis*. Vienna: Manz, 2000. Windisch, B. *Probandenversicherung*. Vienna: Orac, 1995.

Zeinhofer, C. *Der Begriff des Arzneimittels und seine Abgrenzung von anderen Produktkategorien*. Vienna, Graz: NWV, 2007.

(Selected) Medical Literature in English

Aigner, G. 'An Overview of Legal Aspects in Organ Transplantation – What Are the Family Rights?' *Mitteilungen der Sanitätsverwaltung* 12 (2003): 8.

Bachinger, G. 'The System of the Patient Advocacies in Austria'. www.patientenanwalt.com. 14 February 2014.

Bernat, E. 'A Cause of Action for "Wrongful Birth" Under Austrian Tort Law: Don't Take the Civil Code too Seriously!' *Journal of International Biotechnology Law* 1 (2004): 161.

Bernat, E. 'Austria: Legislating for Assisted Reproduction and Interpreting the Ban on Corporal Punishment'. *University of Louisville Journal of Family Law* 32 (1994): 247.

Bernat, E. 'Compensation For Medical Injuries: Is There a Need For a Law Reform? An Austrian Viewpoint'. *European Journal of Health Law* 5 (1998): 117.

Bernat, E. 'Legal Aspects of Developments in Human Genetics: An Austrian Viewpoint'. *Law & Hum Gen Rev* 3 (1995): 35.

Bernat, E. 'Liability Risks in Gynaecology and Obstetrics under German and Austrian Law'. *Medicine and Law* 14 (1995): 413.

Bernat, E. 'Marketing of Human Organs?' *Medicine and Law* 14 (1995): 181.

Bernat, E. 'Opting-in, Opting-out, and Necessity: The Law of Organ Transplantation in Germany, Austria, and Switzerland'. *International Journal of Bioethics* 5 (1994): 101.

Koch, B. & Koziol, H. 'Compensation in the Austrian Health Care Sector'. In *No-Fault Compensation in the Health Care Sector*, edited by Dute, J., Faure, M.G. & Koziol, H. Vienna: Springer, 2004.

Koch, B.A. & Koziol, H. 'Country Report – Austria'. In *Cases on Medical Malpractice in a Comparative Perspective*, edited by Faure, M.G. & Koziol, H. Vienna: Springer, 2004.

Koch, B.A. 'Austria'. In *Digests of European Tort Law*, edited by Winiger, B., et al., vol. 1. Vienna: Springer, 2006.

Koziol, H. 'Problems of Alternative Causation in Tort Law'. In *Developments in Austrian and Israeli Private Law*, edited by Hausmaninger, H., et al. Vienna: Springer, 1999.

Steininger, B.C. 'Austria'. In *European Tort Law 2006*, edited by Koziol, H. & Steininger, B.C. Vienna/New York: Springer, 2008.

Steininger, B.C. 'Austria'. In *European Tort Law 2008*, edited by Koziol, H. & Steininger, B.C. Vienna/New York: Springer, 2009.

Selected Bibliography

Index

The numbers here refer to paragraph numbers.

Index

Made in the USA
Monee, IL
13 September 2026

62974277R00129